Ripley's
Believe It or Not!®

2010

Executive VP Norm Deska

VP, Exhibits and Archives Edward Meyer

Archives Assistant Anthony Scipio

Researcher Lucas Stram

Publisher Anne Marshall

Managing Editor Rebecca Miles

Picture Manager Gemma Simmons

Picture Researcher James Proud

Researcher Rosie Alexander

Text Geoff Tibballs

Editors Judy Barratt, Sally McFall

Interviews James Proud

Factchecker Kevin King

Indexer Hilary Bird

Art Director Sam South

Design Dynamo Design

Reprographics Stephan Davis

First published in Great Britain in 2009 by
Random House Books
Random House, 20 Vauxhall Bridge Road,
London SW1V 2SA

www.rbooks.co.uk

Addresses for companies within The Random
House Group Limited can be found at:
www.randomhouse.co.uk/offices.htm

The Random House Group Limited Reg. No. 954009

ISBN 9781847945853
10 9 8 7 6 5 4 3 2 1

The Random House Group Limited supports The
Forest Stewardship Council (FSC), the leading
international forest certification organisation. All
our titles that are printed on Greenpeace approved
FSC certified paper carry the FSC logo. Our paper
procurement policy can be found at
www.rbooks.co.uk/environment

A CIP catalogue record for this book
is available from the British Library

Printed in China

PUBLISHER'S NOTE
While every effort has been made to verify the
accuracy of the entries in this book, the Publishers
cannot be held responsible for any errors
contained in the work. They would be glad to
receive any information from readers.

WARNING
Some of the stunts and activities in this book
are undertaken by experts and should not be
attempted by anyone without adequate training
and supervision.

Ripley's Believe It or Not!®

2010

SEEING IS BELIEVING

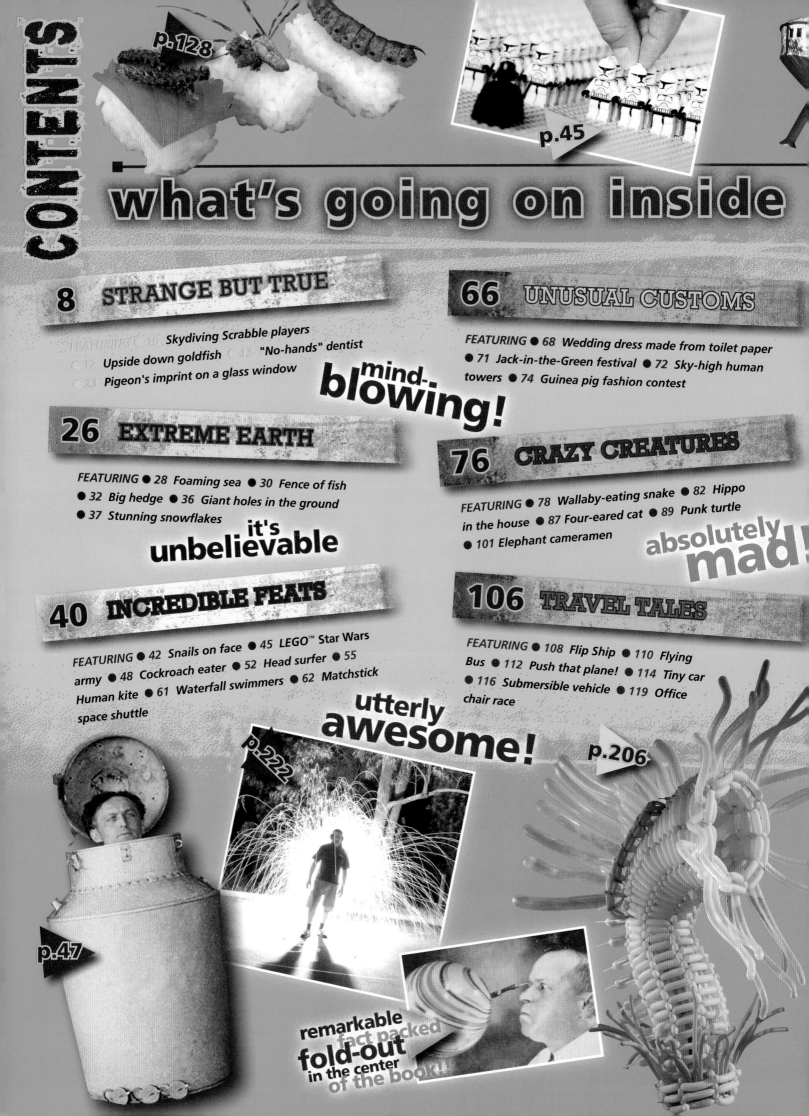

p.128

p.45

CONTENTS
what's going on inside

mind-blowing!

it's unbelievable

absolutely mad!

utterly awesome!

p.222

p.206

p.47

remarkable fact packed fold-out in the center of the book!

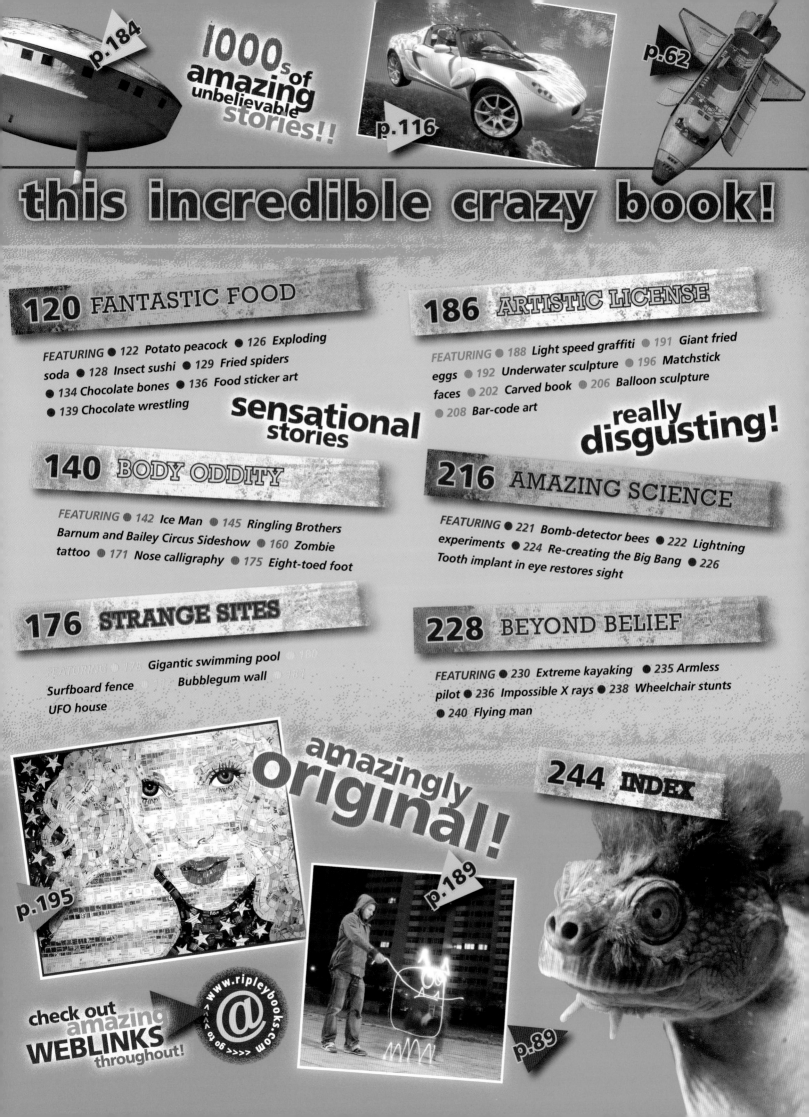

p.184

1000s of amazing unbelievable stories!!

p.116

p.62

this incredible crazy book!

amazingly original!

p.195

p.189

check out amazing WEBLINKS throughout!

www.ripleybooks.com
go to >>>>

p.89

Ripley's
welcome you to their amazing world

Robert Ripley poses alongside an impressive display of his newspaper cartoon proofs in 1929.

Ever played the game where you decide who, out of all the famous people that ever lived, you would like to invite round for dinner? You'd think, perhaps, of Nelson Mandela, Julius Caesar, maybe Neil Armstrong? Here's a top tip. If you want a guest who would entertain the others with the best, jaw-dropping stories that have ever been told—tales of miracles and monstrosities, wonder and weird-ities—you should look no further than Robert Ripley.

In 1918, Robert Ripley became fascinated by strange facts and feats while working as a cartoonist on the *New York Globe*. At first, his column concentrated on unusual achievements in athletics, but once letters from readers who loved the illustrations started to pour onto his desk, Ripley broadened his search for unbelievable stories into every aspect and every corner of the world.

Ripley was passionate about travel and, by 1940, he had visited no less than 201 countries and covered over 464,000 mi (747,000 km), accumulating artifacts and searching for stories that would be right for his column, which he named "Believe It Or Not!" The cartoons were wildly popular—they had a worldwide readership of 80 million and were translated into 17 languages. His weekly mailbag could exceed 170,000 letters and Ripley reveled in them all, encouraging his readers to send him unusual material and photographs. He was a true celebrity of his time.

Ripley bought a magnificent island estate at Marmaroneck, New York, approached only by a long, semi-secret causeway, and filled the gigantic house with luxurious furnishings, strange objects collected on his travels and exotic creatures, such as a 28-ft (8.5-m) boa constrictor! The house is long gone but the artifacts have been re-housed in the 30 Ripley's Believe It or Not! museums that cover the globe from Tokyo to Chicago.

Robert Ripley died in 1949, but his research staff tirelessly continue the search for the quirks of life, ever expanding the Ripley collection.

The main Ripley storeroom houses curiosities old and new from around the world, ready to be processed and placed in Believe It or Not! museums worldwide.

OBAMA ART!

One of Ripley's most recent acquisitions is a portrait of President Barack Obama made from 12,784 gumballs. Ninety children came together to feed gumballs into plastic tubes, which were then assembled to form an image of Obama's face. Artist Franz Spohn from Ohio used a computer program to design the piece, which measured 6 x 6 ft (1.8 x 1.8 m), so that each gumball represented a pixel. The work is being shown at various Believe It or Not! museums around the United States.

An exhibit in the Ripley's museum in London, England, recreates an old Ripley storeroom, with its many-legged and many-headed animals and other remarkable creatures.

check out the ripley website!!

LOOK OUT FOR OUR EXCITING NEW WEBSITE

www.ripleys.com

Where you see this symbol stamped on some of the pages in this book it indicates that there is more information on the subject available on our book website. Check out the extra images, features, and videos, as well as an abundance of new BION stories. **Put yourself on the mailing list** *so we can keep you posted.*

www.ripleybooks.com

get involved!!

If you have a strange fact that could be included on our web pages, in our books, on our shows or in our museums you can…
Write to us (including photographs where possible)
BION Research, Ripley Entertainment Inc.
7576 Kingspointe Parkway, 188
Orlando, Florida 32819, U.S.A.
Or send an email bionresearch@ripleys.com

WELL OVERDUE

LIBRARY BOOK 288 YEARS OVERDUE
A book about the Archbishop of Bremen that was borrowed from a university library in Cambridge, England, in 1667, was finally returned in 1955.

LETTER DELIVERED 286 YEARS LATE
A letter sent in 1718 from a church in Eisenach, Germany, to the nearby town of Ostheim was eventually delivered to the correct address in 2004.

WATCH RETURNED AFTER 90 YEARS
An engraved watch that U.S. soldier William B. Gill lost in France during World War I was finally returned to his grandchildren in Sioux City, Iowa, in 2007.

POSTCARD DELIVERED 58 YEARS LATE
A postcard that was mailed in 1948 was delivered to a home in Spiceland, Indiana, in 2006—after the town's postmaster bought it on eBay.

CLASS RING RETURNED 53 YEARS LATER
Helen Swisshelm lost her class ring in 1948 while swimming in the Hudson River. A man with a metal detector found it and it was returned to her in 2001.

SUITCASE RETURNED AFTER 44 YEARS
In 2004, Beverly Sherman of Lakewood, Washington, got back a suitcase containing her belongings that had been lost when she was involved in a car accident in 1960.

STOLEN BIRD'S EGG RETURNED AFTER 43 YEARS
A rare bustard's egg that was stolen from a museum in Devon, England, in 1963 was sent back in mint condition in 2006—along with an anonymous letter of apology.

LOST WALLET TURNED UP 39 YEARS ON
James Lubeck lost his wallet in Marblehead Harbor, Massachusetts, in 1966. It was reeled in 25 mi (40 km) away by a fisherman in 2005—with all the credit cards intact.

HOW ECCENTRIC!

KING THOUGHT HE WAS MADE OF GLASS
Charles VI of France (1368–1422) was convinced that he was made of glass. So he dreaded traveling anywhere by coach in case the vibration caused him to shatter into a thousand pieces.

SOLDIER THOUGHT HE WAS PREGNANT WITH AN ELEPHANT
Prussian Field Marshal Prince Gebhard Leberecht von Blücher (1742–1819) was haunted by the belief that he was pregnant with an elephant, which he thought had been fathered by a French soldier.

ACTRESS SLEPT IN A COFFIN
Famous French actress Sarah Bernhardt (1844–1923) used to practice her lines and sleep in a pink silk-lined coffin that accompanied her everywhere.

OBSESSED WITH NUMBER 13
The life of California rifle heiress Sarah Winchester (1839–1922) was so governed by the number 13 that when she built her mansion near San Francisco, it had 13 bathrooms, 13 hooks in every cupboard and 13 candles in every chandelier. In the sewing-room, she insisted on there being 13 windows and 13 doors. There were even 13 parts to her will—which she signed 13 times.

PRINCESS BELIEVED SHE HAD SWALLOWED A PIANO
Princess Alexandra of Bavaria (1826–75) was convinced that as a child she had swallowed a full-sized grand piano made of glass.

CIVIL WAR GENERAL THOUGHT HE WAS A BIRD
U.S. Confederate General Richard Stoddert Ewell (1817–72) experienced episodes of believing that he was a bird, during which he would cock his head to one side, peck at his food and emit chirping noises.

EARL DINED WITH DOGS
Naturalist Francis Henry Egerton, Earl of Bridgewater (1756–1829), loved his dogs so much that he used to invite them to dine with him at his stately home in Hertfordshire, England. The dogs would sit at the table with napkins around their necks and be waited on by servants.

Japanese jazz pianist Yosuke Yamashita wore a flame-retardant suit while playing an improvised piece for ten minutes on a piano on fire—until the blaze snapped the strings.

STRANGE »
BUT TRUE

Climbers Jon Ratcliffe and Steve Franklin played Scrabble while perched precariously 200 ft (60 m) above the ground on a cliff ledge in Anglesey, North Wales.

SCRABBLE FACTS

> If all the Scrabble tiles ever produced were placed in one long line, they would stretch 50,000 mi (80,500 km)—that's twice around the world.

> A giant game of Scrabble covered most of the soccer field at London's Wembley Stadium in 1998, and used letter tiles that were the size of dining tables.

> In a 1982 competition in Manchester, England, Dr. Karl Khoshnaw scored 392 points with the word "caziques"— the plural for a West Indian chief.

Even a watching alligator cannot ruffle the concentration of these two keepers at Gatorland Theme Park, Florida. "We don't set any parameters in anything that we do," said park owner Tim Williams. "We would even put the board on an alligator's back."

To celebrate the 60th anniversary of Scrabble in November 2008, extreme enthusiasts played the word game in some stunning locations—including while skydiving at an altitude of 13,000 ft (4,000 m), swimming beneath the ocean surrounded by sharks, and even just a few feet from the jaws of huge alligators!

Invented by New York architect Alfred Butts in 1948, Scrabble is produced in more than 29 languages and has sold more than 150 million sets. At least 30,000 games begin somewhere in the world every hour—but few in such crazy settings as these.

In the Lion Park, Lanseria, South Africa, gamekeepers Kevin Richard and Helga van der Merwe enjoy a game of Scrabble watched by lionesses Meg and Amy.

Using a specially reinforced wooden board and adhesive glue to make their moves, skydivers Nicole Angelides and Ramsey Kent play Scrabble at 13,000 ft (4,000 m) after throwing themselves out of a plane above Florida.

SCRABBLE

EXTREME

UPSIDE DOWN GOLDFISH

Drinkers at a pub in Devon, England, have been watching pet goldfish Aussie swim upside down for four years in a tank on the bar. The fish has become a tourist attraction, with some naturally thinking it is drunk, but experts say Aussie's unusual swimming style is down to a problem with his "swim bladder," which regulates buoyancy, and that he is as healthy as his tank companion Eddie—who swims the right way up.

HOW DO FISH SWIM UPSIDE DOWN?

The ability of fish to float in water is controlled by their swim bladders, a sac filled with gas in the top part of the fish. In some fish the swim bladder can have an effect on their hearing and their sense of depth. Sometimes fish develop problems with their swim bladders, which can result in swimming to one side or even swimming upside down. From an evolutionary perspective, swim bladders are probably developed from the same air sacs that led to lungs forming in mammals.

BRACELET RETURNED ■ When Aaron Giles of Fairmont, Minnesota, lost his identity bracelet as a small boy, he never expected to see it again, but more than 25 years later it turned up—in the gizzard of a chicken. The shiny object was spotted by a meat cutter and all of the engravings were still legible.

MUMMIFIED BODY ■ A Croatian woman had sat dead in her armchair for 42 years before her mummified remains were discovered in 2008. Hedviga Golik was found in her apartment in Zagreb sitting in front of a black-and-white TV set. Neighbors had last seen her in 1966.

ARCTIC CIRCLE ■ George Porter, a British gunner, was buried in an ice floe during the 1875–76 British Arctic expedition and his body has likely been circling the North Pole for more than 130 years.

CASH DROP ■ Indonesian businessman Tung Desem Waringin dropped $10,700 in banknotes from a plane in 2008 to promote his new motivational book and help the country's poor people. His plane circled eight times over a sports field in the town of Serang, scattering bills to the crowds who had gathered below.

NAME CHANGE ■ Chicago school bus driver Steve Kreuscher filed a petition to change his name to "In God We Trust" because he was worried that the phrase might be removed from U.S. currency.

BANK ERROR ■ In 2007, a New York bank accidentally gave $2 million of a client's money to another customer with the same name. Benjamin Lovell tried to explain to the bank attendant that he did not have a $5-million account, but the bank insisted it was his money and that he was able to withdraw it, so he did. He was later brought before a court on a charge of grand larceny.

UNIDENTIFIED FLYING OBJECT ■ A hook-shaped piece of metal, 16 in (40 cm) in length, fell from the sky in October 2007 and crashed through the roof of an unoccupied car in Stanton, Delaware. The mysterious object was too hot to handle after its descent and left ash on the driver's seat. The Federal Aviation Authority said it had definitely not fallen from an airplane.

Gum Sucker

Despite the increased use of Western medicine, blood-sucking leeches are still a popular medical procedure in India. Applied to the gums, or elsewhere on the body, they are thought to cure a variety of ailments, including blood and immunity disorders.

BATHROOM GIFTS ▧ In the summer of 2007, an anonymous man left more than 400 envelopes in bathrooms of public buildings all across Japan, each containing a letter and cash worth $85.

LEG THIEVES ▧ Thinking it was a source of holy healing powers, thieves in Tirupati, Andhra Pradesh, India, sawed the leg off an 80-year-old holy man and stole it. They plied their victim with alcohol and removed his leg when he had passed out drunk. Despite heavy loss of blood, the holy man survived his ordeal.

FISHY FIND ▧ On January 24, 2008, ship captain Kiyoshi Kimino found a 15-year-old handwritten letter from a schoolchild, which read, "I'm a first-grade student. Our school is 120 years old. We are now celebrating it. If you happen to find this letter, please write back to me." Even more unusual, the letter was found stuck to the back of a flatfish off the coast of Japan.

HAIR CUT ▧ Scissor-wielding bandits aboard a bus in Rio de Janeiro, Brazil, grabbed a 22-year-old woman's hair, twisted it into a ponytail and cut it off. Police think the thieves were hoping to sell the long black hair, which the woman had been growing for four years, to wig-makers or to hair-transplant centers.

FORGETFUL THIEF ▧ A shoplifter seeking to make a quick getaway from a Dutch supermarket after stealing a packet of meat left behind a crucial piece of evidence—his 12-year-old son. The thief was in such a hurry that he forgot all about the boy, who quickly furnished the police with his father's details.

SECRET TUNNEL ▧ A man wanted for the murder of a neighbor hid for 17 years in a tunnel he dug under his home. Hui Guangwen was eventually discovered at the house in Suinan, China, in 2007, following a tip-off to police. He told them: "It was really boring down there."

STUD STUNNER ▧ Three days after losing a nose stud in a fall while kneeboarding from a speedboat off Tasmania, Kirsty Brittain was standing next to her fiancé when he filleted a fish he had just caught—and inside the fish was the missing stud.

SNAKE MAN ▧ A 19-year-old Kosovan prisoner, who weighed less than 121 lb (55 kg), escaped from a jail cell in Linz, Austria, in 2008 by squeezing through a narrow food hatch in the cell door.

MISSING TEETH ▧ After Qin Yuan from Chongqing, China, woke up missing his dentures and with a strange feeling in his body, he consulted doctors who discovered his false teeth lodged in one of his lungs. After operating, they suggested that he take them out before sleeping.

EGG SURPRISE ▧ When Mr. Cao from Changchun, China, cracked open an egg to make his supper, he was shocked to find a live chick inside—and he was even more surprised to find that the chick had four legs!

ROOF REPAIRS ▧ A man who was trying to repair the roof of his home in Beijing, China, was blown up a nearby tree by a sudden gust of wind. He was left clinging to the 45-ft-high (14-m) tree for 20 minutes until firefighters rescued him.

ANCIENT STRING ▧ Unearthing a Stone Age settlement on the Isle of Wight, England, archeologists found an 8,000-year-old piece of string. It was made from twisted plant stems.

COFFIN HOME ▧ Despite having a morbid fear of being buried alive, a Brazilian man has set up house in a large coffin. Freud de Melo has equipped the coffin with a TV, a water pitcher, an air vent and two plastic tubes that he attaches to megaphones to contact the outside world.

UNINVITED GUEST ▧ Over Christmas 2008, a stranger spent several days secretly living in the roof of a family's house in Wilkes-Barre, Pennsylvania. The Ferrance family discovered the uninvited guest only when he emerged from their attic wearing their clothes. He had been staying with neighbors but, when they told him to leave, he went through a trap door into the shared attic.

SLEEP SURFER ▧ A woman turned on her computer, typed in her username and password, then composed and sent three emails—all while she was asleep. Researchers from the University of Toledo, Ohio, said the sleepwalker learned what she had done when someone contacted her about one of her emails the following day.

Daring Dentist

The fact that he lacks hands has not deterred Seke, who for almost 30 years has worked as a local dentist. The 42-year-old from Jarkarta, Indonesia, has no formal training but has done a lot of reading on the subject, since starting to drill teeth when he was a teenager. Seke uses a television to help distract his patients.

HORSE WON'T FIAT

When a Polish farmer bought a foal at auction in Warsaw in January 2009, the only way to get it back to his farm, 150 mi (241 km) away, was to put it in the back of a small hatchback with the rear seats strapped to the roof! Luckily, the police found the car on the highway after it had broken down, and took custody of the 260-lb (117-kg) horse until they could find a better means of transport.

FATAL FLAW ■ A man who copied an episode of *CSI: Crime Scene Investigation* by committing suicide but trying to make it look like murder was found out because he didn't attach enough helium balloons to the gun with which he had shot himself. Planning for the gun to float away, Thomas Hickman drove from Dallas, Texas, into New Mexico and put duct tape over his mouth before shooting himself in the head. However, the bundle of balloons, with the gun still attached, was found snagged on bushes nearby.

FLORAL APOLOGY ■ A prisoner who escaped from jail in Crawford County, Arkansas, in June 2008, left behind an origami flower—made from toilet paper—as his way of saying sorry for breaking free.

GROUP TRANCE ■ Fifty female workers at a garment factory in Tangerang, Indonesia, went into an involuntary collective trance in 2007, during which they wept uncontrollably and jerked their bodies around.

RADIOACTIVE CAFÉ ■ Police in the Ukraine foiled a plot to smuggle a highly radioactive helicopter from the site of the Chernobyl disaster area and turn it into a unique coffee shop. Several people were detained in May 2008 while transporting the scrap helicopter—which seated up to 28 people but emitted 30 times the legal level of radiation—from within the exclusion zone set up around the Chernobyl nuclear power station that exploded in 1986.

Dog Girl

Oxana Malaya acts like a dog, walking on all fours, panting with her tongue hanging out and whining and barking at will. Her canine behavior is a legacy of her feral childhood. For five years from the age of three, she was raised by a pack of wild dogs near the village of Novaya Blagoveschenka, Ukraine, after apparently being abandoned by her parents. When she was finally discovered in 1991, she had almost forgotten how to speak.

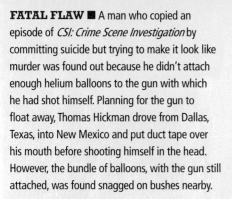

UNLUCKY CAR ■ Hollywood star James Dean died aged 24 in 1955 when he crashed his Porsche Spyder sports car. The car was taken to a garage, where the engine slipped out and fell onto a mechanic, shattering both of his legs. The engine was then bought by a doctor who put it in his racing car and was soon killed in a crash. Another driver in that same race was killed in his car, which had Dean's driveshaft fitted to it. When the shell of Dean's Porsche was later repaired and put on display, the showroom burned down. Exhibited again in Sacramento, it fell off the stand on to a visitor, breaking his hip. Finally, in 1959, the car mysteriously broke into 11 pieces while sitting on steel supports.

NAME GAME ■ Three Englishmen, traveling separately through Peru in the 1920s, found themselves the only passengers in a railroad car. Introducing themselves to each other, they discovered that one man's surname was Bingham, the second man's was Powell, and the third man's was Bingham-Powell. None of the men were related to either of the others in any way.

SICK ROBBER ■ An Australian post office thief was caught by his own vomit. Ahmed Habib Jalloul was so nervous during the robbery in Adelaide that he was physically sick on the spot, allowing police to take DNA from the pool of vomit and match it to him.

PRISON WORSHIP ■ In December 2007, inmate Michael Polk sued Utah prison officials because they wouldn't provide a Thor's hammer, a prayer cloth, a wassail-filled horn, a boar-skin drum and a sword—so that he could worship the ancient Norse gods.

FAKE WIFE ■ When an Indian man went to court in 2008 to obtain a divorce, he took along an impersonator in place of his wife. The supposedly mutual divorce was granted immediately, but when his real wife found out and appealed, the divorce was suspended.

DEAD MAN ELECTED ■ Neculai Ivascu was re-elected as mayor for the village of Voinesti, Romania, in June 2008—despite being dead. He died from liver disease shortly after voting began but still beat his living opponent, Gheorghe Dobrescu, by 23 votes.

GRUESOME DELIVERY ■ Two sisters living a mile and a half apart in Greenville, South Carolina, had bags containing human body parts left outside their homes on the same morning in April 2008. Each bag contained a human hand and a human foot.

LOST BALL ■ When a conifer was felled at the Eaton Golf Club in Norwich, Norfolk, England, in February 2009, the greenkeeper was amazed to discover a perfectly preserved golf ball embedded deep in the trunk. The tree had apparently grown around the ball, which is believed to have lodged in a fork of the tree many years ago following a wayward drive at the first hole.

CORPSE RIDE ■ Two men wheeled their dead friend through the streets of New York City in an office chair in January 2008 to cash his $355 Social Security check. All charges against them were later dropped because they said they didn't know he was dead at the time.

GRISLY DISCOVERY ■ The corpse of Vladimir Ledenev of Tula, Russia, was found sitting at his kitchen table in January 2007—where it had sat undisturbed for six years. In front of him were an empty vodka bottle and a glass.

LONG WAIT ■ Schoolgirl Emily Hwaung of Seattle, Washington, put a note into an ocean-bound soda bottle and received a reply from 1,735 mi (2,790 km) away—21 years later. The bottle, with its message still intact, was washed ashore in Nelson Lagoon, Alaska, and picked up by Merle Brandell, who managed to trace Emily via her old school.

RING RETRIEVED ■ A grandmother from Leicestershire, England, was reunited with her engagement ring—67 years after she had thrown it into a field during an argument. Violet Booth and her fiancé hunted in vain for the ring and had to buy another when they got married a few months later in 1941, but in 2008 her grandson, metal-detector fan Leighton Boyes, amazingly dug up the ring after pinpointing the spot where it had landed.

ROMEO ROBBER ■ An Italian thief who fell in love with the female cashier at a Genoa post office he robbed was arrested when he went back to ask her for a date. The day after forcing the 21-year-old to hand over money at gunpoint, the robber returned to the scene of the crime with a bunch of flowers, an apology and the offer of a date. Instead of immediately accepting his offer, the cashier kept him talking while she activated a silent alarm connected to the police station.

MOVIE MEMENTO ■ Workmen draining a lake beneath a roller coaster in Blackpool, England, in 2005, discovered an earring that had been lost by Hollywood movie star Marlene Dietrich 73 years earlier. The precious pearl earring had fallen off while Dietrich was taking a ride on the Big Dipper at the resort's Pleasure Beach in 1934.

Roadquill

Canadian artist Amy Nugent trawls the streets looking for roadkill, then collects it as material for incredible artwork. She hoarded more than 30,000 porcupine quills from Canadian roads to make a large sphere that she calls Roadquill. Her work is dedicated to recycling and honoring the animals that she encounters.

www.ripleybooks.com
>>> go to >>>

Sting in the Tail

In previous *Ripley's Believe It or Not!* annuals, we saw Thailand's "Scorpion Queen" Kanchana Kaetkaew get married with live scorpions on her dress and survive 32 days locked up with more than 3,000 scorpions. Now she has shocked people further by living in a room for 33 days with 5,000 large scorpions for company from December 2008 to January 2009. The creepy-crawly lover was stung three times in her room at the *Ripley's Believe It or Not!* museum in Pattaya, Thailand, but luckily she has built up immunity to the venom over the years and was unharmed.

Ripley's research

Scorpions are generally timid, but they will defend themselves with the very painful sting on their tail, and some species can produce enough venom to kill a human. In the U.S.A. there are about 1,000 scorpion stings reported each year, although the last known death was in 1968. In Mexico, however, there are more than 1,000 deaths from scorpion stings every year.

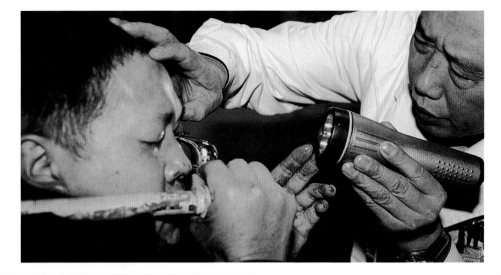

Eye Watering

When Yi Zhao of Chongqing, China, slipped in the bath at his home he impaled his left eye on one of the faucets. After firefighters cut the pipes he was rushed to the hospital with the faucet still stuck in his head. At the hospital it was impossible for Yi Zhao to fit in the scanner, so a plumber was summoned to remove more than a foot (30 cm) of pipe protruding from his eye, but when this did not work, Zhao simply removed the tap himself.

SIXTH SENSE ■ The parents of a three-year-old girl from Middlesbrough, England, are convinced that she has psychic powers. Emilia Rose Taylor had regularly gone into trances as a baby and once she began to speak, she started talking about various people only she could see, including a smelly old man (who it turned out had previously lived at the house) and her father's twin brother, who had died at the age of four.

WRONG DAY ■ A woman from Norfolk, England, discovered in 2008 that she had been celebrating her birthday on the wrong day for more than a century. Lena Thouless, aged 106, had always thought her birthday was November 23, until her daughter discovered that she was actually born on November 22.

PERFECT GAMES ■ In December 2008, brothers Ed and Tom Shircel from Sheboygan, Wisconsin, each bowled perfect 300 games playing for the same team and in the same game.

GHOST STORY ■ A burglar who broke into a house in Malaysia in 2008 told police he was prevented from escaping by a ghost. He claimed that the supernatural figure had held him captive for three days without food and water.

RING RETURNED ■ After losing a gold ring in 1973 when it slipped through a crack in the floorboards of a chapel at Gwyddelwern, Wales, Carys Williams got it back 35 years later when the building was demolished.

TIME RIDDLE ■ Archeologists who opened an ancient Chinese tomb that had been sealed shut more than 400 years ago were alarmed to discover a 100-year-old Swiss watch inside. Believing they were the first people to visit the Ming Dynasty grave in Shangsi since the occupant's death, they were unable to explain the presence of the modern timepiece.

SECRET SISTERS ■ Two women who had been friends for more than 30 years found out in 2008 that they were actually sisters. Deborah Day was adopted at the age of two months, separating her from her sister, Marilyn Morris, but the two met again as teenagers in Weston-super-Mare in Somerset, England, and became firm friends without realizing they were related.

SKULL MYSTERY ■ Scientists on New Zealand's North Island have discovered a skull belonging to a European white woman who lived about 270 years ago—a century before the first-known white settlers arrived in the country.

FATHER FIGURE ■ A one-legged man who has already fathered 78 children is hoping to father 100 by 2015. Born in 1947, Daad Mohammed Murad Abdul Rahman of the United Arab Emirates had already been married 15 times by the age of 60, although he had to divorce his wives as he went along, because under Islamic law he is not allowed to be married to more than four at a time.

BURIED ALIVE ■ Ruby the Border Terrier survived in 2008 despite being buried alive for 16 days in a garden compost heap. She had become trapped under a rock that was meant to stop rabbits from getting into the garden at her home in West Sussex, England.

HAIRY HUMANS ■ There are as many hairs per square inch on your body as on a chimpanzee—but most are too fine or too fair to be visible.

FIRE PROOF ■ Skip and Linda Miller of Cuyamaca, California, have had two houses destroyed by wildfires in four years so have decided to build their third house out of concrete, partially underground and with heat and fire-resistant materials.

VIDEO PUNISHMENT ■ A journalist in Romania can be jailed for up to seven years for recording and showing a video of an official taking a bribe.

UNDERGROUND FIRE ■ An underground fire in coal mines beneath Centralia, Pennsylvania, has been burning since 1962.

NAVAL MYSTERY ■ Although Bolivia has no sea ports and no coastline, it maintains a naval force with more than 150 boats and thousands of sailors.

A Taste for Toothpaste

Dentist Dr. Val Kolpakov from Saginaw, Michigan, collects toothpaste—and since 2002 he has acquired nearly 1,500 different types from around the world. Among his prized possessions are a special Hopalong Cassidy toothpaste and a Scotch whiskey flavored toothpaste.

Incredible Eyeful

Ping Zui of Hubei, China, can blow up balloons using only his eyes. Ping, who discovered his talent as a child while swimming in a river, wears a pair of goggles with a plastic pipeline linked to the balloon.

I Love you

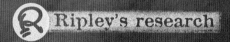

Ripley's research

Ping Zui inflates the balloons through his tear ducts—the only exit for air in the eyes. The tear duct is extremely narrow and winding, and the amount of air that can be expelled in that way is tiny, making his feat all-the-more amazing.

Glandular Fever

This French woman—known as the "Female Gorilla"—suffered from glandular excess, which resulted in huge lumps and masses of dark hair appearing over large parts of her body.

LONG-EARED LADY

Iban women of Sarawak, Malaysia, traditionally wear wooden or metal weights and eardrops around their stretched lobes because elongated ears are a sign of great beauty and status among the tribe.

Star Wars Wedding

When Star Wars fans Rebecca D'Madeiros and Bill Duda were married in their Portland, Oregon, backyard in June 2008, they insisted that all 70 guests come as characters from the 1970s sci-fi movie. The bride and groom were dressed as Mon Mothma and Admiral Ackbar respectively, the wedding was presided over by Yoda, who had recently secured his marriage license over the Internet, and the ringbearer was Princess Leia. The happy couple were led from the house by a line of Imperial Stormtroopers.

DELAYED DELIVERY ■ Michael Cioffi of Boston, Massachusetts, received a postcard of Yellowstone National Park's Tower Falls in February 2008—79 years after it was sent.

FUNERAL FAN Mijo Tkalcec from Peteranec, Croatia, has been to over 2,000 funerals. He has been fascinated by them since he was a child and will travel hundreds of miles just to attend one.

SAME BIRTHDAYS ■ Martin and Kim MacKriell from Gloucester, England, are unlikely ever to forget their three children's birthdays, because they were all born on January 29—at odds of 133,000 to one. Their son Robin was born on January 29, 1994, daughter Rebecca was born on January 29, 1996, and although another daughter Ruby was due to be born on February 7, 2008, she had to be delivered by cesarean section and the only available date was the same birthday as her siblings.

PHOTOGRAPHIC MEMORY ■ Karen and Mark Cline of Mansfield, Ohio, did not have $150 to pay a photographer for their wedding photos when they got married as teenagers in 1980. But when photographer Jim Wagner discovered the pictures during a clearout, he remembered the impoverished couple and sent them their wedding photos just in time for their 27th anniversary.

SPENDING SPREE ■ A nine-year-old Indonesian boy went on a five-day spending spree in 2008 that cost his parents $10,000. Ahmad Legal Civiandi spent his family's cash savings on toys and gadgets.

DOUBLE DEATH ■ After 70 years of marriage, a Syrian couple died of natural causes on the same day in January 2008. The 95-year-old husband died hours after his 90-year-old wife passed away.

JEDI ATTACK ■ A *Star Wars* fan who cofounded the Church of the Jedi in Wales was assaulted in 2008 by a man dressed as Darth Vader. Barney Jones—a.k.a. Master Jonba Hehol—was hit on the head with a metal crutch by Darth Vader impersonator Arwel Hughes.

SECRET GUEST ■ A homeless woman managed to live undetected in the closet of a man's house for a whole year. She sneaked into the house in Kasuya, Japan, when he left it unlocked and set up home in the top compartment of his closet without him having any idea of her presence. She moved a mattress into the small shelf space, took showers while he was out and left no trace of her existence. It was only when food mysteriously began disappearing from his kitchen that he became suspicious and police found the 58-year-old woman curled up on the closet shelf.

SURPRISE DISCOVERY ■ Steve Flaig of Plainfield Township, Michigan, had searched for his birth mother for a long time and in December 2007 he finally tracked her down—finding to his amazement that they had been working for the same company for almost a year. He was a delivery driver for a local home-improvement store and his mother was the woman he simply knew as Chris, the head cashier.

ANONYMOUS DONOR ■ Every month for 33 years, an anonymous donor has left a money-filled envelope at a police station in Tochigi, Japan, with instructions to help the needy.

NO DEATHS ■ In 1946, Mildred West, an obituary writer on New York's *Alton Evening Telegraph*, took a week's vacation. During her absence and for the first time in the newspaper's history, there were no deaths in Alton (population 32,000). Normally, they averaged ten a week.

SKIPPING SCHOOL ■ Ten-year-old Diego Palacios of Monterrey, Mexico, used industrial glue to affix his hand to his bed's metal frame—to avoid going to school.

SINISTER KIMONO ■ A kimono owned successively by three teenage girls, each of whom had died before having a chance to wear it, was considered so unlucky that it was cremated by a priest in 1657. But as the garment burned, a wind fanned the flames and started a fire that destroyed three-quarters of Tokyo, demolishing 9,000 shops, 500 palaces, 300 temples and 61 bridges, and killing 100,000 people.

SNAIL MAIL ■ A postcard from Nebraska mailed on December 23, 1914, finally reached Oberlin, Kansas, in 2007—93 years late!

DOUBLE RESCUE ■ A Chinese man, Wang Weiqing, rescued a seven-year-old boy from a pond in Beicheng in 2008—20 years after rescuing the boy's father from exactly the same spot.

RESTRAINED DRIVER ■ A burglary suspect embarrassed police in Brisbane, Australia, in April 2008 by driving off in their patrol car—even though he had handcuffs on. While the arresting officers were searching for further evidence, the handcuffed man climbed into the driver's seat, started the engine and drove off.

SIBLING RIVALRY ■ The mayor of an Ohio village fought off a challenge for power in November 2007—from her younger brother. Daniel Huffman was hoping to unseat his sister, Charlotte Garman, in the election, but the registered voters of Montezuma stayed loyal to Garman, who had been mayor for eight years, by 43 votes to 24.

CUTLERY ESCAPE ■ In May 2008, 36 prisoners escaped from a jail in N'Zerekore, Guinea, by using spoons to dig through a wall.

WALLET RECOVERED ■ Tom Eichenberg of Elk Grove, California, had his wallet returned to him in 2008—33 years after he lost it. He mislaid the wallet while he was a student at Santa Clara University in 1975 and it was eventually found nestled in a wall by construction workers renovating the student center.

TOILET CORPSE ■ A family lived for two months in 2008 with the decaying body of a 90-year-old woman on the toilet of the only bathroom in their home in Necedah, Wisconsin. They were said to be following the advice of a religious leader who told them the corpse would come back to life.

MACHINERY SPLIT ■ A Serb farmer, angry at a court order forcing him to share everything with his ex-wife, took the judge at his word and cut all his farm tools and machinery in half using a grinder.

Oh baby!

When her daughter said she wanted a sibling, Deborah King made her one—from vinyl. Deborah from Edinburgh, Scotland, is an expert in "reborning," a hobby that creates amazingly lifelike baby dolls. The dolls are painted with multiple layers to give a mottled-skin effect and are weighted and stuffed to weigh and feel similar to a real baby. Customers, who include grieving parents and nostalgic grandparents, can even ask for a heartbeat to be added to their reborn baby.

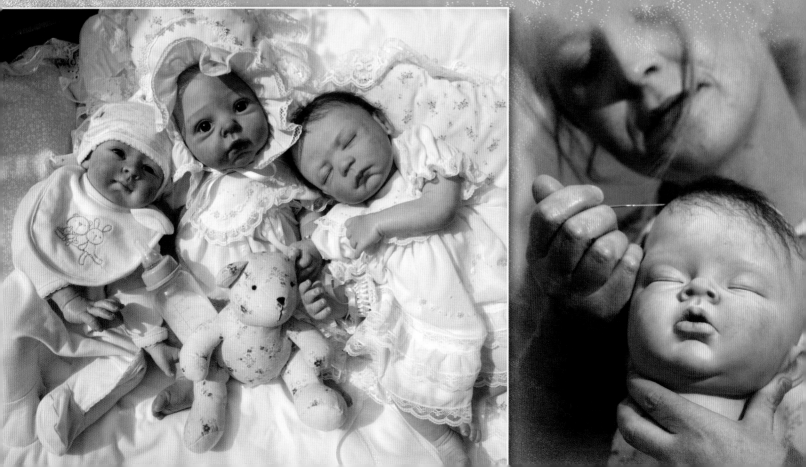

DEAD CAT ■ Edwin Julius Krueger, who ran a general store in Wykoff, Minnesota, for over 50 years, never threw anything away. Following his death in 1989, the store became a museum, full of Krueger's accumulated artifacts including decades of junk mail, 35 years' worth of TV guides, his collection of *Smokey the Bear* posters and even his dead cat Sammy, who died in 1986 and is kept on a shelf in a small cardboard box.

HIP JOINT ■ Prague lawyer Premsyl Donat tried to sell what he claimed was the Czech president's hip joint on eBay in August 2008. Bidding had reached $40,000 when the police swooped in and revealed that the joint was not, in fact, that of President Vaclav Klaus who had undergone a hip replacement operation three months earlier.

CLOSE RELATIVES ■ Lewis Manilow, 81, and Jack Shore, 82, of Chicago, Illinois, who lived only six blocks apart, met randomly in 2008 and then discovered that they were brothers.

ESCAPE BID ■ A daring escape bid through the air-conditioning ducts of the Alton city jail, Texas, in 2008, ended abruptly when one of the two prisoners crashed through the ceiling into the office of Police Chief Baldemar Flores.

HIDING PLACE ■ After spending four years on the run from police on suspicion of robbery, Petru Susanu was finally found in 2009—hiding under his mother's bed. He had used floorboards and carpet to construct a makeshift hideaway under the double bed at the family home in Vladeni, Romania.

License Plate Omen

In an incredible coincidence, Dominic Calgi of New Rochelle, New York, owned a car with the license plate 5V 17 32, which spelled out the exact date of his death—May 17, 1932.

UNTIMELY PROPHECY ■ A bag snatcher in Venice, Italy, died from a heart attack in 2008, minutes after his 66-year-old victim had yelled at him: "I hope you drop dead!"

JUNK PILE ■ Police carted away more than two tons of garbage from the home of Hiroshi Sekine of Gyoda, Siatama, Japan, after he was arrested for blocking the sidewalk with junk.

EDIBLE ORGANS

It looks like a prop from an old horror movie, but it's actually a tasty cake painstakingly made to look like a bloody chest cavity. The "Thorax Cake" was created by horror enthusiast Barbara Jo from San José, California. Different flavor cakes were filled with raspberry, strawberry, kiwi, mango and blueberry sauces designed to ooze out of the organs when sliced into. The gruesome creation was held together by a white-chocolate rib cage before being devoured at Barbara's annual pumpkin-carving party.

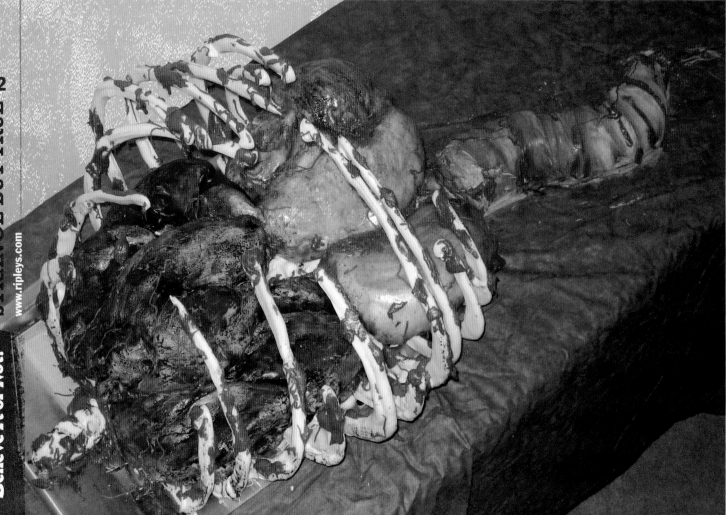

HAIR-RAISING RIDE ■ Fifth-grader Mason Calderhead from Mooresville, Indiana, was surprised to hear a familiar meow when he got out of his mom's car after traveling from his home to karate class in February 2009. His pet cat Gurdy had somehow attached herself to the underside of the car and had taken a hair-raising 5-mi (8-km) ride. Luckily, Gurdy suffered no injuries, but was just a little shaken up from her experience.

KLINGON KEYBOARD ■ A keyboard featuring letters from *Star Trek's* Klingon alphabet has been marketed in Britain. It has been designed for science-fiction fans who have learned the alien tongue Klingonese, the most widely spoken fictional language in the world. The Bible and the works of Shakespeare have already been translated into Klingonese.

LATE VERDICT ■ Although her son had been deceased for two years, Julie Strange of Cumbria, England, carried his ashes into a courtroom so he could answer a summons charge that the judge refused to drop.

BUN FIGHT ■ After arguing with his girlfriend in 2008, a 22-year-old man from Vero Beach, Florida, was charged with assaulting her—having shoved a cheeseburger in her face.

BARBER LAW ■ It's against the law in Houma, Louisiana, to operate barber shops on Sundays and Mondays. Just ask barber Clyde Scott, who was caught working on Monday, May 19, 2008—and ticketed.

EMU CRASH ■ A woman from Largs Bay, South Australia, was killed in January 2008 when her motorbike crashed into an emu that was running across the highway in broad daylight.

KEEN COP ■ Having been in the police force for only six days, P.C. John Nash of Greater Manchester Police, England, was so keen to make his first arrest that he chased, and apprehended, a suspect despite having a 6-in (15-cm) twig impaled in his left eye.

CHEAP HIT ■ Oofty Goofty, a 19th-century sideshow performer in San Francisco, California, carried a baseball bat with him and offered to let people hit him with it for 50 cents a swing.

TATTOO CLUE ■ Arrested in St. Paul, Minnesota, in December 2008, a 25-year-old driver tried to get away with his crime by giving a false name to the arresting police officers—forgetting that his real name was tattooed in large letters on his neck.

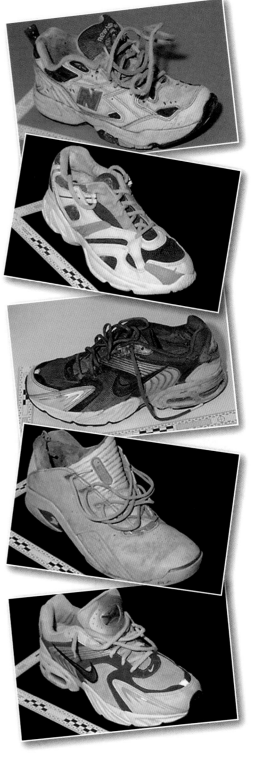

Pigeon Impact

Pigeons can fly at 50 mph (80 km/h), so when a pigeon flew at full tilt into a second-floor window in Washington, D.C., in October 2008, it left an almost perfect impression on the glass, including wings, beak and tail.

Washed-up Feet

Police were mystified by the grisly discovery of five feet washed up in different locations in Canada between August 2007 and June 2008. Each of the sneakers had human feet still inside, which eventually enabled a coroner to identify two pairs, belonging to two unidentified persons. The fifth shoe remained a mystery. It is estimated that a foot separated from a drowned body could travel by strong currents around 1,000 mi (1,600 km) before reaching land.

JACK AND JACKIE ■ Jack and Jackie Reppard from Nokomis, Florida, were born at the same time, in the same room, and were delivered by the same doctor. This may not have proved exceptional in itself, but they went on to attend the same school, graduated together, got married and have recently celebrated their 40th wedding anniversary!

HEDGEHOG HURLER ■ A man was charged with assaulting a teenage boy in Whakatane, New Zealand, in 2008—with a hedgehog. He picked up the creature and threw it at the boy from a distance of 15 ft (4.5 m), causing a large, red welt and several puncture marks on the victim's body.

PALM ROBBER ■ A man tried to rob a store in DeLand, Florida, in June 2008 with a palm frond as a weapon. He threatened to stab the clerk with the frond if he didn't hand over cash. A customer chased him out of the store with a bar stool.

UP FOR SALE ■ Ian Usher from Perth, Australia, sold his entire life for $380,000 on eBay following the breakdown of his marriage. The sale price included his home, his car, his motorcycle, a two-week trial in his job and even his friends.

VANISHING POOL ■ Thieves stole a swimming pool containing 1,000 gal (3,785 l) of water from the backyard of a house in Paterson, New Jersey, without spilling a drop. The Valdivia family awoke to find the hip-high, inflatable, 10-ft-diameter (3-m) pool gone, but with no sign of any of the water.

LETTER RETURNED ■ In July 2008, Xan Wedel of Lawrence, Kansas, received a return-to-sender letter that had originally been sent by a previous resident at that address—60 years earlier! The letter, postmarked November 11, 1948, described the town's dismay at Harry S Truman's presidential victory.

GNOME RUSTLER ■ A man was arrested in Brittany, France, in 2008 on suspicion of stealing 170 ornamental gnomes from various people's gardens.

Alas Poor André

A concert pianist whose dying wish was to be part of a stage production of Shakespeare's *Hamlet* has finally realized his ambition. When André Tchaikovsky died in 1982, he left his body to medical research but requested that his skull be given to the Royal Shakespeare Company "for use in theatrical performance." Many actors and directors were uncomfortable with using a real skull but, in 2008, British actor David Tennant held aloft André's skull in *Hamlet* in Stratford-upon-Avon, England.

FIGHTING GRANNY ■ Italian soldiers are prepared for army life by being beaten up on a daily basis by a tiny 77-year-old grandmother. Japanese granny Keiko Wakabayshi may be only 5 ft (1.5 m) tall, but she is a trained master in a variety of martial arts, including judo and karate.

FASHIONABLY LATE ■ Kenneth Smith attended his high school prom in Chester, Pennsylvania, in June 2008—more than 60 years late. The 84-year-old was drafted into military service in 1943 before finishing high school and, although he returned home after World War II, he never received his high school diploma.

HYPNOTIC HEIST ■ An Italian criminal hypnotized supermarket checkout staff into handing over money from their cash registers, leaving them with no memory of the robbery. The last thing they remembered before finding the till empty was the thief leaning over and saying "Look into my eyes."

SAME INITIALS ■ All 11 members of the Lawrence family from Derby, England, have the same initials—T.J. In 2007, Tim James and Teresa Jean called their ninth child Tillie Jasmine—following on from Timothy John, Tara Jessica, Thomas Joseph, twins Taylia Jade and Travis James, Taylor Jake, Thad Jack and Trey Jacob.

DIRTY LAUNDRY ■ The laundry of a man in Kaiserslautern, Germany, was so foul-smelling that his neighbors called the police, thinking someone had died in the apartment.

REELED IN ■ A man drowning in Maine's Kennebec River in July 2008 was rescued by someone reeling him in with a fishing rod. Bob Greene of Hallowell snagged the man's shirt with a fishing lure and saved him.

Canine Miracle

Marco Menozzi could not believe his eyes when he discovered a dog stuck in the front bumper of his car in Cozze, southern Italy. Traveling at 70 mph (113 km/h), he had struck the animal so hard that it became lodged in the grill. Incredibly, the lucky dog suffered only a broken leg and thankfully is now fully recovered.

Cough Shot

In 1863, W.V. Meadows of West Point, Georgia, was shot in the eye at the Battle of Vicksburg during the American Civil War. He survived, and 58 years later was surprised to cough up the bullet.

Enlarged photo of bullet

Mr. W.V. Meadows West Point - Ga

CHANCE CANCELLATION ■ Elsa Oliver from Gateshead, England, canceled a vacation to New York just before takeoff because she had a premonition that something really good was going to happen to her. Later that day, she heard she had been selected to appear on the TV quiz show "Who Wants To Be A Millionaire?," and she went on to win £64,000.

FORESAW DEATH ■ In 1980, U.S. actor David Janssen, star of the TV show *The Fugitive*, had a bad dream in which he saw himself being carried away in a coffin following a heart attack. The dream unnerved him so much that he consulted a psychic, who advised him to have a medical. Two days later, Janssen died from a sudden heart attack.

LUCKY FIND ■ While at summer camp in Connecticut, Brandon Lavallee found 21 four-leaf clovers and two with five leaves—in one day.

TURKEY BOWL ■ Cincinnati, Ohio, prepares for Thanksgiving each year with its traditional Turkey Bowl, where competitors use frozen turkeys instead of bowling balls to play the game.

CLEARED NAME ■ New Jersey lawyer Adam Goodmann took nearly two years and went through five judges to clear himself of a shoplifting conviction. The amount in the dispute was just $3.76 on a special-offer set of photo prints.

Name Dropper

When George Garratt from Somerset, England, wanted to do something different, he officially changed his name to "Captain Fantastic Faster than Superman Spiderman Batman Wolverine The Hulk and the Flash Combined!"

Captain Fantastic Faster than Superman Spiderman Batman Wolverine The Hulk and the FLASH COMBINED!

EXTREME WEATHER

BY THE YEAR 2100: POSSIBLE EFFECTS OF CLIMATE CHANGE

SUDDEN TEMPERATURE RISE	At Spearfish, South Dakota, on January 22, 1943, the temperature rose 49°F (27°C) from −4°F (−20°C) to 45°F (7°C) in just two minutes.
DRAMATIC TEMPERATURE FALL	On January 10, 1911, the temperature plummeted 47°F (26°C) from 55°F (13°C) to 8°F (−13°C) in 15 minutes at Rapid City, South Dakota.
SIX-STATE STORM	On March 12, 2006, a single thunderstorm tracked 790 mi (1,271 km) across six U.S. states. It began in Oklahoma and ended in Michigan.
TRIPLE TORNADO BLAST	The town of Codell, Kansas, was hit by a tornado on the exact same date (May 20) three years straight—1916, 1917 and 1918.
ONE-MINUTE DELUGE	1.5 in (38 mm) of rain fell in just one minute on a village in Guadeloupe on November 26, 1970.
1,720-FT-HIGH WAVE	On July 9, 1958, an earthquake created a tsunami wave 1,720 ft (525 m) high in Lituya Bay, Alaska. Millions of trees were swept away in its path.
15-INCH SNOWFLAKE	A snowflake that measured 15 in (38 cm) in diameter was seen at Fort Keough, Montana, on January 28, 1887.
300-MPH WIND	A three-second gust of wind during a tornado near Oklahoma City, Oklahoma, on May 3, 1999, reached a speed of over 300 mph (483 km/h).
95 FT OF SNOW	During the 1998–99 season, Mount Baker Ski Area in Washington State had 1,140 in, or 95 ft (29 m), of snowfall.
7-IN HAILSTONE	A hailstone 7 in (18 cm) in diameter with a circumference of 18.75 in (47.6 cm) fell at Aurora, Nebraska, on June 22, 2003—that's almost three times the size of a tennis ball.

ONE MILLION SPECIES WILL BE EXTINCT	Up to 35 percent of all current species—plants and animals—could be extinct. Among the most threatened are polar bears, because the Arctic ice is melting by nine percent every decade. Arctic summers could be ice-free by as early as 2050.
MILLIONS WILL SUFFER WATER SHORTAGES	Up to five billion people—more than half the world's population—will suffer water shortages. Among the worst affected areas could be Central and Southeast Asia, where, as Himalayan glaciers vanish, rivers will run dry.
IT WILL BE TOO HOT TO EXIST	The Arctic will have a benign climate, but the whole central region of the world will be almost uninhabitable owing to excessive heat and lack of water. Increased droughts could create new dust bowls in the southwest U.S.A., northern Mexico, and parts of Europe and Africa. In Nigeria alone, 1,350 sq mi (3,500 sq km) of land is turning to desert each year—that's almost the size of Rhode Island.
200 MILLION PEOPLE WILL LOSE THEIR HOMES	People who live in coastal areas or in river basins are likely to be forced out of their homes by the increased risk of floods and rising sea levels. Some Pacific Ocean islands such as Tuvalu (population 12,000) may have to be completely evacuated as it could be too expensive to build flood defences.
HEAT-RELATED DEATHS WILL RISE	As global temperatures rise by as much as 11°F (6°C), in Australia at least 5,000 more people a year will suffer heat-related deaths. In New York City, 1,000 more people a year will die from the heat. Elsewhere, floods and landslides resulting from increased rainfall may lead to a dramatic rise in the number of deaths from infectious diseases.
NEW YORK CITY WILL FLOOD	Sea levels around New York City could rise by more than 3 ft (90 cm), flooding low-lying areas such as Coney Island, Lower Manhattan and parts of Brooklyn and Queens. Pumping systems may be needed to keep the city's subway system dry.

Sandstone rock at Coyote Butte on the border between Arizona and Utah makes stunning natural waves and stripes. The distinctive patterns were formed as light sand piled up with heavier sand and grit over millions of years, eventually becoming compacted into rock and eroded into smooth waves.

EXTREME EARTH

FOAM BATH

In August 2007, bathers in the sea at Yamba, Australia, found themselves in what looked like a giant bubble bath, when thick sea foam started to wash in on the beach. This rare phenomenon is not fully explained, but it is thought to be caused by elements in the sea, such as microscopic organisms, dead fish and seaweed, being churned to a froth by large waves as they near the shore. The foam at Yamba was thought to extend 165 ft (50 m) out to sea.

Deer Cloud

A cloud in the shape of a reindeer graced the skies over Wellington, New Zealand. A light cirrus cloud, it formed at an altitude of around 30,000 ft (9,100 m).

EXPLOSIVE CLOUD ■ The center of our galaxy has a cloud 10,000 light years across made of antimatter, a material which explodes into pure energy on contact with normal matter.

UPLIFTING EXPERIENCE ■ An earthquake in April 2007 measuring 8.1 on the Richter scale lifted the South Pacific island of Ranongga 10 ft (3 m) higher out of the ocean.

WATER PRESSURE ■ The pressure of water on the sea floor can crush a foam cup to the size of a thimble.

MIGHTY ERUPTION ■ Io, one of Jupiter's moons, has volcanoes that erupt up to 190 mi (305 km) into the sky.

METEORITE CRATERS ■ To date, scientists have found around 200 major meteorite impact craters on Earth, ranging from dozens of feet to hundreds of miles in diameter.

LONG CANYON ■ The Valles Marineris canyon system on Mars is 3 mi (5 km) deep and 200 mi (320 km) wide in some places and is over 3,000 mi (4,830 km) long—that's long enough to stretch from California to New York.

FLOOD POWER ■ Just 6 in (15 cm) of rapidly moving flood water is enough to knock a person down.

LARGE CLOUD ■ A single cumulonimbus cloud can stretch 6 miles across and 11 miles high (10 x 18 km)—almost twice the height of Mount Everest. A large cloud can hold enough water for 500,000 baths and weigh 700,000 tons—equal to the weight of more than 110,000 full-grown elephants.

ELECTRICAL STORM ■ In 1859, a ferocious storm disconnected the batteries running the telegraph system between Portland, Oregon, and Boston, Massachusetts. The storm, however, was so powerful it generated massive natural electrical currents that enabled the telegraph system to operate as normal.

MUD SLIDE ■ Mud avalanches can move at speeds in excess of 100 mph (160 km/h). On November 13, 1985, a volcano mudslide traveled 62 mi (100 km) and killed more than 23,000 people near Nevado del Ruiz, Colombia.

FISH FOSSIL ■ A stone that had sat for 15 years on an ornamental rockery in a garden in Kent, England, was identified in 2008 as being the fossilized head of an 80-million-year-old haddock. The homeowner, Peter Parvin, had found the valuable fossil on a beach during a family holiday.

DAMAGE PATHS ■ Tornadoes can cause damage paths more than a mile (1.6 km) wide and 60 mi (96 km) long. Once a tornado in Broken Bow, Oklahoma, carried a motel sign 30 mi (48 km) and dropped it in Arkansas.

HURRICANE FORCE ■ A hurricane possesses as much energy as 10,000 nuclear bombs. A single hurricane's energy can equate to a power supply of 360 billion kilowatt hours a day—enough to supply electricity for the entire U.S.A. for six months.

FISH FENCE

In September 2008, dozens of fish were found dead, stuck headfirst in a chain-link fence in West Orange, Texas, when the waters receded following a storm surge from Hurricane Ike.

Tornado Terror

A huge tornado funnel cloud touched down in Orchard, Iowa, in June 2008. A witness said the funnel spiraled down close to the ground before going back up into the clouds.

NEARLY FRIED ■ Dave Fern of Pueblo, Colorado, was frying a tortilla in his home in 2001 when lightning struck a tree in his yard and traveled down a power line to his stove, burning a hole in his frying pan.

METEORITE MALAISE ■ A meteorite that crashed in Peru in September 2007—creating a crater 15 ft (4.5 m) deep and 65 ft (20 m) wide—apparently caused headaches, vomiting and nausea among dozens of local people.

Ripley's research

Swept inland as the area flooded and water levels rose alarmingly, the fish were swimming along in the swollen waters until they came to a fence and, being up to 10 in (25 cm) long, were too big to get through. Many of the fish were still stuck in the 4-ft-high (1.2-m) fence two days later.

NARROW BOLT ■ Although the length of a lightning bolt can be as much as 5 mi (8 km), its diameter is usually between just ½ in and 1 in (1.2 cm and 2.5 cm).

HERDERS RESCUED ■ Two reindeer herders were rescued in 2005 after being buried under snow for six days following an avalanche in Kamchatka, Russia.

RAPID REBUILD ■ When a tornado destroyed Chris Graber's home in Marshfield, Missouri, in 2006, his Amish neighbors helped him build a new one in fewer than 15 hours.

POSITIVE GIANTS ■ Some lightning strikes hit the ground up to 20 mi (32 km) away from the storm—and because they appear to strike from a clear sky they are referred to as "bolts from the blue." Known as "Positive Giants," these flashes carry several times the destructive energy of a normal lightning strike.

ACE VACUUM ■ A person exposed to the vacuum of space will fall unconscious after about 15 seconds, but is likely to survive a minute or two with little permanent effect.

COLLISION COURSE ■ The Martian moon Phobos orbits less than 6,000 mi (9,660 km) from Mars. Within 50 million years, it will either crash into the planet or break apart.

LIGHT SATURN ■ With the smallest density of any planet in the Solar System, Saturn is so light that it could float on water—if there were an ocean large enough to accommodate it!

RAPID ACCELERATION ■ An avalanche of snow can reach a speed of 80 mph (130 km/h) within five seconds after it fractures away from the mountainside.

QUAKE DAMAGE ■ There are 500,000 detectable earthquakes each year. Of these, 100,000 can be felt, but only 100 cause damage.

WEATHER EXTREMES ■ In the first half of 2007, floods, landslides and mudslides triggered by torrential rain killed 652 people in China and destroyed 452,000 homes. At the same time, nearly one million people in the country's Jiangxi Province were suffering shortages of drinking water after a month-long drought.

SPACE JUNK ■ More than 6,000 tons of man-made items, including more than 200 derelict satellites, are floating in orbit above our planet.

IGUANA FALL ■ An unusual night of cold weather in January 2008 caused dozens of chilled iguanas to drop unconscious out of trees in Key Biscayne, Florida.

LIGHTNING STRIKE ■ A three-year-old boy slept through a lightning strike in May 2008 that sounded like "a massive explosion" and blew a hole in his bedroom wall. The lightning blew all the lightbulbs and electrical equipment in the house in Flint, North Wales, but, remarkably, Elis Roberts remained fast asleep in his room, even though it was covered in masonry, plaster and dust.

RODE AVALANCHE ■ A veteran ski patroller from New Zealand survived an avalanche in 2007 by riding down it for more than 1,200 ft (365 m). He was finally buried by the snow, which carried him an additional 500 ft (150 m), but he managed to dig himself out with the help of two companions.

EXPLODING TOILETS ■ Hundreds of thousands of hailstones suddenly exploded out of toilets in an Austrian apartment block in July 2008, forcing startled residents to flee the building. One man, who was sitting on a toilet at the time, was blasted off it as the avalanche of ice quickly filled the entire building. The freak incident—at Eisenstadt—was caused by hailstones flooding into and blocking a local drain during a torrential downpour.

COAL FALL ■ In 1983, lumps of coke and coal mysteriously fell out of the sky and landed on yachtsmen in Poole Harbour, Dorset, England.

VALUABLE METEORITES ■ For many years, the standard price for meteoritic material was $1 per pound, but now many meteorites are worth as much as gold. Unsuspecting finders have used fallen meteorites as such things as blacksmith anvils and dog bowls, and for propping up autos.

BELL DEATH ■ Jean Rugibet of Trouille, France, rushed to the local belfry during a lightning storm in 1807 to prove that his beloved bells could drive away bad weather. The storm passed but the bells continued to ring, and friends found his body, fused by lightning to the bell ropes.

BEACH GARBAGE ■ In July 2007, a shift in ocean currents began dumping up to 300 tons of floating garbage every day on the Juhu Beach area near Mumbai, India.

FOSSILIZED FOREST ■ While digging for lignite, or brown coal, in 2007, miners in northeastern Hungary discovered an eight-million-year-old swamp cypress forest. Sixteen fossilized trees were found—the tallest around 20 ft (6 m)—and, amazingly, they had not petrified, or turned to stone, as preserved trees usually do—instead, they had retained their original wood.

Branching Out

These incredible trees are specially grafted to grow into sophisticated shapes by Peter and Becky Cook of Queensland, Australia. Peter once wondered if he could grow a chair and, over many years, his idea came to fruition. The Cooks meticulously plan all their creations, and among their shaped living trees are action figures that have green leaves sprouting from their heads as hair, and the amazing living wooden chair that is strong enough to support a fully grown man.

A Cut Above

Trimming the biggest hedge in Britain is a tall job, and it takes gardener Peter Pidgley a week to tidy up each side. The yew hedge grows in Dorset, England, and was planted during the reign of King Edward VI in the 16th century. The work creates a huge pile of cuttings, but the cuttings don't go to waste—they are sent to France to be used in the development of anti-cancer drugs.

GLOBAL DANGER ◼ More than one million species of plants and animals—a quarter of all life on land—could become extinct in just decades as a result of man-made climate change. Australia alone could lose more than half of its 400-plus butterfly species by 2050.

MIRACLE BERRY ◼ Known also as the miracle fruit, the berry of *Synsepalum dulcificum* creates a chemical reaction that raises your sense of sweetness, making lemons taste like candy, beer taste like chocolate and hot sauce taste like donut glaze. The effect lasts for about an hour. The berry is native to West Africa, but is now being harvested in South Florida where a single berry sells for $3.

ANCIENT SEED ◼ Botanists in Israel have managed to germinate a seed that is 2,000 years old. The 5-ft-tall (1.5-ft) Judean date palm was grown from the seed of a date eaten by Jewish rebels who once occupied the Roman garrison at Masada. The seed was discovered in a jar of discarded date pits during excavations of Masada in the 1960s.

Tree Wheel

A Phoenix tree in China has an unusual growth: a bicycle wheel rim. According to locals in Mengcheng Town, Anhui Province, a bicycle repairman used to ply his trade nearby and nailed the rim to the tree as an advertisement. Over the years, the tree grew around the wheel, which now looks as if it has been there forever.

SPACE DUST ◼ Every day around 40 tons of space dust enter the atmosphere and fall to the Earth's surface—that's the equivalent of the weight of eight African elephants.

OLD SPRUCE ◼ A spruce tree root system in Sweden has been sprouting new trees for nearly 10,000 years. Scientists think the tree in Dalarna originally took root around the year 7542 BC.

WATER FORCE ◼ Tsunami waves travel across oceans at speeds of up to 500 mph (800 km/h). Waves hitting coastlines have shifted 20-ton rocks hundreds of yards inland.

IN THE DARK ◼ On September 28, 2006, street lights across Iceland were shut off to give citizens a better view of the stars—while an astronomer explained what they were seeing over the country's national radio station.

25-HOUR DAYS? ◼ Because of the Earth's decelerating rotation, in the future days may have 25 hours. A British astronomer has proved the Earth's spin has been slowing down since 700 BC.

Bioluminescence

Venture out at night and you might see some of the unbelievable organisms that look like regular citizens of the natural kingdom in the light, but can produce stunning luminous colors in the darkness.

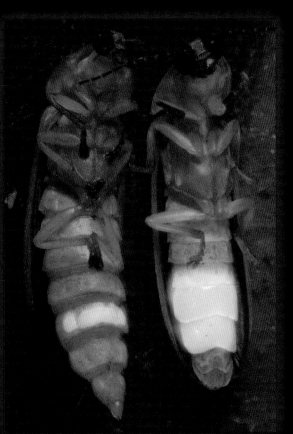

Incendiary Insects

Both the male and female firefly have vivid luminous bodies that can easily be spotted in bushes at night. The female has only one bioluminescent glowing segment, and the male has larger eyes to help him to see it. He also has two bright body segments of his own, which flash in a regular pattern to attract a mate.

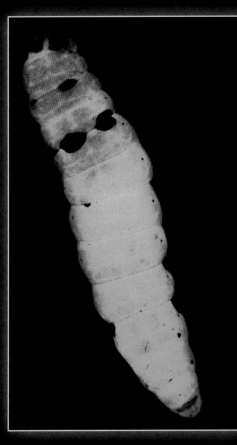

Death Light

Moth grubs don't glow until they're dying. The light is not from the grub itself but from bacteria expelled by a roundworm that burrows into it. The bacteria spread and digest the grub from the inside, turning it into a luminous corpse, before the worm swallows both and lays eggs in the dead larva.

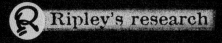
Ripley's research

Bioluminescence is the result of chemical reactions that convert energy into visible light. It has evolved in different creatures and organisms for various reasons, including communication, to warn predators off, to lure unsuspecting prey and to attract mates. The natural light can also provide camouflage in the ocean, as some deep-sea creatures hide from predators below by blending in with the brighter water above.

Fiery Fungi

Many types of mushrooms, including these Australian fungi, can glow brightly in the right conditions. Just don't pick one; they are usually as toxic as their color suggests.

Deep-sea Dazzler

The Tetrorchis is a type of jellyfish about ¾ in (1.9 cm) long. Bright bioluminescence in the creature, along with its thin tissue layers, produces a rainbow effect similar to oil on water.

The ground gave way under houses in Guatemala City, Guatemala, in February 2007. A sinkhole formed when broken water pipes washed underground soil away, leaving a void that collapsed, causing the death of three people and swallowing at least 12 houses. The resulting hole was more than 200 ft (61 m) deep and 65 ft (20 m) wide.

This vast pit, a diamond mine, is located south of the Arctic Circle in Canada's Northwest Territories. The hole is actually located on an island, and is so remote that it has its own airport. When the surrounding water freezes over in the winter, a supply road is opened up—usable for just two months of the year—which stretches 600 km (372 mi) over frozen lakes to the mine.

A Whole Lot of Holes

One of the biggest manmade holes in the world, the Mir diamond mine in Russia, dominates the nearby town of Mirny, which sits perched on the edge of a 1,722-ft (525-m) drop. The mine is an incredible 3,937 ft (1200 m) in diameter, equivalent to 12 soccer fields lying end to end. It was Russia's biggest source of diamonds, and is so deep that it takes mining trucks more than two hours to get to the bottom of the hole.

With a diameter of 1,519 ft (463 m) and a surface area the size of 225 baseball fields, it's easy to see how the "Big Hole" in Kimberley, South Africa, got its name. Originally a large hill, 50,000 diamond miners worked with pickaxes and shovels from 1866 to 1914 to dig 2,625 ft (800 m)—that's almost half a mile—down into the ground. The hole was then infilled with 115-ft (35-m) of rubble and, later, filled with water to within 130 ft (40 m) of its brim, which leaves a whole lot of hole still under the water!

LIGHTNING STRIKE ■ Kent Lilyerd from Mora, Minnesota, was struck on the top of the head by a bolt of lightning in June 2008—and lived to tell the tale. The bolt knocked him out on his lawn for an hour, but when he came round, he had nothing worse than a small head wound. He was saved by the three layers of wet clothing he was wearing, because the bolt, which also caused a hunting bullet in his pocket to explode, charged through his drenched clothing instead of through his vital organs and exited through his boot's steel toe.

MOVING CRUST ■ In addition to causing tides at sea, the Moon's gravity moves the Earth's crust up and down by up to 12 in (30 cm).

GREEN LAND ■ D.N.A. collected from beneath half a mile (800 m) of ice in Greenland reveals that 500,000 years ago the island really was green. The D.N.A. shows that Greenland was once covered by lush forests of spruce, pine, and yew, which were filled with butterflies, moths, and the ancestors of beetles, flies, and spiders.

FIERY SKY ■ In Sussex, England, in 1958, nearly 2,000 flashes of lightning were recorded in just one hour.

BLACK HOLE ■ Sagittarius A, the black hole at the center of the Milky Way, has a mass that is four million times greater than our Sun.

OLD MAN ■ A natural rock formation at Corner Brook, Newfoundland, Canada, resembles a craggy-faced old man and is known as The Old Man in the Mountain.

COLD DESERT ■ The McMurdo Dry Valleys of Antarctica receive fewer than 4 in (10 cm) of snow per year and are the most ice-free places on the continent. The unique conditions in this extreme desert are caused by katabatic winds, which occur when cold, dense air is pulled downhill by the force of gravity. These winds can reach speeds of 200 mph (320 km/h), evaporating all moisture—water, ice and snow—in the process.

SPACE GRAVITY ■ The Earth's gravity is only about ten percent weaker on the International Space Station, which orbits 200 mi (320 km) up in space, than it is here on the ground.

ROCK OF AGES ■ The Nuvvuagittuq rock belt, on the eastern shores of Hudson Bay, Quebec, Canada, is 4.28 billion years old—almost as old as the Earth itself. Most of the Earth's original surface has been crushed and recycled through the movement of giant tectonic plates, but the Nuvvuagittuq rocks, which have been found to contain ancient volcanic deposits, have survived.

VANISHING ROCK ■ Although the Earth's crust consists of solid rock, if you were to break it down into its component elements, nearly half of it would vanish into thin air, because 46.6 percent of the Earth's crust is made up of oxygen.

FLOATING ROCKS ■ Some rocks can actually float. In the course of a volcanic eruption, the violent separation of gas from lava produces a frothy rock called pumice, which is full of gas bubbles and can float on water.

LONG DRINK ■ It would take a person 143,737,166,324 million years to drink the 2,662 million trillion pints (1,260 million trillion liters) of water on Earth, at a rate of two pints (one liter) per hour and with no bathroom breaks.

LIGHTNING QUICK ■ In a storm, lightning is heard before thunder because light travels faster than sound. The difference between the speed of light and the speed of sound is so great that light could travel right round the world before sound finished a 100-m sprint.

POISON LAKE ■ On August 21, 1986, a highly concentrated amount of carbon dioxide bubbled to the surface of Cameroon's Lake Nyos and suffocated 1,746 people and thousands of animals as far as 15 miles away.

LUCKY GIRL ■ Sixteen-year-old BreAnna Helsel survived being struck by lightning at her home in Blanchard, Michigan, in June 2008—and the next day she won $20 in the state lottery.

ICE SHOT

Kenneth Libbrecht from Pasadena, California, is an expert on ice and snow, and takes incredibly detailed photographs of real snowflakes using a specially designed photomicroscope that illuminates the clear flakes with colored lights. The professor of physics braves sub-zero temperatures to catch snowflakes from the air and take photographs in the short time before they melt.

ICE MASS ■ Iceberg B15, which broke off from the Ross Ice Shelf in Antarctica in 2000, measured an amazing 183 mi (295 km) long and 23 mi (37 km) wide and weighed about 3 billion tons. Covering around 11,000 sq mi (28,500 sq km), it was approximately twice the size of the state of Delaware.

DISTANT FORCES ■ Iceberg B15 broke apart in 2002 and the largest remaining piece of it, B15-A, split up in 2005, its demise caused by an ocean swell generated by an Alaskan storm that took place six days earlier and over 8,000 mi (12,875 km) away.

WATER SUPPLY ■ An iceberg that broke free from Antarctica in 1987 weighed around 1.4 trillion tons and could have supplied everyone in the world with half a gallon (2 l) of water a day for 330 years.

TOURIST ATTRACTION ■ An iceberg that floated past New Zealand's South Island in 2006 became a tourist attraction. People paid $330 a person to fly over the unusual iceberg, the first to be visible from the New Zealand shore since 1931.

LONG JOURNEY ■ An iceberg once floated an amazing 2,500 mi (4,000 km) all the way from the Arctic to Bermuda—without melting.

MONUMENTAL 'BERG ■ Although only one-eighth of an iceberg actually lies visible above the waterline, an iceberg in the north Atlantic Ocean stood an incredible 550 ft (168 m) tall—almost the height of the Washington Monument. By contrast, the iceberg that famously sank the cruise liner *Titanic* in 1912 measured just 75 ft (23 m) above the surface of the water.

SHIPWRECK RESCUE ■ In 1875, the schooner *Caledonia* was wrecked 9 mi (14.5 km) off Newfoundland, Canada, but her crew of 82 survived by climbing onto an iceberg so that they could be rescued.

SINGING ICEBERGS ■ A team of German scientists has discovered that some icebergs can sing. The sounds, which resemble the violin section of an orchestra, are too low to be heard by humans, but have been picked up by seismic recordings. They occur during an iceberg tremor, when water squeezes through the iceberg's crevasses, forcing the walls to shake.

QUICK MELT ■ An iceberg 80 ft (24 m) high and 300 ft (91 m) long would melt in 70°F (21°C) weather in only four days.

'BERG SPEED ■ The average speed of icebergs off Newfoundland, Canada, is 0.4 mph (0.7 km/h), although with favorable conditions they have been observed moving at up to 2.2 mph (3.6 km/h)—nearly as fast as a human can walk.

AIRCRAFT CARRIERS ■ During World War II, British scientist Geoffrey Pyke came up with the idea of using icebergs as aircraft carriers, thinking they would be impossible to sink. Although a model was built in 1943 on Patricia Lake, Alberta, Canada, the secret plan (code-named "Habbakuk") was scrapped because the ice split too easily.

Icebergs don't just come in white, as these photographs from the Antarctic prove spectacularly. Nor are they uniformly "mini-mountain" in size and appearance.

Rather, icebergs can vary from being the size of a small car—these are called "growlers"—to icy formations that have the dimensions of a ten-story building. Familiar shapes include pinnacle 'bergs (with one or more spires), domes (rounded top), wedges (a steep edge on one side with a slope on the opposite side) and blocky 'bergs (steep, vertical sides with a flat top).

However, some of the most spectacular icebergs are actually striped, like giant candies. These stripes are often formed by layers of snow that melt and refreeze, and the stark colorings can be the result of more than a thousand years of shaping and compacting by the ice. Blue stripes are created when a crevice in the ice sheet fills up with melted water and freezes so quickly that no bubbles form. Other stripes are created from dust and soil picked up when the ice sheet from which the iceberg comes grinds downhill toward the sea. As ice crystals form a new layer at the base of the shelf, the resultant stripes can be black, brown or yellow or, if the trapped sediment is rich in algae, green. The stripes then move through the structure as it changes shape in the water to create stunning effects.

INCREDIBLE ICEBERGS

HOW MANY?

231,635	Canadians walked 1.6 mi (1 km) at more than 1,000 different venues on October 3, 2007.
40,000	Children across the U.K. staged a mass sleepover on June 14, 2008.
32,681	People took part in a tea party in Indore, India, in 2008.
26,924	Students performed a quadrille dance in Zagreb, Croatia, in 2008.
18,000	People created a human depiction of the Portuguese national flag in Lisbon in 2006.
15,756	Players took part in a single game of bingo at the Canadian National Exhibition in 1983.
13,446	People played games of chess simultaneously in Mexico City's Zocalo Square in 2006.
12,965	People dressed as Santa Claus in Derry, Northern Ireland, in 2007.
12,000	Students from Ottawa, Ontario, Canada, took part in a group hug in 2008.
7,451	Couples kissed simultaneously in Budapest, Hungary, in 2007.
5,441	Scarecrows present in the town of Hoschton, Georgia, U.S.A. in 2008.
4,572	Tractor drivers plowed a field simultaneously at Cooley, County Louth, Ireland, in 2007.
4,083	Air guitarists mimed to "Sweet Child of Mine" by Guns N' Roses at Guildford, Surrey, England, in 2005.
3,745	People enjoyed a snowball fight at Houghton, Michigan, in 2006.
3,500	Priests took part in a single religious ceremony at Jaipur, India, in 2007.
3,249	Residents of Taipei, Taiwan, simultaneously administered the kiss-of-life in 2007.
3,000	People helped draw a teapot on a giant Etch A Sketch® at Boston, Massachusetts, in 2006.
1,706	Harmonica players performed "Twinkle, Twinkle, Little Star" at Seattle, Washington, in 2005.
1,488	People with the surname Gallagher gathered at Letterkenny, County Donegal, Ireland, in 2007.
1,124	People dressed up as zombies in Pittsburgh, Pennsylvania, in 2007.
1,072	People did simultaneous handstands at Indianapolis, Indiana, in 2005.

HOW LONG?

113 DAYS	Martin Smit of South Africa spent 113 days with poisonous snakes in 2008.
20 DAYS	Cathie Llewellyn of Wintersville, Ohio, lived in a car for 20 days in 2005.
11 DAYS	Tony Wright of Penzance, Cornwall, England, stayed awake for 11 days in 2007.
180 HOURS	A team from Edmonds Community College, Washington State, flew a kite for 180 hours in 1982.
120 HOURS	Jayasimha Ravirala lectured for 120 hours at Hyderabad, India, in 2007.
120 HOURS	Norman Perez typed for 120 hours in Manhattan, New York, in 2007.
103 HOURS	Daniel Messier of Canada surfed the Internet nonstop for 103 hours in 1997.
80 HOURS	24 people played basketball for 80 hours at Sibiu, Romania, in 2007.
76 HOURS	Suresh Joachim balanced on one foot for 76 hours in Sri Lanka in 1997.
52 HOURS	Chris Dean and Mike Dudek of Grand Rapids, Michigan, watched TV nonstop for 52 hours in 2004.
48 HOURS	Mike Nabuurs played air hockey for 48 hours at Hamilton, Ontario, in 2005.
48 HOURS	Brian Jahrsdoerfer, Michel Lavoie, Peter Okpokpo and Warner Tse played doubles tennis for 48 hours at Houston, Texas, in 2006.
28 HOURS	Joe Defries of Abbotsford, British Columbia, played the handbells for 28 hours in 2005.
26 HOURS	Joseph Odhiambo from Phoenix, Arizona, dribbled a basketball for 26 hours through the streets of Houston, Texas, in 2006.
8 HOURS 27 MINUTES	Andrea Holt played a nonstop table tennis rally with Alex Perry and Mark Roscaleer for 8 hours 27 minutes at Manchester, England, in 2007.
7 HOURS 43 MINUTES	Joseph Cervantez of Gurnee, Illinois, kissed a car for 7 hours 43 minutes in 2005.
7 HOURS 1 MINUTE	Ashrita Furman of New York managed to spin a top for 7 hours 1 minute in 2006.

To celebrate the 2008 Olympic Games in Beijing, a Chinese man, Dr. Wei Sheng, pierced his head, face, hands and chest in the five colors of the Olympic rings with 2,008 needles.

INCREDIBLE FEATS

Nine-year-old Tiana Walton from Cheshire, England, managed to fit 25 garden snails on to her face at once. The slimy creatures covered her eyes, nose and mouth. "It was relaxing," she said, "but it felt a bit cold. They were quite smelly and you could see their big, long eyes."

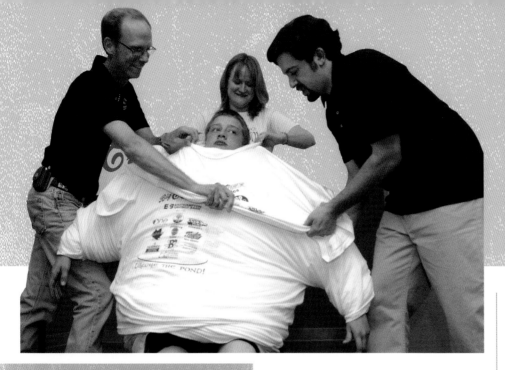

Tight Fit

Austin D. Crow, age 12, of Easthampton, Massachusetts, wore no fewer than 168 T-shirts at the same time—and became so wide that he couldn't make it through the door of his house. It took him nearly three hours to get dressed and the shirts—the largest of which were size 7X—weighed more than 80 lb (36 kg). Austin himself weighed only 111 lb (50 kg).

POWER OF PRAYER ■ Reverend Les Davis of Headland, Alabama, possesses such strong jaws that he can bend steel bars in his teeth.

BIG PICNIC ■ In 2008, a woolen mill in Pembrokeshire, Wales, took three weeks to create a picnic blanket that weighed one ton and was large enough to cover four tennis courts.

FLYING VISIT ■ A U.S. pilot keeps her long-distance relationship alive by making 8,318-mi (13,386-km) round trips to visit her husband in Scotland twice a month. Donna Clark uses planes, trains, buses, cars and ferries to make the 24-hour, 4,159-mi (6,693-km) trip from Cleveland, Ohio, to the remote Isle of Skye, where husband Bryan is a hotel manager.

TREE PLANTING ■ Around 300 villagers in Assam, India, planted 284,000 saplings in 24 hours in July 2008.

BUSINESS CARDS ■ Ryan John DeVries of Sarnia, Ontario, Canada, has been collecting business cards for longer than 20 years and has accumulated more than 224,000.

BASEBALL SHRINE ■ Paul Jones of Las Vegas, Nevada, started collecting baseball cards in 1997 and now has a collection of more than 520,500. He also collects photos of players and autographed baseballs.

ELVIS TOUR ■ Elvis Presley fan Matt Hale from Hertfordshire, England, spent a year traveling the world dressed as his hero—in a white jumpsuit, black bouffant wig and shades. He joined in Brazil's Rio Carnival, posed next to the statues on Easter Island and trekked to the lost Inca city of Machu Picchu in Peru.

FILM FAN ■ Retired painter and decorator Gwilym Hughes, from Dolgellau, Wales, has watched over 28,000 movies in his lifetime. The first movie he ever saw was *King Solomon's Mines*, starring Deborah Kerr and Stewart Granger, and he also has more than 1,000 books on the subject of cinema.

BASEBALL ODYSSEY ■ Josh Robbins of Redondo Beach, California, visited all 30 Major League baseball parks in just 26 days in 2008. Starting in Seattle, Washington, on June 16 and finishing in Milwaukee, Wisconsin, on July 11, he traveled 14,212 mi (22,870 km) and spent more than $2,000 on gas.

DEADLY COMPANIONS ■ At a zoo in Hartbeespoort Dam, South Africa, Martin Smit spent 113 days in a glass enclosure with 40 deadly snakes.

JUNK RACER ■ Two Chinese brothers spent 20 years building their own Formula One racing car out of cooking pots, bicycles and steel doors. Zhao Xiushun and Zhao Baoguo hand-built the car, which manages a top speed of 100 mph (160 km/h), entirely from materials they found on and around their farm in Tangshan.

TRUCK ROLL ■ Known as the "Human Speed Bump," Tom Owen from Birmingham, Alabama, allowed eight trucks—the last of which weighed 30,000 lb (13,607 kg)—to roll over his stomach at the 2008 Arizona State Fair. As the eighth truck passed over him, the ramps failed but although his lower body and legs were crushed beneath the wheels, five different X-rays showed that he hadn't broken a single bone. Owen has now been run over more than 1,000 times.

ECONOMY DRIVE ■ Australians John and Helen Taylor drove a Volkswagen 9,419 mi (15,158 km) through all 48 contiguous states of the U.S.A. in 20 days in 2008 and used only $653 worth of diesel, working out to about 6.9 cents per mile. They achieved an average 58.82 mi (94.66 km) to the gallon.

YOUNG MOZART ■ Talented pianist Curtis Bushell from London, England, has won a recording contract to perform Mozart—even though he is just four years old. He started learning the instrument at the age of three and in July 2008 he passed his grade-one piano exam after nine months' tuition. Within another three months, the little maestro had already reached grade-three standard.

STRIKING EYES ■ Ling Chunjiang of Kaifeng, China, can blow out candles with his eyes. By pinning his nose, he is able to blow air from his eyes through a hose and extinguish 12 candles in one minute. The martial arts enthusiast can also slice off the bottom of a beer bottle with his hand while keeping the rest of the bottle intact.

SOCCER JUGGLER ■ Graeme Lightbody from Johnstone, Scotland, juggled a soccer ball for an amazing six and a half hours in 2008 without letting the ball touch the ground once, achieving a total of 61,100 "keepie-uppies." To take in fluids during his marathon stint, he balanced the ball on his head. He maintained concentration by listening to an MP3 player of his favorite musical artists, including Tina Turner and Phil Collins.

SNAKE BOAT ■ In May 2008, boat makers in Kerala, India, launched a steel rowing boat that carried no fewer than 141 people. The snake boat—so called because the shape of the stern resembles the raised hood of a cobra—measured 143 x 6 ft (43.5 x 1.8 m) and weighed nearly nine tons.

CAN CREATION ■ Five architecture students from Montana State University created a huge sculpture from 45,725 cans of tuna fish and beans. The sculpture, which depicted a hand holding a can, measured a whopping 16 x 32 x 10 ft (5 x 10 x 3 m) and took a painstaking 41 hours to build.

FAMILY TREE ■ Roy Blackmore from Somerset, England, spent nearly 30 years tracing all his ancestors—and ended up creating a family tree that dated back 1,500 years and featured 9,390 of his relatives. His research, which covered around 45 generations, revealed him to be the great-grandson 37 times distant of King William the Conqueror, who invaded England from France in 1066.

HOP THE FENCE ■ Yo-yo expert Arron Sparks from London performed 144 "hop the fence" tricks in just one minute at an event in Suffolk, England, in July 2008—that's faster than two per second.

PILLOW FIGHT ■ No fewer than 3,872 fans took part in a mass pillow fight at the end of a Kane County Cougars baseball game at Geneva, Illinois, in July 2008.

TIGHT SQUEEZE ■ An attempt in August 2008 to see how many Texan cheerleaders could fit into an elevator together ended in panic when the elevator doors got stuck at the first floor. Even though signs clearly stated that the safety capacity was 15 people, 26 teenage girls had managed to squeeze into the confined space at the University of Texas in Austin, but they then had to wait 25 minutes before a repairman was able to release them.

DEAD MOSQUITOES ■ A Chinese man set up an online business in 2008 selling dead mosquitoes that he had killed personally. Nin Nan, of Shanghai, advertised them for around $1 a head, suggesting that the insect corpses could be used for scientific study, decoration or collection. He had 10,000 orders in two days.

www.ripleybooks.com
go to @

WAUL BALL

Joel Waul of Lauderhill, Florida, has spent more than five years creating a huge ball from more than 700,000 rubber bands. The multicolored ball, which he calls Nugget, weighs around 9,000 lb (4,082 kg) and stands over 6 ft (1.8 m) high. He has already suffered for his art—when the ball was a mere 400 lb (181 kg), it rolled over his hand, spraining his wrist.

Toy Soldiers

An army of 35,310 LEGO™ Star Wars figures stood guard at LEGO™ headquarters in Slough, England, in June 2008. A group of employees spent a whole day assembling the miniature army—without use of "the force." The vast collection of Clone Troopers were the centerpiece of a charity event that helped celebrate the toy company's 50th birthday.

SOCK LINE ■ In July 2008, students at King Edward's School in Birmingham, England, created a washing line of socks that stretched for nearly a mile. They pegged out more than 28,000 socks.

THUMBS UP ■ Using only his thumbs, Elliot Nicholls of Dunedin, New Zealand, can type a 160-character message into his cell phone in just 45 seconds—while blindfolded!

MODEL AUTOS ■ Suhail Mohammad Al Zarooni of Dubai, United Arab Emirates, has a collection of more than 7,000 miniature model autos, including models of the limo in which John F. Kennedy was shot, Hitler's Mercedes, and the cars driven by James Bond and Mr. Bean.

PENNY AUCTION ■ In February 2008, Walter Husak of Van Nuys, California, sold 301 antique pennies at an auction in Long Beach for $10.7 million. First place for value went to two coins dating back to the 18th century, which each sold for $632,500.

BANANAS BECKY ■ Becky Martz of Houston, Texas, is fascinated by bananas—not the fruits themselves but the labels. She began collecting banana labels in 1991 and now has more than 7,000. She has even started branching out to collect asparagus and broccoli bands.

FAST ROUND ■ In July 2008, more than 40 golfers representing a local radio station completed a round of golf at Boyne Falls, Michigan, in under eight minutes! Golfers were carefully placed on the course's tee boxes, along the fairways and on the greens. The timing started once the tee-shot was struck, with players on the fairway then running to hit the ball as it came to rest. Three holes were played six times in a row to achieve a total yardage of 6,096 (5,574 m).

PUZZLE SOLVED ■ Pensioner Eric Smith of Staffordshire, England, spent six months completing a 24,000-piece jigsaw puzzle. The 12 x 6 ft (3.6 x 1.8 m) picture of dolphins and boats took the retired sales manager 537 hours and was so big that he had to build a table to accommodate it and move it to his garage.

TUG-OF-WAR ■ More than 100,000 people took part in a tug-of-war contest in Lintan, China, in March 2007. To cope with the numbers, the "rope" was made of steel cables and at 5,850 ft (1,800 m) measured more than a mile long.

MIGHTY MUFFLER ■ Ray Ettinger of Independence, Missouri, spent nearly five years knitting a scarf that is 3,523 ft (1,074 m) long and weighs 75 lb (34 kg). His grandmother had taught him to knit when he was ten.

BOTTLE BANK ■ Since starting his collection in the mid-1970s, Tom Bates has amassed more than 36,000 beer and soda cans and 9,000 different bottles. They were displayed for a time at the Museum of Beverage Containers and Advertising in Millersville, Tennessee.

SKATER BOY ■ Chester Fried of South River, New Jersey, has visited every roller-skating rink across the U.S.A.—more than 300 in total. He put on his first pair of roller skates at age seven and now in his sixties owns more than 300 pairs.

BALANCING ACT ■ Nine-year-old Joe Allison of Devon, England, balanced 16 spoons on his face at the same time in April 2008. He balanced five on his forehead, one on each ear, two on his lips, four on his cheeks, two on his chin and one on his nose. Joe, who discovered his talent when his cousin challenged him to balance a spoon on his nose, is looking forward to growing so there is more space on his forehead.

HIGH RIDER ■ Nik Wallenda, the seventh generation of the Flying Wallendas circus family, walked along a high-wire suspended 135 ft (41 m) above the streets of Newark, New Jersey, and then cycled back along the wire—all without a safety net. He even made a cell-phone call halfway through the walk.

Escape Artist

Escaping from a locked milk can 3 ft (0.9 m) high, bound by the feet in a water-filled torture cell with no air supply, Harry Houdini always made sure that his audience was shocked and thrilled.

Born in Hungary 1874, Houdini moved to the U.S.A. when he was very young, and his dedication to the art of illusion soon made him one of the most famous names in the country. The original escape artist inspired countless imitators but always stayed one step ahead by copyrighting his pioneering illusions and continually inventing new tricks. These included being buried alive on stage and swallowing needles and thread. Houdini would escape from the coffin in less than two minutes, and regurgitated the needles one by one, each threaded with cotton.

Houdini's most vital skill was escaping from handcuffs and picking locks; he offered rewards to anyone who could provide cuffs or ropes he could not escape from. In 1904, a London newspaper produced a unique pair of cuffs that had taken five years to make, yet Houdini still wriggled free. In more than 30 years of performing, he never had to pay a challenger.

The daredevil magician defied death on hundreds of occasions and it was not his famous escapes that killed him. Houdini was renowned for his resistance to pain, and in 1926 an over-zealous member of the public asked to punch him in the stomach to test his strength. Houdini was caught unprepared and, wanting to continue with performing, he didn't seek medical attention for days. Tragically, he had been suffering from appendicitis when he'd been hit and he never recovered.

Water Torture

In 1912, Houdini unveiled his most daring escape yet. Secured by the feet inside a watertight chamber, he would escape within minutes. Such was the force required that he once broke his ankle in escaping. Although Houdini requested that the cell be burned upon his death, his brother kept it intact. The magician got his wish, however, as a museum fire destroyed the torture cell in 1995.

Extraordinaire

Rope Escape

Houdini never failed to extricate himself from a chair onto which he'd been bound with rope. He revealed that he tensed his body and leaned forward slightly from the chair to achieve some slack in the rope. He explained that people assumed that longer ropes would hold him, but the more rope used, the more slack available. Houdini was incredibly strong and flexible and did not need much room to free his hands.

HOUDINI'S STUNTS

> Locked inside a water-torture cell

> Escape from a locked milk can full of water

> Suspended from a building in a straitjacket

> Handcuffed inside a nailed-shut packing crate, and thrown in a river

> Escape from a jail cell

> Swallowing needles and thread

> Buried alive on stage

> Escape from any pair of handcuffs

Milk Can Escape

One of Houdini's most famous performances was the escape from a locked milk can full of water. He would be hidden behind a curtain, and emerge drenched in water.

BOLLYWOOD EPIC ■ Ashish Sharma of Uttar Pradesh, India, watched 48 Bollywood movies for over 120 hours straight in June 2008.

FULL HOUSE ■ Jim Purol of Anaheim, California, sat in all 92,542 seats at the Pasadena Rose Bowl in five days in July 2008. Armed with a pad to cushion his backside against the plastic seats, and an umbrella-hat to shield his face from the sun, he sat for 12 hours each day and, despite the blisters he picked up along the way, he fulfilled the dream he had held for 20 years—ever since he sat in all 107,501 chairs at the University of Michigan's football stadium.

WEDDING VOWS ■ In February 2008, in Pittsburgh, Pennsylvania, 624 couples simultaneously renewed their wedding vows.

BRAINY HUG ■ Alan Baltis of Lakewood, Ohio, hugged 833 people in an hour at the Mensa annual conference in Denver, Colorado, in 2008—that's nearly 14 people a minute. Standing more than 6 ft (1.8 m) tall, he had to squat to complete many of the hugs.

MEDICAL DEVICES ■ Dr. Douglas Arbittier of New York collects old medical equipment. His collection includes amputation saws—some dating back to the 1730s— bloodletting artifacts, old stethoscopes, hearing devices and dental instruments.

RED RALLY ■ In September 2008, some 2,000 redheads from 20 countries gathered in Breda, Holland, for a celebratory red-haired day.

Cram in the COCKROACHES

When Travis Fessler fancied a crunchy snack, he decided to pop 11 live Madagascar Hissing Cockroaches into his mouth at once. The insect fan from Kentucky intended to raise awareness for charity and said, "Madagascar Hissing Cockroaches don't bite or sting, but they do have tiny hooks on the ends of their legs that they use to help them climb. When used on the soft flesh of the inside of the mouth, it was a bit like Velcro rubbing on my tongue and cheeks." The creatures all survived Travis' mouth and now live in a terrarium in his house.

www.ripleybooks.com

Game of Squash

A basketball game between Dallas and Utah went from the tall to the small when a contortionist squeezed himself into a box in the half-time break in March 2006.

LOTTERY LOVER ▦ Telecom engineer Victor Paul Taylor from Manchester, England, has been collecting scratchcards since 1995. He specializes in U.K. National Lottery scratchcards and could be sitting on a fortune because none of the cards have actually been scratched.

FIVE BRUSHES ▦ At Changsha, China, in September 2008, Ye Genyou simultaneously used five brushes to write calligraphy on a piece of paper. He held two brushes in each hand and one in his mouth. He once wrote 7,659 characters on a piece of paper 330 ft (100 m) long and 31 in (80 cm) wide without lifting the brush for 17 hours 13 minutes.

GIANT JIGSAW ▦ Some 15,000 jigsaw puzzle enthusiasts assembled a giant puzzle that almost covered the town square in Ravensburg, Germany. The 6,500-sq-ft (600-sq-m) puzzle consisted of 1,141,800 pieces and was put together in just five hours.

24-HOUR RELAY ▦ Nearly 3,850 people took part in a 24-hour, 100-meter relay race in Riga, Latvia, in October 2008. The youngest competitor was a one-year-old toddler who walked the entire 110 yards (100 m) accompanied by his mom.

POOL CONTEST ▦ At Spring Lake, North Carolina, in October 2008, Brian Lilley and Daniel Maloney played pool for 52 hours nonstop—completing more than 600 games.

BUILT COFFIN ▦ Grady Hunter, 75, won a blue ribbon in the crafts and hobbies competition at the 2008 North Carolina State Fair—by making his own coffin. Hunter wanted to make the coffin more comfortable than most proprietary brands and he incorporated his signature into the wood.

EYES WRITE ▦ A Chinese man can write calligraphy by shooting water from his eyes. Ru Anting from Luoyang, Henan Province, sucks up the water with his nose and then sprays it through his tear ducts onto a board covered with dark paper. He discovered his unusual talent as a child while swimming in a river and after three years of training, he can now shoot water accurately from his eyes over a distance of up to 10 ft (3 m).

TOMATO PASTE ▦ Erik van de Wiel of the Netherlands collects tomato paste cans. He has hundreds in his collection, many sent to him by friends traveling in Europe and North America. Most of the cans are empty now because, if stored too long, they might eventually explode.

HUMAN TORCH ▦ Dana Kunze from Minneapolis, Minnesota, dives from a height of 80 ft (24 m) into a pool—while on fire. Dressed in several layers of cotton shirts, pants and hoods soaked with water, Kunze is doused with gasoline before being set on fire. He then delays his dive for up to 30 seconds, by which time he is feeling like toast!

COLD COMFORT ▦ In 1996, four UPS workers from Calgary, Alberta, Canada, made a $400 bet to see who could go longest over the course of the year wearing shorts in his delivery job. In January 2008, as the temperature dropped to −50°F (−45°C) with wind chill, a winner finally emerged—Shaun Finnis who had happily worn shorts to work every day for more than 11 years, even in subfreezing weather.

HEAD CONTROL ▦ Cuban women's soccer player Yeniseidis Soto managed to control a ball with her head for 2 hours 12 minutes 32 seconds in Havana in 2008—without it once touching the ground or any part of her body other than her head.

Human Flag

Daniel Ulizio from Midland, Pennsylvania, had the strength and sheer nerve to act as a human flag and "fly" from the top of a 100-ft (30-m) chimney in 1937.

Levitation Act

New Yorkers couldn't believe their eyes when Dutch magician Wouter Bijdendijk, also known as Ramana, levitated several feet above the ground in Times Square in October 2007, his only support apparently being a stick held in his left hand.

CONTINUOUS CHANT ■ Worshipers at the Shri Bala Hanuman temple in Jamnagar, India, have been chanting the name of Lord Hanuman continuously for more than 44 years. The chanting began on August 1, 1964, and by August 2008 it had been running for 16,070 days nonstop.

DAY-LONG SERMON ■ Rev. Eric Delve, the vicar of St. Luke's Church in Maidstone, Kent, England, gave a sermon lasting a full 24 hours in August 2008. His outdoor preaching marathon—reading passages from the Bible—was billed as "creation to the end of the world in 24 hours."

SAND CASTLE ■ More than 1,000 people helped creator Ed Jarrett build a sand castle that reached 31 ft 7 in (9.6 m) tall at Casco, Maine, in September 2007. Forty dump-loads of sand—weighing in at around 500 tons—went into building the castle.

CHAMPION BAGGER ■ Erika Jensen, a Macey's grocery-store employee from Utah, won the 2008 International Best Bagger Competition held in Las Vegas, Nevada, judged on her speed, weight distribution and appearance. Three years earlier, her older sister Emily had won the title, and the 2007 champion bagger, Brian Bay, also came from Erika's store.

TWO-HANDED ■ Liam Doherty of Galway, Ireland, can write simultaneously with both hands, forward, backward, upside down and mirror image.

MANY MOHAMMADS ■ More than 20,000 people—all named Mohammad—gathered simultaneously in the Libyan city of Zawia in July 2008. The participants included one man with six Mohammads in his own name. He is called Mohammad Mohammad Mohammad Mohammad Mohammad Mohammad Al Wish.

STRONG BOY ■ Seventeen-year-old Kye Thomas of Bristol, England, can lift loads of up to 476 lb (216 kg)—that's more than twice his bodyweight. The 210-lb (95 kg) boy—dubbed Superkid—won the title of Britain's Strongest Schoolboy in 2008 by picking up a 168-lb (76-kg) log seven times, flipping 700-lb (317-kg) truck tires and lugging 210-lb (95 kg) barrels across fields. He trains by partially lifting cars that are an incredible 15 times his body weight.

STARTING FROM SCRATCH ■ Gideon Weiss has a collection of more than 230 back scratchers. He has amassed his unusual treasures over the past ten years, and they include back scratchers from as far afield as Norway, Spain and Thailand.

CALCULATING RUSSIAN ■ Sergei Frolov from St. Petersburg, Russia, has built up a collection of more than 150 Soviet-made calculators, as well as vintage computers, watches and slide rules.

NECK DEEP ■ Mark McGowan spent 30 hours buried neck-deep in sand on the beach in Margate, Kent, England, in May 2008.

OREGON OREGAMI ■ Joseph Wiseman of Eugene, Oregon, folds paper airplanes that are just over ¼ in (7 mm) long—about the length of a grain of rice.

PRESSING BUSINESS ■ The owner of a dry-cleaning store, Ben Walton of Hampshire, England, ironed nonstop for 60 hours in July 2008, during which time he ironed 923 items—and suffered only a bad back.

PLANE SAILING ■ Motorcycle stuntman Doug Danger has jumped over a jumbo jet airplane. Danger from Palmer, Massachusetts, launched his bike from a narrow ramp at a speed of more than 70 mph (113 km/h) and sailed over the 160-ft (49-m) wingspan of the parked plane.

STRANGE SCORING ■ Scoring only three-point shots and foul shots, the Annandale (Minnesota) High School boys' basketball team amazingly won a game 51 points to 48 in February 2007.

SCIENCE DAY ■ To commemorate 2008 Science Day—a day set aside by school governors in Missouri, Illinois and Tennessee to raise interest in science—children and adults managed to inflate 852 balloons in one hour at West Park Mall, Cape Girardeau, Missouri.

ELEPHANT MAN ■ Ed Gotwalt received his first ornamental elephant as a good-luck gift from his sister-in-law in 1967 and now has collected 6,000 elephant artifacts from all over the world and in every imaginable type of material. He keeps them at Mister Ed's Elephant Museum in Orrtanna, Pennsylvania, where visitors can marvel at an elephant potty chair, an elephant hair dryer, elephant lamps and even an elephant pulling a 24-carat-gold circus wagon.

BIRTHDAY GREETINGS ■ James Bridges of Cadiz, Kentucky, has a contact list of more than 2,600 people—all of whom he calls on their birthday to sing "Happy Birthday."

FAST FEET ■ In November 2008, fleet-footed Martina Servaty created 11½ pt (5.4 l) of juice by furiously treading grapes for just one minute at Mesenich, Germany.

NAPKIN QUEEN ■ Helena Vnouckova from Prague, Czech Republic, has a collection of more than 16,000 napkins.

COIN TRICK ■ Tyler Johnson of Salisbury, Massachusetts, can drop 39 coins off his right elbow and catch them all in his right hand!

FAST TRACK ■ In 2008, Corey Pedersen from Montana and Californian Mike Kim traveled a total of 1,813 mi (2,901 km) on a series of high-speed Japanese trains in a 24-hour period.

GUITAR SESSION ■ Akash Gupta, age 14, played the guitar nonstop for 53 hours in Agra, India, in June 2008.

CUFF COLLECTOR ■ Joseph W. Lauher of New York collects vintage handcuffs. His collection, which also contains leg irons, nippers and thumbcuffs, includes specimens from the U.S.A., Europe and the Far East.

DESERT RACES ■ Finishing in Morocco in March 2007, Sandy McCallum of Edmonton, Alberta, Canada, ran six desert ultramarathons—covering a total of 875 mi (1,408 km) in scorching heat—in the space of just 12 months.

Driving Dangerously

Liu Suozhu of Henan Province, China, performed a breathtaking stunt by driving a family car across two unsteady steel ropes that were suspended 150 ft (46 m) over the Minluo River in Pingjiang, in central China, in April 2008. It took Suozhu 30 minutes to complete the amazing 755-ft (230-m) journey.

NATIONAL FLAGS ■ Climbers from around the world—each carrying their national flag—scaled the Sydney Harbour Bridge in September 2008 and flew 137 flags from the summit of the Australian landmark. Each flag represented a country with a member who had joined BridgeClimb, an organization which, among other things, enables couples to exchange their wedding vows at the top of the bridge.

MOVIE SESSION ■ Suresh Joachim and Claudia Wavra sat through 123 continuous hours of movies—that's watching movies for more than five days—in New York City's Times Square in October 2008. They diligently watched 57 movies from the opening titles until the final credits rolled in each.

Hoopla!

A performer displays incredible hula-hooping skills during a cultural presentation in Beijing to celebrate Chinese New Year in February 2008.

Lava Surfer

Surfers need nerves of steel to brave huge waves, but C.J. Kanuha wasn't looking for the big one when he paddled off the coast of Hawaii in April 2008. Instead, the extreme surfer decided to take his surfboard to within 20 ft (6 m) of molten lava. The Kilauea Volcano on Big Island, Hawaii, literally boils the sea to 400°F (200°C) in places—it melted the wax on Kanuha's surfboard and scalded his feet before he paddled away.

Heads Up

Sri-Lankan-born surfer Dulip Kokuhannadige is trying to start a topsy-turvy craze riding waves off the south coast of England—surfing on his head for as long as 15 seconds at a time. He discovered the new style when teaching young people to surf in the aftermath of the 2004 tsunami, in which he lost all his possessions, and took the upside-down idea to England when he moved to the coastal town of Bournemouth a year later.

WHALE SCARE

Kiteboarder David Sheridan was 300 ft (100 m) from shore off New South Wales, Australia, when he noticed a dark shape loom from the depths. A Southern Right Whale wacked him in the back of the head with its tail, almost knocking him off his board, but luckily for Sheridan from Nambucca, it is thought that the huge whale was just issuing a warning.

WEEKEND LESSON ■ To raise money for charity, teacher Giovanni Cogollo and 120 students at a school in Turbaco, northern Colombia, endured a 74-hour science lesson in 2008. The lesson began on Friday, August 8 and ended on Monday, August 11.

BUBBLE WRAP ■ In London, England, in November 2007, British bubble artist Sam Heath managed to fit 50 schoolchildren—all more than 5 ft (1.5 m) tall—into a single soapy bubble. He made the bubble, which measured 11 ft (3.4 m) across, with a large metal hoop that had a 39 ft (12 m) circumference.

SKATING CHAIN ■ An incredible 1,483 people lined up in single file on the Assiniboine River in Winnipeg, Manitoba, Canada, in February 2008 to form a human skating chain.

UPSIDE DOWN ■ Hairdresser Rustam Danilchuk from Kiev, Ukraine, cuts hair while hanging upside down.

GUITAR ENSEMBLE ■ In July 2008, 2,052 electric and acoustic guitarists, led by folk singer Country Joe McDonald, performed Woody Guthrie's "This Land Is Your Land" in Concord, California.

SNOW GIANT ■ Over the winter of 2008, hundreds of volunteers from Bethel, Maine, teamed up to build a snow woman that towered over the town at 122 ft 1 in (37.2 m) tall. Constructed from 13 million lb (6 million kg) of snow, the snow woman, named Olympia, had 5-ft (1.5-m) wreaths for eyes, 16 skis for eyelashes, five red auto tires for lips, a huge "carrot" nose made of muslin, chicken wire and wood, a 48-ft (14.6-m) fleece hat, a 130-ft (40-m) scarf, 2,000 ft (610 m) of rope hair, three truck-loader tires for buttons and 30-ft (9-m) spruce trees for arms. The residents of Bethel are no strangers to giant snow sculptures—in 1999 they built a snowman, Angus, who stood more than 113 ft (34 m) tall.

MAGIC CARPET ■ A total of 1,200 craftsmen in Khorasan, Iran, spent 18 months weaving a 60,546 sq ft (5,625 sq m) carpet, worth $5.8 million, for a mosque in the United Arab Emirates.

UGLY SWEATERS ■ In December 2007, a portrait studio in Minneapolis, Minnesota, encouraged people to come in for a picture in their ugliest sweater. The winning sweater was shades of brown with some floral design, two masks and a large "U.S.A." on the sleeve.

HOT CONTEST ■ In temperatures above 86°F (30°C), three dozen soccer players from Edmonton, Alberta, Canada, took part in a match that lasted for 33 hours in August 2008. The participants played in three-hour shifts—the equivalent of two full games—and went through around 1,000 bottles of water overall.

NOSE BLOWING ■ Andrew Dahl, age 13, of Blaine, Washington, inflated 213 balloons in an hour in April 2008—with his nose! He blew through one nostril at a time and each balloon was inflated to at least 8 in (20 cm). Andrew, who was just seven when he first used his nose to blow up a balloon, attributed his achievement to determination, perseverance, a strong nasal cavity and lung endurance acquired by playing trumpet in the school band.

PAPER TRAIL ■ In Guangzhou, China, in 2008, Han Yan unveiled a paper tapestry that was more than 700 ft (213 m) long. Titled *Hundreds of Family Names*, it consisted of 288 papercut patterns, with each symmetrical pattern symbolizing one family name in China.

TENNIS RALLY ■ In August 2008 at North Haven, Connecticut, twin brothers Ettore and Angelo Rossetti played a continuous tennis rally that lasted nearly 15 hours—with a total of 25,944 shots. The rally had nearly come to an end hours earlier at around 12,000 strokes when Angelo awkwardly hit a shot as he simultaneously tried to eat a PowerBar, but Ettore raced forward to save the day.

CONSECUTIVE CARTWHEELS ■ Don Claps from Broomfield, Colorado, can perform more than 1,200 consecutive cartwheels. He can even drink water from a paper cup while doing so. He explains: "I pop it in my mouth and throw down my hands, hold the water in my mouth and swallow on the next cartwheel."

LOUD WHISPER ■ A total of 1,330 children took part in a game of Chinese whispers at Arsenal Football Club's Emirates Stadium in London, England, in 2008. The message being passed around was "Together we can make a world of difference." It took 2 hours 4 minutes for it to reach the end of the line, by which time it had changed to "Haaaaaaa!"

ASPHALT ENTHUSIASTS ■ Scott Gordon and Marie Vans founded the Asphalt Museum in Sacramento, California, in 1991 and have managed to collect samples of road from such famous highways as Route 66, Highway 1 and the ancient Roman road the Appian Way.

HONEYMOON GARBAGE ■ An English couple paid for their honeymoon flights by collecting and recycling garbage for three months in 2008. John and Ann Till from Petersfield, Hampshire, took thousands of cans and bottles to a recycling plant and in return amassed 36,000 air miles, which they used to fly back from their honeymoon in the United States.

EVEREST DIVE ■ Holly Budge from Bristol, England, skydived over the world's highest mountain—Mount Everest—in 2008. The 29-year-old jumped from a plane at 29,500 ft (8,990 m) and plunged toward the Himalayas. During her descent, she reached speeds of up to 140 mph (225 km/h) and endured temperatures of −40°C (−40°F).

STREET SIGNS ■ Steve Salcedo of Indiana has more than 350 street signs and traffic lights—all collected legally. His enthusiasm for his unusual hobby started when his brother gave him a street sign that he had found lying by the side of the road and which was riddled with bullet holes.

TRUCKERS' PARADE ■ A total of 292 tow trucks—including flatbeds, wreckers and 50-ton rotators—rumbled through New York City in an awesome drivers' parade in September 2008. They set off from Shea Stadium and finished at an abandoned airport where they parked to spell "New York" on the tarmac.

QUICK KNIT ■ Hazel Tindall of Shetland, Scotland, is so nimble with knitting needles that she can knit an incredible 255 stitches in just three minutes.

BRAND LOYALTY ■ Joseph Macko from Flint, Michigan, has bought or leased a new Cadillac every year since 1955—the same year that Disneyland opened in California. The 84-year-old retired General Motors worker saves up all year to pay for his new car.

LAWN-MOWER MAN ■ Ever since he was given a plastic lawn mower when he was one year old, Samuel Buswell has been obsessed with lawn mowers. The boy from Cornwall, England, who is now four, reads mower catalogues instead of comics and can reel off the specifications, model number and make of hundreds of different types of mowers. Every Saturday he goes with his mother to his local garden store to admire the latest models and he was recently given his first working mower, which he puts to good use trimming the family's lawn every day.

HUMAN KITE

Hurtling through the air only inches from each other, skydivers made a spectacular sight over Florida in November 2007 in a successful attempt to break the world canopy formation record. One hundred jumpers left five planes at different altitudes, grabbing the lines of the canopy below and wrapping them round their feet for a secure grip to form a diamond from the top down, breaking the record by 15 people. There was an 11-minute window from plane to the ground to complete the formation, which required years of practice and planning, including the difficult task of finding 100 skydivers from 14 countries skilled enough to join the group. After four attempts, the jumpers held for 12 seconds, stretching 290 ft (88 m) high and 175 ft (53 m) wide—the size of a football field in the sky.

The most dangerous part of the stunt is the "starburst," when the jumpers must break away from each other without getting entangled in each other's lines. During practice for the attempt, several participants had to cut away their main parachutes when they became entangled and landed using their reserve chutes. When asked about the risks, organizer Brian Pangburn replied: "Well only about 5 percent of the skydivers do canopy formation like we do—and if you ask the other 95 percent if they want to try canopy formation most of them will reply 'No way—you guys are crazy,' and that is coming from people who jump out of airplanes."

Spinning Around

Escape artist Rick Meisel needed all his unique talents when he was locked in a spinning washing machine full of soapsuds in September 2008. Incredibly, he survived long enough to free himself from six pairs of handcuffs and two leg irons before extricating his body from the tiny drum. The space inside was so small that the daredevil had himself surgically altered so that he could fit in it.

FEELING THE PINCH ■ Mark Billington, an eight-year-old boy from Braidwood, New South Wales, Australia, managed to clip 64 clothespins to his head.

LONG SMOKE ■ In Havana, Cuba, in May 2008, José Castelar Cairo hand-rolled a cigar that was nearly 150 ft (45 m) in length—that's longer than four buses standing nose-to-tail.

HAIR-RAISING ■ In May 2008, Shailendra Roy of India pulled a train engine and three coaches—a combined weight of more than 40 tons—using only his hair, braided into a ponytail. Roy, who has also pulled cars, trucks, logs and buses by the same method, keeps his hair strong by rubbing it with mustard oil.

NOSE WHISTLER ■ Brandon Baugh of Tampa, Florida, can whistle "The Star-Spangled Banner"— through his nose. He discovered his unusual talent at school when, taking a deep breath one day, he heard a whistle coming from his nostrils. After a little practice, he found he could nose-whistle at will and now boasts an extensive repertoire of tunes.

BOUND TO SUCCEED ■ In April 2008, friends and fitness fanatics Heather Derbyshire and Karen Fingerhut ran up 54 flights of stairs with two of their legs tied together—in under 15 minutes. The pair ascended the 1,188 stairs of the winding fire escape of the UK's tallest building—London's Canary Wharf Tower—in 14 minutes 34.69 seconds.

SHOE DRIVE ■ No fewer than 10,512 shoes were displayed at the National Geographic Society in Washington, D.C., in July 2008, in a chain of footwear stretching 1.65 mi (2.65 km). Among the contributors was eight-year-old Peter Wajda from Mount Laurel, New Jersey, who organized a shoe drive and collected 509.

COUCH POTATO ■ Manhattan librarian Stan Friedman started 2008 by watching sports on TV for 29 hours continuously. He won a New Year's couch potato contest staged by a restaurant in Times Square, New York City. Four contestants sat in recliners and watched sports with unlimited food and drink, but they weren't allowed to sleep and could take a bathroom break only every eight hours. Friedman took home $5,000 in prizes, including a TV, a recliner and a trophy adorned with a potato.

ETERNAL TRIANGLE ■ In May 2008, students and math teachers at Ironton High School, Ohio, built a paper tower 10 ft (3 m) tall, consisting of 16,384 tetrahedrons. They spent a month cutting out thousands of triangles from construction paper, decorating them and taping them together.

TEEN TEXTER ■ Drew Acklin, 17, from Cleveland, Ohio, sent or received 19,678 text messages in just 30 days in 2008. On average, he handled a text every two minutes during his waking hours over the entire month.

PENNY CHAIN ■ In July 2008, hundreds of volunteers in Fort Scott, Kansas, worked for three days to lay a chain of pennies that stretched for an incredible 40 mi (64 km) in a school parking lot. The line consisted of 3,406,234 coins.

HIGH HEELS ■ Thirty-eight-year-old Jill Stamison of Grand Haven, Michigan, ran a 150-m (164-yd) sprint in 21.95 seconds in New York's Central Park in July 2008—while wearing 3-in (7.6-cm) high heels.

SMURF GATHERING ■ More than 1,200 people descended on Castleblayney, Ireland, on July 18, 2008—to dress up as Smurfs. The participants wore blue and white clothes and any visible skin was painted blue with colored greasepaint.

BOUNCING BOYS ■ Operating in shifts of two people at a time, eight boys, aged between 8 and 11, bounced nonstop for 24 hours on an inflatable castle in Flat Rock, Michigan, in August 2008.

RUBBER BANDS ■ After two years spent collecting rubber bands, Étienne Anglehart of Montreal, Quebec, Canada, had so many that, when they were placed end to end in 2008, they stretched for about 12 mi (19 km). For easy transportation, he keeps them in 19 rolls—each the size of a basketball.

MILLION POSTMARKS ■ The Post Mark Museum in Bellevue, Ohio, houses examples of more than a million different postmarks collected from around the world.

INCREDIBLE FEATS
www.ripleys.com
Ripley's Believe It or Not!®

RUM LABELS ■ Petr Hlousek from Prague, Czech Republic, has collected more than 6,600 rum bottle labels from 98 different countries.

A–Z OF CHOCOLATE ■ Martin Mihál of Germany has been collecting empty chocolate wrappers from around the world since 1996. He has almost 40,000 wrappers from approximately 100 different countries—everywhere from Andorra to Zimbabwe.

TRASH MISER ■ To determine how much waste he creates over a 12-month period, Ari Derfel of Berkeley, California, saved every piece of his non-food garbage throughout 2007, right down to tissues, drinking straws and till receipts. Friends were ordered not to give him any gifts, especially bottles of wine or anything in wrapping paper, but he still managed to accumulate 96 cubic ft (2.7 cubic m) of garbage in his house.

WALL OF FIRE ■ At an air show in Terre Haute, Indiana, in 2007, a crew of 35 people used more than 2,000 gal (7,570 l) of gasoline to create an instant wall of fire that was 6,637 ft (2,023 m) long.

ANGEL DISPLAY ■ Joyce Berg of Beloit, Wisconsin, has collected around 13,000 angels since 1976. Her collection, which is displayed in a local museum, includes angels made from cornhusks and spaghetti, angels adorning bells, music boxes and banks, and angels depicting everything from musicians to sports figures and Biblical to cartoon characters. Joyce loves angels so much that she has even been known to don wings and a halo to greet visitors.

MELON HEAD

The brother of sharpshooter John Richmond truly trusts him with his life. John, from Granger, Indiana, claims to have shot—and missed—his brother Ken more than 100 times. He blew a watermelon off the top of Ken's head with a rifle from 25 ft (7.6 m) and has also successfully targeted objects placed on his brother's chest and face.

This photograph shows **The Human Liberty Bell**, *made with the help of 25,000 troops.*

This machine-gun insignia was made with 22,500 officers and men, some lying, some sitting and some standing, at Camp Hancock, Augusta, Georgia, in 1918.

Mole's **Human Statue of Liberty** *was almost eight times the height of the real statue in New York.*

58
INCREDIBLE FEATS
www.ripleys.com
Ripley's— Believe It or Not!®

Bird's Eye Art

Arthur Mole was a photographer with an unusually large imagination, taking pictures of tens of thousands of painstakingly organized soldiers on the ground using a regular camera from an 80-ft (24-m) tower.

Viewed from this height, the troops formed vast portraits of patriotic and military symbols. Working as a commercial photographer in Chicago in the early 20th century, Mole saw an opportunity to make inspiring pictures that would encourage support for U.S. troops during World War I.

He would spend at least a week organizing each photograph with his colleague John Thomas, directing the assembled troops with a megaphone according to a picture drawn on the lens of his camera. Assistants would then trace the outline with extremely long pieces of lace, enabling him to determine precisely how many troops he would require for each photograph.

Arthur Mole's most famous creations were captured in 1918. Twenty-five thousand soldiers from Camp Dix, New Jersey, stood as one to create *The Human Liberty Bell*, and 18,000 men assembled to Mole's orders in a vast rendering of the Statue of Liberty that stretched for 1,200 ft (365 m). Possibly his most dramatic image involved 21,000 men at Camp Sherman, Ohio, to make *The Living Portrait of Woodrow Wilson*—the U.S. president at the time.

Mole's largest work saw 30,000 men carefully placed to create this **Human U.S. Shield** *at Camp Custer in Battle Creek, Michigan.*

Mole's incredible portrait of President Woodrow Wilson.

Sincerely Yours,

Woodrow Wilson

000 OFFICERS AND MEN
MP SHERMAN, CHILLICOTHE OHIO
IG GEN. MATHEW C. SMITH, COMMANDING

LIVING PHOTOGRAPHY

> The Mayhart Studio of Chicago enlisted the services of hundreds of people to form *A Living Flag*—the Stars and Stripes—in 1917.

> In 1947, Eugene Omar Goldbeck of San Antonio, Texas, arranged 21,765 men at his local air base to represent the American Air Force insignia.

> Advertising agency executive Paul Arden created the 1989 British Airways TV commercial in which thousands of people from all over the world converged on Utah to form a smiling face.

> New Yorker Spencer Tunick has been photographing masses of naked people in public locations since 1992. In 2007, he posed 18,000 nude people in Mexico City—all crouched in the fetal position.

BIKINI REEF ■ A coral reef now thrives in the Pacific atoll of Bikini, where the Castle Bravo, a U.S. thermonuclear test bomb, exploded in 1954. The bomb vaporized three islands, raised water temperatures to 99,000°F (55,000°C), shook islands 125 mi (200 km) away and left a crater more than a mile wide on the ocean floor.

TRANSATLANTIC DUST ■ Some of the dust that blows over Florida has come all the way from Africa. The dust is kicked up by high winds in North Africa and carried to an altitude of 20,000 ft (6,100 m), where it becomes caught up in the trade winds and is transported across the Atlantic. Dust from China also makes its way to North America.

TORNADO TERROR ■ Dan and Jennifer Wells of Northmoor, Missouri, were married in Kansas City in 2003 three days after a tornado completely destroyed their home—Jennifer's wedding dress, hanging in a nearby shed, was untouched.

WHITE RAIN ■ On January 7, 2008, a white-colored rain fell across Grant and Catron counties in New Mexico. The strange rain, which contained high levels of calcium and left milky puddles and a milky white residue over a large area, was thought to have been caused by lake-bed dust from a dry lake in Arizona. The dust particles may have penetrated the clouds and fallen as rain.

DISTANT SHOCK ■ In 1985, a swimming pool at the University of Arizona in Tucson lost water from sloshing caused by the Michoacan earthquake taking place 1,240 mi (1,995 km) away in Mexico.

TORNADO TUESDAY ■ Eighty seven tornadoes combined to devastate areas of five U.S. states—Arkansas, Tennessee, Kentucky, Mississippi and Alabama—on "Super Tuesday," February 5–6, 2008. Two of the tornadoes had wind speeds of up to 200 mph (320 km/h) and the storms created hailstones as big as softballs—around 4½ in (11.4 cm) in diameter.

TRAVELER'S TREE ■ Thirsty travelers in Madagascar need only pierce the thick end of the leaf stalk of the tropical plant *Ravenala madagascariensis* to obtain plenty of water. Owing to its unusual leaf formation, with a vessel-like shape at the base of each stalk, a single specimen of the traveler's tree, as it is popularly known, can store up to 2½ pt (1.2 l) of water.

WATER SUPPLY ■ A newly discovered Mexican plant species has no chlorophyll and gets all its water and nutrients from the trees on which it feeds.

SUBWAY FLOODS? ■ Even in dry weather, the New York City subway system pumps out ten million gallons of water a day. Scientists say that owing to rising sea levels caused by global warming, the city's subways could be completely flooded by the end of the century.

SOLE DEATH ■ Around 500 meteorites, ranging in size from marbles to basketballs, hit the surface of Earth each year—but the only reported fatality over the past 100 years was a dog that was hit by one in Egypt in 1911.

FLYING BABY ■ In February 2008, a tornado in Castalian Springs, Tennessee, ripped 11-month-old Kyson Stowell from his mother's arms and threw him 400 ft (120 m) into a muddy field—where he was found alive and healthy. He was discovered among a collection of plastic dolls that had been picked up by the twister as it destroyed a nearby house.

LIGHTNING MAGNET ■ The Empire State Building in New York is struck by lightning some 500 times a year. It was once hit 12 times in 20 minutes, disproving the theory that lightning never strikes twice in the same place.

BURNED BUTT ■ In October 2006, Natasha Timarovic of Zadar, Croatia, survived a lightning strike to her mouth as she brushed her teeth. She was saved because she was wearing rubber-soled bathroom shoes, so instead of grounding through her feet, the electricity shot out of her backside, miraculously leaving her with only minor burns to her body.

MOVING CLOSER ■ Los Angeles, California, is moving toward San Francisco, also in California, at a rate of about 2 in (5 cm) a year, because the San Andreas Fault, which runs north–south, is slipping. Scientists predict that Los Angeles will be a suburb of San Francisco in around 15 million years.

VAST VOLCANO ■ The Olympus Mons volcano on Mars rises 16 mi (26 km) into the Martian sky, its base being so big that it would cover nearly the whole of Arizona.

GHOST ORCHID ■ The Ghost Orchid has no leaves and no stem. When it isn't flowering, the plant is just a system of roots.

BLACK HOLE ■ Located 3.5 billion light years away from Earth, OJ287, the largest black hole ever discovered, has a mass equivalent to 18 billion Suns.

TREE MOVE ■ To save a 750-year-old boab tree from becoming a casualty of a road-widening scheme, Australian Aboriginals arranged for it to be uprooted from its home in Western Australia in 2008 and moved a distance of 1,900 mi (3,060 km) by truck with a police escort to a park in the state capital Perth. The bottle-shaped tree, which has religious significance to the local people, stands 46 ft (14 m) high, measures 8 ft (2.4 m) in diameter and weighs around 36 tons. Boabs can live for up to 2,000 years.

MOON LAKE ■ A newly discovered lake at the south pole of Saturn's largest moon Titan is bigger than Lake Ontario. Covering an area of 7,800 sq mi (20,200 sq km), the lake is filled mostly with methane and ethane, which are gases on Earth, but liquids on the ice-cold surface of Titan.

FAST FRONT ■ A cold weather front can move at speeds of up to 30 mph (48 km/h)—faster than Olympic sprinters can run.

METEORITE HUNTER ■ Steve Arnold of Kingston, Arkansas, has dug up more than 1,000 meteorites in 15 years of searching. In 2005, he found one in Kiowa County, Kansas, that weighed nearly three-quarters of a ton.

ZAP CHAP! ■ Peter McCamphill of Warwickshire, England, survived a lightning strike in 2007 that burned off his hair, blackened his clothes, and tore one of his shoes into pieces.

SAFEST STATES ■ Between 1975 and 1995, there were only four U.S. states that did not have any earthquakes—Florida, Iowa, North Dakota and Wisconsin.

FLASHLIGHT DIG ■ Trapped beneath 20 ft (6 m) of snow from an avalanche near Ouray, Colorado, it took Danny Jaramillo 18 hours to dig his way to safety—using a flashlight as a shovel.

The Devil's Swimming Pool

Possibly the most dangerous swimming pool in the world, the "devil's pool," as it is known, is a dip in the rocks found on the very edge of Victoria Falls on the Zambezi River in Africa. Local guides lead tourists to the pool on the Zambian side of the falls, where it is possible to bathe only inches from a terrifying 328-ft (100-m) drop, despite a fast-moving current and the vast volume of water that rushes over the falls.

SCORPION QUEEN ■ In December 2008, Thailand's "Scorpion Queen," Kanchana Kaetkaew, held a venomous scorpion in her mouth for more than two minutes. She allowed her husband to place the live scorpion on her tongue, where it remained for 2 minutes 3 seconds before she spat it out.

EIGHT-HOUR SPEECH ■ An Australian politician made an eight-hour speech to delay a vote on changes to workers' compensation laws. Mark Parnell, a member of South Australia's Greens party, started his speech at 11a.m. on May 8, 2008, and finished 12 hours later, having paused only for lunch and dinner.

MASKED MAN ■ Gerold Weschenmoser of Germany has over 5,000 masks in a collection that he started more than 50 years ago, in 1957.

AGILE FEET ■ Anssi Vanhala of Finland can solve a Rubik's Cube puzzle in less than 40 seconds using only his feet.

MATCHSTICK SHUTTLE

Ken Applegate from St. Petersburg, Florida, spent 12 years making a 1:10 scale replica of the *Challenger* space shuttle from over half a million matchsticks. More than 12 ft (3.6 m) long and weighing about 800 lb (365 kg), the matchstick model was completed in 2008 and even has moving features, including opening cargo bay doors and retractable wheels.

26-HOUR GAME ■ Twenty-four members of Havering Field Hockey Club in Essex, England, played indoor hockey for 26 hours nonstop in December 2008.

HAND WALKER ■ At the age of 96, Fred Birchmore of Athens, Georgia, kept fit by walking 3 mi (4.8 km) every day, going swimming—and walking on his hands. In his youth, he once cycled around the world.

SNAKE EATER ■ Wen Xide from Zhumadian, China, enjoys eating live snakes and washing them down with a bottle of beer. He started eating snakes more than ten years ago to win a bet with friends and soon became addicted to them, even though he describes the experience as "a bit smelly." His son is now following in his footsteps and devoured eight live snakes in 2008.

TRACTOR WHEELIE ■ In July 2008, Mike Hagan of Whitehall, Montana, drove his 1994 Ford tractor for a distance of 5.3 mi (8.5 km) on just its two rear wheels. His endurance wheelie lasted 35 minutes.

LEGO™ LOVER ■ Darren Smith of Exeter, Devon, England, started collecting LEGO™ bricks when he was five—and now, 28 years later, he has more than two million of them. His collection fills his large garage and a specially converted loft, and even threatens to spill over into the rest of the house. His wife Claire says: "If Darren had his way, we'd have a LEGO™ extension built."

LEI LINE ■ In May 2008, volunteers in Waikiki, Hawaii, strung together flowers to form a lei (flower garland) that measured over a mile (1.6 km) long.

SEAT FEAT ■ Just weeks after undergoing a triple hernia operation, Terry Twining from Hampshire, England, sat on 40,040 seats at Belgium's national soccer stadium in 48 hours—an average of one seat every four seconds.

BAND-AID® TINS ■ Kevin Savetz from Blue Lake, California, has a collection of Band-Aid® tins. The idea for the collection started in 1994 when he found two dozen Band-Aid® tins dating back to the 1950s in the garage of the house he had just bought.

BALL GAME ■ Organized by Rick Thistle, 40 participants—male and female—played a softball game that lasted a staggering 96 hours 4 minutes at Charlottetown, Prince Edward Island, Canada, in 2008. The marathon game comprised 467 innings and 1,941 runs.

UNDERWATER CYCLIST ■ Helped onto his bike by local scuba divers, 62-year-old Italian Vittorio Innocente cycled underwater at a depth of 213 ft (65 m) in the sea near Genoa, Italy, in July 2008.

REVERSE SKATING ■ Rafael Mittenzwei roller-skated more than 130 mi (209 km) in 24 hours in August 2008—backward. He completed 685 laps of the track in Gross-Gerau, Germany, skating right through the night.

RUNNING BACKWARD ■ Xu Zhenjun of China ran a marathon in 3 hours 43 minutes 39 seconds—while facing backward!

PUB CRAWL ■ Since 1984, four men from West Bromwich, England, have visited more than 14,000 pubs across the U.K. and the Republic of Ireland. In that time, Peter Hill, John Drew, Karl Bradley and Joe Hill have each drunk around 21,000 pints of beer.

HIGH JUMP ■ To mark the start of 2009, Australian stunt motorcyclist Robbie Maddison sped up a ramp in Las Vegas, Nevada, and catapulted 120 ft (37 m) through the air to land on top of a 100-ft-high (30-m) replica of the Arc de Triomphe.

YOUNG BUSINESSMAN ■ While being treated for leukemia, 10-year-old Brandon Rayner of Phoenix, Arizona, has collected more than 900,000 business cards.

Beads Galore

British artist and jeweler Alayna Slater used 10,000 multicolored beads to create a 262-ft-long (80-m) bracelet. It took Alanya 40 hours to make the incredible piece while she was at a fashion show in Birmingham, England, in 2008.

How long do you think you can hold your breath? Imagine diving down an incredible 702 ft (214 m) into the ocean with no breathing apparatus and only fish for company! This is what free diver Herbert Nitsch from Austria did. A champion in the extreme sport of free diving, Herbert dived to this depth in Spetses, Greece, in June 2008, using only the air in his lungs.

Herbert used a weighted sled on the way down, in order to reach this depth. While still in relatively shallow water, he used a soda bottle to help equalize the pressure in his ears, but as he went deeper he had only his own intense training techniques to prevent him from passing out.

As the water pressure increases, Herbert's lungs can shrink to the size of a fist, the blood vessels there eventually flooding with blood to stop the chest cavity from collapsing as the pressure at 656 ft (200 m) reaches almost 300 lb (136 kg) per square inch. The entire Spetses dive took 4 minutes 24 seconds. Descending at a rate of 10 ft 6 in (3.2 m) per second, it took him 1 minute 45 seconds to reach this incredible depth, where he waited three seconds before ascending with the aid of a rope at a speed of 13 ft (4 m) per second.

Safety precautions are vital in the dangerous sport of free diving—when he is deep enough, Herbert removes the nose clip to flood his sinuses with water.

Descending into the depths, Herbert is helped downward by a heavy-weighted sled.

A bulbous "helmet" helps to improve Herbert's hydrodynamics.

Herbert is meticulous in his preparation for a dive and tests all of his equipment carefully.

Ripley's research

Surprisingly, it is not at crushing depths that free divers are in most danger, but just before they resurface. Fit and healthy athletes can succumb to unconsciousness with no warning as the brain finally becomes starved of oxygen.

The air pressure underwater means that the human body loses its buoyancy at only 32 ft (10 m) down and the lungs shrink to half their size. When a free diver drops below 100 ft (30 m), the lungs shrink again to about the size of an orange. Below 328 ft (100 m), some divers counteract painful water pressure by actually flooding the sinus passages in their head. At this point, the heart rate can drop below 20 beats per minute (the normal rate is about 70). An extreme phenomenon observed in super-deep dives is that the body allows blood to pass into organs to keep pressure from literally squashing vital organs; for example, the shrunken lungs are flooded. Some have warned that this means that extreme free divers who sink too deep are at risk of drowning not in seawater but their own blood, should these blood vessels burst under the pressure.

WAY TO GO!

ICE-CREAM VAN CORTEGE
Ice-cream salesman Derek Greenwood of Rochdale, England, had a funeral cortege consisting of 12 ice-cream vans all playing jingles on their way to the cemetery.

SCOTTY'S ASHES BLASTED INTO SPACE
Actor James Doohan, who played Scotty in *Star Trek*, had his ashes scattered in space in 2007 after they were beamed up aboard a rocket launched in New Mexico.

WATCHING CORPSE ROT
When a Mambai tribesman from Indonesia died, the custom was to sit the corpse in the family house while relatives sat around and watched it decompose for as long as they could bear the smell of the rotting flesh.

COFFIN ON CAR ROOF
A man from Schopfheim, Germany, saved on funeral costs by tying his dead mother's coffin to the roof rack of his car and driving along the highway to the cemetery.

BODY TOO BIG FOR COFFIN
Alexander Douglas, the tenth Duke of Hamilton, spent a vast sum of money on a genuine ancient Egyptian coffin, but when he died in 1852, he proved too long for the coffin, and so his legs had to be hacked off before undertakers could fit him inside.

PICKLED IN RUM
Following the Battle of Trafalgar, the body of Admiral Horatio Nelson (1758–1805) was brought back to England pickled in a barrel of rum to prevent it decomposing on the way home.

LEFT FOR THE HYENAS
Masai tribesmen from Africa traditionally leave their dead relatives outside for hyenas to eat.

FIREWORK BURIAL
American writer and journalist Hunter S. Thompson had his ashes blown sky high amid a spectacular firework display at his memorial service in Woody Creek, Colorado, in 2005.

BURIED WITHOUT HIS HEAD
Austrian composer Joseph Haydn (1732–1809) was buried without his head after two of his friends bribed the gravedigger to let them keep it. The head was stored in a Vienna cupboard for 60 years after his death.

BODY IN A JAR
A tradition among the Berawan tribe of Borneo was to squeeze the deceased's body into a large earthenware jar and keep it in the relatives' house for a year before the "official" burial.

ANCIENT FESTIVALS
(NUMBER OF YEARS HELD)

5,000 — THE NEVRUZ FESTIVAL, TURKEY
Homes are cleaned and new clothes are bought every year on March 21, the day when, according to tradition, all diseases and troubles disappear to mark the start of spring.

3,000 — THE DAY OF THE DEAD, MEXICO
Families take flowers and foodstuffs—including chocolate coffins and sugar skeletons—and enjoy a picnic around the graves of departed relatives.

2,300 — ESALA PERAHERA, SRI LANKA
Dancers, acrobats, drummers, flame throwers and more than 100 elegantly decorated elephants parade through the streets of the hill city of Kandy in honor of the Tooth Relic of Lord Buddha.

2,000 — THE LANTERN FESTIVAL, CHINA
Thousands of lanterns in the shapes of birds, animals, fish, fruit, flowers and even space rockets adorn homes, restaurants and temples to celebrate the return of spring and light.

1,500 — THE MARRIAGE OF TREES, ACCETTURA, ITALY
In a centuries-old fertility rite and celebration of new growth in spring, two magnificent trees—the king and queen of the forest—are cut down and carried through the town, where the queen is hoisted on top of the truncated king.

900 — THE DUNMOW FLITCH, GREAT DUNMOW, ENGLAND
A side (or flitch) of bacon is awarded to any couple who can convince a jury of six bachelors and six spinsters that they have been happily married for a year and a day.

850 — FESTIVAL OF CANDLES, GUBBIO, ITALY
Statues of three saints are carried through Gubbio on top of 30-ft-high (9-m) poles and raced up a nearby hill to the Church of St. Ubaldo—and the result is the same every year, the rules dictating that St. Ubaldo must finish first, followed by St. George and St. Anthony.

600 — DUCASSE, ATH, BELGIUM
Eight 12-ft-tall (3.6-m) human statues made from reeds are led through the streets for a ceremonial Wedding of the Giants.

South African Paseka Hlatshwayo thought that the dead should have a different view below ground so he created a sit-down coffin, inspired by an ancient method of burial traditionally reserved for high-ranking people in African culture.

UNUSUAL CUSTOMS

Foam Fun

Every August, as part of an annual festival in the Gracia district of Barcelona, Spain, locals try to outdo each other by decorating their streets in outlandish ways. Filling this street with gallons of foam proved particularly popular with the district's younger inhabitants.

SAME NAME ■ When Ronald Legendre married his girlfriend Hope in Kissimmee, Florida, the best man was an unrelated man named Ronald Legendre and the judge was another unrelated Ronald Legendre.

NO SUPERSTITION ■ A bridegroom born on Friday the 13th made the supposedly unlucky number a key part of his big day. Aiden Edwards cast superstition aside by marrying Zoe Adams at St. Austell, Cornwall, England, at 1300 hours on Friday, April 13, 2007. The Bible reading was from Corinthians, chapter 13.

MACABRE VENUE ■ John Leonard and Margaret Gross of Fremont, Ohio, were carried in caskets to their wedding, which took place in a haunted house.

NO NAMES ■ In Australia, it is against the law to give a name to any animal that you plan to eat.

ANNIVERSARY CELEBRATION ■ In rural Saskatchewan, Canada, mock weddings are staged to celebrate anniversaries—with the husband and wife assuming each other's role and even clothing while re-enacting the marriage ceremony.

Toilet Paper Gown

Katrina Chalifoux of Rockford, Illinois, picked up a $1,000 prize for creating a stunning wedding dress—fashioned entirely out of toilet paper. Katrina's design was one of six dresses on display in the "Cheap and Chic" Toilet Paper Wedding Dress Contest held at the Ripley's Believe It or Not! museum in New York's Times Square in June 2008. She spent two weeks creating the winning sheath dress with a raised flower pattern, modeled here by her niece Francea Maravich, from seven rolls of molded toilet paper.

BACK FROM THE DEAD ■ In January 2008, 81-year-old Feliberto Carrasco of Angol, Chile, woke up to find himself in a coffin at his own wake amid mourning family. Once helped out of the coffin he asked for a glass of water.

STAR SIGN ■ In Sedona, Arizona, it is illegal to lie about your astrological sign.

STRESS RELIEF ■ To help parishioners escape the stress of daily life, Pastor Thorsten Nolting of Dusseldorf, Germany, came up with the idea of allowing them to lie for seven minutes in a 6-ft-6-in-long (2-m) open grave.

DECAYED BODIES ■ Police in Omuta, Fukuoka, Japan, discovered a house with five decayed bodies, where relatives had stored them anticipating their resurrection.

LONGEST SALE ■ The World's Largest Yard Sale extends 450 mi (725 km) through four states! Every August, stalls line the roadside along the U.S. Highway 127 Corridor and the Lookout Mountain Parkway between Covington, Kentucky, and Gadsden, Alabama.

BODY PAINT ■ As part of Fantasy Fest at Key West, Florida, every October, 60,000 revelers cover themselves in body paint—and sometimes not much else!

MURDER LEGAL ■ It is legal to murder a Scotsman within the ancient walls of the city of York, England, if he is carrying a bow and arrow.

CROSS DRESSING ■ At the Ose Festival, held in Shizuoka, Japan, each April, all of the male participants dress up in women's clothes.

NAKED CHARGE ■ A couple of days before the Running of the Bulls Festival at Pamplona, Spain, there is a Running of the Nudes—where naked people charge through the streets of the town!

FUNERAL CUSTOMS ■ The Museum of Funeral Customs at Springfield, Illinois, displays coffins and caskets—including a full-sized reproduction of Abraham Lincoln's coffin—plus embalming instruments and post-mortem photos.

OFFICIAL NAMES ■ Until 1984, Belgians had to choose their children's names from an official list of 1,500 drawn up in the days of Napoleon Bonaparte around the beginning of the 19th century.

SMILE, PLEASE ■ A law that is still on the books in Milan, Italy, requires citizens to smile at all times in public or risk a hefty fine. Exemptions from the rule include visiting patients in hospital and attending funerals.

REINCARNATION BAN ■ China's state administration of religious affairs has regulations that ban reincarnation without first attaining government approval!

COMPULSORY SOCKS ■ In Britain, it is illegal to stand within one hundred yards of the reigning monarch when not wearing socks.

PARTY POLITICS ■ A row over a birthday party invitation led to a complaint being made to the Swedish Parliament in 2008. An eight-year-old boy in Lund, Sweden, had the birthday party invitations he was handing out at school confiscated by his teacher because he failed to include two of his classmates. The two were apparently left out because one did not invite the boy to his own party and the boy had fallen out with the other one. However, the school said that he had violated the children's rights and complained to Parliament.

WEDDING X-RAY ■ When Liza, a Labrador dog, accidentally swallowed Hillary Feinberg's wedding ring the day before she was due to marry Mark Feinberg of Boston, Massachusetts, the groom gave his bride an X ray of the ring instead.

TAKING THE PLUNGE ■ Fifteen couples got married in a joint ceremony while riding down the waterslide at a North Carolina theme park.

Snowman Army

More than 200 snowmen lined up at the annual Sapporo Snow Festival in Sapporo, Japan. Every February as many as two million visitors come to admire statues and sculptures around the city that are made from around 30,000 tons of imported snow.

Bags of colored powder are prepared for the festival in New Delhi, India.

Indian soldiers celebrate the festival at a camp in Amritsar in the northwest of the country.

Rainbow Revelers

Thousands of people across India enjoy more than a splash of color at the Hindu "Holi" spring festival. On the second day of the festival, revelers scatter brightly colored powders over the streets, and everybody is covered head to toe in the rainbow clouds. Water is often sprayed onto the crowds and covers the streets in bright liquid. Traditionally, the powder was made from medicinal herbs and the festival was thought to ward off spring illnesses brought on by the change in weather.

Water is sprayed from the roof of the Krishna temple in Nandgaon, central India, during the Hindu Festival of Colors, "Holi."

PHONE WEDDING ■ Safikul Islam married Irin Biswas in 2008—via cell phone. With relatives huddled around Irin's phone at her home in Murshidabad, India, and an official in attendance, she exchanged vows with Safikul, who was working 2,500 mi (4,025 km) away in Kuwait.

GROOM REPLACED ■ When a groom turned up drunk for his wedding in Arwal, India, in 2007, he was chased out of the village and replaced by his more sober younger brother!

SOCCER RUN ■ In honor of Austria co-hosting the Euro 2008 soccer championships, a funeral company in Vienna created a soccer-ball cremation urn.

RELATIVELY DEAD ■ The Association of the Dead is a political party in Uttar Pradesh, India, dedicated to helping those who have been falsely declared dead by greedy relatives.

VIDEO PROPOSAL ■ New Jersey software programmer Bernie Peng proposed to his girlfriend by hacking into her favorite video game. He reprogrammed *Bejeweled* so that a ring and a proposal popped up on screen when girlfriend Tammy Li reached a certain score.

RANDOM WILL ■ When Luis da Camara of Lisbon, Portugal, died in 2007, he left all his money to 70 people he had randomly picked out of the phone book. Having no family, he left each of the strangers around $12,000.

SKATER GIRLS ■ In a Louisiana version of Spain's famous Pamplona bull run, hundreds of men, women and children, dressed in white and wearing red scarves around their waists and red bandannas around their necks, are chased through the streets of New Orleans by roller-skating girls wearing horned helmets.

MARE'S HEAD ■ In southeast Wales, as part of an ancient New Year's celebration known as Mari Lwyd, singers and dancers parade a mare's skull draped in a white sheet and fixed to the end of a pole through the streets of local towns and villages. The horse's eye-sockets are often filled with green bottle tops and the lower jaw is sometimes spring-loaded so that it can be made to snap at passersby.

WHISTLING BAN ■ Organizers of the 2008 Scottish Traditional Boat Festival banned whistling in the town of Portsoy, Aberdeenshire, for a month in a bid to ensure good weather. An old maritime superstition states that whistling at sea mocks the devil and brings ill winds.

SOUL MATE ■ An unmarried Chinese man—Mr. Li of Nanjing—advertised on the Internet for a female tomb-mate so that he would not be lonely after death. He posted a message online, pointing out that he was not looking for a relationship, just somebody to share a tomb.

SHIN KICKING ■ On a hill in Gloucestershire, England, they still practice the 17th-century sport of shin kicking. Competitors, wearing white shepherds' smocks, grasp each other by the shoulders and try to land blows on their opponent's shins. In olden days, they used to harden their shins with hammer blows beforehand and wear iron-capped boots, but now players stuff their trousers with straw and must wear soft shoes.

WOOL-SACK RACES ■ Every May in the town of Tetbury in Gloucestershire, England, in a ceremony dating back 400 years, men and women run up and down a steep, 25-degree hill carrying heavy sacks of wool—60 lb (27 kg) for the men and 35 lb (16 kg) for the women.

BIG YAWN ■ At the Quiet Festival in Ocean City, New Jersey, instead of a traditional sing-along, participants have a yawn-along. The festival opens with people yawning in time to the tune of "Beautiful Dreamer" before enjoying other peaceful artistic pursuits such as silent movies and mimes.

NATIVITY NAMES ■ During the 2007 Christmas holidays, Travelodge, a British hotel chain, offered a free stay for couples named Mary and Joseph, just like the parents of Jesus Christ in the story of the Christian nativity.

FAT FIRE ■ A 600-lb (272-kg) man produced so much fat when he was cremated at a Salt Lake City, Utah, funeral home that he started a fire. The oven was unable to handle all the fat, with the result that fluids seeped onto the floor and ignited in a grease fire.

SWALLOWED RING ■ A woman in Fuqing, China, passed out in June 2008 after accidentally swallowing a surprise engagement ring that her boyfriend had hidden in a cake. Doctors at the local hospital had to use a catheter to retrieve the ring from her stomach.

MISS GOAT ■ A Most Beautiful Goat Contest is held in Riyadh, Saudi Arabia. Only the Najdi breed of goat may enter and they are shampooed and styled before being paraded. The winners are chosen for their overall appearance and particularly the whiteness of their eyes.

HOMELESS SOCCER ■ In 2006, homeless men and women representing 48 countries competed in the fourth annual Homeless World Cup Soccer Tournament, which was held in Cape Town, South Africa.

Green Man

The "Jack in the Green" procession in Hastings, England, is a May Day tradition featuring a man completely covered in a tall suit of leaves. Its origins lie in the 18th century when workers used to create ever more extravagant May Day garland displays. The enormous garland produced by a guild of chimney sweeps covered an entire man who became known as Jack in the Green. Today, the tradition continues as hundreds of costumed locals follow the Jack amid much May Day revelry.

UNUSUAL CUSTOMS

www.ripleys.com

Ripley's—
Believe It or Not!®

What Goes Up

Hundreds of acrobatic individuals at the Tarragona Castells festival in Spain climb over each other to form gravity-defying human towers in a tradition that dates back to the 18th century. Prizes are awarded for the highest and most complex structures at the biennial festival. Unsurprisingly, they often come crashing down as they teeter on each others' shoulders.

NOVEL NAVELS ■ The town of Shibukawa, Japan, hosts an annual Belly Button Festival, where children and adults paint their navels in bright colors, often in the shape of mouths. The Japanese believe that because the belly button is located in the middle of the torso, it is the most important part of the body.

RED SOCKS ▥ The Red Hose Race in Carnwath, Scotland, was founded 500 years ago to select the fastest runner to warn Edinburgh of invasions from the south. The winner receives a pair of long red socks.

AQUATIC OLYMPICS ▥ In 2008, an aquarium in Qingdao, China, held underwater Olympics with aquatic versions of fencing, cycling, gymnastics and shooting.

DIRTY WORK ▥ Participants in a festival in Laza, Spain, throw ashes, flour and dirt filled with ants at each other! Amid the ant-throwing, a person in a carved wooden mask, masquerading as a brown cow, butts people.

ROMANTIC GESTURE ■ A Ukrainian man paid $20,000 to hire an entire theater company so that he could star in a play and propose to his girlfriend. Gennady Zaleskiy took to the stage in Zaporozhie behind a mask but instead of declaring his love for his leading lady, he turned to face his girlfriend in the audience and asked her to marry him.

MOUNTAIN GOLF ▥ There is only one hole at the Pillar Mountain Golf Classic—but it's a par-70! That's because the course at Kodiak, Alaska, is the 1,400-ft (427-m) mountain itself, and at the time of the annual tournament—on April Fool's weekend—it is often still covered in ice and snow. Consequently, players are advised to carry a set of crampons and are warned about the dangers of frostbite.

SNAKE FESTIVAL ▥ Every May in Cocullo, Italy, as a stone statue of Saint Domenica is paraded through the village, local people drape live snakes around its neck. When the Festival of Snakes is over, the serpents are released into the bush, leaving villagers supposedly immune from snakebites for another year.

ABSEILING GROOM ■ Outdoor enthusiasts Mark and Lena Brailsford chose to make their way to their 2008 wedding service in unusual fashion—Mark abseiled down the tower of the church in Cromford, Derbyshire, England, and Lena, resplendent in wedding dress, paddled a canoe along the River Derwent.

FUNERAL PRIZE ▥ At a baseball game in Grand Prairie, Texas, in June 2008, Elaine Fulps, 60, won a $10,000, all-expenses-paid funeral.

GRAVESIDE HUMOR ■ A parking meter placed on the Okemah, Oklahoma, gravesite of Barbara Sue Manire, who died in 2005 on the day of her 64th birthday, reads "64 Year Limit" and "Time Expired."

CREMATION TATTOO ■ Russell Parsons of Hurricane, West Virginia, has his funeral and cremation instructions tattooed on his arm. His recipe for cremation reads "Cook @ 1700–1800 for 2 to 3 hours."

Grab the Pig

At the 38th Annual Stephensville Round-Up held in Stephensville, Wisconsin, in summer 2008, participants valiantly attempted to wrestle squirming pigs to the ground in thick mud.

LIAR, LIAR ■ Each year since 1929, Burlington, Wisconsin, has held an annual contest to reward the city's best liar.

GRAPE FIGHT ■ In 2007, a farm in Wangcheng, China, filled a large wading pool with two-and-a-half tons of grapes to set the stage for a mass fruit fight. The battle was part of a local grape festival, which also featured a grape speed-eating contest, won by Wang Peng who ate 3 lb 4 oz (1.5 kg) of grapes in 90 seconds.

HERNIA OP ■ An angelfish underwent a $1,000 lifesaving operation in October 2008 to cure a hernia. The 10-in-long (25-cm) fish, named Carla, was anesthetized at England's London Aquarium before veterinarian Sue Thornton repaired the hole in the fish's side.

RUBIK'S RIDDLE ■ The World Cube Association holds an annual contest for solving a Rubik's Cube—while blindfolded. In 2008, the winner solved the puzzle in just 48 seconds. There are even people who can solve a Rubik's Cube in under a minute using only their feet!

DIRT BAGS ■ On Dirt Bag Day in March, visitors to the exclusive ski resort of Bozeman, Montana, deliberately wear scruffy, crazy costumes. The event finishes with the annual Dirt Bag Ball and the coronation of the Dirt Bag King and Queen.

CHOW DOWN

Competitors taking part in the Shepherd's Shemozzle race in the annual Huntaway Festival in Hunterville, New Zealand, need either a starving appetite or a very strong stomach. As part of the endurance race, the shepherds must bite into bulls' testicles and carry them 165 ft (50 m) along the course—they also have to wolf down dry breakfast cereal and raw eggs.

Dressing for Dinner

At the annual Guinea Pig Food Festival in Huacho, Peru, breeders from all over the country bring their prized guinea pigs to compete in races and fashion contests. The incentive for the winning rodents is that they will escape the frying pan, because the other main ingredient of the festival is a demonstration of how to cook guinea pig. A native of the Andes, guinea pig has been a staple part of the Peruvian diet in rural communities since the time of the Incas, and it is estimated that Peruvians consume 65 million guinea pigs each year.

A proud owner shows off her guinea pig in the hope that it might be spared the pot.

FISH BAIT ■ When keen fisherman Peter Hodge of Somerset, England, learned he was dying, he asked for his remains to be turned into fish food. So, after his death in 2008, he was cremated in a wicker fishing basket and his ashes were mixed with 30 lb (13.6 kg) of fish bait—so that he could swim up and down his local river where he had spent 40 happy years.

SOCCER PLOT ■ A cemetery in Iraola, Argentina, has 3,000 burial plots set aside for dedicated fans and members of the Boca Juniors soccer team.

MARRIED MONKEYS ■ Around 3,000 villagers attended a lavish Hindu wedding ceremony in the Indian state of Orissa in 2008—for two monkeys. The bride—a female monkey named Jhumuri—wore a 16-ft-long (5-m) sari decked with flowers. The groom—a male monkey called Manu—was taken by procession to the temple, where he was greeted with loud music, dancing and fireworks. The newlyweds were showered with gifts, including a gold necklace for the bride.

IDENTITY CRISIS ■ After becoming engaged to their longtime boyfriends on Christmas Day 2006, identical twins Francine and Maria Munafo got married to them in a double ceremony in New York in June 2008. Both brides wore white strapless dresses, but to enable the grooms to tell them apart, Maria's was tinged with magenta and Francine's had a touch of green.

ROLLER TOUR ■ The Pari-Roller Club hosts a weekly roller-skating tour through the streets of Paris, with thousands regularly attending.

GRUMPY CLUB ■ A pub in Hampshire, England, hosts a weekly Grumpy Club where members—mostly middle-aged men—meet to air their grievances about everything from the stodginess of trifles to the price of beer.

BURIED LEG ■ Hallie Broadribb of Valleyview, Alberta, Canada, had her leg amputated as a result of cancer and kept the limb in a freezer for a year, then held a funeral and buried it in its own casket.

BABY DROP ■ Villagers in Musti, Maharashtra, India, follow a 500-year-old tradition of dropping infants from a temple tower onto an outstretched sheet held by the crowd below.

CARING CARP ■ At an annual Shinto ceremony in Toyama, Japan, carp are caught, fed sake and released, the locals believing that the fish will swim away taking their own hardships with them.

HEADLESS GOAT ■ Buzkashi is an Afghan team sport played on horseback—where riders use the carcass of a headless goat as the ball.

MISER PUNISHED ■ In 2008, an Iranian court ordered a man to buy his wife 124,000 roses—at a cost of more than $250,000—as punishment for being mean with his money during their ten years of marriage. Under Iranian law, *mahr*, a dowry offered by the man to the woman at the time of marriage, can be claimed at any time during the couple's married life or divorce proceedings.

High Bride

The bride at a traditional wedding in China is carried high above crowds of well-wishers by men on stilts at a ceremony in the city of Qinyang in January 2009.

TABLE CARRIERS ■ Every year, members of the Low Table Club of Jane Franklin Hall College in Hobart, Tasmania, carry a wooden dining table to the top of a mountain and back down to raise money for a cancer charity.

UNDERWATER RUGBY ■ Dozens of teams in Switzerland have signed up for a new sport—underwater rugby. The six-a-side game is played by both men and women, who wear flippers, snorkel and goggles. The ball is filled with saltwater and weighs 13 lb (6 kg), the goal being to place it in the opposing team's basket on the floor of the swimming pool. Players need to come to the surface to breathe.

SLICE OF LUCK ■ Italians believe that a loaf of bread placed upside down will bring bad luck, especially on board fishing boats where it could mean a poor catch.

RUBBER DUCKS ■ At the annual Great Topeka Duck Race in Kansas, some 10,000 rubber ducks are launched from a barge into Lake Shawnee and drift on the current toward the finish line.

FISH THROW ■ The highlight of the annual Tunarama festival at Port Lincoln, South Australia, is the tuna toss, where competitors toss a tuna that tips the scales at 17–22 lb (8–10 kg). In 1998, former Olympic hammer thrower Sean Carlin hurled his fish 121 ft (37 m).

PURE PUN-ISHMENT ■ Since 1977, wits of the world have converged on Austin, Texas, in May for the O. Henry Pun-Off World Championships to determine who can deliver the most excruciating play on words.

BONFIRE RITUAL ■ At June's Las Hogueras Festival in Alicante, Spain, people protect themselves from illness by running and jumping around lighted bonfires seven times and then taking a dip in the sea. The bonfires were originally made from old scrap, but now they are constructed of wood and papier mâché.

SHELL POWER ■ At a bar in Marion, Indiana, they race hermit crabs. The crabs' shells are painted for easy identification, and the crustaceans race around a table while spectators bet on the outcome.

DOG DAYS ■ The town of Whistler, British Columbia, Canada, opens its doors to man's best friend during a two-day Dog Fest in April. There are contests for the best-dressed dog as well as for dog dancing.

UTE MUSTER ■ In October 2007, a total of 6,235 utility vehicles (or utes) gathered for the annual Ute Muster at the Play on the Plains Festival at Delinquin, New South Wales, Australia. The festival also features a contest to see how many people show up wearing a blue undershirt—in 2007 it was more than 1,500!

CHOSEN GIRLS ■ Members of both the Buddhist and Hindu communities of Nepal worship the Kumari—young girls who are selected in a temple to temporarily fulfill the role of a living goddess.

CAT CARE ■ Larry Johnson of California left his finances and possessions to Juniata College, including his car, his $1.3-million condominium, his handgun and a collection of 1,500 CDs—along with the task of caring for his cat.

UNDERWATER CEREMONY ■ In July 2008, Brian Wilson and Christina Gunn got married 20 ft (6 m) below the surface of the Illinois River in southern Oregon. The bride wore a white veil, a red garter and black neoprene and the groom, too, was in diving gear, adorned with a red bow tie. The vows for the underwater ceremony were written in pencil on a white slate, and cards saying "I do" were displayed for Pastor Jim Bard, also a diver. When he pronounced them man and wife, the newlyweds took off their breathing gear and exchanged an underwater kiss. They chose the location because it was where they had first dived together.

WEDDING CLASH ■ When a Chinese bride found that a compulsory teaching exam clashed with her wedding day in May 2008, she had a simple solution—she sat the test in her wedding dress. As the wedding had been arranged for months, Luo Yingchao switched the venue of the ceremony to her school in Zhengzhou City and changed the time to fit in with the end of the exam.

FUNERAL SPEAKER ■ Minister Andrew Hoover of Columbus, Ohio, works as a full-time eulogist—speaking at over 250 funerals a year.

AGE GAP ■ In 2006, 104-year-old Wook Kundor of Kuala Berang, Malaysia, married her 21st husband—a man 71 years younger than herself.

HOW FAST?

270 MPH	435 KM/H	Peregrine falcon (diving)
145 MPH	233 KM/H	Trap-jaw ant (jaws snapping shut)
106 MPH	170 KM/H	Spine-tailed swift
100 MPH	160 KM/H	Racing pigeon
70 MPH	113 KM/H	Cheetah
68 MPH	109 KM/H	Sailfish
64 MPH	103 KM/H	Dolphin
61 MPH	98 KM/H	Pronghorn
60 MPH	96 KM/H	Mako shark
50 MPH	80 KM/H	Lion, American quarter horse, Wildebeest
48 MPH	77 KM/H	Killer whale
45 MPH	72 KM/H	Thomson's gazelle, European hare
43 MPH	69 KM/H	Greyhound, Ostrich
40 MPH	64 KM/H	Zebra
36 MPH	58 KM/H	Australian dragonfly
33 MPH	53 KM/H	Hawk moth
30 MPH	48 KM/H	Grizzly bear
21 MPH	34 KM/H	Spiny-tailed iguana
18 MPH	29 KM/H	Tyrannosaurus rex
12 MPH	19 KM/H	Black mamba
5.6 MPH	9 KM/H	Australian tiger beetle
0.23 MPH	0.37 KM/H	Giant tortoise
0.1 MPH	0.16 KM/H	Three-toed sloth
0.03 MPH	0.05 KM/H	Garden snail
0.01 MPH	0.016 KM/H	Sea horse

DEADLY (MEASURED BY AVERAGE NUMBER OF HUMAN DEATHS PER YEAR)

1 MOSQUITO 2,000,000
Only female mosquitoes suck blood and they transmit disease to more than 700 million people annually.

2 SNAKE 100,000
The Asian cobra alone contributes half of this figure, even though it is not as venomous as Australia's Fierce snake, which has enough poison to kill 250,000 mice.

3 SCORPION 5,000
One component of the venom of the most deadly of scorpions—the deathstalker of North Africa and the Middle East—is being prepared to treat human brain tumors while another component could be used to tackle diabetes.

4 CROCODILE 2,000
Saltwater crocodiles measure up to 23 ft (7 m) long and can swim at speeds of 18 mph (29 km/h) in short bursts—that's more than four times faster than a human swimming champion. Even on land they can run almost as fast as humans.

5 ELEPHANT 600
An Indian elephant was hunted in 2006, after a two-year reign of terror in which he destroyed hundreds of homes and killed 27 people.

6 BEE 400
The Africanized or "Killer" bee was accidentally released in Brazil in the 1950s and now swarms across South America and the southern U.S.A. Killer bees are far more aggressive than the European honey bee and will even wait for you to surface if you hide underwater.

7 LION 250
In 1898, two man-eating lions ate 28 railway workers and a number of local people in Kenya.

8 HIPPOPOTAMUS 200
An adult hippopotamus can open its mouth so wide that a 4-ft-tall (1.2-m) child could stand inside. It possesses such powerful jaws that it could bite a 12-ft-long (3.6-m) crocodile in half.

9 JELLYFISH 100
Even when dead, a jellyfish can sting, and the sting from the Australian box jellyfish can kill a human in just four minutes.

10 SHARK 80
Sharks can detect one part of blood in 100 million parts of water and the biggest—such as the Great White—can bite through steel cables.

A kitten was born in Perth, Australia, in November 2008 with two faces—giving it two mouths, four eyes and two noses. The kitten was able to meow out of both mouths simultaneously.

CRAZY CREATURES

JAW-DROPPING

A monster Amethystine python, thought to be over 16 ft (4.9 m) long, swallowed a fully grown wallaby and her joey in February 2008. Darren Cleland encountered the creature on the banks of the Barron River, west of Cairns, Australia, and said, "We figured if it could eat the wallaby, it could easily eat our 5-year-old."

® Ripley's research

HOW DO PYTHONS SWALLOW SUCH BIG PREY?

Unlike most animals, the jaws of a python are loosely connected to the skull with elastic ligaments, allowing them to open wide to an angle of 180 degrees. The lower jaw is separated into two and unconnected at the chin, so that it can break apart sideways. This means that, amazingly, pythons can swallow prey ten times the size of their mouths.

Pythons wrap their bodies around their prey until it suffocates. As it can take hours for a snake to consume a large animal, they can extend their windpipe beyond the mouth to ensure they can still breathe. Pythons need to eat only once every few weeks, depending on the size of the meal, and they have the rare ability of being able to digest all the bones.

Pythons can open their jaws to such dimensions that a greedy specimen can swallow amazingly large prey relatively easily. This snake wouldn't have to eat again for weeks.

SERPENT SNACK ■ The body of a 32-year-old man from Mindoro Island in the Philippines was recovered inside a 23-ft (7-m) python in 1998.

DOG FOOD ■ An Australian family watched as a 16-ft (4.8-m) python swallowed their pet Chihuahua in front of them in February 2008.

DEADLY BATTLE ■ A 13-ft (4-m) python exploded after trying to swallow a 6-ft-6-in (2-m) alligator in the Florida Everglades in 2005.

HEADFIRST ■ In 2003, a 10-ft (3-m) python in Rangamati, Bangladesh, swallowed a 38-year-old woman up to her waist until local villagers beat it to death.

SWALLOWED WHOLE ■ A 20-ft (6-m) African rock python swallowed a 10-year-old boy in Durban, South Africa, in 2002.

WRONG MOVE ■ A 2-ft-7-in (80-cm) carpet python swallowed four golf balls in Australia after mistaking them for chicken eggs. The balls were safely removed by surgery.

BELLY ACHE ■ An 18-ft (5.5-m) python got into trouble when it swallowed an entire pregnant sheep in Malaysia in 2006. Afterward, it was too full to move and firefighters were called in to move it off the road.

STOMACH SIGNALS ■ A python measuring 22 ft 9 in (7 m) swallowed a 51-lb (23-kg) Malaysian Sun Bear in Malaysia. The bear was being electronically tracked and when it didn't move for four hours scientists became concerned. They retrieved the radio collar in a surgical operation and let the snake go.

HORROR SQUEEZE ■ Twenty-nine-year-old Ee Heng Chun was partially swallowed headfirst by a 308-lb (140-kg) python in Malaysia in 1995. The python was scared off and shot by police.

HOT MEAL ■ A 12-ft (3.6-m) Burmese python needed surgery after it swallowed an entire queen-size electric blanket—with the electrical cord and control box still attached. The blanket was in the cage so that the 60-lb (27-kg) snake could keep warm.

DOGGIE SNACK ■ A man from Merced, California, got a shock when he returned home to find both his snake and dog missing, before discovering his 200-lb (91-kg) Burmese python with a bulge in its stomach about the size of his 30-lb (14-kg) Pit Bull Terrier. The massive reptile escaped from its cage, swallowed the dog and then hid under the house while it digested its meal.

Australian Darren Cleland was alerted by his neighbor's dog to the incredible scene of a 16-ft (4.9-m) python wrapping its elastic jaws around a full-size wallaby and its baby joey. Wallabies can grow to a length of 2 ft 7 in (80 cm)—not including the tail—and weigh up to 44 lb (20 kg).

Wild Ride!

It may look like he is hunting for his next meal, but this lion has been trained to ride on the back of a horse in an amazing display for visitors at a zoo in Xiamen, China. Tigers also hitch a ride on horses as part of the show. The horse is protected from the big cat's claws by a rug on its back.

MINI EGG ■ Andy Jarrell of Taylorsville, North Carolina, discovered a fully developed chicken egg smaller than a grape in his chicken coop in December 2007.

HORSEPITAL VISITOR ■ In a bid to cheer up a sick relative in Hawaii's Wilcox Memorial Hospital in 2008, a man tried to take the patient's favorite horse into the ward. Horse and man were eventually stopped by security guards on the third floor.

ARROW ORDEAL ■ Lucky Jack, a dog from Hot Springs Village, Arkansas, was shot through the head with an arrow and survived—without any permanent damage. He lived with the steel-tipped arrowhead in his jaw for five months until it could be surgically removed.

BLOODSUCKERS ■ Female fleas can drink 15 times their weight in blood every day. Fleas can also pull 160,000 times their own bodyweight, the equivalent of a human pulling 2,679 double-decker buses.

NO LUNGS ■ A species of frog discovered in a remote corner of Indonesia in 2007 has no lungs and breathes through its skin. Scientists believe the aquatic frog *Barbourula kalimantanensis* has adapted itself to reduce its buoyancy in order to keep from being swept down the fast-moving rivers where it lives.

SIX-LEGGED ■ A six-legged deer with two tails was found in the wild near Armuchee, Georgia, in 2008. Animal experts believe it had an identical twin that didn't form completely.

UNICORN BORN ■ In 2008, a nature reserve in Tuscany, Italy, claimed the world's first unicorn deer after a roe deer was born with a single horn in the center of its head. The condition that conjured up images of the mythological creature is thought to have been caused by a genetic flaw in the deer. Its twin was born with the usual two horns.

DRACULA BIRD ■ The ground finch of the Galapagos Islands is a vampire. Using its sharp beak, it pecks holes in the wings of nesting masked boobies and drinks their blood.

SPLIT LEG ■ Angel, a dog from Cleveland, Ohio, was born with a split leg. Her lower leg parts are located side by side, rather than end to end, giving the impression that she has five legs.

Snappy Surgeon

Beatrice Langevin performed the world's first major surgery on the jaw of a crocodile after it was badly injured in a fierce fight on a crocodile farm in Pierrelatte, France. The veterinary surgeon put a plank of wood in the jaws of the 12-ft (3.7-m) creature and used a regular domestic drill to perform the operation.

SERPENT VILLAGE ▥ A village in India boasts one snake to every two people. The 6,000 villagers of Choto Pashla, West Bengal, share their habitat with as many as 3,000 snakes—mainly highly venomous monocled cobras, which can grow up to 6 ft (1.8 m) long. Not surprisingly, neighboring villagers are scared to visit.

PIGEON FANCIER ▥ A monkey in China found salvation by developing a close friendship with a pigeon. Abandoned by his mother, the baby macaque was close to death when taken to an animal hospital in Goangdong Province in 2007 but pulled through after bonding with his new feathered friend. The two became inseparable.

RADIO FROG ▥ Researchers at the University of Illinois have discovered that the concave-eared torrent frog, from China, can tune its ears to different sound frequencies—like tuning in to a radio. Its selective hearing, achieved by opening and closing eardrum canals, enables it to listen to high-frequency mating sounds against the low-frequency noise of rushing water in its habitat.

HERBAL REMEDY ▥ Orangutans in Indonesia have been observed preparing their own plant-based soothing balm. They have been seen to pick a handful of leaves from a plant, chew the leaves and use saliva to produce a soapy foam. Then they scoop some of the lather in their hand and apply it to their arm, as if putting on sunscreen. The leaf is not part of the orangutans' usual diet, but local people are aware of its anti-inflammatory properties.

Deer Dane

Cindy the baby roe deer found an unlikely father figure in Rocky the Great Dane when she was found wet, cold and close to death by staff at the Secret World Rescue Centre in Somerset, England. The fawn was cared for before leaving her 125-lb (57-kg) companion to join a deer herd in the wild.

HIPPO in the House

Imagine sharing your home with a one-ton teenage hippo, complete with huge appetite, who eats up to 175 lb (80 kg) of food a day.

That was the task facing the South African couple who took on an unusual addition to their family almost ten years ago. Park ranger Tonie Joubert and his wife Shirley discovered Jessica the hippo on the banks of a river in Limpopo Province when she was only a few hours old. She weighed a mere 35 lb (16 kg) and still had her umbilical cord attached.

She had been swept away from her mother in devastating floods that hit Mozambique and South Africa in 2000. Knowing that young hippos stay with their mothers for at least four years in the wild, the Jouberts decided to take Jessica home.

They gave the young hippo heavy-duty massages and allowed her to wander about the house before she grew prohibitively large, breaking beds in the house three times.

Over time, Jessica moved out to join the wild hippos that visit the Joubert residence, but she still lives close by her adopted family and when they return from a trip they often find her waiting by the house for a meal. Jessica still eats some of her meals in the house—she's allowed in the kitchen and the lounge—and drinks more than 2½ gal (10 l) of coffee a day.

DID YOU KNOW?

❯ While young hippos are buoyant and swim quite happily, heavy adult hippos can't actually swim at all. They can hold their breath for up to six minutes at a time and move through the water by pushing off the bottom. They can sleep underwater and surface for air automatically without waking up.

❯ Despite their huge bulk and the time they spend in the water, hippos can easily outrun a human on land. They can reach speeds of up to 30 mph (50 km/h).

❯ The oldest living hippo in captivity is 57-year-old Donna, who resides in a zoo in Evansville, Indiana. She has a while to go to clinch the record for the oldest ever, held by a hippo that lived to the age of 61 in a zoo in Germany.

❯ After the elephant and the white rhino, the hippo is the third largest land animal, with some adult males reaching 8,000 lb (3,628 kg) in weight.

CHICKEN SWEATERS ■ Jo Eglen, from Norwich, Norfolk, England, has rescued 1,500 chickens from battery farms—and has had woolly sweaters knitted for each of them to protect them from the cold. Many battery farm birds lose their plumage because of stress.

WOLF POSTER ■ Unable to afford another dog after his old one died, shepherd Du Hebing from Xi'an City, China, controls his flock of sheep using just a poster of a wolf.

CONTACT LENSES ■ The eyesight of a 15-year-old cat from the Isle of Wight, England, has been restored by fitting the animal with contact lenses. Ernest suffered from a condition whereby his lids turned inward and scratched his eyeballs, and veterinarians suggested the innovative solution because he was too old to risk an operation.

BAT LATTE ■ A woman from Iowa drank a pot of coffee, unaware that a dead bat was inside the filter. After drinking the coffee in the morning, she discovered the bat only that night when she went to clean the filter.

GREEN BLOOD ■ A new species of frog with green blood and turquoise bones has been discovered in Cambodia. The Samkos bush frog owes its unusual coloring to biliverdin, a pigment that is usually processed in the liver as a waste product but, in the case of this frog, is passed back into the bloodstream. The green blood helps with the frog's camouflage and makes it taste unpleasant to predators.

SCOOBY IN COURT ■ A dog named Scooby appeared as a courtroom witness during criminal proceedings in 2008. The animal is thought to have been with his owner when she was found dead in her Paris, France, apartment, and on being led into the witness box he barked furiously at a suspect who was led into the room.

MIGHTY MOUSE ■ A little mouse that was put into a viper's cage as a tasty snack for the venomous snake turned the tables and killed the snake instead. The mouse repeatedly attacked the 14-in (35-cm) viper in the cage in Nantou, Taiwan, and after a 30-minute fight, incredibly, the snake was dead and the brave little mouse was left with hardly a scratch.

MONKEY MINDER ■ An orphaned monkey that was being bullied by bigger monkeys was given its own guard dog at Jiaozuo City Zoo in China. Whenever it felt threatened, the baby monkey would jump on the dog's back and hold tight until the bullies gave up.

MONKEY WAITERS ■ A sake restaurant near Tokyo, Japan, employs two monkeys as waiters. One of the macaques takes customers' drinks orders and brings them to their table while the other hands the customers hot towels. The animals receive tips of boiled soya beans.

SNAKE MASSAGE ■ For $80 a visit, customers at a spa in northern Israel can receive a snake massage. Ada Barak uses nonvenomous king and corn snakes to produce a relaxing kneading sensation over the face and body.

CHIPMUNK HOARD ■ When Hope Wideup of Demotte, Indiana, looked under the hood of her car to see why the indicator and windscreen wipers were not working and why the engine was making a strange noise, she found thousands of nuts that had been stored there by a chipmunk.

Hotel Trunks

They may look like unwanted guests, but staff at a hotel in Zambia have spent ten years since the lodge was built watching a herd of elephants wandering through the lobby. The hotel was built on the elephants' traditional route to a mango-tree feeding ground in South Luangwa National Park. For the four weeks when the mangos are ripe and ready for eating, the elephants make their way twice a day through the lodge. Guests are allowed to watch but are kept at a safe distance.

LUCKY BREAK ■ An Australian cat used up one of its nine lives in 2008 when it survived a 34-story fall from the window of a Queensland apartment building. Seven-year-old Voodoo liked to perch on a narrow ledge outside owner Sheree Washington's high-rise flat, but this time he toppled over the edge, and was saved only because he landed in some bushes.

FISH OUT OF WATER ■ After leaping from its bowl, a pet goldfish in Gloucester, England, somehow survived for 13 hours out of water. When Barbara Woodford found Ginger lying on the floor, she feared the worst, but once she put him back in water, he swam around happily. A goldfish expert said: "This is the longest I've heard of a goldfish staying alive out of water. It's quite astonishing."

SKIING APE ■ An orangutan at the Institute of Greatly Endangered and Rare Species in Miami keeps active by riding an inflatable jet ski. Four-year-old Surya wears a child's lifejacket to stay warm and to prevent him going underwater, because he doesn't like getting his head wet.

NO SALT ■ Although they often live their entire lives in saltwater, sea snakes cannot drink saltwater.

EXPERT MIMIC ■ A wild blackbird living in Weston-super-Mare, Somerset, England, is an expert mimic—and can copy the sounds of a cell phone, a car alarm, a wolf-whistle and even an ambulance siren.

POINTLESS TEETH ■ The whale shark, the world's largest fish, grows to be more than 60 ft (18 m) long and has thousands of teeth—but it doesn't bite anything.

Lizard Mystery

Peter Beaumont, a doctor from Darwin, Australia, cracked open an egg for dinner and found a dead lizard inside. He believes the tiny gecko may have crawled into the chicken to eat an embryo and become stuck. The egg then formed around the lizard.

PREDICTIVE TEXT ■ Elephants in Kenya send text messages as a warning if they are straying too near farms. The elephants have had cell phone SIM cards inserted into their collars and these automatically send text messages to rangers if they step out of the 90-acre (36-ha) Ol Pejeta conservancy.

FISHING PIG ■ A pig in China has learned how to catch fish from a pond. The pig steps into the shallow water of the specialist tropical fish pond in Zhenping, catches the fish in its mouth and eats them on the spot.

BUTT ID ■ Chimpanzees are able to identify other chimps by their butts. Research indicates that they probably identify animals they know by their entire bodies instead of just their faces—something that no other primates, including humans, are known to do.

WOMAN'S BEST FRIEND ■ Angelina the Labrador saved the life of her owner Maria Tripodi by knocking her out of the way just as the roof of her Rivoli, Italy, house collapsed. The dog probably felt tiny tremors too small for humans to detect.

SEX CHANGE ■ The Kushiro Municipal Zoo in Hokkaido, Japan, bought a male polar bear pup in 2005, only to find out three years later that it was a female.

NOSEY DOG ■ A poodle in Forli, Italy, bit off its owner's nose before running around the garden with it. Police chased the dog around Loredana Romano's garden before finally managing to retrieve the remains of the nose. Surgeons later reattached the chewed nose to Mrs. Romano who says she has forgiven her pet.

COUNTING BEES ■ By conducting controlled tests with nectar, researchers at the University of Queensland, Australia, have discovered that honey bees can count to four.

Swift Shrimp

An energetic crustacean was given a workout by scientists at a laboratory in Charleston, South Carolina, as part of an experiment. They discovered that the shrimp could run on an underwater treadmill nonstop for three hours.

www.ripleybooks.com >>> go to >>>

GREEDY FISH

The Great Swallower fish certainly lives up to its name. A man fishing in the Cayman Islands spotted a dead 35-in-long (90-cm) Snake Mackerel that burst the expandable stomach of a Great Swallower measuring only 7 in (18 cm) in length. It's unknown how the smaller fish managed to swallow the predator without itself being eaten.

GREEDY SNAKE ■ A python bit off more than it could chew after attempting to swallow a fully grown wallaby on a university campus in Cairns, Australia, in November 2008. The beast had to give up on its meal and slithered off.

RATS' URINE ■ British children's author Emily Gravett made her work *The Little Mouse's Big Book of Fears* look more authentic by yellowing the pages with rats' urine. Gravett, who used to own two pet rats, also got them to chew the pages of the book to make it appear as if they had been nibbled by a nervous mouse.

FACING EXTINCTION ■ Polar bears could be extinct within 100 years owing to global warming. Arctic sea ice is melting at a rate of up to nine percent per decade, and Arctic summers could be ice-free by 2050. As the ice disappears, so will the polar bears' natural habitat.

COW TOWER ■ Designed by local artist Josée Perreault and perched high on a hill at St.-Georges-de-Windsor, Quebec, Canada, is an observation tower built in the shape of a cow lying in a field.

BLUE DUCKLINGS ■ In Kentucky, it is illegal to dye a duckling blue and offer it for sale unless more than six are for sale at once.

Deer in the City

You might not expect to see a reindeer accompanying a man on his daily business around a London suburb, but that's exactly what Dobbey does with owner Gordon Elliott, who takes his pet for walks in Enfield and rides on local trains each weekend of the winter holiday season.

GREEN BEARS ■ Three polar bears at a Japanese zoo turned temporarily green in 2008 after swimming in an algae-filled pond. The algae, which entered hollow spaces in the bears' normally white fur, infested the animals' enclosure following two months of particularly high temperatures.

RAM RAIDER ■ A 300-lb (130-kg) ram that lives with a family in Cardiff, Wales, has his own specially built bungalow, complete with carpet and windows. Rescued by David Palmer as a lamb in 2005, Nick the sheep is now so much a part of the family that he rides in the back seat of David's car and most evenings settles down on the sofa with him to watch television. He has also been known to raid the cookie jar by butting it until the contents spill out.

RODENT INTERLOPER ■ In 2008, a pet cat in Yantai City, China, adopted a rat and brought it up alongside her four kittens. The rat drank the cat's milk and also played happily with its new feline siblings.

BOOMERANG'S BACK ■ A pigeon that had been away for ten years returned home to the man who had raised her—and on Father's Day. Boomerang earned her name in 1998 when she flew the 1,200 mi (1,930 km) back to Dino Reardon's house in North Yorkshire, England, after being given to a breeder in Spain. Later that year, Mr. Reardon gave her to a friend in Lancashire, but she reappeared in June 2008. She inherited her homing instincts from her father, who once walked 60 mi (95 km) back home after having his wings clipped by thieves.

SINGING WOLVES ■ A Chinese zoo has formed a new singing group—made up of 30 wolves. Luo Yong, a keeper at Chongqing Wild Zoo, was amazed to discover the animals' musical ability when he was playing guitar and a young wolf began howling along to the rhythm and patting the strings with its claws. Next Luo Yong wants to teach them to dance, too!

DOG TIRED ■ Charlie, a standard poodle from Chilliwack, British Columbia, Canada, delivered a litter of no fewer than 16 puppies in March 2008. The exhausted dog gave birth to ten female and six male pups.

CLEVER CHIMP ■ Panzee, a highly intelligent chimpanzee from Georgia's Language Research Center, has a vocabulary of at least 150 English words. She is also able to use a computer to identify objects and even barters for food using symbols.

FLYING LESSONS ■ Gary Zammit of Cornwall, England, taught a bird to fly by running alongside it with food in his pockets, flapping his arms, squawking and pretending to try to take off. He found the orphaned baby gray heron after a storm, which killed the rest of its family. The heron, named Dude, eventually responded to his surrogate father's unusual tuition by copying his actions and then taking to the skies, first at a height of 3 ft (1 m) before graduating to 70 ft (21 m).

IT'S A HEXAPUS! ■ Henry, an octopus at an aquarium in Blackpool, England, was born with just six legs.

MUSICAL CAT ■ A cat in Philadelphia, Pennsylvania, has been playing the piano for more than three years. Adopted from an animal shelter, Nora, a gray tabby, moved into the home of music teacher Betsy Alexander and used to sit under the piano and watch intently until each lesson was over. Then one day she climbed up on the bench herself and began playing the keys with her paws. Playing piano became a daily routine and Nora's exploits were posted on the Internet, where they soon achieved more than ten million viewings. The musical cat also has her own CD, DVD, downloadable ringtone and line of e-cards.

THREE BEARS ■ A 350-lb (160-kg) brown bear and her two cubs walked into a crowded restaurant in Sinaia, Romania, in June 2008 and sat down at tables. As terrified diners abandoned their meals and fled, the three bears tucked into the leftovers before raiding the kitchen for more food.

Hen Hypnosis

Psychological counselor Xu Yiqiang demonstrated the art of hypnotizing chickens at a medical university in Xi'an, northwest China, in 2007. The bird lay motionless after a series of gestures and massages until released from its trance.

Stylish Swimmer

Pierre, an aging African penguin living at the California Academy of Sciences in San Francisco, really felt the cold because he had lost many of the waterproof feathers that keep penguins warm. His keeper, Pam Schaller, came up with an unusual solution to his problem and arranged for Pierre to be fitted with a specially designed neoprene wetsuit. The suit was a great success and Pierre was soon back swimming with the rest of his colony without shivering—and some of his feathers have even grown back.

ARTIFICIAL BEAK ■ A bald eagle was given an artificial beak by Idaho veterinarians in 2008 after its real one was shot off by a hunter. The bird, named Beauty, was found scrounging for food and slowly starving at a landfill site in Alaska in 2005. Without a beak, it had been impossible for her to pick up food, drink or preen her feathers.

HOMICIDAL HORNETS ■ The Japanese giant hornet can kill 40 honey bees in just one minute, thanks to its large mandibles, which can swiftly decapitate a bee. It takes only half a dozen of these hornets a little more than two hours to exterminate the entire population of a 30,000-member hive.

www.ripleybooks.com >>>> go to >>>>

Extra Ears

Valerie and Ted Rock, from Chicago, Illinois, own a cat with four ears. Yoda has two extra flaps behind his normal ears, although they are not attached to the base of his skull and are not thought to help his hearing. They are probably the result of a genetic mutation.

Twisted Tails

One of the best examples of a mysterious "Rat King" is on display at the Otago Museum in Dunedin, New Zealand. It was found in the 1930s in a shipping shed. The strange specimens are formed when the tails of several rats become tied together in a knot in the nest and they cannot free themselves. Despite expert research, nobody is sure how this happens or if it is even a natural occurrence.

Ripley's research

RAT KINGS

Rat Kings are an unexplained phenomena with the earliest report dating back to the 16th century. Some experts think that rats become entangled when they are forced into a small space, with the animals naturally facing outward to protect themselves. Eventually, their tails become stuck together and they starve. Some believe that the specimens in museums are hoaxes, but people who have studied them say that the rats have broken tails and calluses that suggest that they were alive for a long period tangled together. The museum Mauritianum in Altenburg, Germany, owns the largest known mummified Rat King, which was found in 1828 and consists of 32 rats.

TRAPPED PIG ■ A pig survived for 36 days buried beneath rubble in the earthquake that devastated southwest China in May 2008. The pig, which lost two-thirds of its weight during its ordeal, existed on water and a bag of charcoal that had been buried alongside it in the ruins of Pengzhou City, Sichuan Province. Although charcoal has no nutritional value, it filled the pig up.

CHEWED TOE ■ A miniature dachshund chewed off its owner's right big toe in 2008 while she was asleep. Linda Floyd of Alton, Illinois, woke from a nap to find her toe missing. She had no feeling in her toes because of nerve damage from diabetes.

BACK BIRTH ■ Female Surinam toads of South America absorb their eggs into the skin of their backs, where the young remain until bursting forth as fully developed amphibians.

PAINFUL JOB ■ U.S. entomologist Justin Schmidt, who helped create the Schmidt Sting Pain Index, has been stung by about 150 different species of bugs on six different continents in the course of his research.

RAT TRAP ■ Pest control officers trapped and removed 788 rats from an infested house in Sutherlin, Oregon, in the spring of 2008.

PIGCASSO ■ Holding the brush in his mouth, Smithfield the pot-bellied pig has created hundreds of paintings, which sell for $16 each over the Internet. His proud owner, Fran Martin from Richmond, Virginia, says blue is his favorite color to paint with.

TEN-YEAR FAST ■ The olm, a cave-dwelling European amphibian, can live more than 58 years and survive a decade without food.

RAT REWARD ■ To mark the Year of the Rat in 2008, authorities in Kuala Lumpur, Malaysia, offered a bounty on rats, dead or alive.

CANINE TOOTH ■ An 11-year-old Brazilian boy bit a Pit Bull that attacked him—and lost a canine tooth in the process. Gabriel Almeida's tooth was dislodged when he grabbed the dog's neck and bit into it after the animal savaged him while he played in his uncle's backyard in Belo Horizonte in July 2008. Gabriel said later, "It is better to lose a tooth than one's life."

SURF'S UP

When 14-year-old Boomer Hodel of Haleiwa, Hawaii, took his pet rats to the beach to wash them, he never expected they would enjoy the experience so much that it would lead to a whole new hobby. The rats—Fin and Tofu—loved splashing around in the shallow water, so Boomer taught them how to surf and they now make regular trips to the beach with their custom-built surfboards to ride 4-ft (1.2-m) waves.

MONKEY PIG ■ A piglet born in China in 2008 had the face of a monkey! One of five piglets born to a sow owned by Feng Changlin of Xiping, the newborn had two thin lips, a small nose, two big eyes and its rear legs were considerably longer than its front ones, causing it to jump rather than walk. While Feng's family were too scared to look at it, villagers flocked from miles around to see the curiosity.

LONG HOP ■ Southern cricket frogs, which come from the southern U.S.A., can jump 36 times their own body length.

STRANGE FAMILY ■ The elephant shrews, or sengi, are a family of tiny, insect-eating African mammals that are more closely related to elephants than to shrews.

LIFESAVER ■ A dog saved his master's life in 2008 by fetching his cell phone. Albert Hoffman suffered serious back injuries and a punctured lung after falling 20 ft (6 m) from a tree while bird hunting in Upper Austria. Unable to move, he called for his pet Labrador to fetch his phone from his nearby backpack so that he could call emergency services.

BACK LEGS ■ A farmer from Kunming, China, was offered nearly $6,000 for a bull with six legs. Li Guolin says the 18-month-old bull, which was born with two small extra legs on its back, has become a tourist attraction.

CAMEL COMFORT ■ A tiny 18-oz (510-g) baby gibbon found starving to death after her mother failed to produce milk for her was nursed back to health with the help of a stuffed toy camel. The tiny, ten-day-old Sumatran Siamang gibbon was taken away from her mother at a zoo in Bristol, England, and given the soft toy camel to cuddle up to while being fed baby food.

MISS PIGGY ■ Nellie, a pig owned by pig trainers Steve and Priscilla Valentine of Gig Harbor, Washington State, can perform over 70 tricks. She can play baseball, golf, soccer and piano; she skateboards; she can put coins in a bank; and she can spell words. She is such a star that she even has her own credit cards. Priscilla Valentine started teaching her pet pigs tricks to keep them from getting bored. She says: "These animals are sensitive and intelligent. They use logic. They're creative, in bad ways of course. They'll learn to open the refrigerator. Having a pig is like having a two-year-old child for 15 years."

Turtle Power

Amateur photographer Chris Van Wyk had quite a surprise when he spotted this punk turtle swimming in the Mary River in Queensland, Australia, in 2008. The unusual creature is an endangered Mary River Turtle and its crazy green "hair" is in fact algae growing on the turtle's head.

GARDEN DOLPHIN In July 2008, a dead dolphin was found in the back garden of a house, perched high up a steep hill, half a mile (0.8 km) from the sea. Gary Harvey of Portland, Dorset, England, who saw the body of the 3-ft-long (1-m) dolphin lying there, said there was no tidal wave at the time.

FISHING CAT The fishing cat, or *Felis viverrina*, of India, has water-resistant fur, webbed feet and dives headfirst into the water to catch fish.

EEL LIGHTS The Aqua Toto Aquarium in Gifu, Japan, used an electric eel to power the lights on a Christmas tree in December 2007.

BEACHED WHALE An 18-ft (5.5-m) minke whale, weighing around 12 tons, swam nearly 1,000 mi (1,600 km) up the Amazon River in November 2007, before beaching itself on a sandbar.

FEMALE PRESERVE The Amazon molly, *Poecilia formosa*, of Texas and Mexico, is practically an all-female species of fish with no need of males for reproduction. Instead, it mates with males from a different species, but the offspring are clones of their mother and do not inherit any of the male's DNA.

FISH CATCH Orangutans on the island of Kaja, Borneo, have developed the art of stabbing at fish using spears that the local fishermen have discarded.

TREE FISH In times of drought, mangrove killifish, native to Florida and Central America, crawl up into trees and hide among the moist, rotting wood of branches and trunks. They temporarily change their biological makeup so they can breathe air, enabling them to survive out of water for several months of the year.

CATFISH SHUFFLE A school of 30 catfish walked along a street in Pinellas County, Florida, in July 2008 after crawling out of a sewer that had become flooded by heavy rainfall. The catfish, which can travel on land provided they stay moist, propelled themselves along the street using their pectoral fins.

MONSTER SQUID In 2008, New Zealand fishermen caught a colossal squid— *Mesonychoteuthis hamiltoni*—that was 33 ft (10 m) long and weighed 990 lb (450 kg). The monster specimen took two hours to land in Antarctic waters. One expert said that calamari rings made from it would be like tractor tires.

FALSE EYE A miniature horse in Lawton, Oklahoma, that lost one of its eyes a few days after birth was fitted with a $3,000 prosthetic eye. The plastic eye was made from a mold of the horse's eye socket and was hand-painted to look exactly like the other eye, with deep blue features and tiny red veins.

DRUM BEAT Low-frequency mating calls of the black drum fish of the eastern U.S.A. are so strong and loud that they can be heard in homes near the shore.

DOLPHIN GUIDE In March 2008, a dolphin managed to rescue a pair of beached pygmy sperm whales at Mahia Beach, New Zealand, by remarkably leading them around a sand bar and then back out to sea.

HUGE HALIBUT Fishing off Norway in 2008, Danish vacationer Soren Beck caught a giant Atlantic halibut. The monster fish weighed a massive 443 lb (200 kg) and was 8 ft 1 in (2.5 m) long— more than twice the size of an average halibut.

This small army of colorful lumpfish makes for an eye-catching display in the Tokyo aquarium where they swim.

TOY STORY Louis, a giant Pacific octopus at the Blue Reef Aquarium in Newquay, Cornwall, England, becomes aggressive if someone comes too close to his favorite toy— a Mr. Potato Head.

PERPETUAL MOTION Tuna fish never stop moving, swimming at a steady rate of 9 mph (14 km/h) for their entire life. Scientists estimate that a 15-year-old tuna will have swum more than one million miles (1.6 million km).

BALLOON SUCKERS

Lumpsuckers, or lumpfish, will take any opportunity to stick themselves to virtually anything, as they did when balloons were introduced into their tank at an aquarium in Tokyo, Japan. The fish get their name because of the pelvic fins under their body that they use as a "sucker" pad to attach themselves to rocks and seaweed. Such is the strength of their suction that scientists in the 18th century claimed that they could lift a bucket of water by a lumpfish attached to it!

Cage of Death

Have you ever wondered what it would be like to be stalked by a crocodile in its element? Visitors to Crocosaurus Cove in Darwin, Australia, have the chance to find out. Locked inside an acrylic tank a mere 1½ in (4 cm) thick and lowered into the water, they are companions of Choppa, an 18-ft (5.5-m) saltwater crocodile who lost his front feet fighting other crocodiles, but retains his formidable jaws to snap at the tantalizing snacks appearing in his pool.

DOG DRIVER ■ Charles McCowan left his truck in the parking lot of a convenience store in Azusa, California, in February 2008 with his 80-lb (36-kg) Boxer dog named Max in the front seat. When he emerged from the store a few minutes later to discover both truck and dog gone, he immediately reported the theft to the police. Shortly after the police arrived, they found the truck parked just across the street in front of a fast-food outlet with Max still in place. A security video showed that Max had accidentally knocked the gear shift into neutral, sending the truck sloping gently backward.

TRAMPOLINE ESCAPE ■ A dog escaped from his owner's garden in York, England, in June 2008 by bouncing over the fence on a child's trampoline. Harvey, a three-year-old Staffordshire bull terrier, bounced into a neighbor's garden but was free for only four days before he was found and returned home.

HOMING INSTINCT ■ Australian scientists have found that crocodiles have an inbuilt satellite navigation system to enable them to find their way home. Three crocodiles were monitored after being moved 250 mi (400 km) from their territory but, swimming between 6 and 19 mi (10 and 30 km) a day, they returned home within weeks.

TOAD'S ESCAPE ■ A cane toad emerged unharmed after being swallowed by a dog and spending 40 minutes in the animal's stomach. The toad was gobbled up in Darwin, Australia, in June 2008 by a dog that mistook it for a meat pie. The toad regained its freedom when the dog vomited it back up. The dog, too, had a lucky escape as cane toads have toxic glands in their skin which can kill animals that try to eat them. Fortunately, the dog swallowed the toad whole instead of chewing it.

FAT STORE ■ Crocodiles store fat in their tails, so they can go quite a while without eating—as long as two years in the case of some large adults.

GROUP ACTIVITY ■ White pelicans use teamwork to capture food. They surround fish and herd them into shallow water where they can feed on them more easily.

CROC'S BEER ■ When a crocodile wandered into a bar in Noonamah, Australia, in 2008, the regulars didn't run for cover—instead they gave it a beer. Then they taped up its mouth and put the 2-ft-long (60-cm) reptile in a box.

HELPFUL HOUND ■ A dachshund in Zhengzhou, China, has learned to push a wheelchair. Little Guai Guai takes his owner's father for a ride by running underneath the wheelchair with his hind legs on the ground and his front legs pushing the foot rests. He is so small and fast that most passersby assume the wheelchair is motorized.

SIR PENGUIN ■ A penguin at Edinburgh Zoo, Scotland, received a knighthood from the Norwegian Army in 2008. Nils Olav, a King penguin, is the mascot of the Norwegian King's Guard and inspects the troops when they perform at Edinburgh's Military Tattoo.

SCUBA-DIVING CAT ■ Whereas most cats steer clear of water, Hawkeye has gone scuba-diving with her owner on more than 20 expeditions. Gene Alba has built a special diving suit so that Hawkeye can join him beneath the surface of his swimming pool in Redding, California. An air tube connects his own oxygen tank with the cat's glass mask, enabling her to stay underwater for up to an hour. Alba reckons that, provided her face is dry, Hawkeye is happy in her new pastime—particularly if it means putting one over on Mutley, his scuba-diving dog.

SIXTH SENSE ■ Sharks and rays have an extra sense, courtesy of the ampullae of Lorenzini, special organs that enable them to detect electromagnetic fields. Whenever a living creature moves, it generates an electrical field and Great White sharks are so sensitive they can detect half a billionth of a volt in the water.

TURTLE POWER ■ A leatherback turtle swam 12,774 mi (20,560 km) in 647 days from Indonesia to the northwest coast of North America—tracked by a satellite.

WATER SUPPLY ■ Dolphins don't drink seawater—they obtain all the water they need from the bodies of the fish they eat.

ICE PACK ■ Some American and Chinese alligators can survive the winter by freezing their heads in ice, leaving their nose out to breathe.

TIRE RIDE ■ A cat survived a two-and-a-half-hour truck journey by clinging onto a spare tire. Gil Smith drove 70 mi (113 km) from Gilbert, Arizona, to Kearny, unaware that his cat Bella had climbed onto the tire beneath his truck.

NO BOARD REQUIRED

Deciding that swimming looks like too much hard work, Gentoo penguins in the Falklands took wildlife photographer Andy Rouse by surprise by surfing into shore on top of the waves rather than below them, "I was sitting on the beach laughing at them… it was just awesome." He speculates that they may put on the display in order to escape predators lurking under the breakers, and it might be the best way for them to land under certain conditions in the Falklands where the waves can reach 20 ft (6 m) high. Andy notes that the penguins often swim back out when they reach the beach and surf back in again, suggesting they, like us, do it for the adrenaline rush as well as the practical benefits. Gentoos are the only birds known to catch waves on a regular basis; Andy says Chinstrap penguins tried to copy the Gentoos, but wiped out.

BEAGLE ADVENTURE ■ A dog that went missing in New York mysteriously turned up over five years later in Hinesville, Georgia—more than 850 mi (1,370 km) away. Rocco the beagle slipped under the garden fence of his Queens home in the spring of 2003 and although his owners, the Villacis family, covered the neighborhood with posters, there was no trace of the dog until July 2008, when a Georgia animal shelter was able to return him thanks to an identity microchip under his skin.

CONJOINED SWALLOWS ■ A pair of conjoined barn swallows—a rarity estimated at more than one in a million—was discovered in White County, Arkansas, in July 2008. The birds, which fell out of a nest and died shortly afterward, were fully formed and attached at the hip by skin. At first they appeared to have only three legs, but a fourth leg was found tucked up underneath the connecting skin.

TWO-FACED KITTEN ■ Renee Cook of Amarillo, Texas, found a two-faced kitten among a litter of seven otherwise normal kittens born to her Persian-mixed cat Amber in February 2008. The kitten, which had two mouths, two noses, and four eyes, died the following day.

EXTRA LEGS ■ Hex the kitten was born in Cooper City, Florida, in April 2008 with six legs and two sets of intestines.

CANINE PACEMAKER ■ A dog trained to help authorities search for murder victims and survivors of natural disasters had to be saved herself in May 2008. Search-and-rescue dog Molly, a five-year-old chocolate Labrador retriever from Saginaw, Michigan, was fitted with a pacemaker by veterinarians after suffering a suspected heart attack. Such was Molly's popularity and value to the community that the device was donated by a medical technology company while an anonymous businessman from Kansas paid for most of the surgery fees.

SURVIVED CRUSHER ■ A puppy survived with nothing worse than a bruised paw in 2008—despite being crushed among cardboard in the middle of a garbage truck. A Kentucky recycling company worker found the dog peering out through mangled cardboard after it had been deposited from a truck armed with a ramming device that exerted 35,000 lb (15,875 kg) of pressure.

HELPFUL PARROT ■ When Yosuke the African gray parrot flew out of his cage in Nagareyama, Japan, in 2008 and got lost, he recited his name to his rescuers, just as his owners had taught him to. He told a veterinarian, "I'm Mr. Yosuke Nakamura" and went on to provide his full home address, right down to the street number.

GINGER'S JOURNEY ■ In 2008, a cat survived a 6,500-mi (10,500-km), five-week journey in a shipping container by lapping up condensation. Ginger crept into the container in Taiwan and did not see daylight again until the consignment of yarn was opened by staff at a textile firm in Nottinghamshire, England.

HELPING PAWS ■ Cavendish, a Leonburger dog, can load the washing machine, pick up items from the floor, and fetch the phone. He is the trusted helper of Dr. Nicola Hendy, a research fellow at England's University of Nottingham, who has cerebral palsy and is blind.

SPORTING GOLDFISH ■ Comet the goldfish can play basketball, soccer and rugby, slalom expertly around a series of poles, play fetch with a hoop, swim through a narrow tube and even limbo under a miniature bar on the bottom of his tank. The talented goldfish has been trained by Los Angeles computer scientist Dr. Dean Pomerleau, who rewards each correct maneuver with food. He says: "Fish are more intelligent than people give them credit for."

TERRIER TERROR ■ A tiny Yorkshire terrier received the shock of his life in March 2008 after chewing through the wires of a bedside lamp at his home in Lancaster, England. When pup Dylan Thomas was zapped by electricity leaving him stiff and motionless, his owner tried to pull the wire from the animal's mouth, only to be flung across the room by the shock. Emergency chest massage brought the dog back to life and he made a full recovery, despite needing to have part of his frazzled tongue amputated.

ODD COUPLE ■ Although in the wild a goat would be prey for a wolf, the two animals have become sweethearts at a zoo in Nanchong, China. They even share a cage and if the goat decides to wander off for a while, the wolf howls and runs frantically around the cage until she comes back.

DIFFERENT EARS ■ Many species of owl have one ear bigger than the other and one ear higher than the other. This makes it easier for them to judge exactly where a sound is coming from and to pinpoint prey at night.

DIFFERENT STINGS ■ A scorpion's first sting is made up of different toxins to its subsequent stings. Whereas the first is usually powerful enough to incapacitate a vertebrate prey or predator, later stings tend to be milder or employed merely to stun smaller invertebrates.

MIRACLE COW ■ A cow in the Indian state of Gujarat releases milk from its udders without any assistance from her owner. The cow—named Radha—produces milk whenever she is fed, delivering 8½ pt (4 l) in the morning and the same amount again in the evening.

I LOVE DOTTIE ■ In March 2008, Dottie, a cat in Sacramento, California, gave birth to a kitten with dark markings on its side that from left to right read "I," then a heart shape, followed by a dot.

TITANIC TONGUE ■ Most elephants weigh less than a blue whale's tongue, which tips the scales at three tons. When fully expanded, a blue whale's mouth can hold 100 tons of food and water, but the dimensions of its throat mean that it is unable to swallow anything wider than a beach ball.

SPITTING VENOM ■ A newly discovered species of spitting cobra from Kenya holds enough venom to kill 15 people.

HUMAN STATUS ■ A woman went to court in 2008 to prove that her chimp deserved human status. Paula Stibbe of Vienna, Austria, argued that Hiasl was like a human child—he loves watching TV and videos, playing games, and can use signs and gestures to indicate what he wants.

SNAKE COLLAR ■ Jelly, a cat owned by Wendy Wallis of Tasmania, Australia, came home one day with a new collar—a highly venomous copperhead snake wrapped around her neck. The reptile was removed by snake wrangler Matthew Stafford and, despite receiving a bite from the poisonous creature, lucky Jelly was soon on the mend after treatment at a local veterinary center.

MYNA MIMIC ■ A myna bird at a shop in Nanjing, China, keeps two noisy parrot neighbors quiet by miaowing like a cat. The myna became irritated by the parrots' squawking until it noticed that whenever a cat appeared, they fell silent. Owner Mr. Jiang says: "Whenever the parrots get too noisy, the myna calls their bluff by mimicking the cat, and the parrots hush up right away."

Canine Carts

Two-legged Chihuahuas Venus de Milo, Carmen and Pablo were featured in Ripley's Believe It or Not! Prepare to be Shocked last year, and we are pleased to report that they are now enjoying life with their new dog carts, provided by the North Shore Animal League of America. The devices help them to move around freely rather than stumbling perilously along on their back legs.

LOCUST

A swarm of pink locusts engulfed a beach on the Spanish Canary Island of Fuerteventura in November 2004. Vacationers hurriedly evacuated the area when the locusts arrived. The creatures had been severely battered during their ocean crossing and many arrived with broken legs and wings, dying shortly after landing. They were part of a swarm of more than 100 million locusts that flew in from western Africa in the course of one weekend. One swarm in Morocco was 145 mi (230 km) long and 500 ft (150 m) wide and contained an estimated 69 billion locusts. The insects' numbers were boosted that year by areas of the Western Sahara receiving 100 times more rainfall than usual, creating conditions that were ideal for locust breeding.

GREAT LOCUST PLAGUES

1915 From March to October, a plague of locusts stripped areas in and around Palestine of almost all vegetation.

1954–55 A swarm of locusts in Kenya covered more than 385 sq mi (1,000 sq km), contained 40,000 million insects and weighed 88,000 tons.

1958 Ethiopia lost 167,000 tons of grain to locusts, enough to feed a million people for a year.

1987–89 A plague of locusts that originated in Sudan spread as far as India, affecting 28 countries and costing around $300 million to treat an area of 100,000 sq mi (260,000 sq km).

2000 100 billion locusts swarmed in Australia, affecting 11,500 sq mi (30,000 sq km) in South Australia. They turned the sky so black that outback weather stations gave false readings of heavy rain.

2004 Locust swarms necessitated the spending of $400 million to treat an area of 50,000 sq mi (130,000 sq km) in 20 countries. Harvest losses were valued at $2.5 billion.

2005 Hundreds of thousands of locusts invaded southern France, devouring everything from farmers' crops to flowers in village window boxes.

SWARM

LONG JOURNEYS ■ Desert locusts often travel up to 80 mi (130 km) a day and stay in the air for long periods, regularly crossing the Red Sea, a distance of more than 185 mi (300 km). In 1988, a locust swarm migrated from West Africa to the Caribbean in just ten days—a distance of more than 3,000 mi (4,800 km).

EATS EYELASHES ■ In Brazil, there is a species of cockroach that eats eyelashes, usually those of young children while they are asleep.

VORACIOUS APPETITE ■ A locust can eat its own weight—0.07 oz (2 g)—in plants each day. This means that just a very small part of an average swarm of locusts eats the same amount of food in one day as 10 elephants or 2,500 humans.

RAMPANT RATS ■ A plague of rats ate the entire rice crop in India's northeastern state of Mizoram during 2007 and 2008, despite millions of the rodents being killed after the government paid a bounty of two rupees per rat-tail.

PLAGUE THREAT ■ During plagues, desert locusts can extend into as many as 60 countries—more than one-fifth of the total land surface of the world. A plague of desert locusts therefore has the potential to damage the livelihood of one-tenth of the world's population.

LOW FLYERS ■ Desert locusts can't cross tall mountain ranges, such as the Atlas Mountains in North Africa or the Himalayas, because they can fly only at altitudes of up to 6,000 ft (1,830 m). At higher altitudes, it is too cold for them to survive.

ROCKY EXISTENCE ■ In 1874, a swarm of Rocky Mountain locusts covered an estimated 198,000 sq mi (512,820 sq km)—that's bigger than California. Yet, less than 30 years later, the species was extinct. The demise of the insect was caused by farmers destroying thousands of eggs at a time as they plowed the land to plant crops.

LONG JUMP ■ A desert locust can jump ten times its own body length in one leap. That's like a human jumping around 60 ft (18.3 m)—more than twice the world long-jump record.

FARMERS' REVENGE ■ In some parts of the world, humans have taken revenge on crop-destroying locusts by turning them into a tasty delicacy—usually deep-frying them or covering them in chocolate.

Tremendous Tail

Crystal Socha of Augusta, Kansas, has an equine claim to fame—her 11-year-old American Paint Horse, Summer, has a tail that measures an incredible 12 ft 6 in (3.81 m). The spectacular specimen was shown off during the Equifest of Kansas horse festival in 2008.

SHREW BREW ■ Malaysian tree shrews that drink alcoholic fermented nectar suffer no ill effects from consuming quantities that would inebriate a human. The animals drink daily from the flower buds of a palm. The buds collect yeast, which ferments the nectar to create a potent brew that is 3.8 percent alcohol—as strong as many beers.

HONEY THIEF ■ A bear who repeatedly stole honey from a beekeeper's hives in Macedonia was convicted of theft and criminal damage in March 2008.

MILLIPEDE WALL ■ Villagers in Obereichstaett, Germany, built a specially designed wall in 2007 to keep out the thousands of millipedes that have overrun the town each fall for centuries.

MOUTH-TO-MOUTH ■ The life of a cat trapped in an apartment fire at New Bedford, Massachusetts, in September 2008, was saved when heroic firefighter Al Machado revived the lucky feline using mouth-to-mouth resuscitation.

Prime Mate

Two rare white tiger cubs reared at an animal institute in Myrtle Beach, South Carolina, have an unusual surrogate mother. Anjana, a two-year-old chimpanzee, helped the tiger's keeper to raise Mitra and Shiva since their birth, including feeding them with a bottle. She has also had a hand in caring for leopards, lions and orangutans.

ELEPHANT BAN ■ Twelve-year-old Jack Smithies of the U.K. got 655 people to sign his petition that would allow families to keep elephants as pets in their backyard. However, the British government rejected the 2008 petition on the grounds that elephants were too big and dangerous to be suitable as pets.

BIKER OWL ■ When wildlife-center worker Jenny Smith goes for a ride on her bicycle around the lanes of Staffordshire, England, she has an unusual passenger—a tawny owl called Treacle. He hops on to the handlebars whenever she gets on the bike and stays perfectly still throughout the ride.

PINK POOP ■ Volunteers at a scenic spot in the town of Mansfield in Nottinghamshire, England, painted dog poop bright pink in 2008 in an attempt to shame pet owners into cleaning it up.

BEE ALERT ■ Twelve million swarming bees forced the closure of a California highway in March 2008 after a truck carrying crates of the insects overturned near Sacramento. The bees stung officers, firefighters and tow-truck drivers trying to clear the accident.

MUMMIFIED CAT ■ In December 2008, an Australian man was arrested at an airport in Cairo, Egypt, with a 2,000-year-old mummified cat in his suitcase.

NON-SWIMMER ■ Pfeffer's Flamboyant Cuttlefish, which lives off the coast of Indonesia, walks along the sea floor on its tentacles and fins—because it can't swim.

HEARING ANTLERS ■ Researchers from the University of Guelph, Ontario, Canada, have discovered that a moose's antlers act as giant hearing aids, boosting the animal's hearing by nearly 20 percent. With ears 60 times the size of human ears, moose are renowned for their exceptional hearing, enabling them to hear for distances of up to 2 mi (3.2 km)—but now experiments have shown that antlered bulls can locate moose cows much more accurately than males without antlers or other females.

PRAYERY DOG ■ Conan, a two-year-old Chihuahua, joins in daily prayers at a Buddhist temple in Japan. He sits on his hind legs, raises his paws and puts them together at the tip of his nose. He has proved so popular with worshipers that attendances have increased by 30 percent since his introduction as temple pet.

The interior of the doghouse, with its themed wallpaper and furnishings, is every bit as stylish as the outside.

Pooch Palaces

A U.S. firm builds luxury houses, complete with air conditioning, custom-made beds and superbly designed interiors—all for dogs. La Petite Maison designs $50,000 homes for pampered pooches and once built an Alpine chalet for a St. Bernard. In 2008, supermodel Rachel Hunter commissioned a deluxe doghouse that was a scaled-down version of her own Californian home, with terracotta floors and wrought-iron balconies.

KICKBOXING TERRIER ■ A Russian Black Terrier named Ringo Tsar has been learning to kickbox. His owner, former martial arts champion Russ Williams from Holywell, North Wales, has been training the dog to jump up on command and kick at a punch bag with his front legs. He says that while many dogs bite people, Ringo will surely be the first to knock out a human with his paws.

COW ARRESTED ■ A cow was arrested in Cambodia in 2007 for causing traffic accidents that had resulted in the deaths of six people. The cow kept wandering into the road on the outskirts of the capital Phnom Penh, forcing drivers to swerve to avoid it.

SWAN CHAOS ■ Police held up traffic and roads were closed around the town of Langney in East Sussex, England, in June 2008, because a family of swans went on a three-hour walkabout. Under the Act for Swans introduced back in 1576, no one could touch the birds as they legally belong to the Queen.

PISTOL CRACK ■ Despite being less than 1 inch (2.5 cm) long, the pistol shrimp that swims in the Mediterranean emits a noise measuring 218 decibels—that's louder than a gunshot. The deafening crack is caused by a jet of water that spurts out of the shrimp at 60 mph (100 km/h), creating a bubble that momentarily soars to a temperature of 8,000°F (4,426°C). When the bubble collapses, the surprisingly loud explosion occurs.

SWIMMING CHAMP ■ A water-loving sheepdog named Paris has been made an honorary member of a Chinese swimming club—and even has her own shower cubicle. She swims up to 15 mi (24 km) every day in the Jialing River in Chongqing and has so far swum over 6,500 mi (10,460 km).

JAWS GLUED ■ A dog glued his jaws together after sinking his teeth into a diner menu. Cymbeline, a Scottish Terrier, had been trained to pick up the mail from the doormat of his home in Essex, England, and to hand it to his owner, but the high-gloss paper menu glued his jaws shut for half an hour until a veterinarian managed to free the gum from his teeth.

MUSICAL WALRUS ■ A walrus at a zoo in Turkey has learned to play the saxophone. Sara amazes visitors to the Istanbul Dolphinarium by gripping the instrument between her flippers and blowing out a series of notes.

PET REUNION ■ A woman was reunited with her missing cat in 2008—after nine years. Gilly Delaney from Birmingham, England, thought her beloved pet Dixie had been killed by a car in 1999, so she was amazed when animal welfare officers turned up with the cat after finding it wandering the streets.

SHARK ATTACK ■ A dog in Florida had a lucky escape in 2008 when his owner dived into the water to save him from a 5-ft (1.5-m) shark. Greg LeNoir had taken his Rat Terrier Jake for a swim at the Islamorada marina when the shark surfaced and grabbed the dog in its mouth.

MAN'S BEST FRIEND ■ A German Shepherd dog saved his owner's life in 2008 by hitting the speed-dial button on the phone for 911 to call Emergency and then barking to raise the alarm. Buddy had been trained by his owner, Joe Stalnaker of Scottsdale, Arizona, to act in an emergency.

ENGINE ORDEAL ■ Luna the cat lived to tell the tale after spending a week in the engine of her owner's car in November 2008. She had survived more than 300 mi (480 km) of motoring through Austria but had hidden so deep inside the engine that the whole thing had to be dismantled in order to get her out.

TOURISM JOB ■ A chimpanzee in Radkow, Poland, has been given a paid job promoting tourism. Seventeen-year-old Bobby receives $140 a month to walk around with a sign on his back advertising a local beauty spot known as Monkey Rock.

TUNEFUL PARROT ■ Leonard, an African Gray parrot from Bristol, England, has learned to whistle "Dock of the Bay" and the theme tune from *Mission Impossible*. He also does a rendition of "YMCA" by The Village People. His owners describe him as "great fun."

EGG-STREMELY LARGE ■ Children at a school in Gloucester, England, were amazed in January 2009 when their class pet, a hen named Little Lil, laid an egg the size of a tennis ball. The egg, which was three times bigger than normal, measured 4 in (10 cm) from top to bottom and 2¾ in (7 cm) across.

TWO-HEADED FISH ■ Thousands of bass larvae at a fish farm in Noosa River, Queensland, Australia, spawned with two heads. The mutant larvae survived for just 48 hours before they died en masse.

PENGUIN WEDDING ■ An aquarium in Wuhan, China, staged a wedding ceremony for two black-footed penguins in January 2009. The groom, who brought his own tuxedo, was dressed in a tie and his bride wore a red blouse. At the reception, the happy couple dined on their favorite dish—spring fish.

IN A SPIN ■ When spiders are first taken into space, they spin a tangled, messy web—but as they adapt to microgravity, they begin spinning normal, symmetrical webs.

NONSTOP FLIGHT ■ The bar-tailed godwit, a Pacific coastal bird, makes flights of more than 7,000 mi (11,250 km) without stopping to eat.

Fishy Friend

A moray eel took part in New Year celebrations at the Sunshine International Aquarium in Tokyo, Japan, in 2009 when it swam with a diver who had plunged into the tank to feed the fish while dressed in a traditional Japanese kimono. Moray eels are normally harmless, but with razor-sharp teeth they can give a painful bite that can be particularly susceptible to infection.

DOGGY WIGS ■ A Santa Barbara, California, firm called Total Diva Pets sells a range of $30 hairpieces for dogs. Sisters Jenny and Crissy Slaughter sell the doggy wigs in eight different designs—including Afro and green spiky punk—and in five sizes from Chihuahua to Great Dane.

OCTOPUS VANDAL ■ Otto, an octopus at the Star Aquarium in Coburg, Germany, caused electrical short circuits by crawling to the rim of his tank and squirting a jet of water at a light fixture.

BEASTLY BEETLE ■ A species of Peruvian dung beetle has turned from scavenger to carnivore. Whereas it once ate only animal feces, the ferocious scarab has been observed decapitating and eating live millipedes ten times its size.

SINGING FISH ■ Researchers at Indiana University have discovered that the art of singing originated in lungfish. They say that the pattern of beak and throat movements in birds, as well as mouth, tongue and lower-jaw motions in humans, all started to evolve when lungfish began gulping and swallowing air.

AQUAPHOBIC PENGUIN ■ A penguin at the Blackbrook Zoological Park in Staffordshire, England, has become a celebrity because he is afraid of water. While his 23 penguin pals swim around happily, Kentucky stands on a rock and refuses to take the plunge. Keepers say the Humboldt penguin was born smaller than his siblings and has lost a lot of feathers since birth, which might make the water a bit cold for him.

KEEN VISION ■ Jumping spiders of the genus Portia have incredible vision for their small size. Their tiny primary eyes have better visual acuity than lizards, pigeons or cats.

NEVER TOO OLD ■ A reptile in New Zealand has become a father at the age of 111. Henry, a tuatara living at the Southland Museum and Art Gallery, was aggressive toward female lizards until having a cancerous growth removed from his genitals in 2002. Since then, he has mellowed and after mating with a female named Mildred, he became the proud father of 11 baby tuataras.

Two-faced Cow

A young calf born with two faces due to a genetic abnormality attracted attention from locals in Lintao county, China, in 2007 because it had four eyes and two mouths.

When elephants carried cameras hidden in logs into the jungle, some creatures were intrigued to see their reflection in the glass, while others, such as the rare Bengal tigers (below), barely noticed them at all.

ELEPHANT CAM

Elephants at Pench National Park in Madhya Pradesh, India, were specially trained as over-sized cameramen for a TV documentary. The elephants were hired to carry the cameras, which had been disguised as logs and rocks, with their tusks and trunks, and walked deep into the jungle where they captured some unparalleled images of elusive Bengal tigers. Wild tigers are used to sharing their habitat with elephants, so they were oblivious to the filming, viewing the cameras with mild curiosity rather than suspicion.

Bulging Belly

A bulge in a python's belly was all that could be seen of 8-week-old tabby cat Kohl after he was swallowed whole in the garden of the McLaren family in Darwin in Australia's Northern Territory in 2008. X-ray photographs taken after the 6-ft-long (1.8-m) snake was removed clearly show the kitten stretched out inside its stomach. The unfortunate pet was swallowed by the hungry snake despite having a head three times as large as that of the python.

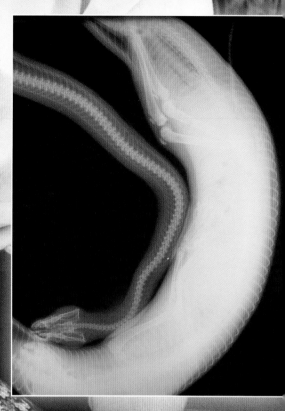

DEVOTED MOM ■ When her six little ducklings were swept down a drain cover in Newcastle upon Tyne, England, in 2008, a mother mallard duck followed their panicked cheeps for more than a mile (1.6 km)—across roads, roundabouts, train lines, two school fields and the grounds of a hospital.

DOG SPARED ■ Ordered to be put down after attacking a child, Ozzy the German shepherd had his sentence commuted to life imprisonment in 2007—and landed a job patrolling the perimeter of a correctional facility near Media, Pennsylvania.

SNAKE SCARE ■ Hearing her baby cry, Cari Abatemarco peered into the crib at the family home in Brentwood, New York—and found a 12-in (30-cm), non-venomous kingsnake wrapped around her seven-month-old daughter's leg.

RUBBLE RESCUE ■ A dog was found alive in April 2008 having spent eight days trapped beneath 15 ft (4.5 m) of rubble after a two-story building exploded in Breckenridge, Colorado. Springer Spaniel Lulu survived the ordeal by drinking melting snow and eating food she found in the debris.

SURPRISE PACKAGE ■ A cat was accidentally posted 450 mi (725 km) in 2008 after it crawled unnoticed into a parcel and fell asleep. Gitti Rauch from Rottach-Egern in southern Germany said her cat climbed into a box filled with presents for relatives in Dorsten, but she didn't spot him as she sealed the package and sent it off. Janosch emerged unharmed two days later.

BATHTUB ORDEAL ■ A four-year-old cat from Stadthagen, Germany, survived despite being walled in beneath a bathtub for seven weeks. She lost 9 lb (4 kg) during her ordeal.

HEROIC PARROT ■ A parrot saved his owners from a house fire in July 2008 by squawking loudly enough to raise the alarm. Bob, a three-year-old African gray, alerted the Hall family that fire was spreading through their house in Hampshire, England. Thanks to Bob, the Halls managed to flee the blaze in time, grabbing their savior's cage on the way out. Sam Hall said: "I used to find Bob very annoying with his growling and squawking, but not now. He's a legend. He saved our lives."

BEAR SAVED ■ A 364-lb (165-kg) black bear that had been shot with a tranquilizer dart was saved from drowning in 2008 by a wildlife officer who dived into the sea to rescue it. Seeing the drowsy bear run into the water, Adam Warwick of the Florida Fish and Wildlife Commission stripped to his underwear, swam out to sea and put his arm around the animal's neck to keep its head above water.

SIZZLING SNAKE ■ A snake was treated for third-degree burns in Australia in 2008 after hitching a ride under the hood of a car. The 8-ft (2.4-m) python had wrapped itself around the car radiator for warmth, but was then taken by surprise when the vehicle embarked on a long journey from northern New South Wales. The overheated car broke down and when the owner looked under the hood, he was shocked to find a broken fan belt—and a very hot and very cranky snake.

Hungry Heron

Known to eat small mammals and frogs, this hungry Gray Heron horrified onlookers in Vianen, Holland, when it made a grab for a baby rabbit on the banks of a river. The squealing creature was carried to the water, quickly drowned, and much to the disbelief of onlookers, swallowed whole!

LAUNDRY SHOCK ■ Removing clothes from the washing machine at her home in Gorham, Maine, in July 2008, Mara Ranger was horrified to find an 8-ft (2.4-m) reticulated python among her laundry. The snake is believed to have entered the machine through water pipes. It was removed by an officer from the local animal control department before being taken to New York's Wild Animal Kingdom.

RAGING BULL ■ A bull that was swept into a raging river during floods in Australia in January 2008 survived a 56-mi (90-km) trip downstream with tree trunks, logs and fences before being rescued. Two-year-old Barney was found in an exhausted state at the mouth of the Tweed River near the ocean in New South Wales.

DEER SURGEON ■ John Polson of Saskatoon, Canada, performed a roadside cesarean section on a white-tailed deer in 2008. Spotting a deer alive but badly injured beside a vehicle, he decided to end the animal's suffering and then remembered that it was the season for female deer to be giving birth. So he cut open her womb, discovered two live fawns and took them home to be hand-reared before being released back into the wild.

BUNNY ALARM ■ A pet rabbit—named Rabbit—saved a couple from a fire in Melbourne, Australia, in 2008 by scratching furiously on their bedroom door to wake them as they slept while smoke poured through the house. The six-month-old floppy-eared rabbit was allowed to roam the house unless its owners, Gerry Keogh and his partner Michelle Finn, had guests. Firefighters went back into the burning building to rescue the heroic pet, because the smoke had prevented its owners finding him.

PIG BOOTS ■ A piglet in North Yorkshire, England, was fitted with little gum boots in 2008 so that she could conquer her fear of mud. When the piglet appeared reluctant to get her trotters dirty, Debbie and Andrew Keeble solved the problem by giving her four miniature gum boots that had served as novelty pen and pencil holders in their office.

SNAIL COMPANION ■ A Chinese man is so devoted to his pet snail that he takes it for walks. Yang Jinsen from Dongwan, found the snail by the roadside on his way home from school in 1997 and has looked after it ever since, building it a nice home, playing with it, taking it for walks in the fields and, in 2007, introducing it to his new wife. The snail has responded to the loving care by living for more than twice its normal life span.

DONKEY JAILED ■ A donkey spent three days in a Mexican jail in May 2008 after it bit and kicked two men in Chiapas State. It was released from the prison, which normally houses drunks, when its owner paid a fine and the injured men's medical bills.

DONKEY RETIRES ■ Russia's prestigious Mariinsky ballet bade farewell to one of its longest-serving artistes in 2008—a 21-year-old donkey named Monika. Pensioned off after 19 years of carrying the overweight Sancho Panza around the stage in productions of *Don Quixote*, at her retirement party she danced a waltz with one of the company's ballerinas and was presented with a carrot cake.

HAMSTER HUNT ■ Roborovski's hamster, a native of northern China, forages so keenly for food that in a single night it covers over 100 mi (160 km)—a distance equivalent to almost four human marathons.

ELECTRIC ANTS ■ Many ant species nest near electrical equipment owing to an affinity for magnetic fields created by electricity.

SAVINGS EATEN ■ An Indian trader lost his life savings after the paper bills were eaten by termites infesting the bank's safe deposit boxes. Dwarika Prasad had deposited more than $16,000 with the Central Bank of India in 2005, but when he opened the box in January 2008, there was little more than termite dust.

HEAT DETECTORS ■ The heat-sensitive pit located on each side of a rattlesnake's head enables it to detect items of prey that are as little as one-tenth of a degree warmer than the environment around them.

PIGEON SERVICE ■ A pigeon called Spitfire—capable of flying at speeds of up to 60 mph (95 km/h)—is used by Rocky Mountain Adventures in Colorado to carry memory cards containing pictures of white-water rafters back to base so that the day-trippers' photographs can be developed in time for them to take home.

BLOOD DONOR ■ The American Red Cross honored one of its most unusual blood donors in February 2008—a 200-lb (90-kg), two-year-old English Mastiff named Lurch. Owned by Joni Melvin-Thiede from Howell, Michigan, Lurch has donated blood more than 20 times, helping to save the lives of dozens of dogs.

TIGHTROPE WALKER ■ In Chongqing City, China, in 2008, a two-year-old Tibetan Mastiff called Hu Hu demonstrated his skill as a high-wire artist. The dog climbed to the top of a platform 13 ft (4 m) high and, balancing his paws on two thin steel wires, walked 33 ft (10 m) to the other side.

UPSIDE DOWN ■ Africa's mochokid catfish can swim upside down to enable it to feed on the underside of rocks and branches that have fallen underwater.

HOSE ESCAPE ■ A spider monkey briefly escaped from Washington Park Zoo in Michigan City, Indiana, in 2008 by climbing up a garden hose left there while workers were cleaning a moat. He was recaptured at a nearby boat dealership, perched on top of a speedboat.

RELIGIOUS BUZZ ■ Beekeeper Slobodan Jeftic from Stari Kostolac, Serbia, builds beehives in the shape of tiny monasteries and churches so that, besides giving his bees somewhere beautiful to live and make honey, he can look after their souls.

SOLDIER BEAR ■ During World War II, a brown bear named Voytek captured a spy in Iraq and helped transport ammunition in Italy for the Polish Army. The 250-lb (115-kg) bear, who stood more than 6 ft (1.8 m) tall, was such a valued member of the armed forces that he was given his own name, rank and number. Like most other soldiers of that era, he enjoyed a beer and a cigarette when off duty.

DOGGIE SCHNAUZER, M.D. ■ A dog has predicted the deaths of 40 people at a Canton, Ohio, nursing home over a three-year period. Staff noticed that Skamp the schnauzer seems to know when people are about to die and will spend hours, even a couple of days, with a dying resident.

CAT LOVER ■ A dog risked his life to save a litter of newborn kittens from a house fire in Melbourne, Australia, in October 2008. Leo, a Terrier cross, refused to leave the burning building without the four kittens—and after his bravery he had to be revived with oxygen and heart massage. Happily, the kittens also survived.

LUCKY KOALA ■ A koala bear survived being hit by a car at 60 mph (97 km/h) and dragged with his head jammed through the grill for 8 mi (12 km). The eight-year-old bear was struck north of Brisbane in Queensland, Australia, in July 2008 and was freed only after the car was flagged down by another motorist.

Hamster Power

Super Pet has created the "Critter Cruiser" for pet hamsters who are bored with going round and round the wheels in their cages. The cruiser is a fully hamster-powered car that enables our furry friends to race around a specially designed track, going as fast or slow as they like.

CRAZY CREATURES
www.ripleys.com
Ripley's Believe It or Not!®

Blowing Bubbles

Dolphins are known as the playful animals of the sea, but visitors to an Orlando sea-life center were amazed to see them making bubble rings with an expert touch before following them through the water. The dolphins create the bubbles by churning the water in swift movements and blowing through their blowhole, swimming through the rings and nosing them into different shapes. They will even make more than one ring and join them together, apparently all just for fun.

HOW FAST?

2,193 MPH (3,529 KM/H)	JET AIRPLANE	In 1976, Eldon W. Joersz flew a jet airplane at 2,193 mph near Beale Air Force Base, California—that's 2,188 mph (3,521 km/h) faster than flight pioneer Wilbur Wright's fastest air speed in 1903.
760.3 MPH (1,223.6 KM/H)	CAR	In 1997, Andy Green hit a top speed of 760.3 mph while driving *Thrust SSC* (Supersonic Car) at Black Rock Desert, Nevada.
360.9 MPH (580.8 KM/H)	MOTORBIKE	In September 2008, Rocky Robinson rode his *Ack Attack* motorbike at 360.9 mph at Bonneville Salt Flats, Utah.
317.6 MPH (511 KM/H)	SPEEDBOAT	Driving his speedboat *Spirit of Australia*, Ken Warby reached a speed of 317.6 mph at Blowering Dam, Australia, in 1978.
164.9 MPH (265.3 KM/H)	MOTORBIKE, WHILE BLINDFOLDED	In 2003, Billy Baxter rode a 1,200cc motorbike at 164.9 mph at Boscombe Down, Wiltshire, England—while blindfolded.
130.7 MPH (210.3 KM/H)	MOUNTAIN BIKE, DOWNHILL	Riding a mountain bike down a snow-covered mountain in Chile in 2007, Austrian Marcus Stoeckl hit a speed of 130.7 mph.
92 MPH (148 KM/H)	SOFA	Marek Turowski drove a rear-engined sofa at 92 mph at an airfield in Leicestershire, England, in 2007.
81 MPH (130 KM/H)	BICYCLE	In 2002, Canada's Sam Whittingham clocked 81 mph on his aerodynamic recumbent bicycle at Battle Mountain, Nevada.
80 MPH (129 KM/H)	LAWN MOWER	At Bonneville Salt Flats, Utah, in 2006, Bobby Cleveland drove at over 80 mph on his lawn mower.
63 MPH (101 KM/H)	SKATEBOARD	In 1998, Gary Hardwick reached a top speed of 63 mph on a skateboard during a race in Arizona.
60 MPH (96.5 KM/H)	SHOPPING CART	In 2005, Edd China of Berkshire, England, drove a motorized shopping cart at 60 mph.
46 MPH (74 KM/H)	OUTHOUSE	Paul Stender of Brownsburg, Indiana, has reached speeds of 46 mph on his jet-powered portable toilet, the *Port-o-Jet*.

EPIC JOURNEYS

16,865 MILES (27,142 KM)	ATV	From August 2007 to March 2008, Josh and Anna Hogan of San Francisco, California, drove 16,865 mi on an all-terrain vehicle, starting in Mombassa, Kenya, and finishing in Elche, Spain.
14,594 MILES (23,487 KM)	LAWN MOWER	Gary Hatter drove 14,594 mi on a lawn mower, leaving Portland, Maine, in May 2000 and traveling through all 48 contiguous states, plus Canada and Mexico, before finally arriving in Daytona Beach, Florida, in February 2001.
13,172 MILES (21,198 KM)	TRACTOR	In 2005, Vasilii Hazkevich drove a tractor 13,172 mi on a three-month round trip starting and finishing in Vladimir, Russia.
13,000 MILES (20,921 KM)	JET SKIS	In 2006, South Africans Adriaan Marais and Marinus Du Plessis traveled 13,000 mi from Anchorage, Alaska, to Miami, Florida, on jet skis.
12,163 MILES (19,574 KM)	SNOWMOBILE	Robert G. Davis rode a snowmobile for 12,163 mi on a 60-day journey in 2008 through Maine and Canada.
12,000 MILES (19,312 KM)	UNICYCLE	In 1983–84, Pierre Biondo of Montreal, Quebec, Canada, rode a unicycle around the entire perimeter of North America—a journey of more than 12,000 mi.
12,000 MILES (19,312 KM)	TUK-TUK	In 2006, Jo Huxster and Antonia Bolingbroke-Kent drove a tuk-tuk (a three-wheeled motorized taxi) 12,000 mi from Thailand to England.
5,045 MILES (8,119 KM)	SAILBOARD	From May 2004 to July 2005, Flavio Jardim and Diogo Guerreiro windsurfed 5,045 mi along the coast of Brazil.
3,618 MILES (5,823 KM)	SKATEBOARD	In 2006, Welshman Dave Cornthwaite skateboarded 3,618 mi across Australia from Perth to Brisbane, a journey that took him 90 days.
2,580 MILES (4,152 KM)	PARAGLIDER	In 2004, Bob Holloway managed to fly 2,580 mi in a powered paraglider from Astoria, Oregon, to Washington, Missouri.
1,500 MILES (2,414 KM)	TIRE TUBE	For 44 days in 2007, Cheng Yanhua paddled more than 1,500 mi down China's Yangtze River—from Chongqing City to Shanghai—on a tire inner tube.
23 MILES (37 KM)	POGO STICK	Ashrita Furman covered 23 mi by pogo stick in New York City in 1997—a journey that took him more than 12 hours.

For Kerry McLean of Walled Lake, Michigan, you need only one wheel to travel, provided you ride inside it. The most extreme vehicle of its kind, the Mclean Monowheel was first produced in 1970 and has been improving ever since. Some models are now powered by V8 engines and are capable of speeds of more than 50 mph (80 km/h). Monowheels can be difficult to control, and the McLean model is one of the few such machines to be road-legal.

TRAVEL TALES

FLIP SHIP

It's not every day that you see a ship sink into the ocean, right itself and then go back to shore, but that is the job of the remarkable Flip Ship, which has doors in the floor, tables bolted to the walls and portholes in the ceilings. FLIP is technically not a ship but a "floating instrument platform," used for ocean research by scientists at the Scripps Institute of Oceanography in San Diego, California, who live and work on the craft for weeks at a time. Extending from the living area is a 355-ft-long (108-m) tank that fills with seawater, sinking deep into the sea and flipping the bow 90 degrees into the air, providing stable quarters five stories high in the middle of the ocean.

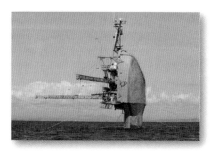

Ripley's
Believe It or Not!®

HOMEMADE SUB ■ A Chinese laborer spent a year hand-building an operational submarine from metal barrels and other improvised parts. Tao Xiangli's sub is 20 ft (6 m) long, weighs 1.6 tons, seats one person and comes complete with a TV, monitoring cameras and headlights. Able to dive up to 33 ft (10 m), it cost him $4,500 to build, the equivalent of his annual salary.

TWO WHEELS ■ Stuntman Dave Ackland of Devon, England, drove an old Vauxhall Viva car up on two wheels through a gap 6 ft 6 in (2.02 m) wide in March 2008. The width was just 2 ft (67 cm) more than the height of the car.

JUNK VOYAGE ■ Marcus Eriksen and Joel Paschal completed a three-month, 2,600-mi (4,185-km) voyage from Long Beach, California, to Hawaii in 2008 on a raft made of plastic bottles. Their 30-ft (9-m) junk vessel had a deck of salvaged sailboast masts, six pontoons filled with 15,000 plastic bottles and a cabin made from the fuselage of a Cessna airplane.

PEDAL AMERICA ■ In 2006, at age 80, Bill Anderson of Yuma, Arizona, completed a cycle ride from the Mexican border to the Canadian border and back—a round trip of 3,000 mi (4,830 km).

FLYING CAR ■ A car in China was blown onto the roof of a house in May 2008 by a gust of wind. The driver, from Yanbian City, Jilin Province, had just turned a corner when wind lifted his car off the road and onto the roof of the building with the vehicle remaining right side up. The driver said later that he had felt like he was in a flying car.

Body Control

Teenager Ben Gulak from Milton, Ontario, Canada, has developed an electric motorbike called the "Uno" that is controlled entirely by body movements. Although it looks like a unicycle, the machine actually has two wheels, side-by-side, and uses gyroscopic technology to stay upright. It moves in the direction that the rider leans—and the more Ben leans, the faster he goes, up to 25 mph (40 km/h) on the prototype. The environmentally friendly Uno weighs just 120 lb (54 kg) and has a range of two-and-a-half hours after it has been charged.

REDNECK STONEHENGE ■ In 2008, as part of an ongoing feud with neighbors, farmer Rhett Davis from Hooper, Utah, erected a backyard fence of three old cars sticking up in the air. After digging three large holes on the edge of his property, Davis took the cars, which had competed in demolition derbies, and planted them nose-first into the ground, calling the end result his "redneck Stonehenge."

CRAZY RIDE ■ A woman was arrested in August 2008 for driving around the parking lot of a store in Marathon, Florida, with her three-year-old granddaughter sitting on the car roof.

CARDBOARD BIKE ■ University student Phil Bridge from Stockport, England, has come up with the ultimate in recycling—a cardboard bike. He says the cardboard components would be replaced every six months free of charge, while the tougher elements—the steel wheel rims and rubber tires—would simply slot into a new cardboard frame. His invention, which can bear the weight of a 168-lb (76-kg) adult, is also waterproof to withstand rainy days.

FAMILY TANK ■ Joachim Schoeneich of Neu Anspach, Germany, enjoys taking his family for shopping and day trips—in a six-ton military tank. The tank is armed with a disabled 30-mm (1.2-in) gun, has 3-in-thick (7.6-cm) armor plating plus a baby seat for Joachim's two-year-old son. Joachim admits: "It's a bit hard to find a parking space, but we get the right of way at every junction!"

HANDS-FREE ■ Eranna Kundaragimath from Bagolkot District, India, can ride a motorbike for 150 mi (240 km)—over a period of five hours—without touching the handlebars. He has been practicing riding without using his hands for 10 years and can reach speeds of 50 mph (80 km/h). He uses his waist and legs to balance the machine and turn corners.

TRUCK JUMP ■ Robbie Knievel—son of legendary motorbike stuntman Evel Knievel—surpassed his late father in May 2008 by jumping a distance of 200 ft (61 m) over 24 trucks at a theme park in Kings Island, Ohio. His father had managed 115 ft (35 m) over 14 buses at the same venue in 1975.

OUTSIZE YACHT ■ John Melling from Cornwall, England, spent five years building a yacht 26 ft (8 m) wide in his backyard knowing that, because of its size, he would never be able to move the finished boat to the street.

SEWER TRIP ■ Until 1975, visitors could take boat trips through the sewers of Paris, France—an underground network of tunneling that stretches for 1,300 mi (2,090 km).

PAPER BOAT ■ Inspired by a book on origami, Alan Jones from Bartley, Hampshire, England, built a boat measuring 12 x 6 ft (3.6 x 1.8 m)—from paper. The boat, which has a cabin 9 x 6 ft (2.7 x 1.8 m), is kept afloat by a layer of juice cartons acting as a double hull. With his son Rhys, Alan had planned to sail 4,000 mi (6,437 km) down the Mississippi in the summer of 2008. Although the paper boat proved seaworthy, severe flooding put a halt to the adventure. Instead they donated the boat to the South Dakota scout group who helped test it.

PANTS ON FIRE! ■ A Polish man was cycling so fast he actually caught on fire. The cyclist said he smelled something burning, looked down and noticed his pants were on fire. The flames were probably caused by the friction from his clothes.

CANOE COMMUTE ■ Duncan Crary and Alison Bates regularly make the 7-mi (11-km) commute from Troy to their workplace in Albany, New York, in a 17-ft (5-m) canoe. The journey takes them around three hours each way.

Flying Bus

In a reversal of the Evel Knievel classic motorcycle jump over buses, fearless stunt driver Steve Hudis soared 109 ft (33 m) in Las Vegas, Nevada, in a school bus weighing 28,000 lb (12,700 kg), through a fireball, clearing 15 motorcycles before crash-landing and emerging unscathed.

STATIONARY RIDE ■ Fifty-year-old George Hood of Aurora, Illinois, rode a stationary bike for more than 176 hours over nine days in May 2008. He clocked up a mammoth 2,600 mi (4,185 km) and burned nearly 47,000 calories.

CRUSHED SNAILS ■ Hundreds of migrating snails caused a six-car pile up as they slithered across a busy highway near Stuttgart, Germany, in 2008. The slime from the crushed snails made the road so slippery that cars kept skidding.

CABLE SCARE ■ A retired couple from Munich, Germany, were suspended in their plane from 380,000-volt power lines for nearly three hours after the light aircraft clipped the overhead cables as it came in to land at Durach. With aviation fuel pouring over them dangerously close to the engine, the couple remained hanging 80 ft (24 m) above ground until firefighters were able to cut them free with the aid of an elevated crane.

FAKE FERRARIS ■ Mechanics in Palermo, Sicily, have been turning out the ultimate in counterfeit Italian designer goods—fake Ferraris. Before police stepped in, skilled car workers had been converting the chassis of Pontiacs, Mercedes and Toyotas into imitation Ferraris, which were then sold for around one fifth of the price of the real thing. The customers apparently knew they were buying fake goods—but they just wanted a Ferrari to impress their friends.

BICYCLE PARADE ■ Renowned for being bicycle friendly, the city of Davis, California, held a parade of 1,838 bicycles in March 2008.

EXPENSIVE ERROR ■ While cleaning an airplane at Baton Rouge Airport, Louisiana, in 2008, a mechanic accidentally pressed the starter switch, sending the craft into takeoff mode and crashing into two other planes inside the same hangar. All three planes were destroyed, causing $100 million of damage.

LOST PROPERTY ■ More than 32,000 books, 27,000 handbags and 25,000 items of clothing are left behind on London's transport system every year. Other items turned in include a pair of breast implants, a stuffed puffer fish, a case full of human teeth, a wheelchair, a life-size toy gorilla, a prosthetic arm and a coffin.

VIRTUAL FLIGHT ■ An airline in India offers passengers the experience of flying in a real plane without ever actually taking off. Customers pay $4 a head to watch a safety demonstration, listen to pilot announcements and be served airline meals by cabin crew, but Bahadur Chand Gupta's Airbus 300 stays grounded in Delhi suburb—just as well, as it has only one wing and part of the tail is missing.

ONE OWNER ■ Carl Keller of Clintonville, Wisconsin, has owned the same car for 58 years. When he bought the brand new turquoise blue 1951 Packard convertible for $3,800 at age 26, his mother chided him for wasting his money on cars.

HOT WHEELS ■ In May 2008, a man in Kyushu, Japan, stole a bicycle and rode nearly 300 mi (482 km) from Oita Prefecture to Kogoshima Prefecture because he wanted to visit somewhere warm.

DA VINCI CODE ■ Olivier Vietti-Teppa of Switzerland made a 2,000-ft (610-m) jump from an airplane in 2008, using the design of a 500-year-old parachute. His model was based on Leonardo da Vinci's pioneering parachute of 1485, consisting of four triangles of fabric and a pointed top. Vietti-Teppa also wore a modern reserve parachute in case da Vinci's design failed to open—but in the event it worked perfectly, although the device proved impossible to steer.

FLYING HIGH ■ In February 2008, 81-year-old aviation enthusiast Edwin Shackleton from Bristol, England, flew in his 852nd different type of aircraft when he boarded an Embraer 195 from Exeter to Alicante, Spain. A former RAF engineer, Mr. Shackleton was unable to work as a pilot because of his poor eyesight.

LIGHTNING STRIKES ■ Four airplanes were struck by lightning on June 25, 2008, as New Zealand was hammered by almost 15,000 lightning strikes in just 24 hours. Among the planes hit was a Lan Chile Airbus, which despite having a hole the size of a dinner plate punched in its nose by lightning, still managed to land safely at Auckland.

DEADLY DOSE ■ A motorist stopped by Bulgarian police after a minor accident in August 2008 had a staggering blood-alcohol reading that was more than double the level usually considered fatal. The 25-year-old, who had drunk 42 pt (20 l) of beer, registered a 0.851 percent blood-alcohol content. Bulgaria's legal limit is 0.05 percent and 0.4 percent is often fatal.

Plane Push

While passengers on a plane in China may not have been expecting first-class treatment, they probably didn't think they would have to get out and push! However, when their plane broke down after landing on the runway in Zhengzhou in September 2008, airport staff failed to budge the stricken jet, and eventually it took two hours for the combined efforts of crew and passengers to move the plane half a mile (0.8 km) to safety.

MONSTER MOTORBIKE

Ray Baumann of Perth, Australia, has created a Monster Motorbike that is 10 ft (3 m) high, 30 ft (9 m) long and, at over 14 tons, weighs more than a double-decker bus. The bike, which took three years to build, has a six-speed truck engine and two giant digger wheels. Baumann demonstrates its awesome power at auto shows, where he uses it to flatten cars and even caravans.

TICKET PROTEST ■ To protest against a ticket for parking part of his car in the street beside his house, Ian Taylor from the town of Tredworth, Gloucestershire, England, sawed his car in half to clear the way.

UNPAID FINES ■ Valerie Sanchez of Harlingen, Texas, was arrested in January 2008 for not paying 76 outstanding traffic warrants. She owed $18,896 in unpaid fines and fees.

NUDE FLIGHT ■ A German travel agency has recently started bookings for a small flight from Erfurt, Germany, to a Baltic Sea resort—on which the passengers on the 55-seat plane can travel totally nude. However, the passengers have to be clothed until they board the aircraft and they also have to be clothed again when they disembark.

DISABLED DRIVER ■ When police stopped a truck driver in Qingdao City, China, they were alarmed to discover that he had no hands. Instead, the driver, whose hands were blown off by firecrackers in his youth, was turning the wheel with the stumps on his wrists.

GOAT SACRIFICE ■ In September 2007, when a Boeing 757 airplane owned by Nepal Airlines developed technical problems, officials managed to cure the fault by sacrificing two goats in front of the troublesome plane at Kathmandu airport—in accordance with Hindu tradition, which states that animals should be sacrificed to appease the gods.

CURRY SCARE ■ A British Airways flight from Belgrade to London was forced to make an emergency landing in July 2008 after passengers feared that the fumes wafting through the cabin of the airplane were part of a terrorist attack. It was only when emergency workers wearing breathing apparatus had helped frightened passengers from the plane that the source of the fumes was discovered—a giant container of curry spices in the cargo hold.

DRIVING AT 101 ■ Alden Couch of Langley, Washington, still had a legal driver's license at 101 years of age. Right up until his death in 2008, Couch, who started driving behind the wheel of a Model T Ford, estimated he drove around 7,500 mi (12,000 km) a year.

BAG OF BONES ■ A 62-year-old woman traveling from Brazil to Italy was stopped at Munich airport in Germany in 2008 after baggage control handlers discovered a human skull and other bones in her luggage. The skeleton, which was sealed in a plastic bag, was that of her brother who had died 11 years earlier in Brazil. She explained to airport authorities that she was just trying to fulfill his dying wish to be buried in Italy. The woman and her skeleton were allowed to continue their journey to Naples in peace.

WOODEN CAR ■ A prototype wooden electric car was unveiled in Kyoto, Japan, in 2008. It has bamboo-weave doors, can be driven for 6 mi (9.5 km) when charged up and can reach a top speed of 30 mph (48 km/h).

ADVANCE TICKET ■ In 1973, Gopal Dey of Howrah, West Bengal, India, purchased a train ticket for June 28, 2073, which he intends to will to his grandson.

WOOD BEETLE ■ Momir Bojic of Celinac, Bosnia, has taken a year to cover the bodywork of his old Volkswagen Beetle completely in oak.

CHEAP RIDE ■ The Tata Nano, a car being built in India, costs only $2,500 and is the least expensive new car in the world.

DUMMY PASSENGERS ■ In order to overcome transit lane rules where vehicles must have a minimum of three occupants, drivers in Auckland, New Zealand, have been dressing up mannequins and dogs as children.

SPLINTER SUPERCAR ■ Joe Harmon of Durham, North Carolina, has built a 240-mph (385-km/h) supercar called the Splinter—and it's made almost entirely of wood. The chassis, body, wheels and a large percentage of the suspension components are all made from wood.

HIGH MILEAGE ■ Students from Mater Dei High School in Evansville, Indiana, built an automobile that travels over 1,000 mi (1,610 km) on a single gallon of gasoline.

CAR CUTTER ■ Kelly Breton from East Longmeadow, Massachussetts, can saw a 4-door family car in half in under a minute. However, she has a good teacher because her father is famous car cutter Lee "Hackman" Breton.

ROAD ROBBERS ■ Thieves near Frankfurt, Germany, stole a mile and a half of the central reservation barrier, consisting of four metal strips weighing 20 tons in total, from a busy highway.

DOUBLE SMASH ■ A veteran motorist ended 76 years of trouble-free driving with a bang in 2008 by smashing his Ford Fiesta into two Porsches. Jack Higgs, 93, was parking next to a Porsche showroom in Penarth, Wales, when his car suddenly shot backwards, causing $120,000 damage.

BOY DRIVER ■ A four-year-old boy from Stanford, Kentucky, tried to drive to his grandmother's house in 2008. The boy managed to start the car and turn it around but his adventure ended when he drove the vehicle through a fence and came to rest in some trees. He was unhurt.

PORSCHE PLUNGE ■ A mechanic at Porsche's Hong Kong distributor managed to drive a newly serviced 911 Carrera 4S down an elevator shaft at the company's service center. He wrecked the $160,000 car by accidentally stepping on the accelerator instead of the brake.

SOLD NAME ■ David Partin of Orlando, Florida, won $100 worth of gasoline from a local radio station in 2008 by agreeing to name his unborn son after two of its DJs. The boy was named Dixon Willoughby Partin after hosts Richard Dixon and J. Willoughby. The station was offering free gas to the listener with the most interesting item to trade.

DRIVE-IN WEDDINGS ■ Fifty couples took part in a series of drive-in weddings at a car rally in Vasteras, Sweden, in July 2008. Ten priests from the Church of Sweden were on hand to perform the seven-minute ceremonies next to a procession of 1950s and 1960s cars.

HAIL DAMAGE ■ In June 2008, a hailstorm in northwestern Germany produced stones the size of tennis balls and damaged 30,000 new Volkswagen cars parked at a factory in Emden.

VEHICLE BURIAL ■ A man loved his old Morris Minor car so much that he asked to be buried in it. Indian farmer Narayanswami had bought the car in 1958 and, in accordance with his last wishes, in April 2007 his body was placed in the car, which was then lowered into a huge grave that had been excavated in the Tamil Nadu region.

TRACTOR PROCESSION ■ For the 2004 funeral of Harold Peabody, the founding president of the Maine Antique Tractor Club, his son led a procession of antique tractors to the cemetery.

AUTO SPOTTER ■ When she was just three, Cody Horton of Maricoa, Arizona, could identify the cars of 42 different Nascar drivers and recite their color combinations—from memory.

ATV PARADE ■ More than 1,000 all-terrain vehicles assembled in Silver Bay, Minnesota, in June 2008, snaking through the town at speeds of around 5 mph (8 km/h).

FORKLIFT DRIVE ■ Drivers from China, Germany and Spain took part in the 2007 Forklift Truck Championships at Aschaffenburg, Germany. Competitors had to transport and rearrange boxes in order, in the fastest possible time.

Miniature Machine

Visitors to the Ripley's Believe It or Not museum in Piccadilly, London, should see if they can spot the tiny Peel P50, a one-door coupe just 52.8 in (134 cm) long and 39 in (99 cm) wide. First produced in 1963, the vehicle can accommodate one adult and reach 38 mph (61 km/h). The Peel P50 has no reverse gear but as it weighs only 130 lb (59 kg) the driver can get out, lift the back end and wheel the car in the right direction.

Fishy Vehicle

Not afraid of standing out in a traffic jam, adventurous artist Andy Hazell from Wales fixed a huge model of a sea bass to the roof of his Vauxhall Corsa hatchback. The fishy passenger is 20 ft (6.1 m) long and made from aluminum, with motorized gills, mouth, eyes, fins and tail giving it convincing movement. At night the sea bass creation is illuminated by 140 LEDs. Just don't ask him to park it!

Submersible Convertible

In March 2008, a Swiss auto company unveiled a convertible car that operates totally underwater as well as on the highway. Inspired by James Bond's car in the movie *The Spy Who Loved Me*, the Rinspeed sQuba is an ordinary car that, at the touch of a button, can transform itself into an amphibious vehicle capable of diving to a depth of around 33 ft (10 m).

ENGINE DWELLERS ■ A woman in South Africa took her BMW car back to the dealership because it was full of rodents. Looking for somewhere warm to live, a family of six dassies—rabbit-sized mammals—had set up home in the car's engine bay and spare tire. The woman had tried to dislodge them by going for a high-speed trip down the highway and then by taking the vehicle in for a car wash, but when that too failed, the dealership called Johannesburg Zoo to remove the animals.

LONG JOURNEY ■ In 1982, Jaeyaena Beuraheng boarded the wrong bus in Malaysia and ended up in northern Thailand. It took her 25 years to be reunited with her family.

BUDDHA BUGGY ■ Created by Larry Neilson of Seattle, Washington, the Buddha Buggy art car is a 1987 Honda decorated with some 50 small Buddha statues. The interior has a velvet altarcloth-draped dashboard with brass Tibetan incense burners, statues and gold tassels, while the roof has a detachable 4-ft (1.2-m) Buddhist stupa monument, housing a 13-in-high (33-cm) porcelain Buddha.

LUCKY CAB ■ As a way of wishing his passengers good luck, taxi driver Izumi Imai of Akita, Japan, has handed out more than 8,000 four-leaf clovers since 2004.

BRICK-BUILT CAR

The Swedish car-maker Volvo teamed up with experts from LEGOland™ California to produce a life-size replica of a Volvo SUV using everyday LEGO™ bricks. Built on the chassis of a real Volvo XC90, the car took two months to complete, was made from 200,000 LEGO™ bricks and weighed almost 3,000 lb (1,360 kg).

TRAVEL TALES
www.ripleys.com

SMASHING TIME ■ Kevin Weaver of Danville, Pennsylvania, chose a novel way of asking Karen Slusser to marry him—he painted his proposal on the side of a car and drove the car in a demolition derby.

BIG PUSH ■ Covering up to 70 mi (113 km) a day, Ryan Nichols, a quadriplegic, propelled a handcycle a distance of 776 mi (1,250 km) in 11 days in October 2008 from Salt Lake City, Utah, to Huntington Beach, California.

CHANGE IS GOOD ■ Paul Brant of Frankfort, Indiana, has purchased a new car and two new trucks—entirely with coins. In 1994, he bought a truck and a car for $36,000 in quarters and by 2007 he had again collected enough quarters and dollar coins to pay $25,000 in change for a new Dodge truck.

VW MODELS ■ The Volkswagen Model Museum at Königslutter, Germany, displays Reinhard Sokoll's collection of nearly 6,000 pieces of VW Beetle memorabilia, including VW toothbrushes, ashtrays and butter dishes.

TOY DESIGN ■ Art car designer Kathleen Pearson from Bisbee, Arizona, has covered a 1983 Ford station wagon in hundreds of small toys. Her creation, which she calls Love 23, has 4,000 toys glued to the exterior and another 800 inside.

VIKING FUNERAL ■ Arne Shield of Michigan left instructions for his family to hold a Viking funeral for him—when the time came his ashes were put on a papier-mâché Viking ship, set afire, and cast adrift on Lake Michigan.

FIGHTER CAR ■ Richard Hanner of Hellertown, Pennsylvania, loves American F-15 fighter jets so much that he spent 18 months building a car that looks like one. His three-wheel, road-legal car, which has a cockpit, wings and a tail, cost nearly $10,000 to make.

BOVINE BIKE ■ Larry Fuente of Mendocino, California, calls his three-wheel motor bike Cowasaki—because the frame of the bike fits around a full-size model of a brown-and-white cow. The rider sits on the cow's back, the bike's horn makes a mooing sound and the tail has to be lifted up when the vehicle needs to be filled with gas.

WINGED CAR ■ Ashland, Oregon, artist Konnie May has converted her 1967 Volkswagen Beetle into the Flutterbug, complete with antennae and wings. The bodywork of the car is painted with brightly colored butterflies and, as well as having two antennae protruding from the roof, it has wings attached to either side that flap at the push of a button.

HAND STAND ■ Every September since 1992, 24 contestants stand for as long as possible without leaning, under the scorching Texas sun, with one hand on the body of a brand new truck. The record for the Hands on a Hard Body Contest at Longview is nearly four days, by which time contestants say that hallucinations and swollen ankles start to take hold.

VIKING REPLICA ■ On July 1, 2007, a crew of 65 people set out on a 1,000-mi (1,610-km) voyage from Roskilde, Denmark, in a historically accurate replica of a Viking ship and arrived in Dublin, Ireland, 45 days later.

BEETLE BELLE ■ Edward Smith of Washington state writes poetry about cars, sings to them and talks to them as if they were his girlfriend. He has had romantic feelings toward cars for more than 40 years, his current girlfriend being a white Volkswagen Beetle named Vanilla.

Human Hamsters

Invented in New Zealand, ZORB™ globe riding requires humans to roll down gentle hills inside large transparent plastic spheres—like giant hamster wheels. Some "zorbanauts" have reached speeds of more than 30 mph (48 km/h), while others have traveled over a third of a mile (0.5 km) in their sphere.

Lawn Grower

The new grass field of the St. Louis Cardinals baseball team was the inspiration for Gene Pool's outrageous grass-covered bus, which Gene encourages people to ride in. The grass is real and watered daily, along with the artist's living grass suit.

LOW RIDER ■ Andy Saunders from Dorset, England, converted a Volkswagen Camper Van that stood 7 ft 8 in (2.3 m) high into a mini version just 3 ft 3 in (1 m) tall, with the driver's head sticking out of the roof. The minivan can reach a maximum speed of 80 mph (130 km/h), but is so low that it could be driven under a parking lot barrier.

TRASH NAP ■ Garbage collectors in Indiana were surprised early one morning to hear a man yelling from the top of their truck. William Bowen woke up just in time from his drunken nap in a garbage can, which had landed him in the back of the garbage truck. The late-night reveler was unhurt, but extremely cold and had no recollection of getting into the can.

ODD COMBINATION ■ In what may be a unique accident, an airplane crashed into a boat that was parked in the driveway of a house. The pilot of the single-engine plane was trying to land at Big Bear Airport in California's San Bernardino Mountains in May 2008 when she experienced problems and came down instead between two homes, slamming into the boat. Nobody was hurt in the crash.

$120,000 BICYCLE ■ Scandinavian company Aurumania has launched a 24-carat, gold-plated bicycle priced at $120,000. The limited edition luxury bike is decorated with over 600 Swarovksi crystals, and the company has also created a 24-carat-gold wall bracket, so that it can be displayed as a work of art.

HOMEMADE PLANE ■ Peng Cong from Chongqing, China, has built his own airplane—from reading books and the Internet. His plane is 18 ft (5.5 m) long, has a 32-ft (9.7-m) wingspan and cost him $27,000 to build. It managed to reach an altitude of 1,000 ft (300 m) on only its second flight.

Speedy Seating

Workers in Bad Koenig-Zell, Germany, left their offices, donned costumes and raced each other down crowded streets in the first German Office Chair Racing Championship in April 2008.

FINE FIGHT ■ Simon Belsky, a senior citizen from New York City, has spent $7,500 and more than two years fighting a $115 parking ticket because, now that he has retired, he says he has nothing else to do.

MOTHER SHIP ■ A lost humpback whale calf thought a yacht was its mother. The six-week-old calf tried to suckle from the yacht and refused to leave its side off the coast of Sydney, Australia.

AUTO TEXT ■ Li Zongxiong from Taiwan has covered every inch of his car, two trucks and a motorbike with words from Buddhist texts. Each day for more than nine years he has been adorning the bodywork, doors, wheels, windshields and mirrors—and even the number plates—with virtuous thoughts.

FISHING CAR ■ Wang Hongjun from Qian'an City, China, has spent 13 years and around $200,000 building his own amphibious car. He says he often takes his creation to a lake to fish and has also taken his son on a 10-mi (16-km) drive out to sea.

JET-PACK FLIGHT ■ Eric Scott used a jet pack powered by hydrogen peroxide to fly 1,500 ft (460 m)—the length of five football fields—across Colorado's Royal Gorge in November 2008.

Bride Ride

For Katie Hodgson and Darren McWalter getting married was an uplifting experience, quite literally. Along with the officiating minister, they rode on the wings of biplanes up to 1,000 ft (300 m) above Gloucester, England, and shouted their vows through megaphones while the ceremony was broadcast to wedding guests on the ground.

TANKED UP ■ A Russian tank crashed into a villager's house in the Urals in 2008 shortly after its crew had stopped off to buy two bottles of vodka at a nearby shop. The Russian Army promised to pay compensation but said the tank had skidded on melting ice.

AUTO CELLAR ■ Ken Imhoff took 17 years to build his own Lamborghini sports car in the cellar of his Wisconsin home, only to find that he had no way of getting it out. So he hired an excavator to gouge out a slope in his garden and then dig down into the foundations of the house so that the newly built car could be pulled out.

AIRPORT HOME ■ A Japanese tourist liked Mexico City airport so much that he was still there three months later. Hiroshi Nohara from Tokyo decided to make Terminal 1 of the Benito Juarez International Airport his new home and survived by living off donations from fast-food restaurants and passengers, to whom he became a national celebrity.

TOE TRUCKS ■ The breakdown vehicles owned by Lincoln Toe Trucks of Seattle, Washington, are two pink tow trucks in the shape of human feet—one left and one right. The fiberglass toes sit atop old Volkswagen vans.

MUSICAL FLOAT ■ Jon Large and Spencer Marsden from Manchester, England, have transformed a milk float (delivery van) into a percussion instrument. Their Tone Float has rows of bottles in the rear section, each fitted with an electronically controlled striking hammer. The bottles are tuned to pitch by the volume of liquid inside.

HOW LARGE?

130,000-LB BIRTHDAY CAKE
To celebrate the centennial of Las Vegas, Nevada, in 2005, chefs made a birthday cake 102 ft (31 m) long that weighed 130,000 lb (59,000 kg).

54,917-LB ICE-CREAM SUNDAE
In 1988, Mike Rogiani of Edmonton, Alberta, Canada, created a mammoth ice-cream sundae that weighed 54,917 lb (24,909 kg) and was so big it had to be mixed in an empty swimming pool.

44,457-LB PIZZA
In 1987, at Havana, Florida, Lorenzo Amato and Louis Piancone cooked a pizza that weighed a whopping 44,457 lb (20,165 kg) and was later cut into more than 94,000 slices.

26,455-LB PIE
In 2000, the Denby Dale Pie Company of West Yorkshire, England, baked a meat-and-potato pie that was 40 ft (12 m) long and weighed 26,455 lb (12,000 kg).

8,377-LB KEBAB
In 2007, students in Cyberjaya, Malaysia, prepared a kebab that weighed 8,377 lb (3,800 kg) and was more than 1¼ mi (2 km) long.

6,510-LB OMELET
In 2002, the Lung Association of Brockville, Ontario, Canada, produced an omelette weighing 6,510 lb (2,953 kg) from 60,000 eggs.

5,440-LB SANDWICH
In 2005, Wild Woody's Chill and Grill of Roseville, Michigan, made a sandwich that weighed 5,440 lb (2,467 kg).

5,038-LB SLAB OF FUDGE
The Northwest Fudge Factory of Levack, Ontario, Canada, made a slab of fudge 45 ft 6 in (13.8 m) long, weighing 5,038 lb (2,285 kg), in 2007.

3,415-LB POPCORN BALL
A popcorn ball 24 ft 6 in (7.5 m) in circumference and weighing 3,415 lb (1,550 kg) was manufactured at Lake Forest, Illinois, in 2006.

2,534-LB PUMPKIN PIE
In 2007, farmers in Cullinan, Pretoria, South Africa, made a pumpkin pie 27 ft (8.2 m) long and weighing 2,534 lb (1,150 kg).

2,319-LB STIR FRY
In 2005, pupils at Wesvalia High School in Klerksdorp, South Africa, made a mixed stir fry weighing 2,319 lb (1,052 kg).

315,261 LB OF KIMCHI
Using 58,000 cabbage heads, 2,200 cooks in Seoul, South Korea, in 2008, prepared a dish of kimchi—spicy pickled cabbage—that weighed 315,261 lb (143,000 kg).

PECULIAR TASTES

LIVE SCORPIONS
Father-of-two Hasip Kaya of Turkey has been addicted to eating live scorpions since he was a boy.

FLY FEAST
In protest at his town's garbage collection service, a man named Farook from Tirunelveli, India, started eating nothing but flies.

LIVE TREE FROGS AND RATS
For over 40 years, Jiang Musheng of China has eaten live tree frogs and rats to ward off abdominal pains.

A POUND OF SAND
Ram Rati of Lucknow, India, eats 1 lb (454 g) of sand every day to fight stomach complaints.

23,000 BIG MACS
Don Gorske of Fond du Lac, Wisconsin, has eaten more than 23,000 Big Macs in the last 36 years. To prove his addiction, he keeps all the sales receipts in a box and says the only day he didn't eat a Big Mac was the day his mother died.

CHICKEN FEED
Jan Csovary from Prievidza, Slovakia, eats chicken for breakfast, lunch and tea, and has consumed over 12,000 chickens since the early 1970s.

NOTHING BUT CHEESE
Dave Nunley from Cambridgeshire, England, has eaten nothing but grated mild Cheddar cheese for over 25 years and goes through 238 lb (108 kg) of it every year.

DIET OF WORMS
Wayne Fauser from Sydney, Australia, regularly eats live earthworms, either in sandwiches or just plain.

CHOCOLATE-COVERED LETTUCE
Danny Partner of Los Angeles, California, used to eat 12 iceberg lettuces covered in chocolate sauce every day.

DAILY GRASS
Gangaram from Kanpur, India, eats 2 lb (907 g) of grass every day because he says it gives him energy.

CARROT CRUNCHER
Julie Tori from Hampshire, England, has eaten at least 4 lb (1.8 kg) of carrots every day for over ten years. On the one day she didn't have her favorite vegetable, she was seized by a panic attack.

Tofu garnished with spring onion and a generous helping of preying mantis is on the menu at the home of alternative chef Shoichi Uchiyama, from Tokyo, Japan, who collects insects from around his home. He advises that deep frying is the best way to cook them, and thinks that school children should be taught the benefits of eating creepy crawlies, as they are plentiful and nutritious.

FANTASTIC FOOD

Potato Peacock

This colorful 8-ft-tall (2.4-m) peacock-shaped lantern made of potatoes appeared at a department store in Shenyang, China, in January 2008. The vegetables were finely sliced until translucent and then arranged so that multi-colored lights shone through.

EXCLUSIVE POTATO ■ An exclusive French potato can sell for $800 per kilo. Only 100 tons of the La Bonnotte variety are cultivated each year and it is grown only on the island of Noirmoutier, off the west coast of France, where the fields are fertilized with nothing but seaweed.

FISH LUNCH ■ A retired couple from England have traveled 60 mi (96 km) for a fish-and-chip lunch at their favorite seaside resort every day for the past ten years. Cypriot-born Ermis and Androniki Nicholas have visited Weston-super-Mare, Somerset, over 2,600 times, journeying around 160,000 mi (257,495 km) and spending almost £20,000 on fish and chips.

SNAKE VODKA ■ Texan rattlesnake rancher Bayou Bob Popplewell has been selling bottles of vodka containing dead baby rattlers as a healing tonic. He uses the cheapest vodka he can find as a preservative for the snakes and compares the end result to cough syrup.

CHEESE CHANTS ■ An Austrian school for dairy farmers has won a string of prizes for its Grottenhofer Auslese cheese since it began playing Gregorian chants to the cheese while it matures. The head of the school believes the monks' music stimulates the micro-organisms that help the cheese mature.

MIGHTY MEATBALL ■ Gary Travis, owner of Meatball Mike's restaurant in Cranston, Rhode Island, made a pork-and-beef meatball weighing 72 lb 9 oz (33 kg) in August 2008.

GENEROUS GESTURE ■ Eighty-eight-year-old Golda Bechal of London, England, bequeathed the bulk of her estate—more than $20 million—to the owners of her favorite Chinese food restaurant.

HEAVY POTATO ■ A potato grown on the Isle of Man, off the western coast of England, weighed 7 lb 13 oz (3.5 kg)—the weight of a healthy newborn baby.

OUTSIZE EGG ■ In 2008, Titi, a one-year-old hen belonging to the Martinez-Guerra family in Campo Florido, Cuba, laid an egg weighing a colossal 6.34 oz (180 g)—nearly three times the weight of the average hen's egg.

FRY MUSEUM ■ The Belgian city of Bruges has opened a museum dedicated to French fries. The brainchild of Eddy Van Belle, the Frietmuseum chronicles the history of the nation's favorite food from its conception in the 1700s, along with a collection of fry art, a display of the fry in cartoons and an exhibition of kitchen fryers.

COLA CRAVING ■ A Croatian man has drunk nothing but Coca-Cola for more than 40 years. Pero Ajtman of Karanac is now in his seventies and has been drinking up to five glasses of Coke a day since 1968 when he promised his mother he would never touch alcohol. He says he is in perfect health and is happy to drink Coke until the day he dies.

30周年記念

御祝

寿

How did you start carving watermelons?

I was inspired to learn the art of fruit carving when I saw a watermelon sculpture at a Tokyo hotel that was holding a festival celebrating Thai culture. Watermelons have a large area to carve and are stronger than other fruits.

What tools do you use to carve them?

Only one knife—a carving knife made in the Kingdom of Thailand.

What is your favorite watermelon carving?

It is the Japanese crane and tortoise, which are symbols of good fortune.

How long does it take to carve a watermelon?

It takes around 90 minutes.

What happens to your carved fruit?

After appreciating the carvings, we chill them and eat them.

How long do the carvings last?

At room temperature in an exhibition, they last two days. In a refrigerator, they can last for two weeks.

Watermelon Marvels!

Japanese food sculptor Takashi Itoh has been carving amazing art in watermelons for seven years. Entirely self-taught, he became an expert in just three weeks. His carvings include dragons, slogans and Japanese cranes and tortoises. According to Takashi, you can carve many different fruits and vegetables—as well as watermelons he recommends using papayas, pumpkins, carrots and the Japanese radish.

Wobbly Building

St. Paul's Cathedral was molded from jelly for the Architectural Jelly Design Competition 2008 at University College London, where professional architects entered sweet structures including an airport and a bridge. The orange-and-mango-flavored cathedral was created by jelly makers Bompas and Parr, who use architectural techniques in their jelly molds. Entries were judged on their wobbling qualities amid the sound of wobbling jelly piped through the building.

BUTTER SCULPTURE ■ For the Harrisburg, Pennsylvania, Farm Show in 2008, Jim Victor created a sculpture from 1,000 lb (453 kg) of butter. The sculpture—a take on "Mary Had a Little Lamb"—depicted a girl trying to take her cow on a school bus.

EDIBLE MENU ■ The menu at Moto restaurant in Chicago, Illinois, is edible. Chef Homaru Cantu loaded a modified ink-jet printer containing mixtures of fruits and vegetables and then printed tasty images downloaded from the Internet onto edible sheets of soy bean and potato starch. Customers can even flavor their soups by ripping up the menu and adding it to their dish.

Dough Art

Food-artist Prudence Emma Staite celebrated the city of Rome at the launch of a well-known pizza chain's new pizzeria at the Museum of London, England, in 2007. She constructed the Colosseum, the head of Pope Benedict XVI and the Spanish Steps all from pizza dough.

EDIBLE RACE ■ An edible boat race was staged in Eyemouth, Scotland, in 2008, where 30 competitors sent such vessels as an apple raft with a cabbage-leaf sail out to sea. The winner was a chocolate tart, although the most seaworthy was judged to be a coracle of slow-baked lasagne sheets. Some entries, notably melon-skin boats, were disqualified for not being entirely edible.

CHOCOLATE ROOM ■ As part of a Valentine's Day promotion in 2008, a Belgian chocolatier unveiled a room in Manhattan that was made entirely from chocolate—including the walls, furniture, artwork, chandelier, fireplace logs and candles.

CANDY CASTLE ■ In Zagreb, Croatia, in 2008, Krunoslav Budiselic spent 24 hours building a 10-ton chocolate castle from around 100,000 chocolate bars. The finished candy construction stood 10 ft (3 m) high on a chocolate base that measured 20 x 7 ft (6 x 2.1 m). Afterward, the individual chocolate "'bricks" were sold off for charity.

GLOBAL EGG ■ In 2008, a hen in Zaozhuang City, China, laid an egg with a pattern on it that resembled a map of the world. The four oceans, Greenland and the Hainan Islands in the South China Sea were all distinctly recognizable.

ROYAL MAC ▦ Royal accounts revealed in 2008 that Queen Elizabeth II owns a drive-through McDonald's burger restaurant. A retail park in Slough, visible from the Queen's State Apartments at Windsor Castle, Berkshire, England, was recently purchased by the Crown for $184 million and it includes a McDonald's.

BACON FLOSS ▪ Seattle-based novelty dealer Archie McPhee has introduced a new line in dental floss—one that has the flavor of crispy bacon. The company already sells bacon-scented air freshener.

SERIAL EATER ▦ In April 2008, New Yorker Timothy Janus ate 141 pieces of nigiri sushi in just six minutes. He has also devoured 4 lb (1.8 kg) of tiramisu in six minutes and 10 lb 8 oz (4.8 kg) of noodles in eight minutes.

NANO NOODLES ▪ Japanese scientists have created a bowl of noodles so tiny that it can be seen only through a microscope. Students at the University of Tokyo carved the bowl, which has a diameter of just one-25,000th of an inch, from microscopic carbon nanotubes. The noodles inside the bowl measured one-12,500th of an inch in length and were only one-1.25 millionth of an inch thick.

EXOTIC ICES ▦ In 2008, the city of Yokohama celebrated the 130th anniversary of the arrival of ice cream in Japan with a festival showcasing such regional flavors as raw horse, curry, octopus, garlic, prawn, chicken wings, cheese, beer, eel, beef tongue and pit viper.

PIZZA RUSH ▪ A Domino's pizza in Gulfport, Mississippi, sold 7,637 pizzas in a single day in August 2008, customers being enticed by the offer of 10-in (25-cm) pepperoni pizzas for just $2 each.

LARGE BLUEBERRY ▪ A 12-year-old boy from New York State has grown what is believed to be America's biggest blueberry. Zachary Wightman from Kerhonkson exhibited his 0.24-oz (6.8-g) fruit at the Ulster County Fair in July 2008.

BLUE BREAD ▪ Dozens of Australian shoppers were alarmed in 2008 when they put their supermarket-bought garlic bread in the oven to cook—and it turned blue. The mystified manufacturers promptly recalled the bread and blamed the problem on an old batch of garlic.

PORK STAMP ▪ To mark 2007 being the Year of the Pig, China released a scratch-and-sniff stamp that smelled like sweet-and-sour pork—and the glue on the back of the stamp was even flavored like the popular dish.

HOT CURRY ▪ In 2008, chef Vivek Singh from The Cinnamon Club restaurant in London, England, produced a lamb-based curry containing some of the world's hottest chilies, including Dorset Naga and Scotch Bonnet. The end result was so hot that, before eating it, customers had to sign a disclaimer saying they were aware of the nature and risks involved with tasting the curry.

FIRE-EATER

Inspired by a fantasy role-playing game, Misty Doty of Washington State commissioned a masterpiece of a cake in the form of a dragon for her husband John. The tasty creature was made by expert cake-maker Mike McCarey of Redmond, Washington, from chocolate and vanilla with a chocolate buttercream filling. It took 12 hours to complete.

Ripley's research

WHY DOES THE SODA EXPLODE?

There is some dispute over what actually causes carbonated drinks to explode when candy is dropped into the bottle, but most scientists agree that it is a reaction between the carbon dioxide gas in the liquid and the mints. The mints dissolve the surface tension around the individual bubbles of carbon dioxide gas, allowing the bubbles to gather together on the candy. Soon the liquid cannot contain the gas any longer and it explodes out of the top of the bottle. Diet soda works better than regular soda, but nobody knows exactly why.

Soda Shower

In Leuven, Belgium, students donned ponchos and braved a sticky deluge when they simultaneously dropped mints into 1,360 bottles of diet cola and watched as the drink exploded high into the air.

BEAN DIET ■ Neil King from Essex, England, lost 140 lb (63.5 kg) in nine months—by eating six cans of baked beans every day. Eating beans for breakfast, lunch and dinner, he devoured more than 1,500 cans or half a ton of beans and saw his weight drop from 420 lb (190 kg) to less than 280 lb (127 kg).

PANCAKE FEAST ■ The Fargo, North Dakota, Kiwanis Club made nearly 35,000 pancakes in eight hours at its Pancake Karnival in February 2008. The pancakes were served with more than 1,100 bottles of syrup.

DOGGIE BEER ■ A Dutch pet-shop owner has created a new beer—for dogs. Gerrie Berendsen, from Zelhem, has persuaded a local brewery to launch a nonalcoholic, beef-flavored brew called Kwispelbier, which is Dutch for "tail-wagging beer."

EEL DRINK ■ A new energy-boosting drink has gone on sale in Japan—made from eels. The fizzy, yellow-colored drink contains extracts from the heads and bones of eels along with five vitamins that are contained in the fish.

GIANT CHEESECAKE ■ In June 2008, bakers at Eli's Cheesecake World in Chicago created a 2,000-lb (907-kg), three-tiered cheesecake made from 1,330 lb (603 kg) of cream cheese, 300 lb (136 kg) of sugar, 150 dozen eggs, 100 lb (45 kg) of butter cream frosting and 100 lb (45 kg) of marzipan.

BURNED FOOD ■ Harpist Deborah Henson-Conant from Arlington, Massachusetts, runs the online Museum of Burnt Food, dedicated to "accidentally carbonized culinary masterpieces." She started the museum in the late 1980s and her exhibits include inadvertently cremated quiches, pizzas and baked potatoes.

FIERY CHILI ■ Created by vegetable grower Michael Michaud from Dorset, England, the Dorset Naga chili is so hot that cooks are advised to wear gloves at all times when preparing it in order to avoid skin irritation. An extract of the Dorset Naga needs to be diluted in water 1.6 million times before any trace of its heat disappears and it therefore racks up 1.6 million Scoville Units—the measure of chili heat—compared to Tabasco sauce's mere 8,000.

HORNET SALIVA ■ The saliva of Japan's giant hornet is a component in a Japanese sports drink said to reduce muscle fatigue.

Sea-horse Kebabs
Fried sea-horses were among the delicacies sold at markets in Beijing, China, for the 2008 Olympic Games.

BUSY DINER ■ A restaurant in Damascus, Syria, can serve more than 6,000 customers simultaneously. The Damascus Gate Restaurant has a staff of 1,800, a kitchen of 26,900 sq ft (2,500 sq m) and a dining area of 581,250 sq ft (54,000 sq m).

CHEESE WHEEL ■ A wheel of cheese weighing 1,590 lb (721 kg)—that's more than the weight of eight fully grown men—was produced by a factory in Altay, Russia, in 2008.

HAM-BUSH FOILED ■ Caught in the act of stealing meat from the freezer of a restaurant in Gloucester, Massachusetts, a thief tried to beat off owner Joe Scola by hitting him over the head with 5 lb (2.2 kg) of frozen prosciutto. However, Scola sent the would-be thief running for cover by whacking him in the face with a ham first.

UDDER LUXURY ■ Dairy cows at a farm in the Netherlands have been receiving V.I.P. treatment in the hope they will produce better-tasting milk. Nancy Vermeer's 80 cows are pampered with massages and get to lie on soft rubber mattresses sprinkled with sawdust and even water beds.

TUNA ACUPUNCTURE ■ For superior sushi, a Japanese company administers acupuncture to each tuna fish prior to its death, in order to reduce the amount of stress it suffers.

MOOSE MEAT ■ In December 2006, Swedish astronaut Christer Fuglesang became the first person to take dehydrated moose meat into space.

ONION GENES ■ It may be a humble vegetable, but an onion's genetic code is nearly six times longer than a human's.

Crunchy Crawlies
The Japanese have put a creepy-crawly twist on their traditional sushi by adding large and spiky insects. The dish is not for the squeamish, and includes caterpillars, spiders, moth larvae, cockroaches and cicadas on a bed of sushi rice.

FANTASTIC FOOD

www.ripleys.com

Ripley's Believe It or Not!®

NO WASTE ■ Le Spirite Lounge in Montreal, Quebec, Canada, is a vegan restaurant with two strict rules: first, everyone must finish their meal in order to get a dessert; and, second, unless they finish their dessert, they can never return to eat at the restaurant again.

ALCOHOLIC FERMENT ■ People with auto brewery syndrome can become spontaneously drunk when, amazingly, their body ferments normal food into alcohol during the process of digestion.

LUXURY BURGER ■ After six months of development, Burger King® launched a $185 burger in London, England, in 2008. Made using ingredients from seven countries, from Japan to France, The Burger, which is the size of a regular Whopper, combines Japanese beef with white truffles, Cristal Champagne onion straws, Pata Negra ham drizzled in Modena balsamic vinegar, organic white wine and shallot-infused mayonnaise, and pink Himalayan rock salt, all served up in an Iranian saffron and truffle bun.

PIZZA CHAIN ■ In May 2008, Scott Van Duzer and employees of Big Apple Pizza and Pasta in Fort Pierce, Florida, created a chain of pizzas 722 ft (220 m) long.

KANGAROO BURGERS ■ An Australian scientist has recommended that eating kangaroo burgers could help save the planet. Dr. George Wilson says sheep and cows produce more methane gas emissions through flatulence than kangaroos, whose digestive systems produce virtually no greenhouse gas emissions at all.

FRIED SPIDER

Near the town of Skuon, Cambodia, a species of tarantula spider is bred in holes in the ground specifically for food. The spiders are fried until the legs are stiff and the abdomen is not too runny, giving a crispy exterior and soft center said to resemble the taste of chicken. The spiders sell for 500 riel (12 cents) each and their popularity as a foodstuff is thought to stem from the regime of the Khmer Rouge (1975–79), when hunger forced people to eat spiders to survive.

QUICK MIX ■ In Las Vegas, Nevada, in February 2008, bartender Bobby Gleason mixed 253 cocktails in an hour, averaging just over four cocktails a minute.

HALF-MILE SAUSAGE ■ In July 2008, the village of Graus in northern Spain prepared a sausage that was more than half a mile (0.8 km) long. It was made from 1.2 tons of pork and was cooked using 1,323 lb (600 kg) of charcoal.

BATMAN SOUP ■ The Toy and Action Figure Museum at Pauls Valley, Oklahoma, houses an exhibit of unusual food products related to comic books and superheroes. Items include such culinary oddities as Superman Pasteurized Process Imitation Cheese Spread, Spiderman Cookies and Batman Soup.

UPSCALE CANDY ■ Lebanese chocolatier Patchi created boxes of chocolates that went on sale at Harrods department store in London, England, for $10,000 each. The 49 chocolates, which were made from organic cocoa, rested on suede and were separated by gold and platinum linings. In addition, each one was decorated with gold and a Swarovski crystal flower or handmade silk rose. The boxes themselves were personalized for the buyer and wrapped with leather and handmade silk.

CANDY BOWL ■ U.S. rock band Van Halen had it written into their contract that at every concert they played they were to be provided backstage with a bowl of M&M's®—but with the specific instructions that they were to have all the brown candies removed.

LOBSTER LOVERS ■ A 22-lb (10-kg) male lobster named Big Dee-Dee was rescued from the pot after becoming a popular tourist attraction in Shediac, New Brunswick, Canada. The monster lobster, believed to be over 100 years old, was caught in July 2008. More than 1,000 tourists a day visited the fish market to see him, prompting Laura-Leah Shaw of Vancouver, British Columbia, and two anonymous organizations in Ontario to pay $3,000 to buy him and put him back in the sea.

MARS MAD ■ Keith Sorrell of Liverpool, England, has eaten nothing but his favorite chocolate bar for more than 17 years. Every day he eats at least a dozen Mars Bars, which combine chocolate, nougat and caramel, in place of meals.

SPACE YOGURT ■ A Japanese dairy has been selling space yogurt, made using two types of lactic acid bacteria that spent 10 days in space aboard a Russian Soyuz rocket. Half of the bacteria died inside the rocket, but the strong, surviving bacteria are said to give space yogurt a more full-bodied flavor than that made with standard earthbound bacteria.

Cheesy Politicians

Working eight hours a day for a week in a 40-degree cooler, Wisconsin artist Troy Landwehr carved his own version of John Trumbull's historic painting *Declaration of Independence*—from 2,000 lb (907 kg) of Cheddar cheese.

M&M® Eminem

Mexican artist Enrique Ramos made this 40 x 30 in (100 x 76 cm) portrait of rapper Eminem from over 1,000 M&M's® colored candies.

CHEESE MITES ■ The manufacture of Milbenkäse, a variety of German cheese, includes the intentional introduction of cheese mites. The mites look like crumbs on the cheese's rind.

BACON-FLAVORED CHOCOLATE
■ Chicago chocolatier Katrina Markoff creates unusual-flavored bars of candy, including curry and chocolate and chocolate with mushrooms. Her company's latest offering, Mo's Bacon Bar, which contains chunks of smoked bacon combined with milk chocolate, sold out within 48 hours when it went on sale at Selfridge's department store in London, England, in November 2008.

Snake Wine

In Vietnam, you can buy snake wine— often with a dead snake preserved inside the bottle. Venomous snakes are usually chosen for the reptilian brew, but because their poison is protein-based, it is inactivated and therefore rendered harmless by the ethanol in the rice wine. The wine is popular because snakes are said to have medicinal qualities, curing everything from poor eyesight to hair loss.

CHAMPAGNE DELIVERY ■ When guests on the beach at the Cap Maison Hotel on the Caribbean island of St. Lucia want to order champagne, they raise a red flag and the drink is then delivered to them by zip-wire.

CHILI BUG ■ New research from the University of Washington has revealed that bugs are responsible for the heat in chili peppers. The spiciness is a defense mechanism developed by some peppers to combat a microbial fungus that invades through punctures made in the outer skin by insects. If unchallenged, the fungus would destroy the plant's seeds before they could be eaten by birds and widely dispersed.

EASTER EXTRAVAGANZA ■ A decorated Easter egg, measuring 48 ft 6 in (14.8 m) long and 27 ft 6 in (8.4 m) in diameter, was created in Alcochete, Portugal, in 2008.

GARLIC MENU ■ Garlic's Restaurant in London, Ontario, Canada, has a menu with the emphasis on garlic, offering such dishes as garlic ice cream and garlic cloves dipped in chocolate, which can be washed down with garlic martinis.

DRIED SAFFRON ■ It takes between 50,000 and 75,000 saffron crocus flowers to make just 1 lb (450 g) of dried saffron spice—that's the equivalent of an entire football field of flowers.

EXPENSIVE WATER ■ There is a type of water that sells for nearly $17 an ounce. Kona Nigari water—a desalinated water rich in minerals from the deep seas off Hawaii—is much prized by the Japanese and is sold in concentrated form to be mixed with regular water.

DIVAN INTERVENTION ■ There is a new restaurant in New York where customers eat on king-size beds. Created by Sabina Belkin, Duvet is furnished with beds, pillows and sheets instead of tables, chairs and tablecloths.

LOBSTER OMELET ■ An omelet at the Le Parker Meridien restaurant in New York sells for $1,000. It contains 10 oz (280 g) of sevruga caviar, a whole lobster and six eggs.

ROBOT BARTENDER ■ A Japanese beer maker has devised a robot bartender, Mr. Asahi, who can serve customers with a smile in less than two minutes. Mr. Asahi, who weighs a quarter of a ton, can pull pints, and open bottles and pour them for customers. He works behind a specially designed bar and can politely respond to questions via an operator-controlled system that includes more than 500 vocal effects.

TOP BANANA ■ Broadview Heights, Ohio, disk jockey Ross Cline peeled and ate five bananas in one minute in March 2008.

BUSY CHEF ■ Working alone, Donnie Rush of Bay St. Louis, Mississippi, made 142 pizzas in a single hour in August 2008.

PORTLY PATTY ■ A 115-lb (52-kg) sausage patty—big enough to serve more than 450 people—was made in Hatfield Township, Pennsylvania, in February 2008. The huge patty, which was 6 ft (1.8 m) in diameter and 1½ in (3.8 cm) thick, was cooked over 160 lb (72.5 kg) of charcoal for about 40 minutes. It took several people to flip it halfway through cooking.

DEATH DINER ■ A death-themed restaurant has opened in Truskavets, Ukraine—housed in a 65-ft (20-m) windowless coffin. The brainchild of funeral parlor director Stepan Pyrianyk, the restaurant, called Eternity, takes the form of a huge casket decorated with dozens of wreaths and smaller coffins.

CRUSTY MAYO ■ Spanish chefs have devised a new method of making mayonnaise from colloidal silicon dioxide—the substance that comprises 60 percent of the Earth's crust. They have also created a nutritious sausage from the leftovers from dragnet fishing, roasted prawns in beach sand and designed edible plates made from wheat, rice and maize.

ANGER RELEASE ■ Customers at Isdaan restaurant in the Philippines can release their anger by throwing cups, saucers, plates, even working TV sets, at a wall.

CANDY MURAL ■ More than 4,000 office workers used a quarter of a million Smarties—colored chocolate candies—to create a 500-sq-ft (46-sq-m) mural depicting major London landmarks, including the Big Ben tower, the London Eye and Wembley Stadium.

Oyster Fan

On his way to winning an oyster-eating competition in New Orleans, Louisiana, champion gobbler Patrick Bertoletti scoffed an incredible 420 oysters in just eight minutes. The Chicago-based chef has also won jalapeno-pepper and chicken-wing eating competitions.

TWO-FOOT SCONE ■ Bakery shop owner Helen Hallett and her family from Torquay, Devon, England, created a scone that weighed 57 lb (26 kg) and measured 2 ft (60 cm) in diameter. The colossal cake was made from a 100-year-old recipe and it included 22 pt (10.4 l) of clotted cream. At 700 times bigger than a standard scone, it had to be baked in a mold specially constructed by welders.

LONG CHOPSTICKS ■ The Marco Polo Hotel in Dubai, United Arab Emirates, has manufactured a pair of chopsticks that are 22½ ft (6.85 m) long—that's equal to the size of the tallest pair of stilts!

THE 134-POUNDER ■ In 2008, Mallie's Sports Grill & Bar of Southgate, Michigan, created a giant burger weighing 134 lb (61 kg). The 24-in (60-cm) burger needed three men using two steel sheets to flip it and went on the menu at a price of $399.

JAIL BAIT ■ The Jail restaurant in Taiwan has been designed to resemble a prison. Customers enter via a big metal door and are greeted by staff wearing prison uniforms. Handcuffed, the guests are then led to their cell, which is complete with metal floor, rusty iron bars on the window and sliding prison door.

CAFÉ CHAOS ■ Two women were rushed to hospital with burning sensations in their mouths in July 2007 after a café in Queenstown, New Zealand, mistakenly served dishwashing detergent as mulled wine.

TEQUILA BOTTLES ■ Since he started his collection in 1994, Ricardo Ampudia from Tepoztlan, Mexico, has amassed more than 3,600 tequila bottles, including over 500 different brands. His oldest bottle dates back over 100 years, while his most expensive—made of pure gold poured over hand-blown glass—is worth $150,000. He also has a 3-ft-long (90-cm) tequila bottle in the shape of a rifle and another containing the tail of a rattlesnake.

MEATY COLOGNE ■ Burger King™ made a novel Christmas gift in 2008—a men's cologne called Flame, which smells of barbecued meat.

Spaghetti Contest

It was forks at the ready as competitors furiously tucked into bowls of pasta at a spaghetti-eating competition held at a festival in Sydney, Australia, that celebrated all things Italian.

FISH ATTRACTION ■ To entertain diners, a restaurant in Changchun, China, has around 20 carp swimming in the 13-ft-long (4-m) urinal in the men's bathroom.

DEPRESSION-ERA PRICES ■ An Italian restaurant in Harlem, New York City, where Frank Sinatra and Tony Bennett were once regulars, marked its 75th anniversary in 2008 by charging 1933 prices. Patsy's Restaurant was selling a 12-oz (340-g) steak and grilled salmon for 90 cents, a slice of pizza for 60 cents and most beverages for 10 cents.

TOMATO CANNERS ■ California is by far the largest producer of processed tomatoes in the U.S.A. California's prolific canners process more tomatoes in a few days than Ohio, the second-largest producing state, processes during the entire season.

TWO-TON CAKE ■ In January 2009, 55 cooks from Mexico City spent 60 hours making a two-ton cheesecake, which they cut into 20,000 slices.

WINNING DOG ■ In the patisserie showpiece section of the International Culinary Olympics, held in Erfurt, Germany, in 2008, Michelle Wibowo from West Sussex, England, won gold with a life-sized sugar sculpture of a hound dog. It took her four days and 44 lb (20 kg) of sugar to make the dog, which even had drool.

SEABED CHAMPAGNE ■ Two hundred bottles of champagne sat on the seabed off Finland for over 80 years before being sold in 2008—for around $300,000 a bottle. The 1907 vintage champagne was en route to the Russian royal family when the ship carrying it sank.

PEARL FIND ■ Raymond Salha and his wife were eating oysters at their restaurant in Tyre, Lebanon, in 2008, when they discovered 26 pearls inside one shell on her plate.

A TASTE FOR TOMATO

Guinness Rishi from Delhi, India, is always striving to achieve unique feats. Recently he finished off a bottle of tomato ketchup in less than 40 seconds. In 2001, Rishi personally delivered a pizza from Delhi to the Ripley's Believe It or Not! museum in San Francisco, California.

CHOCOLATE CREATIONS

It's hard to imagine wanting to consume the incredible works of art produced by Jean Zaun of Lebanon, Pennsylvania, even though they are made out of chocolate, sugar and food-coloring. Jean worked as a candy coater in the family confectionery business, but now makes edible copies of famous works of art and eerily lifelike three-dimensional reproductions, including a pair of boots worn by Vincent van Gogh and a white-chocolate deer skull with antlers that look remarkably real.

FANTASTIC FOOD

www.ripleys.com

Ripley's—
Believe It or Not!®

Deer Skull

This piece was part of a three-dimensional still life for a wedding reception that looked like a forest floor. Jean used a real deer skull and then added white chocolate for the head and antlers.

CHOCOLATE BACON ■ There's a new snack on sale at the Santa Cruz Boardwalk seaside amusement park in California—chocolate-covered bacon. The unusual combination was created by fourth-generation candy-maker Joseph Marini III in the belief that most people love bacon and most people also love chocolate.

108 VARIETIES ■ A restaurant in Mindoro, Wisconsin, serves more than 100 different types of burger. Located on Highway 108, Top Dawg's, run by Paul and Sue Kast, offers 108 burgers on its menu, including the Ginza Burger (made with teriyaki sauce and water chestnuts). The owners are even printing T-shirts for those who can eat their way through all 108—not in one sitting!

CRAB CAKE ■ Chef Fred Bohn of Dover, Delaware, spent nine hours cooking a giant crab cake that weighed in at 235 lb (106.5 kg). The crab cake was cooked in a 3-ft (90-cm) rotisserie-style pan and was later divided into 600 crab sandwiches.

SEEING DOUBLE ■ A restaurant in Yiwu, China, is run by two couples in which both the man and the woman of one couple is the identical twin of the man and the woman in the other. The twin brothers married the twin sisters in 2005, leading to confusion for their customers, who could not understand how the same couple could work for 21 hours every day.

WINE-TASTING ■ In May 2008, the British pub chain J.D. Wetherspoon conducted a synchronized wine-tasting in its inns across the U.K.—and 17,540 people turned up to drink a free glass of Coldwater Creek Chardonnay.

LUCKY TIP ■ In February 2008, a customer presented a racehorse, named Mailman Express, to 71-year-old waitress A.D. Carrol of Houston, Texas, to thank her for good service.

SHARP COOKIE ■ Fifteen-year-old Girl Scout Jennifer Sharpe from Dearborn, Michigan, sold 17,328 boxes of her scout group's signature cookies in 2008 by setting up shop daily on a street corner.

Van Gogh's Boots

These boots are based on a pair depicted in one of Van Gogh's paintings. Jean used a pair of worn work boots as molds, welding the parts together with dark chocolate.

SUPER GRAPES ■ The Kagaya Inn at Ishikawa, Japan, sells grapes the size of table tennis balls for $26 each. The tomato-colored Ruby Roman grapes, which have been under development since 1994 in a state-led project, are so sought after that a single bunch—containing around 35 grapes—sold for $910 in August 2008.

DATE PLATE ■ In July 2008, organizers of the Liwa Date Festival at Abu Dhabi in the United Arab Emirates displayed a vast plate piled with 4,410 lb (2,000 kg) of dates. The oval-shaped steel plate, which was fitted with 15 carrying handles, measured 33 x 6½ ft (10 x 2 m).

BABY RICE ■ Naruo Ono, owner of Yoshimiya, a rice shop in Fukuoka, Japan, sells baby-shaped bags of rice that proud parents can send to friends and relatives as birth announcements. The bags, known as Dakigokochi, are custom made to feature the newborn's face and to weigh the exact amount as the baby.

BRIDAL CAKE ■ After ten years of marriage, Chidi and Innocent Ogbuta of Dallas, Texas, renewed their vows in style—accompanied by a 5-ft (1.5-m) wedding cake made into a life-size model of Chidi in her bridal dress. The $6,000 butterscotch cake took five weeks to create and was made from 2 gal (7.5 l) of amaretto liqueur, 50 lb (23 kg) of sugar and 200 eggs. The cake bride's dress was made of icing and the head and arms were of polymer clay. The end result weighed a whopping 400 lb (180 kg) and it needed four men to lift it into the wedding venue.

HAPPY MEAL ■ Mother-of-two Juliet Lee from Germantown, Maryland, can eat seven chicken wings, 1 lb (450 g) of nachos, three hot dogs, two pizzas and three Italian ice creams in just over seven minutes.

BEEF BARBECUE ■ Around 1,250 people grilled 26,400 lb (12,000 kg) of beef in Montevideo, Uruguay, in April 2008. The grill was nearly one mile long and firefighters lit more than six tons of charcoal to barbecue the beef.

TEARLESS ONION ■ Scientists from New Zealand and Japan have created an onion that doesn't make you cry when you cut it. Using gene-silencing technology, they managed to insert DNA into onions, creating a sequence that switches off the tear-inducing gene in the onion so that it doesn't produce the enzyme that makes us cry.

CHOCOLATE FERRARI ■ A full-size Ferrari Formula One car was unveiled in Italy in 2008—made entirely from chocolate. Confectioners spent more than a year making the $24,000 car out of 4,405 lb (2,000 kg) of Belgian chocolate, but at a Ferrari-owners' club party in Sorrento it was smashed up with hammers and handed out to guests who took bits home in bags.

BEER BATH ■ At the Chodovar Beer Spa in the Czech Republic, guests take soothing, hot, 20-minute baths in dark beer. The beer yeast is believed to be beneficial to the skin.

BLACK MARKET ■ A single black watermelon fetched $6,100 at an auction in Japan in August 2008. The sought-after 17-lb (7.7-kg) premium Densuke watermelon—grown on the northern island of Hokkaido—was one of just 65 from the first harvest of the season.

SCOTCH EGG ■ A London, England, hotel chef created a huge Scotch egg that weighed 13 lb 10 oz (6.2 kg). Lee Streeton prepared the dish from an ostrich egg weighing 3 lb 12 oz (1.7 kg), sausage meat, haggis and breadcrumbs. The egg alone took one and a half hours to boil and the entire cooking process took eight hours.

BIG BOX ■ British chocolatier Thorntons unveiled a box of chocolates in London's Leicester Square in April 2008 that weighed 4,805 lb (2,180 kg). The giant box was 16 ft 6 in (5 m) high, 11 ft 6 in (3.5 m) wide and contained more than 222,000 chocolates.

LATE SUPPER ■ A Canadian couple cashed their coupon for a free dinner at a Canton, Ohio, restaurant—15 years after receiving it. For its grand opening in 1993, Nicky's Restaurant had released balloons with cards attached offering a free dinner for two. One of the balloons sailed across Lake Erie and landed in the backyard of Margaret and Ken Savory in Waterford, Ontario, but ill health prevented them from taking up the offer until August 2008.

Sticker Art

Barry Snyder of Erie, Colorado, creates 4-ft-sq (0.4-sq-m) mosaic artworks using stickers from store-bought fruits and vegetables. An average mosaic takes him around six months to create and uses 4,000 colorful stickers, many of which are sent to him by friends from around the world. His work is so sought-after that an original can sell for around $10,000.

BURGER BRIDES ■ Three couples were married on Valentine's Day 2008 at the same burger restaurant in Columbus, Ohio. Flower girls threw salt and pepper packets and the cake resembled three burgers with fries and a drink.

SECRET RECIPE ■ A hotel in England's Lake District asked guests and kitchen staff to sign a secrecy clause to protect its recipe for sticky toffee pudding after a couple tried to post it on the Internet. The closely guarded recipe has been locked in a vault at the Sharrow Bay Hotel for over 40 years and only a handful of people have ever been taught how to make the dish.

MECHANICAL EATING ■ At Michael Mack's 's Baggers restaurant in Nuremberg, Germany, no humans serve the customers. Instead, orders are taken by customers pressing touch-screen computers and the food is delivered mechanically in little pots on wheels riding on long metal tracks that run from the kitchen to the tables.

NO LIGHTS ■ At O. Noir restaurant in Montreal, Quebec, Canada, customers dine in total darkness. There are no lights, no candles, and all cell phones and glowing watches must be removed.

PUNCH BOWL ■ At an extravagant party during the reign of Britain's King William III (1688–1702), the Honourable Edward Russell used the fountain in his garden as a giant punch bowl for mixing drinks. The ingredients included 560 gal (2,120 l) of brandy, 1300 lb (590 kg) of sugar, 25,000 lemons, 20 gal (75 l) of lime juice and 5 lb (2.2 kg) of nutmeg. Russell's butler rowed around the fountain in a small boat, filling the punch cups for the guests.

CORNDOG CHOMP ■ No fewer than 8,400 people ate corndogs simultaneously at the Iowa State Fair in Des Moines in August 2008.

Humongous Burger

Brad Sciullo of Uniontown, Pennsylvania, managed to eat his way through a 15-lb (6.8-kg) burger—but it took him 4 hours and 39 minutes. The monster burger—the Beer Barrel Belly Bruiser—was prepared by Denny's Beer Barrel Pub of Clearfield, Pennsylvania, and when toppings and the bun were added, it weighed a whopping 20 lb (9 kg).

ELECTRONIC TONGUE ■ Scientists at the Barcelona Institute of Microelectronics in Spain have built an electronic tongue that can determine the variety and vintage of a wine at the press of a button. The handheld device is made up of six sensors that detect characteristic components such as acid, sugar and alcohol.

SNOW BEER ■ Every year Kevin O'Neill, founder of Australia's Snowy Mountains Brewery, collects a bucket or two of the first snow of winter to fall at Charlotte Pass, New South Wales, and adds it to his next batch of beer.

FLAPJACK FLIPPER ■ Canadian TV presenter Bob Blumer, who hosts "Glutton for Punishment" on the Food Network, cooked and flipped 559 flapjacks in one hour at Calgary, Alberta, in July 2008—that's about one every 6.5 seconds.

POTATO CHIPS ■ Bernd Schikora of Vreden, Germany, has a collection of more than 2,000 empty potato chip packets from all over the world, including Europe, the U.S.A. and Asia—and in 2008 they went on display in a cultural history exhibition at a local museum.

RIB MUNCHER ■ Bob Shoudt of Royersford, Pennsylvania, ate 6 lb 13 oz (3 kg) of ribs in 12 minutes in an eating contest at Bridgeport, Connecticut, in August 2008. One competitor was still chewing 10 minutes after the contest had ended, his mouth clogged with rib meat.

MEAL TICKET ■ Takeru Kobayashi from Nagano, Japan, earned $200,000 in prize money and appearance fees from competitive eating in 2007 and has legions of female fans. Showing that he has not lost his appetite for the sport, he devoured 11 lb (5 kg) of chicken satay in 12 minutes in Singapore in July 2008.

TOMBSTONE TEA ■ The New Lucky Restaurant in Ahmadabad, India, is built around, and over, a centuries-old Muslim cemetery—with the graves located in the café floor between the dining tables. The shin-high graves are painted green, have candles on top of them and every day the restaurant manager decorates each one with a single dried flower.

FRUIT SALAD ■ In 2008, around 400 people from Swan Hill, Victoria, Australia, sliced and diced locally grown nectarines, plums, peaches, melons and grapes to create a fruit salad that weighed a whopping 6.2 tons. The finished salad was loaded into a giant fruit bowl on January 25 and then eaten the next day, Australia Day.

CRÊPE TOWER ■ In 2008, Gus Kazakos of Ocean City, New Jersey, made a French crêpe tower that stood 3 ft 4 in (102 cm) tall, weighed around 300 lb (136 kg) and consisted of 510 individual crêpes. He used 120 lb (54 kg) of flour, 140 eggs, 170 pt (80 l) of milk, 80 lb (36 kg) of chocolate, 40 lb (18 kg) of bananas and 40 lb (18 kg) of strawberries to make his edible tower and could have gone higher had the chocolate not started to melt, risking the possible collapse of the entire structure.

CAMEL SPIT ■ Chef Christian Falco from Perpignan, France, spit-roasted a 1,210-lb (550-kg) camel for 15 hours at Safi, Morocco, in November 2007. He used almost 3 tons of wood and 32 pt (15 l) of oil to cook the camel, which was big enough to feed 500 people.

HEART ATTACK GRILL ■ The Heart Attack Grill at Chandler, Arizona, prides itself in offering potentially unhealthy meals, ranging in size from the "Single Bypass Burger" to the monster "Quadruple Bypass Burger"—all served with "Flatliner Fries," which it promises are deep-fried in pure lard. Fittingly, the restaurant's waitresses are dressed as nurses.

MEAT FEAST

More than 30,000 people devoured 61,600 lb (27,940 kg) of meat—that's 2 lb (1 kg) per person—at a giant barbecue near Asunción, Paraguay, in 2008. The fires covered an area the size of a football field.

Glazed Gator

The annual Explorers Club Dinner in New York is renowned for the bizarre delicacies it offers to guests. Along with glazed and oven-roasted alligator, diners have enjoyed honey-glazed tarantula, mealworms, housefly larvae and rattlesnake.

RAT MEAT ■ An Indian welfare minister has advised people to farm rats for food as a way of beating rising prices. Poor people in parts of India have traditionally eaten rats that they hunted in paddy fields, but Vijay Prakesh says rich people should also sample rat meat, which he claims is full of protein and tastes even better than chicken.

PRISON FOOD ■ Convicted murderers staff a luxury Italian restaurant that is located behind walls 60 ft (18 m) high inside the 500-year-old top security Volterra Prison in Tuscany, Italy. The chefs, waiters and even the pianist are all inmates, and every customer has to undergo strict security checks.

HEAVENLY FEAST ■ Phuljharia Kunwar, an 80-year-old widow from Bihar, India, spent $37,500 on a two-day feast for 100,000 villagers in 2008 in the hope that her display of generosity would please the gods and secure a place for her in heaven.

VAMPIRE CAFÉ ■ A restaurant in Tokyo, Japan, has a vampire theme. The Vampire Café is decorated with blood-red walls, as well as skulls, crosses and black coffins dripping with red candle wax. Many of the dishes are served in a similar style, including a Dracula dessert that comes with crucifix biscuits.

SPEEDY SANDWICH ■ Mexican caterers prepared a "torta" sandwich 144 ft (44 m) in length in just five minutes at Mexico City in 2008. The quick-fire sandwich, each section of which had a different flavor, weighed a staggering 1,320 lb (600 kg) and contained 30 ingredients. It featured thousands of pieces of bread, lettuce, onion and tomato mixed with hundreds of gallons of mayonnaise, mustard and spicy sauces.

FOOD COLLECTION ■ Volunteers for the Greater Toronto Apartment Association knocked on more than 160,000 apartment doors in the Canadian city in a single day in April 2008 to solicit food donations—and collected more than 262,500 lb (119,000 kg) of canned and packaged food for charitable causes.

BEER COFFIN ■ Chicago's Bill Bramanti has had a coffin specially built to resemble a huge can of his favorite beer. The 67-year-old paid $2,000 to have the casket painted blue and red like his beloved Pabst Blue Ribbon beer and, in the hope that he won't be needing it for a while yet, he has filled it with beer and ice and is using it as a cooler.

INDOOR STORMS ■ At a restaurant in San Francisco, customers eat against a backdrop of occasional light tropical rainstorms, complete with thunder and lightning—which all take place indoors! The Tonga Room's Polynesian theme extends to the dance floor, which is built from the remains of a lumber schooner that once traveled regularly between the city and the South Sea Islands.

FISH DINNER ■ On May 30, 2008, organizers of the sixth annual Polish Heritage Festival served up 2,552 fried fish dinners at the Hamburg Fairgrounds, New York State.

300 CHEFS ■ The West Lake restaurant in Changsha, Hunan Province, China, employs 1,000 people (including 300 chefs) and seats 5,000 customers.

ASPARAGUS SPEARS ■ Joey Chestnut of San Jose, California, ate 8 lb 13 oz (4 kg) of deep-fried asparagus spears in 10 minutes at the Stockton Asparagus Festival, California, in April 2008.

LEMONADE CUP ■ Arthur Greeno, owner of a Tulsa, Oklahoma, branch of Chick-fil-A, made a 839-gal (3,815-l) cup of lemonade in August 2008. To make the drink, 11,730 lemons were hand-squeezed, yielding 145 gal (660 l) of lemon juice, which was added to more than 1,000 lb (453 kg) of sugar, 250 lb (113 kg) of ice and 580 gal (2,640 l) of water. In 2007, he had made a 131-gal (595-l) hand-spun milkshake.

PRINGLE BURIAL ■ Fredric J. Baur, the designer from Cincinnati, Ohio, who thought up the Pringles tube, was so proud of his invention that he asked to be buried in one. So when he died in May 2008, some of his ashes were placed in a Pringles can that was buried in a grave along with an urn containing the rest of his remains.

CHOCOLATE WRESTLING

Sweet-toothed revelers at a music festival on an island in the Danube River in Budapest, Hungary, let off steam as they wrestled in a pool of chocolate provided by a local confectionery company.

TALL

8 FT 11 IN (2.72 M)
Robert Wadlow (1918–40) of Alton, Illinois, stood 6 ft 2 in (1.88 m) tall at the age of eight. When he died, he needed 12 pallbearers to carry his half-ton coffin.

8 FT 9 IN (2.67 M)
John Rogan (1868–1905) from Sumner County, Tennessee, grew rapidly from age 13 and eventually couldn't stand or walk. He got around by building himself a cart, which was pulled by two goats.

8 FT 9 IN (2.67 M)
Eddie Carmel (1936–72) from New York City made a living in carnival sideshows and movies. By the time he died, his height had fallen to 7 ft (2.13 m) because he suffered from severe curvature of the spine.

SHORT

1 FT 8 IN (51 CM)
Lucia Zarate (1864–90) of Mexico weighed just 8 oz (227 g) at birth—about the weight of a lemon—and at the age of 12 her calf was only 4 in (10 cm) in circumference, that's only 1 in (2.5 cm) more than the size of an adult man's thumb.

1 FT 10 IN (56 CM)
Edith Barlow (1925–50) from Yorkshire, England, weighed just over 1 lb (454 g) at birth and was so tiny that for the first six months of her life she had to be wrapped in cotton wool that had been soaked in olive oil.

1 FT 10½ IN (57 CM)
Gul Mohammed (1957–97), from New Delhi, India, weighed just 37 lb (16.8 kg) as an adult.

HEAVY

1,600 LB (725 KG)
Carol Yager (1960–94) of Flint, Michigan, once lost 521 lb (236 kg) on a three-month diet.

1,400 LB (635 KG)
Jon Brower Minnoch (1941–83) from Bainbridge Island, Washington, was so heavy he needed 13 people just to roll him over in bed.

1,235 LB (560 KG)
Mexico's Manuel Uribe (1965–) has shed hundreds of pounds since his 2006 peak, but has been confined to bed for years.

UNUSUAL

FOUR-LEGGED WOMAN
Myrtle Corbin (1868–1928) from Cleburne, Texas, had two separate pelvises side by side from the waist down, giving her two outer legs and two smaller inner legs.

CAMEL GIRL
Born in Hendersonville, Tennessee, in 1873, Ella Harper was known as "The Camel Girl" because her knees turned backward, a result of which was that she found it more comfortable to walk on all fours.

THREE-LEGGED MAN
Francesco Lentini (1889–1966) was born near Syracuse, Sicily, with three legs, two sets of genitals and one extra rudimentary foot growing from the knee of his third leg. So, he had three legs, four feet and 16 toes. He used his third leg to kick a soccer ball across a stage as part of his theater act.

LOBSTER BOY
Grady Stiles (1937–92) of Pittsburgh, Pennsylvania, had fingers and toes that were fused together to form claw-like extremities, leaving him unable to walk and earning him the nickname "Lobster Boy."

THE HUMAN UNICORN
Wang, a farmer from Manchukuo, China, in the 1930s, had a horn 14 in (36 cm) long growing from the back of his head.

THE HALF LADY
Born in Basle, Switzerland, in 1884, Mademoiselle Gabrielle had a perfectly formed upper body, but no lower torso and no legs.

LION-FACED MAN
Stephan Bibrowsky (1891–1932) had hair 6 in (15 cm) long all over his body, the result of the rare genetic disease hypertrichosis. His appearance led to him being known as "Lionel, the Lion-Faced Man," his mother blaming his condition on the fact that she saw her husband being mauled by a lion while she was pregnant with Stephan.

THE BEARDED LADY
A regular performer with the Barnum and Bailey Circus, Grace Gilbert (1876–1924) from Williams County, Ohio, stood 5 ft 9 in (1.75 m) tall and boasted an impressive beard that measured 10 in (25 cm) in length.

Maxine Rowson appeared as a "half woman" in the P.T. Barnum Circus, where a number of unusual human acts were exhibited in the 19th and early 20th century.

BODY ODDITY

ICE MAN

Burying yourself in ice may not be many people's idea of fun, but for Wim Hof it's all in a day's work—the endurance expert loves pushing his body to its limits and beyond (in search of a completely natural high).

In January 2008, on a cold day in New York, Dutchman Wim stood in 1,550 lb (703 kg) of ice cubes up to his neck for an incredible 1 hour and 12 minutes—longer than he ever had before—wowing onlookers and experts, who say that the human body should not be able to withstand freezing temperatures for that period of time.

Even encased in ice, Wim's body temperature remained over 95°F (35°C)—his heart rate increased to twice his resting rate to retain this warmth. Usually, when there is serious danger of hypothermia, the body starts to sacrifice fingers and toes in order to preserve blood for the important organs as bodily fluids start to freeze. Yet Wim emerged without any signs of hypothermia at all, and, incredibly, required only half an hour to fully recover from immersion in the ice.

Doctors are astounded that Wim can also climb 24,280 ft (7,400 m) up Everest —into the so-called "Death Zone"—in a pair of shorts, when most people would succumb to hypothermia and frostbite. He has also swum 260 ft (80 m) under ice at the North Pole on one breath and wearing only swimming shorts, and run a half marathon in bare feet in the Arctic Circle.

Ripley's research

Wim has been tested by medical experts in an attempt to understand his superhuman ability, but doctors can find nothing out of the ordinary about him. Some speculate that it is a result of his extraordinary mental strength and concentration—Wim has been a master of Tibetan "Tummo" meditation for years. Tummo is an ancient practice that is said to enable its practitioners to raise their body heat by the power of the mind alone, what Wim calls his "inner fire." In all the freezing feats Wim has undertaken, he has never suffered frostbite.

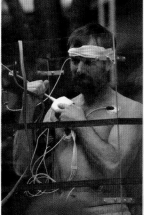

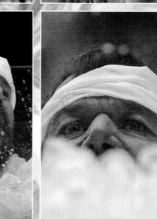

Is spending an hour in ice dangerous?

It is dangerous if you are not prepared for an aggressive impact—cold is equivalent to force, the colder the temperature, the heavier the force.

How do you combat the risks?

It is training and mind focus, and above all, a love for the unseen that helps me face the dangers.

What happens to your body in the extreme cold?

My body transforms, the core remains supplied with heat but the rest is more or less hibernating to save energy.

What further things do you hope to undertake as an ice adventurer?

I plan to break my own record of standing in ice by reaching 1 hour and 35 minutes, and to complete a marathon at the North Pole wearing only shorts.

SALIVA POOL ■ During a typical lifetime, one person will produce around 50,000 pt (23,660 l) of saliva—that's enough saliva to fill two swimming pools.

STRONG NAILS ■ Fingernails are one of the body's strongest components. They contain keratin, which is also found in rhino horns.

BRAIN CAPACITY ■ The human brain has a storage capacity of more than four terabytes—that's 4,194,304 megabytes, or the equivalent of nearly three million standard computer floppy disks.

NEW LINING ■ People get a new stomach lining every three to four days. If they weren't constantly replaced, the mucus-like cells lining the stomach walls would soon dissolve owing to the strong digestive acids in the stomach.

DREAM ON ■ The average dream lasts no longer than 20 seconds and we have 1,460 a year—that's the same as sitting through five full-length movies.

SKIN DEEP ■ In just one square inch (6.5 sq cm) of skin on the human body there lie 12 ft (3.6 m) of nerve fibers, 1,300 nerve cells, 100 sweat glands, three million cells and 20 ft (6 m) of blood vessels.

FAST GROWING ■ Beards contain the fastest-growing hairs on the human body. If a man never trimmed his beard, it would grow to a length of 30 ft (9 m) in an average lifetime.

STOMACH ACID ■ Your stomach acid is strong enough to dissolve razor blades. The stomach contains hydrochloric acid, which not only dissolves the pizza you had for lunch, but is capable of eating through many metals.

BLOOD BROTHERS ■ Ninety-six percent of human DNA is the same as the DNA of chimpanzees. The number of genetic differences between chimps and humans is ten times smaller than that between rats and mice.

VERSATILE LIVER ■ The human liver performs more than 500 functions and will grow back to its original size even if as much as 80 percent of it is removed.

LUNG SURFACE ■ The surface area of a human lung is equal to the size of a tennis court. However, unless you are doing vigorous exercise, you use only about one-twentieth of your lungs' gas-exchanging surface.

SAFE KISS ■ If a person has a cold, you are more likely to catch it by shaking hands with them than by kissing them.

SWEATY FEET ■ Feet have 500,000 sweat glands and can produce more than a pint (half a liter) of sweat every day.

RAPID IMPULSE ■ Nerve impulses travel to and from the brain at a speed of 170 mph (275 km/h)—faster than a sports car.

THIGH PRESSURE ■ When you walk, the amount of pressure you exert on each thighbone is equivalent to the weight of an adult elephant.

TASTE BUDS ■ The average human has about 10,000 taste buds—but they're not all on the tongue. Some are under the tongue, on the insides of the cheeks or on the roof of the mouth. Others—those that are especially sensitive to salt—are located on the lips.

STRONG HAIR ■ A single human hair can support up to 3½ oz (100 g) in weight. So a whole head of hair, made up of 120,000 individual strands, could support 13 tons—the weight of two African elephants.

NEW SKIN ■ You shed and regrow your outer skin cells approximately every 27 days, which means you will have nearly 1,000 new skins in a lifetime.

NECK BONES ■ A human has the same number of vertebrae in the neck as a giraffe: seven. It's just that a giraffe's are much longer.

TOOTH TRUTH ■ The tooth is the only part of the human body that can't repair itself—because the outside layer of the tooth is enamel, which is not a living tissue.

VERBAL SPRAY ■ The average talker sprays about 300 microscopic droplets of saliva per minute—that's about two-and-a-half droplets per word.

TINY VESSELS ■ The aorta, the largest artery in the body, is almost the diameter of a garden hose. However, capillaries—the blood vessels that pass blood from the arteries into the veins—are so small that each is about one-tenth the thickness of a human hair.

LONG LASHES ■ The entire length of all the eyelashes shed by a human in an average lifetime is nearly 100 ft (30 m)—that's over half the length of an Olympic swimming pool.

WATER LOSS ■ On average, you breathe 23,000 times a day and take about 600 million breaths in a lifetime. As your body is composed of between 55 and 75 percent water, you lose around 2 pints (1 l) of water a day through breathing, enough to fill an average watering can in just over a week.

HEARTBEAT ■ The adult human heart beats around 40 million times a year and in one hour it produces enough energy to lift a one-ton weight 3 ft (90 cm) off the ground.

MOUTH BACTERIA ■ There are 50 million bacteria in every teaspoon of human saliva and the number of bacteria in a single human mouth exceeds the human population of the whole of North America—that's more than 500 million mouth bacteria altogether.

CELL REPLACEMENT ■ Except for your brain cells, 50 million of the cells in your body will have died and been replaced by others, while you have been reading this sentence.

ALL-SEEING ■ Our eyes can distinguish up to one million color surfaces and take in more information than the largest telescope known to man.

HARD WORK ■ Your heart uses the same amount of force to pump blood out to the body as your hand does when squeezing a tennis ball hard. Even at rest, your heart muscles work twice as hard as the leg muscles of a person who is sprinting.

FRESH BLOOD ■ There are 2.5 trillion red blood cells in your body at any time. To maintain this number, 2.5 million new ones need to be produced every second by your bone marrow—that's the equivalent of a new population of the city of Toronto, Canada, every second.

BLINKING CRAZE ■ The average human blinks 6,205,000 times each year—that's almost 12 times a minute or once every five seconds.

LONG JOURNEY ■ In a single day, blood travels 12,000 mi (19,300 km) around the human body—that's four times the distance across the U.S.A. from coast to coast. A red blood cell can circumnavigate your body in under 20 seconds.

SUPER PUMP ■ The human heart pumps about one million barrels of blood during the average lifetime—enough to fill more than three supertankers.

BODY ODDITY
www.ripleys.com
Ripley's—Believe It or Not!®

-1933-

CELEBRATING "RING

RINGLING BROTHERS AND BARNUM

BARNUM AND BAILEY
GREATEST SHOW ON EARTH

Wowing circus audiences across the U.S.A. for more than 20 years, the Ringling Brothers and Barnum and Bailey Circus sideshow was a result of a merger between two of the largest circuses in the world, which were combined in 1919 to make the "Greatest Show on Earth." The circus traveled in 100 double-length railroad cars and employed

more than 1,200 people—it was probably the largest traveling circus that there had ever been. It followed that the new, combined sideshow was one of the biggest of its kind and the show's *spieler*, or "talker," boasted that they had "more freaks, wonders, strange and unusual people than any other traveling museum, circus or sideshow in the entire world."

At one point, there were more than 30 oddities on show. Audiences would pay to see the acts before the main event opened in the big tent and could buy merchandise from the performers, such as rings belonging to giants and authentic stories of their unusual lives. Such opportunities meant that popular acts often became very wealthy.

The Bearded Girl

Annie Jones began working on the Barnum stage at only nine months old and stayed for most of her life, becoming a spokesperson for the circus.

Dog Face

"Jojo the Dog Face Boy" was the Russian Fedor Jefticheive who performed with his hairy father at sideshows from the late 19th century and later became a popular act in his own right with the P.T. Barnum Circus. Jojo would play up to his wolf boy character by growling at the crowd, although he was intelligent and could speak five languages. He died of pneumonia in 1905 in Greece.

(1) ELSA VAN DORYSON
7 ft 8 in (2.3 m)—Giant
Born in Berlin, Germany, in 1888, Elsa Van Doryson (real name Dora Herms) was shorter than her theatrical "sister" but still towered over audiences at 7 ft 8 in (2.3 m) tall. She was so tall while still in her teens that she appeared in a German show demonstrating extremes of the body. She joined the Barnum and Bailey Circus in 1914, and toured Europe with her giant husband Werner Syre until she became a fixture in the sideshow from 1922.

(2) ALFRED LANGEVIN
Smoked Through His Eyes
Alfred Langevin was a regular Ripley's oddity, performing his strange optical act for audiences at the Odditorium from 1933 to 1940. Experts believe that an abnormality in his tear glands allowed Alfred to blow up balloons, play the recorder and even smoke a cigarette by forcing air out of his eyes.

(3) (6) (19) & (21) HARRY DOLL
The Doll Family of Midgets
Harry Doll was the head of a "family of dolls" that toured with the Ringling Brothers and Barnum and Bailey sideshow. They were real siblings born to a couple from Stolpen, Germany. Harry and Gracie began in German sideshows where they were spotted by the American Bert W. Earles, who took them to live with him in California and enrolled them in the 101 Ranch Wild West Show in 1914. Some years later they were joined by Daisy and Tiny and became a part of the Ringling Brothers and Barnum and Bailey Circus where they entertained audiences for 30 years. Eventually named the "dolls" after members of the audience described them as such, they would ride horses and sing and dance in the sideshow. The family branched out into Hollywood when all four appeared as munchkins in the 1939 film The Wizard of Oz, and Harry and Gracie played significant parts in the 1932 horror movie Freaks. One of the longest running sideshow acts in the U.S.A., Harry was born in 1902 and died aged 83, Gracie was born in 1899 and died aged 71, Daisy was born in 1907 and died aged 72, while Tiny was born in 1914 and died in 2004 aged 90.

(4) VITO BASSILE
The Vegetable King

(5) MOSSAB HABIB
Egyptian Wonder Worker

(6) GRACIE DOLL
(see Harry Doll, left)

(7) MAJOR MITE
26 in (0.67 m) and 20 lb (9 kg)
As well as being a successful draw on the sideshow circuit, Major Mite was one of the smallest munchkins in The Wizard of Oz film and played a number of other parts in Hollywood films, including the role of a thief disguised as a baby in Free Eats (1932). He died in 1975, aged 62, in Salem where he was born and originally named Clarence Chesterfield Howerton.

(8) JACK EARLE
Claimed to be 8 ft 6 in (2.6 m) tall
Joining the Barnum and Bailey Circus in the mid-1920s, Jack Earle was claimed to be an enormous 8 ft 6 in (2.6 m). Such was his imposing stature that he was recruited to play the role of the giant in the 1924 film Jack and the Beanstalk. After he stopped performing in the Ringling sideshow, Jack became a salesman and a successful photographer and poet.

(9) LIA GRAFF
Smallest Woman on Earth

(10) BARON PAUCCI
24 in (0.6 m)
Baron Paucci had a loud demeanor that belied his tiny stature and earned him a reputation as a gambler and big spender. He performed at Sam Gumpertz's show on Coney Island for 15 years, joining many other midgets in a scaled-down town called Lilliputia named after the place in the book Gulliver's Travels. When his outrageous behavior forced him to leave Coney Island, he found a place in the Ringling Circus sideshow. Baron Paucci married a woman of normal size, but the marriage was short-lived.

(11) JACK HUBER
Armless Man

(12) SUZANNE
Snake Trainer
Suzanne was billed as "the greatest of all the snake trainers!" She is seen here with a baby boa constrictor around her neck but also used to show larger snakes up to 20 ft (6 m) in length.

(13) MISS MAE
Tattooed Girl

(14) CLICO
The Wild Dancing South African Bushman
A skilled dancer, South African tribesman Franz Taaibosh was referred to as Clico because of the clicks he used in his own language on stage. He was discovered by a Captain Heston, who promoted Clico's shows in Europe before the outbreak of World War I. Clico impressed Americans who were watching and he joined Sam Gumpertz's Coney Island show before touring with the Ringling Brothers for many years. He died aged 83 in 1940 in New York.

(15) HILDA VAN DORYSON
8 ft 4 in (2.5 m)
The stage sister of Elsa Van Doryson, Hilda was born Annie Haase in 1906 in Europe. When her early showbusiness career fell flat after a staged marriage to another giant, she joined Elsie in 1926 for the first time as "sisters." They played sideshows together until 1939, and Annie Haase was performing in the late-1960s under her old stage name Kaatje Van Dyk. She was recognized in 1968 as the tallest woman in the world.

(16) DAN BREWER
Inside Lecturer
The show also featured a lecturer, who explained to the amazed audience the extraordinary sights before their eyes.

Clico

Clico's real name was Franz Taaibosh. He was a South African dancer brought to sideshow fame by a Westerner, Captain Heston. He was so called because of the "clicking" sounds of his native language, and performed with the Ringling Circus for many years.

CLICO Wild Dancing

SOUTH AFRICAN BUSHMAN

Anna Haining Bates

The circus performer Anna Haining Bates was born in Canada in 1846 and had grown to over 7 ft 6 in (2.3 m) in height when she was hired by the P.T. Barnum Circus in 1862. It was there that she met and married the 8-ft-tall (2.4-m) Captain Martin Van Buren Bates.

Barnum's Freaks

The "museum" was part of P.T. Barnum's traveling circus: from left to right are featured Laloo, who had two bodies, Young Herman with a hugely expanding chest, J.K. Coffey with the body of a skeleton, James Morris, who could stretch his skin to extremes, and Jojo the Dog Face Boy.

Hairy Woman

Josephine Clofullia was known in P.T. Barnum's Circus as "The Bearded Lady of Geneva," and had a full beard when she was only eight years old. Rumors that she was actually a man led to a court case, during which doctors confirmed that the bearded lady was a bona fide female.

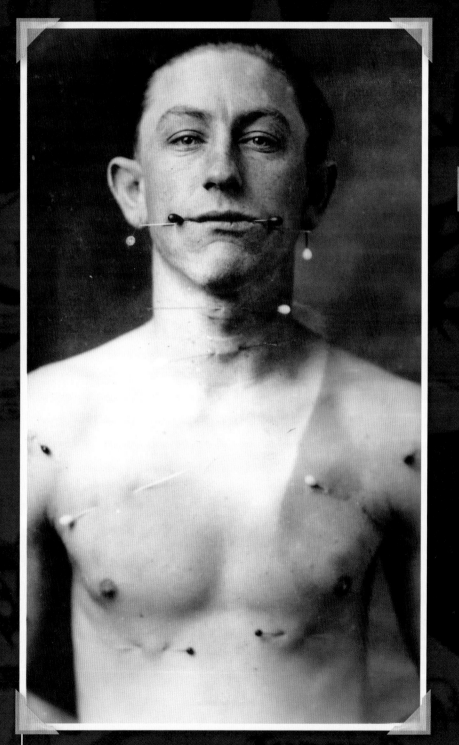

Mortado

Mortado the Human Fountain would spray water out of holes in his hands and feet. During one act, he appeared to be nailed to a piece of wood, spraying capsules of fake blood from the holes.

B.A. Bryant

B.A. Bryant was able to stick pins and needles throughout his entire body, yet feel no pain.

Alfred Langevin

Alfred Langevin could blow up balloons, smoke cigarettes and even blow out candles by forcing air out of his eyes. He was a regular at the Ripley's Odditorium.

Eko and Iko

Albino twins, Eko and Iko were kidnapped by bounty hunters working for sideshow talent scouts in the late 19th century, but were later freed and became wealthy performers for the Ringling Brothers and Barnum and Bailey Circus sideshow.

MAJOR MITE
AGE -- 18 YEARS
WEIGHT - 19 POUNDS
HEIGHT - 26 INCHES

Hairy Family

Known as "The Sacred Hairy Family from Burma," two family members had faces completely covered in thick hair. After performing for the King of Burma, they were discovered by an Englishman and were one of the attractions at the P.T. Barnum Circus in the 1890s.

Major Mite

Major Mite performed at the Ringling Brothers and Barnum and Bailey Circus sideshow and was one of the munchkins in the 1939 film The Wizard of Oz.

WRAPPED UP

Now in her late eighties, Zhou Guizhen from Liuyi, China, had her feet bound when she was young, in an ancient Chinese custom. Girls would have their toes broken and tied underneath their feet before the arch of the foot could develop, so that the toes never grew properly and the feet could fit in tiny shoes.

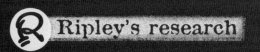

Ripley's research

It is not clear exactly how feet binding came about, but the practice is more than a thousand years old. It was initially encouraged by the upper classes, but spread across the whole of Chinese society. It was used as a way to keep women at home, as it is painful to walk with bound feet, and demonstrated how Chinese women were expected to let men do everything for them. When girls were between four and ten years old, their feet were washed, sometimes in animal blood, and the four smallest toes were broken, then bound tightly with silk. The binding was regularly removed and then tightened, in a process repeated for years. Foot binding largely died out in the early 20th century.

EYEBALL ARTIST ■ Xiang Chen from China's Hunan Province can paint, write and play the piano—all with his eye. He can hold paintbrushes as big as 4 lb 6 oz (2 kg) under his eyelid to create unique artwork and can also write amazing calligraphy with his eye or play the piano by means of holding a stick in his eye. He discovered that his eyes were different from other people's when, at age 16, he felt no discomfort even though they were filled with sand from his job as a construction worker.

TONGUE PAINTER ■ Ani K from Kerala, India, paints with his tongue and spent five months creating an 8-ft-wide (2.4-m) tongue-painted watercolor of Leonardo da Vinci's *The Last Supper*. He was inspired after seeing an artist paint with his foot. He did try painting with his nose, but found that too many other people were doing it already.

COMBOVER PATENT ■ The "combover," in which a partially bald person grows hair long on one side of the head and combs it over the scalp to the other side, to cover the bald spot, is actually a U.S.-patented invention.

TWINS UNITED ■ The annual Twins Day Festival at Twinsburg, Ohio, attracts around 2,000 sets of twins, triplets and quadruplets from all over the world. It features contests for the most alike and least alike twins.

LUCKY DAY ■ On Friday, June 13, 2008, tattoo artist Oliver Peck from Dallas, Texas, completed 415 tattoos in a single day—all of them featuring the number 13.

PATRIOTIC TATTOOS ■ Since arriving in the U.S.A. from Tonga in 1976, Sam Bloomfield of Everett, Washington, has been determined to show his gratitude to his new home. He began by painting his house red and white, later adding a blue shingle roof, and then in 2007 he got a series of patriotic tattoos. Now he has "God Bless America" tattooed under his left eye, "Land of the Free" under his right eye, a large "U.S.A." across his forehead and the Stars and Stripes over the rest of his face. The work took 15 hours over the course of three months and cost $1,500. However, that's not all—Mr. Bloomfield has more than 100 tattoos altogether, including the flags of 20 countries.

UNDERWATER ■ A two-year-old girl survived a fall into a freezing swimming pool in September 2008, despite spending 18 minutes underwater. Oluchi Nwaubani from London, England, was deprived of oxygen for three times longer than the brain can normally survive but miraculously pulled through because, in the cold water, her body entered a hibernation-like state, slowing her metabolism down to almost nothing and protecting her brain cells.

EYEBALL TATTOO ■ Pauly Unstoppable from Whiteland, Indiana, has had his eyeball tattooed—and it took 40 insertions of the needle to turn the body-art fan's eye blue. He is no stranger to body modification—he had his ears pierced when he was seven, he pierced his septum with a sewing machine needle around the age of 11 and has had his nostrils stretched to a whopping 1½ in (3.8 cm) wide.

HYPNOTIZED HIMSELF ■ Alex Lenkei from Worthing, West Sussex, England, hypnotized himself in April 2008, aged 61, and underwent bone and joint surgery on his right hand—without anesthetic. A registered hypnotist, he felt no pain throughout the procedure, which involved the use of a hammer, chisel and circular saw.

DRILL IMPROVISATION ■ A British brain surgeon used a $60 home-improvement drill to carry out a successful operation on a fully conscious patient in the Ukraine. London-based Henry Marsh was halfway through removing a tumor from Marian Dolishny's head when the power ran out. Without his usual equipment, he improvised with a Bosch cordless drill and managed to save the patient's life.

BOGUS DENTIST ■ Ecuador's Alvaro Perez successfully practiced as a dentist in Sampierdarena, Italy, for many years, despite having no qualifications and using home-improvement tools such as a power drill, pliers and screwdrivers in his surgery.

BUTTON FEAR ■ Gillian Linkins of Hampshire, England, suffers from koumpounophobia—a paralyzing fear of buttons. The sight of buttons gives her panic attacks and she can't stand to be in the same room as family and friends who wear them. Consequently, her boyfriend is allowed to wear clothes fastened only with zippers.

ORANGE SKIN ■ Michael Stenning of Sussex, England, drank so much cider—more than 8½ pt (4 l) a day—his skin turned orange.

Tiny Tattooist

A 5-year-old girl got to stick the needle in her dad at a tattooing parlor in Montreal, Canada, in June 2008 to become the world's youngest tattoo artist. Emilie Darrigade took control of the machine and added color to a bumblebee design on her father's forearm. Emilie chose the bumblebee herself, because it is her dad Dave's nickname for her.

154

BODY ODDITY
www.ripleys.com
Ripley's Believe It or Not!®

Creative Crowns

A dental technician from Utah is one of the world's best tooth artists, having illustrated teeth for more than 20 years. Steve Heward's customers can have anything they want to display on their teeth, including many famous faces from the worlds of sports, politics and entertainment. Unlike skin tattoos the dental variety are easily removed with a rubber grinder in the dentist's chair.

Left to right, top to bottom: Tiger Woods, George Washington, Abraham Lincoln, Princess Diana, Queen Elizabeth II, David Beckham, Simon Cowell, Amy Winehouse, John Lennon, Elvis and David Letterman.

Steve's tattoo of Bob Dylan adorns a client's molar.

RAVINE PLUNGE ■ Amber Pennell, a 21-year-old mother of two, survived five days at the bottom of a 100-ft (30-m) ravine in North Carolina in August 2008. Searchers eventually found her inside her wrecked pickup truck after it had veered off U.S. Highway 321 and plunged into an abyss of trees and vines.

FOX ATTACK ■ A woman jogging near Prescott, Arizona, in November 2008 ran 1 mi (1.6 km) with the jaws of a rabid fox clamped on her arm. She then drove herself to hospital after managing to pull the animal off and dumping it in the trunk of her car.

HARD-NOSED ■ Daniel Greenwood was shot in the head by a robber in Manchester, England, in 2008, but escaped death because the hard bone at the top of his nose did enough to slow down the bullet and prevent it being fatal.

FAT CHANCE ■ A 280-lb (127-kg) mugging victim in Dortmund, Germany, survived being shot at close range because the bullet lodged in his rolls of fat. Rolf Mittelhaus didn't even realize he had been shot until he reported the mugging to police two days later and the bullet fell out during a routine medical examination. It had barely pierced his skin, having been smothered by the surrounding mass of flesh.

FLESH-EATING BUG ■ Within 24 hours of brushing her hand across her face while weeding in her garden in Norfolk, England, Tracy Majoram was on life support in the hospital, her body having been attacked by a flesh-eating bug she had caught from the soil. The bug—a bacterial infection—ate the flesh around her right eye and caused her lungs and other vital organs to fail before it was defeated by powerful antibiotics.

BALL BARRIER ■ An Australian girl has been fitted with a Ping Pong ball to keep her alive. When two-year-old Mackenzie Argaet underwent a liver transplant in Sydney in 2008, the donated organ was too big for her tiny body. So to prevent her new liver from pressing against vital arteries, surgeon Dr. Albert Shun erected a plastic barrier in the form of a Ping Pong ball. The ball will remain in Mackenzie's body for the rest of her life.

FARSIGHTED ■ A human eye in Norway still has vision after more than 120 years! Bernt Aune had a cornea transplanted into his right eye in 1958 from the body of a 73-year-old man and is still using it, even though it was expected to last only five years at the time he received the transplant.

TOWEL REMOVED ■ Doctors in Japan carried out surgery on a man to remove what was thought to be a 3-in (8-cm) tumor, only to discover that the "growth" was really a 15-year-old surgical towel. He had been carrying the cloth, which had been crumpled to the size of a softball, since 1983 when surgeons at a hospital near Tokyo had accidentally left it inside him following an operation to treat an ulcer.

PERSISTENT COUGH ■ Nicholas Peake of Lowton, Greater Manchester, England, has coughed continually—up to 100 times an hour—for nearly 14 years, except when he sleeps or chews gum.

RIPLEY RESCUE ■ A bullet struck John Peterson in the buttocks during World War II, but was slowed down as it first went through his map case, which contained a paperback copy of the original *Ripley's Believe It or Not!* book.

WATER ALLERGY ■ Student Ashleigh Morris of Melbourne, Australia, cannot swim, enjoy a shower or go out in the rain—because she is allergic to water. Even sweating causes sore red lumps. She became one of only a few people in the world to develop incurable aquagenic urticaria after a reaction to taking penicillin when she was 14.

MOBILITY REGAINED ■ A double amputee is able to walk again thanks to a pair of prosthetic legs fitted with the type of Bluetooth technology more commonly associated with hands-free cell phones. Marine Lance Cpl. Joshua Bleill from Greenfield, Indiana, lost both his legs below the knees when a roadside bomb exploded while he was on patrol in Iraq in 2006, but now he has computer chips in each leg that send signals to motors in the artificial joints, enabling the prosthetic knees and ankles to move in a coordinated manner.

Artistic Nails

Decorations far beyond nail polish were on show at a nail art competition in Singapore in 2008, where a 3-D swan sits below a tree on wildly extended fingernails painted with flowers and textured with acrylics.

Loose Skin

Agnes Schmidt of Cincinnati, Ohio, suffered from a condition that resulted in a thick growth of extra stretchy skin round her thighs. Ehlers-Danlos syndrome is a rare genetic disorder that causes extreme ■ *skin abnormalities.*

STOOL TRANSPLANT ■ To treat her chronic case of the superbug *Clostridium difficile*, Marcia Munro of Toronto, Ontario, Canada, received a fecal transplant from her sister, so that the "good" bacteria in her sister's feces could fight the disease. Wendy Sinukoff collected stool samples for five days in an ice-cream container and stored them in her refrigerator before taking them as carry-on luggage on an airplane to Calgary, Alberta, where the transplant was carried out.

FACE TUMOR ■ For the past 35 years, the face of José Mestre from Lisbon, Portugal, has been gradually swallowed up by a tumor. It first appeared on his lip in adolescence but, now 15 in (38 cm) long and weighing 12 lb (5.4 kg), the tumor has spread to obliterate his entire face apart from one eye. He is blind in the other eye and eating is an ordeal, yet he has always refused surgical treatment on religious grounds.

Ripley's **Believe It or Not!**®

YOUNG ARMS

A 54-year-old farmer from Germany was given the arms of a teenage boy following a 15-hour double arm transplant operation in Munich, Germany, in July 2008. Karl Merk lost his arms in a threshing machine in 2002 and the donor boy died in a road crash. The operation was a success and within three months Mr. Merk was able to open doors and turn lights on and off.

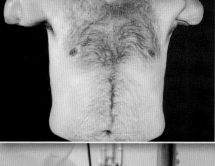

VALUABLE BUTT ■ Grandfather Graham Butterfield from Lancashire, England, has his buttocks insured for $2 million. As the official bouncer for a U.K. bed manufacturer, his job is to bounce on beds to test their softness and texture.

TASTY WORDS ■ James Wannerton from Lancashire, England, can taste words. He suffers from synesthesia, a condition that means that two senses are stimulated at once—in his case, hearing or seeing words stimulates his sense of taste. He chooses girlfriends according to the taste generated by their names. He says "Barbara" and "Helen" are nice juicy flavors, whereas "Colleen" makes him feel nauseous.

SOUND ASLEEP ■ Svetlana Yurkova from Belarus survived being run over by a train traveling 90 mph (145 km/h) in March 2008 after she fell asleep between the tracks. Tired after celebrating her birthday, she lay down in a comfortable spot and didn't even hear when an express train passed over her during the night. If it had woken her up, and she had moved, she could have been decapitated.

CAMEL WALK ■ Ella Harper of Hendersonville, Tennessee, appeared in shows as "The Camel Girl" because her knees turned backward. Owing to this deformity, she struggled to walk solely on her feet and preferred to move around on all fours.

MIRACULOUS SURVIVAL ■ A window cleaner, who survived plummeting 47 stories from the roof of a Manhattan skyscraper, was able to walk again just six months later. Ecuadorian-born Alcides Moreno from Linden, New Jersey, and his brother Edgar fell 500 ft (150 m) on Christmas Day 2007 when cables connecting their cleaning platform to the roof gave way. Sadly, Edgar was killed immediately, while Alcides suffered horrific injuries that required 16 operations to put right. However, amazingly, by June 2008 the only physical signs of his terrible ordeal were a limp and a long scar on his left leg. The death rate from even a three-story fall is about 50 percent, while anyone who falls more than ten floors rarely survives, prompting one of the doctors who treated Alcides to remark: "Forty-seven floors is virtually beyond belief."

BRA SAVIOR ■ An outdoor sports enthusiast was rescued from a German mountain in 2008 by sending an S.O.S. with her bra. Jessica Bruinsma from Colorado Springs, Colorado, had injured her ankle, skull and shoulder falling into a crevasse and was stranded on a crag at an altitude of 4,100 ft (1,250 m). However, after being missing for three days, she alerted the attention of the emergency services by hooking her brightly colored sports bra like a flag on to a cable used to transport logs. One of the workers spotted the bra and quickly told the rescue police, who adjusted their search area and found missing Jessica.

SURPRISE PACKAGE ■ A human eyeball was delivered by mistake to a hotel in Hobart in the Australian state of Tasmania in 2008. A taxi driver took the box—marked "Live human organs for transplant"—to a city hotel, but luckily a quick-thinking member of the hotel staff saved the eyeball by putting it in a refrigerator.

PLASTIC SURGERY ■ Thirty-six-year-old Angela Bismarchi of Rio de Janeiro, Brazil, has had 42 elective plastic surgery treatments.

GROWTH SPURT ■ Dr. Luis de la Cruz of Madrid, Spain, has successfully performed more than 17 operations to make patients up to 2 in (5 cm) taller. The $8,500 procedure involves implanting a piece of silicone between the skull and scalp.

NEW BLOOD ■ Teenager Demi-Lee Brennan from Kiama, New South Wales, Australia, has switched blood groups—at estimated odds of six billion to one. She was born with O-negative blood but then received a replacement liver in 2002 and she is now O-positive after, amazingly, her body adopted the immune system of the organ's donor.

FOUR KIDNEYS ■ Laura Moon from Yorkshire, England, was born with four fully functioning kidneys. She didn't discover them until an ultrasound following a car accident at age 18. About one in every 125 people in the U.K. has an extra organ.

TINY TEEN ■ A teenage girl in Nagpur, India, is shorter than the average two-year-old. Jyoti Amge stood just 1 ft 11 in tall (58.4 cm) at age 14 and, because she has a form of dwarfism called achondroplasia, she won't grow any taller. She has to have her clothes and jewelry specially made and uses special plates and cutlery to eat, as normal-sized utensils are too big. However, she does go to a regular school, where she has her own small desk and chair.

CHANCE DISCOVERY ■ An Internet photo swap between two mothers resulted in cancer being diagnosed in a toddler's eye. Megan Santos from Riverview, Florida, posted the picture of her one-year-old daughter Rowan to Madeleine Robb of Manchester, England, who immediately spotted a shadow behind the little girl's eye. It turned out to be an aggressive form of cancer, which could have proved fatal if left undetected for another week.

NAIL GUN ■ George Chandler of Shawnee, Kansas, had no idea that a 2½-in (6.4-cm) nail had been driven into his skull until his friend noticed it protruding through his cap. Phil Kern had been using a nail gun to mount lattice in Chandler's yard in June 2008, when the gun unexpectedly discharged.

EAR LEECHES ■ In 2007, doctors in the United Arab Emirates removed seven ¾-in (2-cm) leeches from the ear of an Egyptian farm worker. The man had complained of an unpleasant sensation in his head and an X ray revealed the leeches enthusiastically sucking blood from around his eardrum.

CLOSE SHAVE ■ Carlos Juarez survived a shooting by robbers in New Haven, Connecticut, in 2008—thanks to his lunch box. He held up the cooler to protect his chest and it took the full force of two bullets, one leaving a hole in the container, the other piercing a pack of gum.

TASTE BUDS ■ Sanjay Sigat, a curry chef from London, England, has his taste buds insured for $2 million. He uses his ultrasensitive palate to flavor dishes eaten by millions of people each year.

DOUBLE BLOW ■ Scott Listemann of Poughkeepsie, New York, lost his left leg twice in the space of seven months. The leg was amputated below the knee following an accident in November 2007 and then the following June the prosthetic replacement fell off while he was skydiving.

KEEN CLIMBER ■ Dottie O'Connor from Bradford, Massachusetts, was terrified of heights until she received a lung transplant—but now she's an avid climber. She is thought to have inherited the donor's personality in a condition known as cellular memory phenomenon.

FOOT REPAIRS ■ Despite having no hands, a man in China makes a living repairing flat bicycle tires—with his feet. He operates all the necessary tools, including a tube of glue and a hammer, by holding them between his toes.

ICED HAND ■ In –22°F (–30°C) weather, Irina Ivanova of Tyumen, Russia, fell onto a railroad track and her hand froze immediately to the rail. Blowtorches were used to cut away the rail, which went to the hospital with Irina still attached.

BODY ODDITY
www.ripleys.com
Ripley's Believe It or Not!®

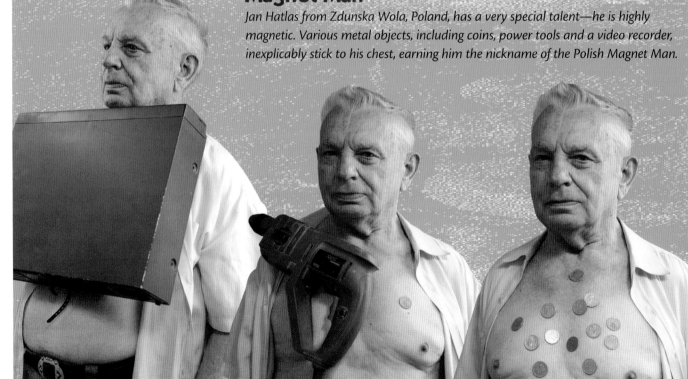

Magnet Man

Jan Hatlas from Zdunska Wola, Poland, has a very special talent—he is highly magnetic. Various metal objects, including coins, power tools and a video recorder, inexplicably stick to his chest, earning him the nickname of the Polish Magnet Man.

MINI MUSCLEMAN

At just 2 ft 9 in (90 cm) and weighing 22 lb (10 kg), Aditya "Romeo" Dev is the smallest bodybuilder in the world. His trainer, Ranjeet Pal, seen here with Romeo, has helped him develop a program tailored to developing his small muscles with care. Every day, crowds watch Romeo train with 3.3-lb (1.5-kg) dumbbells at his gym in Phagwara, India.

TREE MAN ■ In April 2008, medics cut off over 4 lb (1.8 kg) of warts from the body of an Indonesian fisherman, allowing him to see the outline of his fingers and toes for the first time in over a decade. After cutting his knee as a teenager, Dede Koswara watched helplessly as large tree-like roots began growing out of his arms and feet over the next 20 years. Eventually, he was diagnosed as suffering from a virus and a rare genetic fault that had impeded his immune system, allowing the warts to grow unchecked.

SIGHT RESTORED ■ In 2008, surgeons in Glasgow, Scotland, managed to restore the sight of a man who had been blinded in one eye during World War II. John Gray, 87, was injured during a German bombing raid on Clydeside in 1941 and was told he would never see again through his right eye, but developments in optometry have enabled a new artificial lens to be inserted in the eye and his sight to be restored.

METAL BAR ■ When Donovan McGowan had an operation in Glasgow, Scotland, in March 2008 after being hit by a car, surgeons left a 4-in-long (10-cm) metal bar inside his head. After suffering blinding headaches and a swelling on the side of his head for the next three months, he eventually demanded a scan—and that's when doctors discovered the bar.

SULFUR-RICH ■ The average human body contains enough sulfur to kill all the fleas on a dog, enough carbon to make 900 pencils, enough iron to make a 3-in (7.6-cm) nail, enough potassium to fire a toy cannon, enough fat to make seven bars of soap, enough phosphorus to make 2,200 matchheads and enough water to fill a 10-gal (38-l) tank.

PROTRUDING HEART ■ A boy in China has his heart growing on the outside of his stomach. The heart of four-year-old Zhang Weiyuan from Hetai Village, Panjing, is covered with just a thin layer of skin, under which it can clearly be seen beating. His parents have to wrap him in extra clothes to protect his protruding heart.

NO HEART ■ Fourteen-year-old D'Zhana Simmons from Clinton, South Carolina, lived for four months in 2008 without a heart. Treated in Miami for an enlarged heart that was too weak to pump blood efficiently, she underwent a heart transplant, but when the new organ failed to work properly, she survived for 118 days on nothing more than artificial heart pumps until she was finally able to receive a second, successful transplant.

LIVING ZOMBIE

One of the undead is alive and well in Montreal, Canada. Rick, known simply as "Zombie," is covered from head to toe in corpse-like tattoos, complete with a skull etched on his face, a detailed spine down his back and brains painted onto his head. His amazing body-art took more than 24 hours to complete and cost almost $7,000.

HORROR WEDDING ■ Horror movie fans Tracy Fox and Nick Adams were married at a Waterbury, Connecticut, tattoo parlor on Halloween 2008. They sealed their bond by having their knuckles tattooed with significant words—she chose "werewolf" and he chose "wormfood," because he says everyone will be wormfood someday. The couple wore horror movie costumes and were married by a justice of the peace dressed as a witch. Naturally, the wedding cake was in the shape of a black cat.

VOLCANO FALL ■ Snowmobiler John Slemp from Damascus, Oregon, escaped with just leg injuries after falling 1,500 ft (457 m) down the inside of a volcano crater in 2008. He had been climbing the active Mount St. Helens in Washington State with his son and a friend when a cornice overhanging the crater collapsed. After plunging to the bottom, he tried to climb back up, only to be thwarted by an avalanche. Instead, he headed for a steam vent and kept warm while awaiting rescue.

Tattoo Hero

This heavily tattooed chest belongs to one of the pioneers of tattoo art. Charles Wagner was born in Germany in 1875 but later moved to New York, where he began his career by putting sailors under the needle. His designs were hugely influential and he also helped to invent the first electrical tattooing machine.

HUMAN SPIDER ■ Makaya Dimbelelo from Angola is known as the Human Spider. He can squeeze his entire body through the head of a tennis racket.

EXPENSIVE HOBBY ■ Since 2001, Don McClintock from Christchurch, New Zealand, has spent $70,000 on tattoos covering his entire body except the tops of his feet and his inner thighs. He started his body-art obsession by having the names of his children tattooed around his neck and it took off from there.

ELECTRIC SHOCK ■ In May 2008, Sam Cunningham of Wigan, England, survived an electric shock from a 25,000-volt power line that catapulted him from a bridge on to a railway track below when the steel toe caps in his boots attracted a charge from overhead power cables. He had been retrieving a rugby ball.

LAUGHING GIRL ■ A curious medical condition has caused a Chinese girl to laugh non-stop for more than 12 years. Xu Pinghui from Chongqing was stricken by a fever at the age of eight months, and ever since then she has been laughing uncontrollably. Her worried parents say that when she was two she even lost her ability to speak and could only laugh.

MOUTH EXIT ■ A former U.S. marine had his appendix removed in 2008—through his mouth. Jeff Scholtz underwent the groundbreaking procedure at a hospital in San Diego, California, where doctors used a flexible tube to thread miniature surgical instruments down the 42-year-old's throat to his stomach. A tiny incision was made in the stomach wall to reach the appendix, which was then cut away, pulled back into the stomach and out through the throat. Whereas patients given conventional appendectomies through the abdomen can spend up to a week in hospital, Scholtz was back at work two days later and doing sit-ups 24 hours after that.

LOST IN TRANSLATION ■ Vince Mattingley of Hertfordshire, England, spent 26 years proudly showing off a tattoo on his chest that he thought was his name in Chinese writing. However, on a visit to Thailand he discovered that the symbols actually spelled out Coca-Cola!

TWO FACES ■ As a result of his facial deformities, Bob Melvin from Lancaster, Missouri, was known as "The Man With Two Faces." As a child he was barred from attending school because of his appearance, which was subsequently found to be caused by neurofibromatosis, a disorder that causes the spontaneous growth of fibrous tumors.

POOP FACIAL ■ A trendy spa in New York is offering a facial made with bird droppings. The main ingredient in the "geisha facial" is sterilized, powdered nightingale droppings, which are mixed with water and rice bran before being brushed on the face. The method was originally used to remove the thick, lead-based makeup that geishas wore, hence the name.

ACCENT CHANGE ■ Richard Murray from Hereford, England, spoke with a broad Birmingham accent until he suffered a stroke in 2005. When he regained the power of speech after the stroke, he found that he was now talking in a French accent and doctors don't know whether his English accent will ever return.

NOSE INSURED ■ Leading European winemaker and taster Ilja Gort insured his nose for $8 million in 2008. He took out the policy after hearing about a man who lost his sense of smell in a car accident. Under the terms of his policy, Gort is not allowed to ride a motorbike, take up boxing or be a knife-thrower's assistant. The bearded Dutchman must also visit only experienced barbers who will keep their razors steady near his nose.

HIT DVD ■ Barry McRoy was saved from a shooting in Walterboro, South Carolina, by a DVD in his jacket pocket that stopped the bullet.

AMAZING ESCAPE ■ Ryan Lipscomb of Seattle, Washington, is one of the few people alive who can describe what it feels like to have a truck run over your head. He was riding his bicycle when it collided with a truck. As he fell off and landed in the street, the truck rolled over his head, mangling his cycling helmet. Incredibly, he escaped with just a headache and a stiff neck.

EAU DE SPIT ■ Customers at Harvey Nichols, a leading British store, are paying more than $150 for a French perfume called Secretions Magnifiques that smells of blood, sweat and spit.

Leg Language

T.D. Rockwell from San Francisco, California, displayed 25 different languages in tattoos on his legs. His right leg included Chinese, Japanese, English, Hebrew, Aramaic and Greek, and his left leg featured German, Danish, French, Swedish, Icelandic, Finnish, Spanish, Italian, Portuguese, Russian, Czech, Hungarian, Polish, Persian, Turkish and Arabic!

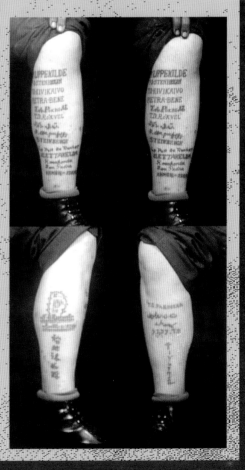

Masculine Mother

Thomas Beattie of Bend, Oregon, became the first man ever to become pregnant, giving birth to a baby girl in June 2008. Beattie was born a woman and underwent gender reversal surgery ten years ago, but was able to complete a regular pregnancy despite years of male hormones that enabled him to grow a beard.

SURROGATE TWINS ■ A 51-year-old Brazilian woman gave birth to her own grandchildren in 2007. Rosinete Serrao acted as surrogate mother for her daughter Claudia and produced twin boys.

SIGNIFICANT BIRTHS ■ In neighboring states in the U.S.A., two babies were born at precisely 8.08 a.m. on 8/8/08, amazingly also weighing 8 lb 8 oz. Xander Jace Riniker, the eighth grandchild for his mother's parents, was born in St. Luke's Hospital, Cedar Rapids, Iowa, while Hailey Jo Hauer made her arrival into the world at Lake Region Hospital, Minnesota. Xander's father said that eight had never before been his lucky number!

DISTANT TRIPLETS ■ A set of triplets in California were born 13 years apart. In 1992, Debbie Beasley of Santa Rosa gave birth to twins Jeffrey and Carleigh, conceived through IVF. The remaining embryos that resulted from her fertility treatment were frozen, and then, in 2004, she and husband Kent had those six embryos thawed and implanted. The following year one of the embryos developed and Debbie gave birth to a healthy baby, named Lania.

EARLY BIRD ■ For two years in a row—January 1, 2007 and 2008—Becky Armstrong gave birth to the first baby of the year at Gettysburg Hospital in Gettysburg, Pennsylvania.

BIG BABY ■ In September 2007, Tatyana Barabanova, from the Altai region of Russia, gave birth by cesarean section to her 12th child —and was stunned to find that baby Nadia weighed in at a whopping 17 lb (7.7 kg), making her one of the heaviest babies ever born. Nadia's father was speechless when he saw the size of his newest daughter. The average weight for a healthy newborn baby is around 7 lb (3 kg).

IDENTICAL QUADS ■ Korie and Scott Hulford of Seattle, Washington, had identical quadruplets in 2002—thought to be one of only 27 sets living in the world at the time.

SIGNIFICANT DAY ■ Lila Debry-Martin of Kingston Peninsula, New Brunswick, Canada, gave birth to triplets on August 10, 2000—three years to the exact day after she had given birth to twins.

UNUSUAL SET ■ In 2008, a woman from Belcamp, Maryland, gave birth to a rare set of quadruplets in which three of the four boys were identical. Two embryos had been implanted into the mother, and both had been fertilized. One of them split, then split again to create the identical triplets.

YAM BOOST ■ The Yoruba tribe of Nigeria has the highest incidence of twins in the world, which they attribute to eating a certain type of yam that contains high levels of a substance similar to the hormone estrogen.

SECOND TRIPLETS ■ In 2000, Crystal Cornick of Baltimore, Maryland, defied odds of about 1 in 50 million to give birth to her second set of triplets in less than two years.

RARE QUADS ■ Karen Jepp of Calgary, Alberta, Canada, gave birth to naturally conceived identical quadruplets in August 2007—a one in 13 million chance! She had her daughters Autumn, Brooke, Calissa and Dahlia by cesarean section at a hospital in Great Falls, Montana, with each weighing over 2 lb (1 kg).

FERTILE STATES ■ American women are more likely to give birth to triplets if they live in Nebraska or New Jersey. Both states have a percentage of triplets that is twice the national average.

STAGGERED BIRTH ■ Joanne March of Kelowna, British Columbia, Canada, gave birth to triplets over an incredible period of 45 days in 1993.

ARNIE'S ARMY ■ Three sets of triplets— three girls and six boys—were born in the space of eight hours on May 4, 2005, at Arnold Palmer Hospital in Orlando, Florida.

MATERNITY MARCH ■ In 1993, during a three-day walk in which she traveled 62 mi (100 km), Bernadette Obelebouli of the Congo, gave birth to triplets—one each day—in three different villages.

Triple Luck

A couple from Peterborough, England, got more than they bargained for when new mother Carmela Testa gave birth to identical triplets—Olivia, Gabriella and Alessia—in the hospital where she normally works as a midwife. You are 100 times more likely to be hit by lightning than give birth to naturally conceived identical triplets.

WHAT ARE THE ODDS?

Twins	1 in 90
Identical twins	1 in 285
Triplets	1 in 8,100
Quadruplets	1 in 729,000
Twins with different color skin	1 in 1 million
Identical triplets	1 in 5 million
Identical quads	1 in 13 million
Double set of identical twins	1 in 25 million
Quintuplets	1 in 65 million
Sextuplets	1 in 4.7 billion

Septuagenarian Mom

Omkali Charan Singh became the oldest mother in the world when she gave birth to twins, a boy and a girl, on June 27, 2008, in Uttar Pradesh, India, at the ripe old age of 70. Despite being old enough to be their great-grandmother, she said her record-breaking title meant little to her and that she just wanted to care for her children.

ELECTRIC MAN ■ Constantin Craiu from Buzau, Romania, has been dubbed "Electric Man" after he gave a public demonstration in which he put two wires into an electrical socket, then used his hands as conductors to turn on a lamp. He is able to touch live wires without protection and, instead of receiving an electric shock, merely feels his fingers getting warm. Doctors say his skin might be unusually resistant to electricity or he may have a mystery condition that protects his heart from shocks.

FOUR EYES ■ In March 2008, an otherwise apparently healthy baby, Lali, was born in Saini Sunpura, India, with two faces. Affected by a rare condition known as craniofacial duplication, where a single head has two faces, Lali had two noses, two pairs of lips and two pairs of eyes. Except for her ears, all of her facial features were duplicated. Her father described how she drank milk from her two mouths and closed all four eyes at the same time. The baby was immediately revered as the reincarnation of the Hindu goddess of valor, Durga, who is traditionally depicted with three eyes and many arms. Sadly, Lali died two months later.

MAGNETIC POWERS ■ Twelve-year-old Joseph Falciatano from Pulaski, New York, has been nicknamed Magneto because his very presence repeatedly causes computers to crash. At home his Xbox console freezes whenever he sits too close to it and a school awards ceremony almost had to be cancelled after a slide show started to crash because he was too near. To combat his talent for crashing its computers, the school put a grounding pad under him and gave him an anti-static wrist-strap. Experts believe his unusual powers are a result of the amazing amount of static electricity he produces.

TOTAL RECALL ■ A woman from Los Angeles, California, can remember where she was, what time she got up, what she did, what she ate, who she met and what made the headlines on any date since 1980. University of California-Irvine scientists found they could give Jill Price a date at random and within seconds she could tell them what day of the week it was, what she did and other key events of the day. However her memory is not photographic. When asked to close her eyes, she could not remember what clothes the researchers were wearing.

MINI MOM ■ Although she is only 29 in (74 cm) tall, 18-year-old Meena Dheemar of India, gave birth to a full-size, healthy baby in the state of Madhya Pradesh in April 2008.

PARALLEL PATHS ■ Identical twins Doris McAusland and Dora Bennett from Madison, Wisconsin, met their husbands at the same church group, got married on the same day, each had one son, retired from the same cafeteria job, had their hysterectomies together, and both hate anchovies! In more than 80 years they have only once been seen wearing different outfits—when they had different shoes on.

BROKEN LEG ■ Welsh senior Roy Calloway was amazed to learn that he had been living with a broken leg for half a century. He smashed his right leg in a motorbike crash in 1958, spending six months in traction and two years on crutches. However, although he remained in pain, he attributed it to the side-effects of the treatment. Then, in 2008, an X ray revealed that the leg had never actually healed and was in fact still broken.

WEIGHT LOSS ■ By steady dieting, Manuel Uribe of Monterrey, Mexico, lost 574 lb (260 kg)—in just over two years. At one point, due to constant over-eating, he weighed 1,257 lb (570 kg), which is the weight of seven fully grown men.

NO LAUGHING MATTER ■ Kay Underwood from Leicestershire, England, collapses whenever she starts giggling. Kay, who once collapsed more than 40 times in a single day, suffers from cataplexy—a muscular weakness triggered by emotion. Victims are often left paralyzed for several minutes, although they can still hear what is going on around them.

TOE DIAL ■ In May 2008, a man from Walton Beach, Florida, got both his arms stuck in an industrial press and was rescued after shaking his belt-clipped cell phone to the floor and dialling for help with his toes.

GLUE REPAIR ■ New York surgeons have repaired a little girl's damaged brain with superglue. Ella-Grace Honeyman, from Norfolk, England, was born with vein of Galen malformation—a rare condition that causes tiny holes in the brain's main blood vessels. After blood seeped through the openings and flooded her skull cavity, she was given just months to live until U.S. surgeons injected an organic adhesive into the holes and managed to plug them successfully.

THE LONG AND SHORT OF IT

3.08 in (7.8 cm)	**Eyebrow hair**	In 2004, Frank Ames of Saranac, New York, had eyebrow hair measuring 3.08 in (7.8 cm) long
3.5 in (8.9 cm)	**Nose**	Mehmet Ozyurek from Artvin, Turkey, had a 3.5-in (8.9-cm) long nose
3.74 in (9.5 cm)	**Tongue**	Stephen Taylor from the U.K. has a tongue that is 3.74 in (9.5 cm) long
4 in (10.2 cm)	**Calf**	At age 12 in 1876, Mexican Lucia Zarate had a calf that measured 4 in (10.2 cm) in circumference—just 1 in (2.5 cm) more than the thumb of an adult man
6.5 in (16.5 cm)	**Leg hair**	Wesley Pemberton of Tyler, Texas, had a leg hair that measured 6.5 in (16.5 cm) in 2007
5.2 in (13.2 cm)	**Ear hair**	Radhakant Bajpai of Uttar Pradesh, India, has ear hair that stretches 5.2 in (13.2 cm) at its longest point
35 in (89 cm)	**Fingernails**	Lee Redmond of Salt Lake City, Utah, has not trimmed her fingernails since 1979 and they are now 35 in (89 cm) long
10.59 in (27 cm)	**Hands**	Somali-born Hussain Bisad's hands measure 10.59 in (27 cm) from his wrist to the tip of his middle finger
15 in (38 cm)	**Waist**	Grandmother Cathie Jung from North Carolina has a tiny, 15-in (38-cm) waist
17 in (43 cm)	**Feet**	U.S. actor Matthew McGrory, who died in 2005, needed shoe size 29½ to house his 17-in (43-cm) long feet
12 ft 6 in (3.81 m)	**Mustache**	After 22 years of growth, Badamsinh Juwansinh Gurjar of Ahmedabad, India, boasted a mustache that measured 12 ft 6 in (3.81 m) in 2004
17 ft 6 in (5.33 m)	**Beard**	When Norway's Hans Langseth died in 1927, his beard had attained a length of 17 ft 6 in (5.33 m)
18 ft 6 in (5.64 m)	**Hair**	China's Xie Qiuping started growing her hair in 1973 and by 2004 it had reached 18 ft 6 in (5.64 m) long

BODY ODDITY

www.ripleys.com

Ripley's Believe It or Not!®

SEEING EYE TO KNEE

It was from one extreme to another in London's Trafalgar Square in September 2008 as tiny He Pingping from Inner Mongolia met Russian Svetlana Pankratova, who has legs an incredible 4 ft 4 in (1.32 m) in length. At only 2 ft 5 in (74 cm) tall, Pingping, who was able to fit in his father's palm when he was born, stands just over half the height of Pankratova's legs—or just past her knees.

Big Baby

In 1936, at just three years of age, Leslie Bowles from Suffolk, England, weighed 142 lb (64 kg)—that's the same weight as many adults.

Clip Art

Believe It or Not, this delicate model of a deer is made from human nail clippings! Murari Aditya of Calcutta, India, used clippings from his own incredibly long fingernails and toenails to make these and other creatures, including bears and dragons.

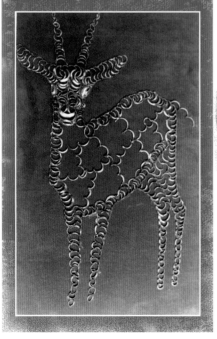

LONG LOCKS ■ Asha Mandela from Davenport, Florida, has dreadlocks that are 8 ft 9 in (2.66 m) long—that's much longer than she is tall. She started growing her hair more than 20 years ago and it would have been 11 in (28 cm) longer had she not accidentally stepped on it and broken a piece off. She uses a whole bottle of shampoo and an entire bottle of conditioner every time she washes her locks.

NAIL SCULPTURE ■ San Francisco artist Tim Hawkinson made a tiny sculpture of a bird's egg from his finely ground fingernail clippings and hair, held together with super glue. He also created a sculpture of a baby bird from his fingernail clippings.

SMILING HEADS ■ Waiters at a restaurant in Beijing, China, had the hair on the backs of their heads shaved into smiling faces to attract more customers.

CAUGHT BULLET ■ A Croatian man took a leaf out of Superman's book by catching a bullet in his teeth and spitting it out. The gunman's bullet ricocheted off Mirna Cavlovic's cheek and lodged in the false teeth of her husband Stipe, who promptly spat out the hot lead. Police say he survived the 2008 attack because the bullet lost a lot of speed when it grazed his wife's face.

KEEPING PACE ■ Lesley Iles from Essex, England, is being kept alive by a pacemaker she was fitted with more than a quarter of a century ago. Whereas most pacemakers, which regulate the wearer's heart rate, last only 12 years, hers had clocked up 25 by 2008, an occasion she marked by running a marathon and completing it in just over six hours.

BANJO ACCOMPANIMENT ■ To test the success of the brain surgery he was undergoing, bluegrass musician Eddie Adcock played his banjo throughout the operation at the Vanderbilt Medical Center, Nashville, Tennessee in October 2008. He had the operation to treat a hand tremor that could have threatened his career. Surgeons placed electrodes in his brain and fitted a pacemaker in his chest, which delivered a current to shut down the region of the brain causing the tremors.

UNIQUE CASE ■ A mystery condition, believed to be the only case in the world, has left a 21-year-old Australian woman blind three days out of every six, because her eyes shut involuntarily and she is unable to open them. When Natalie Adler's eyes are closed, she cannot see except through a slit in her left eye. For two years, doctors treated her by injecting Botox around her eyes, allowing her to see five days out of six, but that method no longer works.

TOO FAT ■ A Canadian prisoner was released early in November 2008—because he was too fat for his cell. Michel Lapointe—known as Big Mike—was less than halfway through a five-year sentence at a prison in Montreal when he was freed because his 450-lb (204-kg) frame was too big for his chair and his bed.

FLEXIBLE SENIOR ■ Wang Jiangsheng, a martial arts expert from Tianshui, Gansu Province, China, can put his leg behind his head—at the age of 83!

MOUTH STYLIST ■ Ansar Sheikh, a hairdresser from Uttar Pradesh, India, cuts hair by the unusual technique of holding the scissors in his mouth. In March 2008, he cut hair by this method for 24 hours straight.

TOE WRITER ■ Born without hands, Sujit Dawn of West Bengal, India, has learned to write by holding the pen between the toes of his right foot. He has to take school exams on a bed, but can write almost as fast with his feet as other students can with their hands. He is also able to use his toes to play musical instruments, such as the harmonium.

SILVER SKIN ■ Rosemary Jacobs from Vermont has had silver skin for more than 50 years. Her rare condition—known as argyria—began at the age of 11 when a doctor prescribed her nasal drops for a blocked nose. The drops contained colloidal silver and soon turned her skin gray.

TATTOO CLUE ■ It didn't take police long to track down car thief Aarron Evans in Bristol, England, in 2008—closed circuit TV cameras revealed that he had his name and date of birth tattooed clearly on his neck.

BOY RECYCLED ■ A 14-year-old boy from Milwaukee, Wisconsin, survived in November 2008 after being accidentally dumped into the back of a recycling truck and compacted. The boy, who had hidden in a recycling bin filled with cardboard, was discovered only when the waste-management truck dumped its load at a processing center.

FOOT IN HEAD ■ Surgeons in Colorado Springs discovered a tiny foot inside the head of a baby boy. They had operated on three-day-old Sam Esquibel after a scan revealed a microscopic brain tumor, but while removing the growth they also found a near-perfect foot and the partial formation of another foot, a hand and a thigh.

TEXT OPERATION ■ A British surgeon performed a life-saving amputation on a boy in Africa—by following text-message instructions from a colleague who was thousands of miles away. The boy's left arm had been ripped off by a hippopotamus and surgeon David Nott knew he had to remove the patient's collar bone and shoulder blade. However, because he had never performed the operation before, he relied on text messages from a colleague back in London who had to guide him through the procedure.

ARROW ESCAPE ■ A schoolboy archer from Changchun, China, had a miraculous escape in 2008 after being shot through the eye with an arrow. The 16-in (40-cm) arrow pierced Liu Cheong's eye socket and sunk more than 4 in (10 cm) into his head, being stopped only by the back of his skull. He survived because the arrow somehow missed his brain.

KEY HORROR ■ A little boy has made an amazing recovery after a freak accident left a set of car keys lodged deep in his brain. Twenty-month-old Nicholas Holderman was playing at home in Perryville, Kentucky, when he fell on to his parents' car keys, one of which pierced his eyelid and penetrated into his brain.

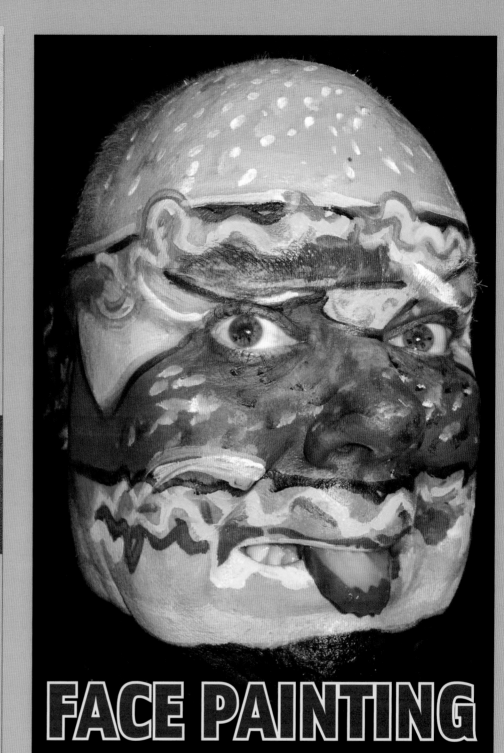

FACE PAINTING

Michigan artist James Kuhn has taken face painting to a new level—by painting his face in dozens of different designs, from Tweety Pie to a zebra. He has shown a particular appetite for food designs, painting himself as a pineapple, a burger (complete with pickle tongue) and a giant carton of popcorn, which he topped with real popcorn for added authenticity. He says the worst part is painting the insides of his nostrils.

EYELID STRENGTH ■ Martial-arts expert Luo Deyuan from Guiyang, China, can pull a one-ton car along the road—with his eyelids. He also pulled the vehicle by fastening a rope to a piercing in his neck. In addition, he can lift two buckets of water with his eyelids and stop electric fans with his tongue.

NEW CHIN ■ An Irish teenager born without the lower half of his face has been given a new chin by surgeons in New York. They took a piece of bone from Alan Doherty's hip and carved it into the shape of a jaw. Despite the facial improvement, he cannot talk yet and must feed himself through a tube.

TOILET PLUNGER ■ An Indian baby survived in February 2008 after falling through the toilet of a moving train and onto the tracks just moments after her unexpected birth. Her mother was traveling on an overnight train near Ahmedabad when she suddenly gave birth on the toilet—a simple hole in the floor—and the premature baby, weighing only 3 lb (1.4 kg), was small enough to slip through. The mother fell unconscious and it was two stations later when staff learned what had happened. A guard found the baby unhurt—despite it having spent nearly two hours lying on the track.

CONSOLATION PRIZE ■ After trying unsuccessfully to pick up a teddy bear with a mechanical crane at an amusement arcade in Skegness, Lincolnshire, England, three-year-old Christopher Air of Sunderland took matters into his own hands—and climbed into the machine by squeezing his body through the flap where the prizes are delivered. He was stuck inside for 30 minutes before he could be rescued, but the arcade owner gave him the bear to cheer him up.

EMBRYONIC TWIN ■ A nine-year-old girl with a stomach ache went to doctors at Larissa General Hospital in Athens, Greece, where they discovered an embryonic twin, which was a fetus complete with head, eyes and hair, in the little girl's abdomen.

STILL ALIVE ■ Ninety-five-year-old Mabel Toevs of Sanford, Florida, was accidentally declared dead by the U.S. social security administration in April 2007 and had to prove to the government that she was still alive in order to receive her medical insurance benefits.

TIME-CHANGE TWIN ■ Peter Cirioli was born before his twin sister Allison in Raleigh, North Carolina, on November 4, 2007, but she is 26 minutes older than him owing to the time change from Daylight Saving.

FINGERS STUCK ■ Curious about bathwater running down the drain, a two-year-old Australian boy stuck two fingers into the drain to experience the sensation and ended up destroying the bathroom of his family's house in Bendigo, Victoria. The suction dragged his fingers in so much that they got stuck and it took emergency services six hours to free him, by cutting away pipes and dismantling the bath.

WIND DRAMA ■ A six-month-old baby survived being run over by a train at Möhlin, Switzerland, in April 2008. A strong gust of wind blew the baby's buggy off a platform and into the path of an oncoming train, but while the buggy was mangled, the infant fell between the tracks and was discovered lying unharmed beneath the train.

RAPID RECOVERY ■ Ryan Ooms, aged 11, of Saskatoon, Saskatchewan, Canada, walked out of hospital just two and a half weeks after he severed his spine in a July 2007 car accident.

SISTER ACT ■ Sisters Sarah Sweeter and Deborah Lewis gave birth to daughters on the same day—July 23, 2008—in the same hospital in Homer, Michigan. Sweeter, who wasn't due for at least another week, had traveled from Kalamazoo to support her sister, but 13 hours after Lewis had her baby, Sweeter gave birth to her own daughter.

SLEEPING SICKNESS ■ A rare spinal condition prevented three-year-old Rhett Lamb of St. Petersburg, Florida, from sleeping more than a couple of minutes at a time until doctors performed successful surgery.

FEET STRAIGHTENED ■ A Filipino teenager who was born with feet so clubbed they twisted backward and upside down took her first steps unaided in 2008. Jingle Luis was treated in New York, where surgeons inserted screws into the bones of her feet and turned them bit by bit to straighten them out.

BABY DELIVERY ■ Delivering a package to an apartment building in Albany, New York, in April 2008, postal carrier Lisa Harrell had just pushed the doorbell when she noticed an open window and glimpsed a baby. Next thing she knew, she had instinctively shot out her arms and was shocked to find that she had caught the baby that had fallen through the window.

LAWN BIRTH ■ Jessica Higgins of Fullerton, California, gave birth on her front lawn in August 2008. She was driving home from the mall when little Mary Claire shocked her by deciding to arrive six weeks early. So she had the baby—alone—on the lawn while her two-year-old son carried on sleeping in the car.

CUDDLY TOY ■ A three-year-old girl who fell from a fifth-floor apartment in Ufa, Russia, in August 2008 was saved by the cuddly toy she was holding. After crawling on to a ledge and opening the window, she plummeted to the ground, but luckily landed right on top of the big, soft toy.

Twin Surprise

In July 2008, a German couple had black and white twins—a one-in-a-million occurrence. Ghanaian-born Florence Addo-Gerth and her German husband Stephan were amazed when baby Ryan was born with light skin and blue eyes, followed by his brother Leo with dark skin and brown eyes.

BIG DADDY

The wedding of Bao Xishun to 5-ft-5-in (1.68-m) Xia Shujuan was featured in *Ripley's Believe It or Not! Prepare to be Shocked* last year. When Xia later became pregnant, Bao said he hoped his son would be at least 6 ft 6 in (2 m) tall so that he could play basketball. At 7 ft 9 in (2.36 m) tall, Mongolian herdsman Bao Xishun is a father to look up to in every respect. Here he towers over his baby son, who was born in China's Hebei Province in October 2008. The little boy was 22 in (56 cm) long at birth—only slightly longer than the average length for a baby.

RIPLEY'S UPDATE

BIRD BOY ■ A boy in Russia communicates only by chirping and flapping his arms after his mother raised him in a virtual aviary. The seven-year-old was found in 2008 living in a tiny apartment in Volgograd, surrounded by cages housing dozens of birds. The boy, who does not understand any human language, is suffering from "Mowgli syndrome," named after *The Jungle Book* character raised by wild animals.

LOVE SYMBOL ■ A Chinese couple tried to name their baby @, because the character used in e-mail addresses is also a symbol of love. When translated into Chinese, it means "love him."

TOE THERAPY ■ A Chinese man bit his wife's toes for ten years to bring her out of a coma. After his wife suffered a head injury in an industrial accident, Zhang Kui of Shenyang tried to wake her by gently biting her toes because he had heard that the feet are the home for many nerves. At last in 2008 his decade of devotion paid off when she suddenly squeezed his wrist.

FAMILY SIZE ■ An Indiana couple who tipped the scales at more than 700 lb (320 kg) combined, underwent weight-loss surgery on the same day at the same Chicago hospital in December 2008. Todd Richmond, 305 lb (138 kg) had gastric bypass surgery and his 402-lb (182-kg) wife Lorie had a duodenal switch.

BRAIN WORM ■ Doctors in Phoenix, Arizona, feared that Rosemary Alvarez had a brain tumor, but instead it turned out that the thing penetrating her brain was a parasitic worm. Thankfully, the worm was successfully extracted and Rosemary made a full recovery.

SELF DIAGNOSIS ■ A ten-year-old girl diagnosed herself with Asperger's syndrome after reading a book about the condition. Rosie King from Wakefield, West Yorkshire, England, was reading *Little Rainman: Autism—Through the Eyes of a Child* when she recognized aspects of herself in one of the characters. Her parents took her to an expert who confirmed that Rosie had mild Asperger's, an autistic condition that can cause communication and emotional problems.

FROG DREAMS ■ The three things pregnant women dream of most during their first trimester are frogs, worms and potted plants!

BORN PREGNANT ■ A baby in Saudi Arabia is one of a kind—because she was born pregnant. Her mother was pregnant with two fetuses, but one grew inside the other and the baby girl was born with the second fetus inside her womb.

Beard Bonanza

Sarwan Singh of British Columbia, Canada, is the proud owner of a beard that stretches so far from his chin that it easily reaches the floor and, at 7 ft ¾ in (2.45 m) in length, is longer than most men are tall.

TIGHT SQUEEZE ■ Transylvanian contortionist Nicole Coconea has such a flexible body that she can squeeze into a 2-ft-tall (60-cm) glass bottle—and still have room to drink a cup of tea!

SNEEZING FIT ■ Twelve-year-old Donna Griffiths of Worcestershire, England, sneezed for 978 consecutive days between January 1981 and September 1983. Sneezing at one-minute intervals, she sneezed more than half a million times in the first year alone. In the later stages, her sneezing slowed to five-minute intervals.

LIFESAVER PURSE ■ When a robber fired at a Middle Tennessee State University student in November 2008, the student's oversized purse stopped the bullet and saved her life. The bullet was found inside Elizabeth Pittenger's purse beside a small case that had also been punctured. She herself was unhurt.

ROLLER LIMBO ■ Nine-year-old Zoey Beda of Oakdale, Wisconsin, can roller-skate backward under a bar that's just 7 in (18 cm) high—that's about the height of three tennis balls stacked on top of each other.

MASS MASSAGE ■ In Taiwan in July 2008, 1,008 reflexologists performed simultaneous foot massages lasting 40 minutes on a total of 1,008 tourists from all over Asia.

FAMOUS BEARD ■ In 2008, wisps of hair from Charles Darwin's beard went on display at London's Natural History Museum—126 years after his death. The hairs are thought to have been collected from the famous naturalist's study desk by his family, then wrapped in tissue paper and preserved for generations in a box.

BUY-A-BODY ■ In areas of rural China, some families with dead, unmarried sons purchase a dead woman's body and bury them together as a married couple.

BODY PAINTING ■ To promote the virtues of a high-fiber diet, former England cricketer Mark Ramprakash had his entire body painted to depict his internal organs and to show how he would look with no skin.

HAIR SHE GROWS ■ Xia Aifeng of Shangrao, China, is 5 ft 3 in (1.6 m) tall—but she has hair that is 8 ft (2.42 m) long. So even when she stands on a bench, her hair touches the ground. She hasn't cut her hair for 16 years and it takes 90 minutes to wash.

SEVERED TONGUE ■ Suresh Kumar was admitted to hospital after cutting off his tongue with a knife inside a temple in Jammu, India, and offering it to a Hindu goddess. Doctors stitched the wound, but said he may never be able to speak again.

MIRACULOUS RECOVERY ■ Velma Thomas from Nitro, West Virginia, miraculously came back from the dead in 2008 shortly after medical staff took her off life support. Her heart had stopped beating three times and for more than 17 hours she had no measurable brain waves. Her skin had started hardening and her hands and toes were curling up. However, ten minutes after staff stopped the respirator— while nurses were removing the tubing—the 59-year-old suddenly woke up.

HUMAN BILLBOARD ■ Tattoo enthusiast Victor Thompson of Laconia, New Hampshire, has rented himself out as a human billboard. He charges $200 per square inch for companies to advertise their products and services with tattoos on his skin. He has also had his head tattooed to resemble the helmets worn by his favorite football team, the New England Patriots.

NO HANDS ■ A teacher in China has won a distinction award for writing a thesis—despite having no hands. Ma Fu Xing from Qinghai Province lost both his hands in a fire when he was four months old and, after first using his toes to write, spent four years mastering the art of holding a pen with the stumps of both hands. When he became a teacher, he also had to learn the art of writing with chalk on a blackboard.

LODGED BULLET ■ Two days after being shot during an attempted robbery, 74-year-old E.T. Strickland from Riviera Beach, Florida, was back at work—with the bullet still stuck in his head.

HICCUP ATTACK ■ Singer Christopher Sands from Lincoln, England, hiccuped an estimated ten million times in a 15-month period from February 2007 to May 2008. He calculated that he hiccuped every two seconds for 12 hours a day, an affliction that meant that he could hardly eat or sleep.

HAWKING TATTOO ■ Science fan Jack Newton from Sussex, England, has Stephen Hawking's face tattooed on his right leg. He decided to have his leg decorated with the theoretical physicist's face after reading his book *A Brief History of Time*—despite not understanding a word of it.

KISS OF DEAF ■ A passionate kiss ruptured a young woman's eardrum in Zhuhai, China, causing her to lose the hearing in her left ear. The deafening kiss reduced the pressure in her mouth, pulled out her eardrum and led to a complete breakdown of her ear.

Bearded Girl

This young girl, complete with long beard and mustache, was a member of the famous Barnum and Bailey's Traveling Circus during the 1930s.

INSECT CLUE ■ Police in Finland trapped a possible car thief as a result of a DNA sample taken from his blood found inside a mosquito. When police inspected the abandoned car at Seinaejoki, they noticed a mosquito. The insect was sent to a laboratory for testing, which showed blood belonging to a known criminal.

FISH SMELL ■ A 41-year-old woman from Perth, Australia, has been diagnosed with a rare and incurable genetic condition that has left her whole body smelling of fish.

LIVING CANVAS ■ Belgian tattooist Wim Delvoye has sold a tattoo he did of the Virgin Mary on the back of Switzerland's Tim Steiner to a collector for $215,000. As a living canvas, Steiner must display his back at various exhibitions, facing a wall so that visitors can enjoy the tattoo.

www.ripleybooks.com
@ >>>> go to <<<<

Nose Artist

After a flash of inspiration six years ago, experienced calligraphy artist Wu Xubin of Changzhi, China, decided to dunk his nose in ink and use it to write poems, and he has been writing without a pen ever since.

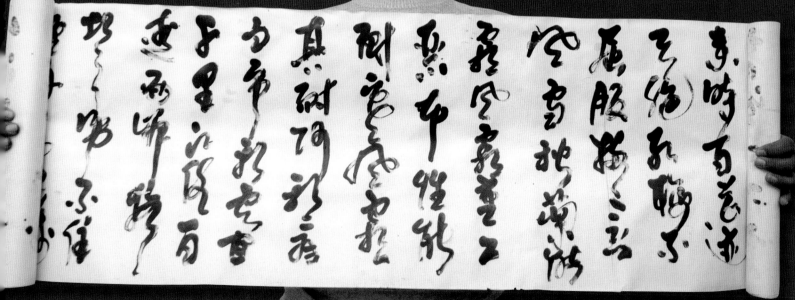

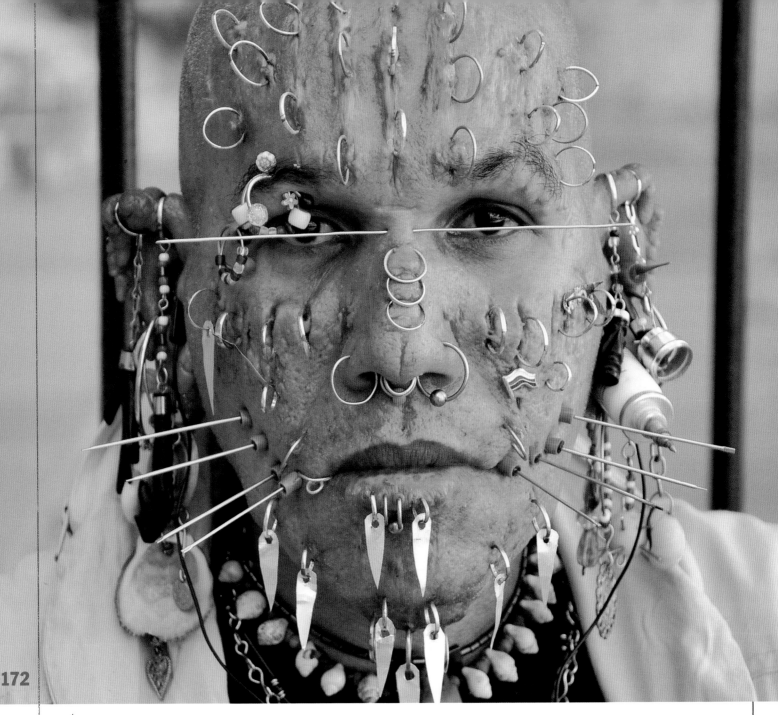

PIERCING STARE

This man from Havana, Cuba, is commonly known to have the most facial piercings of anyone in the city.

GREEN SWEAT ■ In 2008 a man in China perspired green sweat for more than a month. Fifty-two-year-old Cheng Shunguo of Wuhan City noticed that his underwear and bed sheets had turned bright green, as had the water in his shower. After extensive medical tests doctors concluded that Cheng's condition had been triggered by eating a cake that had been colored with green clothes' dye.

NAILED ON ■ Ruben Enaje of the Philippines has been nailed to a cross in 22 annual re-enactments of the Crucifixion of Jesus during the Christian Good Friday holiday.

MEMORY LOSS ■ A golfer in Hsinchu, Taiwan, was so excited after hitting a hole-in-one that he lost his memory. After jumping for joy, Mr. Wang couldn't remember hitting the ball into the hole or even where he was.

ACCIDENT CHANGE ■ As a result of suffering a stroke, a Canadian woman from southern Ontario has started speaking like a Newfoundlander. The phenomenon, known as foreign-accent syndrome, caused 52-year-old Rose Dore's voice to change so much that when she checked into a Hamilton hospital, staff assumed she was from the East Coast.

HAIRY EARS ■ Radhakant Bajpai of Naya Ganj, Uttar Pradesh, India, has ear hair 5.2 in (13.2 cm) long. The tufts, which are so long he could make two small ponytails from them, grew dramatically when he used a special shampoo.

MEXICAN PASSION ■ Jamie Sherman of southern Arizona didn't like Mexican cuisine until she received a heart transplant in 2001. After that she developed a powerful craving for cheese enchiladas, bean burritos and soft tacos. She subsequently learned that her donor, Scott Phillips, had always loved Mexican food.

LIFESAVING HANDSHAKE ■ A doctor in England saved a man's life just by shaking his hand. Essex medic Chris Britt was introduced by chance at a restaurant to Mark Gurrieri, but as the two men shook hands, Dr. Britt immediately recognized Mr. Gurrieri's large, spongy-feeling hand and big facial features as symptoms of acromegaly, a potentially deadly tumor lying at the base of the brain. The rare condition was confirmed by hospital diagnosis, enabling Mr. Gurrieri to receive treatment.

RING CAUGHT ■ As a 22-year-old woman from Sydney, Australia, fell out of bed in the middle of the night in April 2008, her belly-button ring got caught in her nostril. Paramedics managed to untangle her.

FIRST CUT ■ When 59-year-old Ukrainian-born Darka Jakymchuk walked into a Queens, New York, hair salon on December 12, 2007, it was for her first haircut in 45 years. During that time her hair had grown to 5 ft 5 in (1.65 m) long.

SUNBURN MAP ■ Barry Kwok of Hong Kong peeled an 8½-in (21.6-cm) piece of sunburned skin from his chest—in the shape of China. It took his sister 90 minutes to help him peel away the huge strip after he got burned on the beach.

SOFT LANDING ■ Jens Wilhelms of Frankfurt, Germany, survived a 25-ft (7.5-m) plunge down an elevator shaft in April 2008 by landing on a 57-year-old woman who had fallen down it the day before. Doctors say that despite injuring her further by landing on her, Wilhelms probably saved the woman's life by alerting paramedics to her situation.

SOCCER BLACKOUT ■ Jim Coan of Lancashire, England, hasn't watched his favorite soccer team, Liverpool, play in over a decade because of a heart condition that causes him to black out when he gets excited.

SNAKE GIRL ■ Teenage contortionist Nokulunga Buthelezi of Johannesburg, South Africa, has such a flexible body that, dressed in a snakeskin costume, she can bend her arms, legs and entire torso to resemble a python. Even as a ten-month-old baby she could do the splits and would often sleep with her legs behind her neck.

EAR TUG ■ The Inuit people of Arctic North America compete in tug-of-war contests using only their ears. A loop of string is placed over the same ear of each competitor. No jerking is allowed and one person must use a steady pull straight back to try and force the other to give in.

DRANK URINE ■ Brothers Meng Xianchen and Meng Xianyou survived for six days in August 2007 by eating coal and drinking their own urine as they dug themselves out from a coal mine collapse near Beijing, China.

LUCKY DEFLECTION ■ When an armed robber fired his gun, antique dealer Donnie Register of Jackson, Mississippi, threw up his left hand to protect himself—and survived because the bullet deflected off his wedding ring.

METAL MUNCHER ■ When Luis Zarate of Trujillo, Peru, complained of sharp stomach pains in 2008, doctors removed 17 metal objects—which he had eaten. X rays of his chest showed that inside him were screws, nails, bolts, pens, a watch clasp, a knife and barbed wire.

CREATIVE URGES ■ Tommy McHugh from Liverpool, England, was a builder until he suffered a near-fatal brain hemorrhage in 2001. A month later he began feeling sudden creative urges, manically filling exercise books with poetry, and he is now a prodigious artist—despite never having picked up a paintbrush before his illness.

ELECTRIC PRESENCE ■ By her very presence, Debbie Wolf of Sussex, England, causes streetlights to flicker, freezers to defrost, TVs to channel-hop and household appliances to stop working. She has to use a wind-up alarm clock, as her reaction when she wakes scrambles digital models. She says her electrical powers are strongest when she is stressed or excited.

GREAT AGE ■ When Mariam Amash of Jisr az-Zarqa in northern Israel, applied for a new identity card in 2008, it was revealed that she was 120 years old. Mrs. Amash, who has 10 children, 120 grandchildren, 250 great-grandchildren and 30 great-great-grandchildren, attributed her longevity to eating plenty of vegetables.

BASE JUMPER ■ A base jumper survived an 850-ft (260-m) fall from the top of a waterfall in June 2008 after his parachute failed. The man suffered only a suspected broken leg and pelvis, plus internal injuries, when he hit the water of the Wallaman Falls in Queensland, Australia.

ARM IMPALED ■ A woman from Manchester, England, had to be cut free with a hacksaw after accidentally impaling her arm on 3-in (7.6-cm) metal spikes attached to a statue of the Hindu goddess Kali. The goddess is generally associated with death and destruction.

BULLET REMOVED ■ When doctors in Barbastro, northern Spain, performed surgery to remove a painful lump from 88-year-old Faustino Olivera's left shoulder, they discovered that the cause of his problems was a bullet that had been lodged there for 70 years. A veteran of the Spanish Civil War, Olivera remembered being shot during the Battle of the Ebro in 1938, but had thought the lump on his shoulder was a cyst.

Amazing Acrobat

A contortionist rehearses a spine-tingling move for a show in Rosenheim, Germany, in 2007. "Mother Africa—Circus of the Senses" featured acrobatic artists from across Africa, who trained in Tanzania for four years before taking the show on the road.

Lip Tattoo

The latest craze among young people in Nanjing City, China, is to have their lips tattooed with images of heavenly constellations.

MANE ATTRACTION ■ Jean Burgess of Kent, England, hasn't cut her hair for more than 55 years. The last time she had it cut was in 1953, when she was 15, and she hated it so much she vowed to let it grow. By the time she was 30, it reached the floor, and now it is 5 ft 6 in (1.68 m) long, although she tends to wear it in a tight bun. Her hair takes 2½ hours to comb, 45 minutes to wash and 24 hours to dry, which she usually does by laying it out across her garden on a sunny day.

MERMAID GIRL ■ Young Shiloh Pepin goes bowling and has had ballet classes even though she suffers from sirenomelia, a rare condition that caused her legs to fuse together like a mermaid. Shiloh from Kennebunkport, Maine, is one of only three people in the world known to have had the condition, also known as Mermaid Syndrome, and was not expected to live after being born without many of her internal organs, but by 2008 she had survived more than 150 surgeries.

SHOCK RETURN ■ Twenty-seven years after being reported missing, presumed dead, Taiwanese fisherman Hu Wenhu stunned his family by suddenly reappearing. He had been stranded on Réunion Island in the Indian Ocean since 1981 after missing his ship home. While his family back in Taiwan feared the worst, Hu had opened a Chinese restaurant on the island and married three times.

LONG BROW ■ Toshie Kawakami of Tokyo, Japan, has an eyebrow hair nearly 7 in (18 cm) long that she hides behind her ear. A barber once accidentally chopped it down to just more than 1 in (2.5 cm), but it quickly grew back at a rate of ½ in (1.25 cm) a month.

EXTRA DIGITS ■ Haramb Ashok Kumthekar from Goa, India, has 12 fingers and 14 toes. Although he is proud of his unique appearance, it means he cannot wear a pair of ordinary flip-flops on his feet or find a pair of gloves that fit his hands in the winter.

Long Nails

Shridhar Chillal of Poona, India, grew the nails on his left hand for 48 years until they reached a combined length of 20 ft 2 in (6.1 m). The longest was his thumbnail at 4 ft 9 in (1.4 m). He constantly protected his nails, with the result that he didn't get a proper night's sleep for nearly half a century and could not risk being in crowds or hugging his grandchild. In strong winds, he would turn his body so that he shielded his nails from the gusts.

AMAZING BIRTH ■ In January 2008, Stacey Herald of Dry Ridge, Kentucky, gave birth to a baby over half her size. Stacey is just 28 in (71 cm) tall, yet daughter Makya was 18 in (46 cm) long at birth. During her pregnancy, Stacey added 20 lb (9 kg) to her tiny 52-lb (23.5-kg) frame.

BUTTER KNIFE ■ In April 2008, doctors in Vancouver, Washington, removed a butter knife that had become embedded in the head of 11-year-old Tyler Hemmert. The knife, thrown by another boy, was lodged 4 in (10 cm) deep above his right ear so that only the handle was visible. Miraculously, it only grazed his skull.

DRAIN DRAMA ■ In September 2008, three-year-old Leona Baxter survived with only cuts and bruises after being sucked into a storm drain at Chester-Le-Street in County Durham, England. Leona had been playing in shallow floodwater when she fell down the open drain, was carried 230 ft (70 m) underground along a pipe and then spat out unconscious into a raging river, swollen by torrential rain. Her father, who had frantically followed the pipe's path to the riverbank, dived in to rescue her. The sheer pressure of water beneath the storm drain had forced the manhole cover off, resulting in Leona being dragged down into it.

WRONG CHORD ■ Twenty-five-year-old Stacey Gayle of Alberta, Canada, underwent brain surgery in October 2007 to relieve a rare problem—she would have seizures every time she heard music. Her condition, called musicogenic epilepsy, was so bad that medication couldn't control them and she even had to leave the church choir where she sang.

SAFE TOILET ■ A severe phobia kept Pam Babcock of Ness City, Kansas, in her bathroom for two years. She spent so much time sitting on the toilet that she needed surgery to remove the seat from her flesh.

HOW MANY TOES?

This person has eight toes on one foot—a condition known as polydactyly, which means having extra digits on the hands or feet. These extra digits can vary from small pieces of soft tissue to complete fingers or toes with their own bones. The condition, which is sometimes inherited, affects about one child in every 2,000. The surplus digits are usually removed in childhood, but some people prefer to keep them intact.

ODD-SHAPED

BASKET-SHAPED OFFICE BLOCK
The Longaberger Company of Newark, Ohio, has its head office built in the shape of one of its trademark wicker baskets. The seven-story building is topped with two huge metal handles, each weighing 75 tons.

CAR-SHAPED HOUSE
Auto-mad architect Dan Scully built his New Hampshire home in the shape of a car, complete with two round windows as headlights and the bumper from a Volkswagen bus. Inside, old car seats provide Dan with his furniture.

VIOLIN-SHAPED HALL
The Chowdiah Memorial Hall in Bangalore, India, is built in the shape of a giant violin to honor master violinist Tirumakudalu Chowdiah.

SHIP-SHAPED CAR WASH
A car wash at Eau Claire, Wisconsin, is shaped like a cruise liner, right down to its two smoke stacks.

COOKIE JAR HOUSE
Built in 1947, a three-story house in Glendora, New Jersey, is shaped like a cookie jar.

AIRPLANE-SHAPED HOUSE
Said Jammal has built a house in Abuja, Nigeria, that has a 100-ft-long (30-m) jet airplane on the roof.

ELEPHANT LANDMARK
Formerly a restaurant and tavern, Lucy the elephant is now a historic landmark in Margate, New Jersey. The 90-ton elephant-shaped building was hit by lightning in 2006, leaving Lucy's tusks blackened.

SHOE-SHAPED SHOP
In Bakersfield, California, there stands a shoe-repair shop that is built in the shape of a 30-ft-long (9-m), 20-ft-high (6-m) shoe, complete with chain laces.

ROBOT-SHAPED BANK
The 20-story Bank of Asia building in Bangkok, Thailand, is shaped like a giant robot, and even has two 20-ft-high (6-m) lidded "eyes" that serve as windows on the top floor. The eyeballs are made of glass and the lids are metal louvers.

DOG-SHAPED INN
The Dog Bark Park Inn at Cottonwood, Idaho, is a bed-and-breakfast establishment built in the shape of a giant beagle.

BALL-SHAPED HOUSE
Dutch architect Jan Sonkie is such a keen soccer fan that he built his four-story house in Blantyre, Malawi, in the shape of a soccer ball.

FISH-SHAPED MUSEUM
The National Freshwater Fishing Hall of Fame Museum in Hayward, Wisconsin, is housed in a building 143 ft (43.5 m) long shaped like a muskie fish.

MOTHER GOOSE HOUSE
A building in Hazard, Kentucky, is shaped like a goose sitting on its nest. The giant bird's head and neck form the roof, while the windows below are egg-shaped.

STRANGE PLACES

MUSICAL HIGHWAY
A strip of road in Lancaster, California, plays the "William Tell Overture" when cars drive over it at 55 mph (88 km/h). The notes were created by workers carving grooves into the road surface.

CARS APPEAR TO ROLL UPHILL
An optical illusion created by undulating terrain means that cars amazingly appear to roll uphill at Magnetic Hill, near Moncton, New Brunswick, Canada.

SANDS THAT BARK
Barking Sands Beach on the Hawaiian island of Kauai has sand that barks like a dog. The dry sand grains emit the strange sound when people walk on them in bare feet.

WHERE DUCKS WALK ON FISH
So many carp gather at the base of the spillway of the Pymatuning Reservoir, Linesville, Pennsylvania, that ducks walk across the backs of the fish and hardly get their feet wet.

600 HAIRPIN TURNS
The road to Hana on the Hawaiian island of Maui is 52 mi (84 km) long but has over 600 hairpin bends—that's 12 sharp turns every mile, or one every 150 yd (137 m).

CLOCKS DELIBERATELY KEEP WRONG TIME
Churches in Malta have two clocks showing different times. One is correct but the other is deliberately wrong in order to confuse the devil about the time of the next service.

FIRE THAT NEVER GOES OUT
A burning seam of coal that lies 500 ft (152 m) below the surface in the Hunter Valley, New South Wales, Australia, creates a continuous column of smoke from the fire that never goes out.

CITY WITH NO CAR ACCESS
Juneau, the state capital of Alaska, can be reached only by water or air, because there are no roads leading to the city.

Electrician Alex Goodhind has spent more than $60,000 on Christmas lights for his house in the town of Melksham in Wiltshire, England. His dazzling display incorporates 120,000 lightbulbs and takes four months of preparation each year before the big switch-on.

STRANGE >> SITES

TREE HOUSE

This Christmas tree in a house in the town of Bournemouth, England, appears to start on the ground floor and go straight up through the roof. In fact, it is an illusion created by the owner, Greig Howe, who bought a 35-ft (10.6-m) tree and sawed it into three sections before placing the trunk in the living room, the middle in a spare bedroom and the top on a flat roof. He did this to impress his son Harry, who thought that the previous year's 5-ft (1.5-m) tree was a bit small.

TILTING TOWERS ▥ Completed in 2008, the 768-ft-high (234-m) China Central Television Center in Beijing tilts at an angle of ten degrees—almost twice the deviation of the Leaning Tower of Pisa. The steel-and-glass building has been designed in a series of L-shapes to enable it to withstand an earthquake measuring eight on the Richter scale. The building's two towers are connected at their summit by a right-angled bridge—an operation so delicate that it had to be carried out at 4 a.m. when the metal was at its coolest, to avoid the possibility of expansion.

DOLLAR HOUSE ▣ A two-story house in Detroit, Michigan, sold for $1 in August 2008. The abandoned house, described as "the nicest on the block" when it sold for $65,000 in November 2006, was reduced to a bargain price as a result of the U.S. housing market crash.

HIDDEN SKELETONS ▥ A house in Chicago, Illinois, changed hands three times between 2006 and 2008 before someone finally examined a bedroom and discovered the skeletons of a man and his dog.

CHURCH CONVERSION ▣ A Chicago real estate agent converted his $3-million home into a church in 2007. George Michael placed a cross on the side of his lakeside mansion and renamed it the American Church of Lake Bluff, holding services there for a handful of friends and family after acquiring a pastor's degree on the Internet.

SUMMER EXPANSION ▥ Paris's famous Eiffel Tower grows up to 7 in (17 cm) in height each year in summer because the sun's heat causes an expansion of the iron from which the landmark is made.

PLANE ON ROOF ▣ In Abuja, Nigeria, there is a two-story concrete house with a replica of a jet aircraft embedded in the roof, as if it has landed there. The plane on the roof is 100 ft (30 m) long and 20 ft (6 m) high at the top of its tail and was built by Said Jammal to please his wife Liza who loves airplanes. He hopes to build a kitchen inside the fuselage.

FOREIGN ACCENT ▥ The entire population of the tiny Pacific island of Palmerston Atoll in the Cook Islands speaks with an accent from England's West Country—12,000 mi (19,300 km) away. That's because all 63 inhabitants are descended from William Marsters, a Gloucestershire carpenter and barrel-maker who settled on the island in 1863 and who had four wives, 17 children and 54 grandchildren.

BLOOMING BIG ■ The Aalsmeer Flower Auction House in the Netherlands is so big that it covers more than 125 football fields. Eighty percent of the world's cut flowers pass through it each day, a total of 3.5 billion flowers a year.

HONEY DRIP ■ So many bees live in the walls of a stately Tudor home in San Marino, California, that honey drips out of the walls. Thousands—maybe millions—of bees have been sharing the house with Helen and Jerry Stathatos for more than 20 years, discoloring the wallpaper in the dining room and making the whole house smell sweet, like a jar of honey.

CHEEK TO CHEEK ■ The Miniscule of Sound, a nightclub measuring just 4 x 8 ft (1.2 x 2.4 m) in Hackney, London, England, holds only 14 people—including the D.J. Located in the changing booth of a disused outdoor swimming pool, it has a dance floor of 20 sq ft (1.8 sq m) and comes complete with mirror ball.

SMOKE HOLES ■ Following a ban on smoking indoors, Michael Windisch, owner of the Maltermeister Turm Bar in Goslar, Germany, cut holes in his exterior wall so that his customers could lean out and smoke without going outside.

PLAIN OF JARS ■ Scattered around the fields of Xieng Khouang Province in Laos are thousands of stone jars up to 10 ft (3 m) tall. The jars, each of which can weigh as much as 14 tons, lie in clusters, with up to 250 at an individual site. Archeologists believe the jars date back at least 1,500 years and may have been used as funeral urns or to store food.

ROOF GARDEN ■ Designed by Viennese architect Friedensreich Hundertwasser, the Waldspirale apartment building in Darmstadt, Germany, has a roof completely covered with vegetation and also has more than 1,000 windows, each of which is unique.

House Spider

A spider that was as big as a house appeared on the side of a building in Liverpool, England, in September 2008. Made from steel and wood, the 50-ft (15-m), French-designed, mechanical spider was suspended from the building as a work of art. Weighing 37 tons, the giant arachnid—called La Princess—*had sophisticated hydraulics that enabled the dozen engineers strapped to its frame to operate its eyes, legs and abdomen so that it could also crawl along the streets at 2 mph (3.2 km/h).*

OXYGEN CHAMBER ■ The lower house of the Japanese legislature has an oxygen booth in which tired legislators can refresh themselves.

MOVING HOUSE ■ Tim and Jennifer O'Farrell bought a house in the U.S.A.—and then had it shipped to Canada. The 3,360-sq-ft (312-sq-m), two-story waterfront house made a two-day, 280-mi (450-km) journey from Hunts Point, Washington, to its new location across the border on Vancouver Island, British Columbia, by barge. The previous owners had bought the Lake Washington property for $9.4 million in 2007 but wanted only the land, not the house.

LOCKER HOME ■ A German man slept in a lost-and-found luggage locker at a railway station for nine years. Every evening, Mike Konrad climbed feet-first into locker 501 at Düsseldorf station, squeezing his body into the space, 31 x 2 ft (9.5 x 0.6 m), usually reserved for passengers' suitcases. He always left the door ajar while he slept, so that he could obtain a refund on the $3 he had to pay to open the locker.

DIFFERENT TONGUES ■ The tiny Pacific island nation of Vanuatu has only 210,000 people but 110 indigenous languages.

WOODEN SKYSCRAPER ■ A log cabin in Arkhangelsk, Russia, rises 144 ft (44 m) above the ground and has 13 floors. When Nikolai Sutyagin began work on the wooden skyscraper in 1992, he added just three floors, but he then decided it looked ungainly so he added another and then just kept going...

BARGAIN BRIDGE ■ A steel bridge in Soldiers Grove, Wisconsin, was put up for sale for $1 in 2007. The defunct Kickapoo River Bridge was built in 1910 but hadn't carried traffic since 1976 because of its deteriorating condition.

HIGH LIFE ■ The blood of people living on the 3-mi-high (4.8-km) Tibetan Plateau is pumped through their bodies at twice the rate of lowlanders.

Fancy a Dip?

A swimming pool at a resort in Algrarrobo, near Santiago, Chile, is so huge that small boats often sail in it. The pool, which took five years to build, measures 3,323 ft (1,013 m) long, covers 20 acres (8 ha) and holds 66 million gallons of water—and the water is so clear you can see the bottom, even at the 115-ft (35-m) deep end.

LUCKY NUMBER ■ Federal Hill, a plantation house in Bardstown, Kentucky, was built with 13 front windows, 13 steps on its stairs, 13 mantles, 13-ft-high (4-m) ceilings and 13-in-thick (33-cm) walls.

LOST LANGUAGE ■ The last two people in the world who speak the Apayan Zoque language of Apayan, Tabasco, Mexico, are two men in their seventies, who refuse to speak to each other.

TREE HOUSE ■ David Csaky spent two years living in a tree house in Seattle, Washington. He lived 30 ft (9 m) above the ground on a 300-sq-ft (28-sq-m) self-made platform, which was accessible by a ladder counter-weighted with sandbags on pulleys. He fitted his tree house with a tent, wood stove, three chairs, shelves and a counter and shared it with various pets, including a rat, a ferret and a squirrel.

DOG CEMETERY ■ Tuscambia, Alabama, has a cemetery that is reserved exclusively for raccoon hunting dogs.

LAST SPEAKER ■ Eighty-three-year-old Soma Devi Dura of Nepal is the last fluent speaker of the Dura language on the planet. To communicate with her husband, children and grandchildren, she has to use other languages.

OLDEST BEEHIVES ■ Archeologists in Israel have found beehives that are around 3,000 years old. The discoveries in the ruins of the city of Rehov are thought to be the oldest intact beehives ever located.

ISLAND SALE ■ The owners of the European Channel Island of Herm, which measures 1.5 mi (2.4 km) long and 0.5 mi (0.8 km) wide, and has a population of just 50, put the entire island up for sale in 2008 at a price of $30 million.

CONCRETE TREE ■ Architect Madame Hang Nga has designed a guesthouse in the resort of Da Lat, southern Vietnam, which looks like a tree but is actually made of concrete. The five-roomed residence is known locally as the Crazy House.

FIRST CONTACT ■ The Metyktire tribe, located in a remote area of the Brazilian Amazon some 1,200 mi (1,930 km) from Rio de Janeiro, made its first contact with the outside world in May 2007. The isolation ended when two Metyktire members suddenly appeared in the village of a neighboring tribe.

STEPFATHER INCLUDED ■ An apartment was put up for sale in a sought-after district of Stockholm, Sweden, in August 2008—complete with live-in stepfather. The woman who inherited a share of the apartment after her mother died wanted to sell it, but her stepfather refused to move out.

BOARD FENCE

Hawaiian Donald "D.J." Dettloff is a surfer with a big imagination. Almost 20 years ago, with a storm threatening Maui, he tied his surfboards up with wire to prevent them from being blown away, giving him the inspiration for what has become a local landmark—a fence made entirely of surfboards. Over the years it has grown to include 700 boards, with many donated by friends and strangers, who all wanted to contribute their own surfboards, body boards and kite boards to the fence.

STRANGE SITES
www.ripleys.com

MAUI SURFBOARD FENCE
KA'ONO LAU PE'AHI

MAIL BACKLOG ■ Owing to the country's 2002–07 civil war, Ivory Coast's postal service had a five-year backlog of undelivered mail.

CAVE NETWORK ■ The Mammoth Cave National Park in Kentucky houses more than 367 mi (590 km) of caves—longer than the distance between Los Angeles and San Francisco—and the figure is growing each year as new passageways are discovered.

ONLY OFFICER ■ Malcolm Gilbert is the first and only full-time police officer on Pitcairn Island in the South Pacific. The nearest police backup is in New Zealand, which lies 3,300 mi (5,310 km) away.

NO CAPITAL ■ Along with Tokelau and Western Sahara, the South Pacific island of Nauru is one of only three countries in the world without an official capital. Its government offices are all situated in the Yaren District, but no single place has been designated as capital.

HUMAN ROOTS ■ New research has revealed that humans originated from a single point in central Africa. Scientists from Cambridge University, England, studied more than 6,000 skulls of indigenous people from all over the world and concluded that modern humankind developed around Africa's Great Rift Valley.

NOISE ANNOYS ■ The town of Tilburg in the Netherlands has begun issuing 5,000 euro ($6,800) fines to a local Catholic priest for ringing his church bells too loudly when he calls worshipers for early morning Mass.

BUBBLE HOUSE ■ High above Nice, France, in Tourette-sur-Loup sits a home known as the Bubble House. Designed by Antti Lovag, it consists of a series of connected bubble-shaped rooms covered in oval, convex windows and set into the volcanic rock hillside.

Baobab Bar

This enormous Baobab tree is in Limpopo province, South Africa, and stands 72 ft (22 m) high with an incredible 154 ft (47 m) circumference. It is so large that a bar big enough for 60 people has been installed inside the trunk, and there's room for plenty more outside! Baobab trees become naturally hollow over time, and the bar tree in Limpopo has been dated at more than 6,000 years old.

gum wall

Watch out for the alleyway entirely covered in chewed bubblegum next time you are in San Luis Obispo, California. The gum plastered to the brickwork in Bubblegum Alley has been spreading since the late 1950s. Additions have built up over the years and include a bright red face made from the sticky stuff. Visitors are welcome to add to the collection and some even sample some of the secondhand gum on offer.

This red gum face is one of the more artistic offerings in the alley.

While most of the gum on the walls lost its taste and color long ago, there are still fresh submissions every day, if you have the stomach for it.

Sole Survivor

When Hurricane Ike battered the town of Gilchrist, Texas, in 2008, it flattened everything in its path—except for the house of Warren and Pam Adams. It remained the last house standing because it was built on 14-ft-high (4.3-m) wooden columns. The Adams family had learned their lesson in 2005 when their previous home was destroyed by Hurricane Rita.

FAST MOVER ■ Vanda James from Great Yarmouth, England, has moved house a staggering 27 times in four years. Her quest for the ideal home—it included a three-month stay in New Zealand—has seen her move on average once every eight weeks and spend some $60,000 on deposits and removal fees plus 648 hours packing and unpacking. Her shortest stay in a house was one week. "It just didn't feel right," she says.

COMPACT HOME ■ Dee Williams lives in a house in Olympia, Washington, that is no bigger than a parking spot. She built the 84 sq ft (7.8 sq m) cabin herself out of salvaged material and now it sits in her friend's backyard. Two solar panels provide electricity and it takes Dee just four paces to get from one end of her house to the other.

TOWERING LOVE ■ A woman from San Francisco is married to the Eiffel Tower. Erika La Tour Eiffel (she changed her name to cement her union with the French monument) has a condition that causes her to form relationships with inanimate objects rather than people. She is also in love with the Golden Gate Bridge.

Spaceship House

A house in Chattanooga, Tennessee, that is shaped like a flying saucer was sold at auction in 2008 for a down-to-earth bid of $135,000. Built in 1970, shortly after the first Moon landing, the mountainside dwelling has small square windows, directional lights and is perched on six "landing gear" legs. It also has a retractable staircase at the entrance.

UPSIDE DOWN

UPSIDE DOWN

A house with a difference was unveiled to the public at Trassenheide, northern Germany, in 2008—because both the outside and inside are upside down. Visitors to the house, which was designed by Polish architects Klausdiusz Golos and Sebastian Mikiciuk, reported feeling dizzy as they encountered chairs, tables and carpets that had been stuck to the ceiling to create the inverted interior and give people an alternative view of everyday items.

DONKEY LAW ■ South Shields, England, has had a law on the books for 800 years allowing city officials to block construction of any market that is within a day's ride by donkey—and, incredibly, it's still enforced!

HOUSE STOLEN ■ Yuri Konstantinov from Astrakhan, Russia, returned from a holiday in 2008 to discover that his entire two-story house had been stolen. A neighbor had taken down the building brick by brick and sold all the contents.

TIN MAN ■ In a protest against bureaucracy, Geoff Harper of Scorton, North Yorkshire, England, added a 30-ft (9-m) Tin Man to the exterior of his house, choosing his subject because, in his view, the local council, like the Tin Man from *The Wizard of Oz*, had no heart.

ESTATE CONDITIONS ■ Hélène Louart of Pellevoisin, France, offered to will her estate of $2 million to her hometown—but only if officials named a street after her, hung her favorite art in the mayor's office and agreed to sell her house only to Parisians.

SAND HOTEL ■ In the summer of 2008, a hotel opened in the English seaside resort of Weymouth, Dorset, that was made entirely from sand. A team of four sculptors worked 14 hours a day for a week to build the beach structure from 1,102 tons of sand. For $20 a night, guests could sleep on sand beds in either a twin or double bedroom and gaze at the stars—until the rain washed it all away.

SECRET CASTLE ■ Farmer Robert Fidler from the town of Redhill in Surrey, England, hid a mock Tudor castle behind 40-ft-high (12-m) hay bales for more than four years. After the local council blocked Fidler's plans to build his dream home in one of his fields, the determined farmer erected the disguise from hundreds of bales of straw, topped with huge tarpaulins. He moved his family into the completed castle in 2002, but did not remove the straw façade until four years later in 2006.

TOWN RELOCATION ■ The town of Lynn Lake, Manitoba, Canada, was created in the 1950s by dragging 208 buildings on sleds 93 mi (150 km) from the town of Sherridon.

FOUNTAIN HOTEL ■ In 2007, Japanese artist Tatzu Nishi built a temporary hotel around a fountain in the center of the city of Nantes, France. The Hotel Place Royale consisted of a bedroom with bathroom that was 1,400 sq ft (130 sq m) and enclosed the upper part of the square's famous 19th-century fountain.

UNDERGROUND TEMPLES ■ Members of the Damanhur religious organization in northern Italy have spent decades carving out thousands of cubic feet of earth to build a five-story underground complex, complete with nine temples.

OPTIONAL EXTRA ■ After trying in vain for a year to sell her four-bedroom home in West Palm Beach, Florida, 42-year-old Deven Trabosh came up with a novel method of attracting interest in the property—by including herself in the asking price. Looking for love, the single mother, who had been divorced for 12 years, listed the home for $340,000 on a sell-it-yourself website, but increased the asking price to $840,000 if the buyer decided to take her as part of the package.

AUCTION MANIA

$1.5M	**JOHN LENNON'S EYEGLASSES**	A pair of John Lennon's iconic round spectacles fetched $1.5 million at an auction in 2007.
$312,800	**MARLON BRANDO'S GODFATHER SCRIPT**	Marlon Brando's movie script from *The Godfather*, complete with the actor's notes, sold for $312,800 in 2005.
$16,029	**YO-YO SIGNED BY RICHARD NIXON**	A yo-yo signed by President Nixon once fetched $16,029 at an auction.
$10,000	**CHARLTON HESTON'S LOIN CLOTH**	The loin cloth worn by Charlton Heston in the movie *Ben Hur* was sold for $10,000 in 1997.
$8,200	**MADONNA'S BRA**	The black Jean-Paul Gaultier bra that Madonna wore on her 1993 tour sold for $8,200 a mere four years later.
$7,300	**LOCK OF BEETHOVEN'S HAIR**	A 4-in (10-cm) lock of hair from German composer Ludwig van Beethoven was sold for $7,300 in 1994.
$7,000	**LEE HARVEY OSWALD'S BODY TAG**	The body tag from the corpse of Lee Harvey Oswald, President Kennedy's assassin, fetched $7,000 at an auction.
$4,100	**DEAD DOG FROM *THE WIZARD OF OZ***	The stuffed carcass of Toto, the dog that starred in the movie *The Wizard of Oz*, fetched $4,100 at an auction in 1996.
$3,154	**JUSTIN TIMBERLAKE'S HALF-EATEN TOAST**	A slice of singer Justin Timberlake's half-eaten French toast (complete with fork and syrup) sold on eBay for $3,154.
$2,640	**ELVIS PRESLEY'S PRESCRIPTION BOTTLE**	An empty prescription bottle that had belonged to Elvis Presley was sold at an auction for $2,640 in 2007.
$2,000	**A SLICE OF ROYAL WEDDING CAKE**	A 27-year-old slice of cake from the 1981 wedding of Prince Charles to Lady Diana Spencer sold for $2,000 in 2008—even though only the marzipan and icing remained.
$1,400	**CHER'S OLD RECORD PLAYER**	A 1970s record player belonging to Cher sold for $1,400 in 2006.
$575.96	**BOBBY HULL'S FRONT TEETH**	The false front teeth of former Chicago Blackhawks hockey player Bobby Hull fetched $575.96 at an auction in 2004.
	BRITNEY SPEARS' CHEWING GUM	A piece of used chewing gum discarded by Britney Spears in a London hotel fetched $263 on eBay.

WEIRD ART

VEGETABLES	Chinese artist Ju Duoqi creates versions of great paintings from vegetables. Her works include a copy of Leonardo da Vinci's *Mona Lisa* composed of tofu and sea kelp.
HORSE DUNG	An American firm sells individually crafted models of birds made from genuine Californian horse dung.
DEAD PEOPLE'S ASHES	Bettye Jane Brokl from Biloxi, Mississippi, incorporates the ashes of dead people into abstract paintings to create pictorial memorials.
JELL-O	Artist Liz Hickok has built a 32-sq-ft (3-sq-m) model of her home city of San Francisco, California, entirely from Jell-O.
FRIDGES	In Santa Fe, New Mexico, artist Adam Horowitz built a replica of the famous English landmark Stonehenge from more than 100 old refrigerators.
DOUGH	Kittiwat Unarrom of Bangkok, Thailand, makes edible human heads and torsos out of bread dough.
POSTAGE STAMPS	Pete Mason from Staffordshire, England, creates portraits of famous people from thousands of used postage stamps.
PLAYING CARDS	Bryan Berg of Spirit Lake, Iowa, replicated the skyline of New York City—including the Empire State Building, the Chrysler Building and the Yankee Stadium—from 178,000 playing cards.
DUST AND DIRT	Scott Wade of San Marcos, Texas, re-creates old masters by Da Vinci and Van Gogh on the dusty rear windshield of his car.
TREE ROOTS	Shelvaraj, a micro artist from Nagapattinam, India, carves tiny religious figures from the roots of trees.
TOASTED BREAD	Maurice Bennett from Wellington, New Zealand, reproduces great artworks from burned toast and has also made a portrait of Eminem from more than 5,000 candy M&M's®.
POST-IT® NOTES	David Alvarez of Leavenworth, Washington, spent three months creating a 10-ft-high (3-m) portrait of singer Ray Charles from more than 2,000 colored Post-it® notes.
CHEWING GUM	Jamie Marraccini from Sterling, Virginia, makes abstract models of human heads from pieces of used chewing gum.

Yellowdog was made by Herb Williams from Tennessee who uses up to 250,000 coloring crayons to make each of his sculptures. His studio is filled from floor to ceiling with single-color boxes of 3,000 crayons delivered direct from the manufacturer.

ARTISTIC ❯❯
LICENSE

LIGHT SPEED GRAFFITI

A group of German graffiti artists have moved away from daubing walls with spray paint to create dazzling shapes caught on camera, lighting up gloomy cities with energized glowing art. The momentary swirls of light give life to trash cans and create eerie figures on dark streets before dying away into the night.

Based in Cologne, "Lichtfaktor" comprises the graffiti artists Tim Fehske and David Lupschen and video engineer Marcel Panne. Despite the hi-tech-looking result, the images are made using regular flashlights, neon tubes, glow sticks, LED light, sparklers and fireworks. The images are "sketched" rapidly by Tim and David, who wear dark clothing so they can hardly be seen in the final product and move quickly out of shot to avoid disrupting the lights. The group then take pictures, using cameras set to an unusually long exposure—10 to 30 seconds—that allows more light to be captured.

The group also make videos using stop-motion technique, piecing together one light drawing after another to create radiant shapes that come alive on the streets. Their approach to their art is experimental, retaking shots until they get what they want, and they are never sure how the finished pictures will look.

How do you make your pictures?

All our pictures are created with a camera (in one shot). We have a collection of flashlights, biking lights and flashing LED lights that all work with batteries so that we are completely mobile. We also get good results using fireworks and torches. We like the contrast between the different light sources—for example, xenon gives a golden look and LEDs produce thin, precise lines. We put glasses and other things on the flashlights to get different shapes and colors, or use multi-LED lights and color filters. We like to integrate the surrounding into the picture, for example the trash can (Star Wars vs. Star Trek; far right), which we think is much more interesting than just creating effects in the air. Most of the time we know what we want to draw before we go out, but we are always inspired by our surroundings. And because it's a live process, it's always improvised because you can't plan everything before you actually take the pictures. To get the best results, we use a tripod with an exposure of around 10 to 30 seconds, or longer if needed.

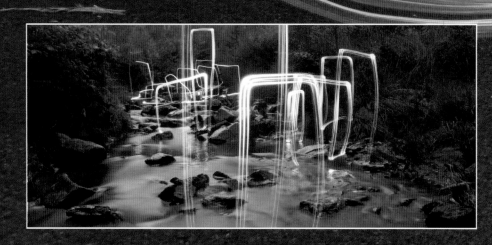

MAIZE MAZE ■ In 2008, a British farmer created a maze in the shape of the Statue of Liberty that was nearly 12 times bigger than the statue itself. Using more than a million maize plants, Tom Pearcy cut a 437-yd-long (400-m) outline of the famous statue in a field near the city of York. His past patterns have included a Viking ship and London's Big Ben clock.

RADIO TWEET ■ A temporary U.K. radio station with nothing but a 20-minute loop recording of birdsong picked up half a million listeners in early 2008.

CHALK TRAIN ■ In January 2009, more than 2,000 schoolchildren and teachers in Cluj, Romania, helped create a drawing on a deserted highway that stretched to around 4 mi (6.4 km) in length. They used 10,000 boxes of colored chalks to draw a 7,000-yd-long train.

POINTLESS TRIP ■ Before making his 1934 epic *Cleopatra*, Cecil B. DeMille sent a team of researchers on a $100,000 trip to Egypt to study the color of the Pyramids—even though the film was in black and white.

KARAOKE MARATHON ■ Anthony Lawson of Wilmington, North Carolina, sang karaoke songs for more than 39 hours straight in June 2008.

JUMBO PROJECT ■ Mark Coreth of Wiltshire, England, has built a full-size sculpture of an African bull elephant in his garden. He created the skeleton of the 13-ft-high (4-m) elephant out of chicken wire before filling it in with polystyrene and giving it a coat of plaster and a bronze finish. It weighs six tons and is so heavy that he needed scaffolding to support the elephant while he was working on it.

METALLIC CLOTHS ■ Ghanaian sculptor El Anatsui specializes in making huge cloths from various recycled objects such as bottle caps, labels and washers. He once created an 18-ft (5.5-m) wide, 16-ft (5-m) high tapestry of aluminum liquor-bottle labels bound together with copper wire and followed that with another giant shimmering cloth, this time made by stitching together thousands of whiskey bottle caps.

MELTING COW ■ In Budapest, Hungary, there is a plastic sculpture of a blue cow that appears to be melting on the ground in the heat. The cow sculpture takes the form of a melting ice cream and even has a stick emerging from the animal's rear.

Knit Knot Tree

Offbeat artists Nancy Mellon and Corrine Bayraktaroglu made sure a tree in Yellow Springs, Ohio, was warm through the winter when they knitted a sweater to cover its branches. The unusual piece of clothing started as a single knitted section and grew day by day, with people adding pockets and vivid colors. It soon began to attract attention from people all around the world.

PHOTO OPPORTUNITY ■ Matt Frondorf of San Antonio, Texas, drove across the U.S.A. from New York to San Francisco—a distance of more than 3,300 mi (5,310 km)—taking a photograph every mile along the way.

PHONEY SHEEP ■ French artist Jean-Luc Cornec exhibits life-sized sculptures of sheep made from recycled telephones and curly phone cables. The twisted cables replicate the wool of the sheep while the old-style phone receiver placed on its rest is used to represent the sheep's head.

PEN FRIENDS ■ Juan Francisco Casas, a Spanish artist living in Rome, illustrates portraits that stand up to 10 ft (3 m) tall—using nothing but blue ballpoint pens. Casas, who started out as a traditional painter, often uses just four cheap ballpoints—costing less than a dollar in total—on one picture, but his works sell for around $7,500.

LIMESTONE LIONESS ■ *The Guennol Lioness*, a 5,000-year-old sculpture from Mesopotamia, sold for $57.2 million in an auction in December 2007 in New York City. The tiny limestone figure, which measures just 3¼ in (8.3 cm) tall, had been on loan to the Brooklyn Museum of Art since 1948.

BLINKING DICTATION ■ Despite being almost entirely paralyzed following a massive stroke, French author Jean-Dominique Bauby wrote his 1997 book *The Diving Bell and the Butterfly* by blinking his left eyelid! A friend slowly recited the alphabet over and over again, and Bauby blinked when the friend reached the required letter, meaning that the book was written one letter at a time. Three days after it was published, Bauby died from heart failure.

DECK-CHAIR DESIGNS ■ Artists and celebrities dreamed up colorful designs as part of an exhibition of 700 deck chairs in London's city parks over the summer of 2008. The oldest designer was 98-year-old Fleur Cowles, a London-based American who was once a friend of the Spanish artist Picasso.

DANNY BOY ■ The song "Danny Boy" was performed continuously for 50 hours at a Ferndale, Michigan, coffee shop in March 2008. There were nearly 1,000 renditions, including classical, folk, blues, rap, spoken word and foreign language versions of the song, played on a variety of instruments including piano, trombone, violin and kazoo.

MONSTER MURAL ■ In 2008, a group of 510 students from a university in Luoyang, Henan Province, China, created a mural of flowers that covered 5,490 sq ft (510 sq m). The color painting consisted of 170 three-ply boards and measured 62 x 80 ft (20.8 x 24.5 m).

CAT HAT ▥ A grandmother has set up a thriving business by making hats from the feral cats that roam the remote Tasmanian island where she lives. Each week Robyn Eades takes delivery of frozen cat carcasses—shot by a local ranger to cull the population—and they are then defrosted and skinned before being tanned and stitched into winter hats, coat-hangers and purses. Her designs are so popular that she has taken orders from as far away as Siberia. She says: "I feel like I am saving them from their fate. They are going to live forever in my creations."

LONG DRAW ▥ For more than a year, Mexican artist Filemon Trevino devoted all his energies to creating a pencil drawing that was ¼ mi (0.5 km) long. He spent 6,000 hours and used 800 pencils to complete his representation of the heart and circulatory system, which incorporated doves and geometric shapes. He worked so hard he lost 35 lb (16 kg) in weight and was hospitalized seven times for dehydration, heart and kidney problems and fainting spells.

QUAKE ALARM ▥ In March 2007, musicians in the Japanese city of Omi played a concert that lasted for 182 hours—that's more than a week—despite a major earthquake rocking the venue during the piano piece. Performers ranging in age from six to 96 took turns in playing some 2,000 tunes, but the most impressive musician was the unflappable pianist. "She was amazing," said one of the organizers." The whole place was shaking quite badly, but she went right on playing. Even an earthquake couldn't stop us."

RHYMING COUPLETS ▥ Dr. Mulki Radhakrishna Shetty of Bangalore, India, wrote 50,000 rhyming couplets in just 24 months.

SUICIDE SCARE ▥ A Chinese artist sparked a suicide scare in 2008 by hanging naked mannequins from the outside of Shanghai skyscrapers. Liu Jin positioned four mannequins with wings on their backs for his work *Wounded Angels*, but passersby mistook them for real people who looked as if they were about to jump.

INTERNET CHAT ▥ In 2008, artists Ben Rubin and Mark Hansen created a work of art to replicate 100,000 people chatting online. The visual and sonic installation at London's Science Museum involved 231 small electronic screens.

HUMAN COMPUTER ▥ Thomas Watts (1811–69), librarian of the British Museum in London, memorized the full title and exact location of every one of the volumes the museum acquired between 1851 and 1860—a total of 680,000 books.

THE BIG ONE! ▥ Angler Mike Wallis of Warner, Oklahoma, must have been hoping to hook the big one! He built a steel fishing rod 83 ft (25 m) long with a fully functioning reel.

MASTER SAMPLER ▥ British D.J. Osymyso (a.k.a. Mark Nicholson) sampled 50 different songs in one track in 2008. He had previously created "Intro-Inspection," which put intros to 101 well-known songs into a 12-minute track.

Henk's egg creations were so large that children could sit high up on the yolks.

Sunny Side Up

Fried eggs measuring 100 ft (30 m) wide were the order of the day when Dutch artist Henk Hofstra left them on city squares in Leeuwarden, Holland, for six months in 2008 as part of a city project. The artist dubbed his creations the *Art Eggcident*, and is no stranger to unusual artistic stunts, having once painted an entire street blue.

Hidden

Scuba divers venturing under the sea in Moliniere Bay, Grenada, will get a watery surprise when they see the eerie figures erected on the seabed by British artist Jason Taylor. Situated up to 80 ft (25 m) deep underwater, the figures can be found holding hands in a circle, typing at a desk, or as spooky faces peering out from coral reefs.

Made of metal and cement, the sculptures are designed to become part of the seabed over time, to encourage the growth of corals and other sea life and provide an attraction for scuba divers as well as fish. The figures can be hard to see when the weather is dull, but when the sun is high and visibility is good they can be seen clearly. They appear to be different colors depending on their depth—those in shallower water generally look red and yellow, while deeper statues are green and blue. Some are partly hidden by the shifting sand found on the seabed and underwater visitors are encouraged to dig to see the entire creation.

Ripley's ask

Why did you decide to make underwater sculptures?

I wanted to create artwork that had specific environmental goals. I also wanted to show how man's interventions could create a positive impact on our planet.

Did you encounter any problems when installing the sculptures?

The heavier they are underwater the better, but they can be impossible to deploy from a boat without huge financing. Many of the pieces are designed with this in mind, made in sections and fixed underwater.

The ring of children took me over a week underwater to connect all the components. When I surveyed the site it was fairly level, but when I came to place the children I found a slight gradient, which meant I had to excavate huge areas of sand with a shovel—not easy in diving gear!

How do your underwater sculptures differ from art on dry land?

Many of the pieces were constructed hollow to allow current to pass through, and making them lighter on land. One of the difficult areas is working with changing weather patterns—which means I always have to make back-up plans.

How long do you expect the sculptures to last?

Some of the metal sculptures I predict will last around ten to 15 years but the cement ones should become a permanent fixture to the environment, as they have many similar qualities to natural reefs.

Do you have any plans for future artwork?

All my new projects are about exploring new underwater environments. I also hope to start growing figures out of coral. A piece I recently constructed in Kent has become a kind of barometer for the health of the river in which it sits, as the more algae that form on its surface the more indicative it is of the amount of chemicals that are in the water.

on the seabed

Curious fish ponder Jason's Fish and Chip sculpture on the seabed.

The Lost Correspondent features a lonely figure typing at a desk.

A row of sleeping heads becomes part of the underwater scenery.

It was painstaking work to complete every hair on each of Bluey's eight legs.

Elizabeth Thompson adds yet more putty to her detailed replica spider.

Arachnid Art

British artist Elizabeth Thompson is seen through the legs of a giant spider that she made from blue putty for a display at England's London Zoo in 2007. The creature was made from 4,000 packs of the putty, measures 4 ft (1.2 m) in width and weighs more than 440 lb (200 kg)—as much as three people. Nicknamed "Bluey," the sculpture is a much larger, and scarier, version of the common house spider.

BLIND PHOTOGRAPHER ■ Alison Bartlett takes amazing photographs of wildlife—even though she has been blind for more than 16 years. Alison, from Hampshire, England, "sees" with her ears, listening for sounds such as rustling in the grass, a bird's wings flapping, or a squirrel nibbling. Her assistant points her in the right direction and gives distances, but the art is all hers. She says: "Of course others have to tell me whether the pictures are any good."

POETIC JUSTICE ■ In December 2007, a large group of teenagers from Vermont were prosecuted for vandalizing the former home of U.S. poet Robert Frost (1874–1963), and their sentencing included classes to learn about Frost's poetry.

GUMMY BEAR ■ Artist Maurizio Savini from Rome, Italy, creates intricate sculptures, which have included a life-size buffalo and a grizzly bear, from thousands of pieces of chewed bubblegum. Maurizio works the gum when it is still warm and manipulates it with a knife. His sticky sculptures have been exhibited all over the world and have sold for as much as $70,000 each.

COLORFUL COLLECTION ■ Sculptor John McIntire of Memphis, Tennessee, donated 700 Hawaiian shirts—collected over the course of 50 years—to the Memphis College of Art.

LIST MANIA ■ Artist and author Hillary Carlip from Los Angeles, California, has been collecting abandoned shopping lists for many years, but in 2008 she took her hobby a step further by turning some of those lists into performance art. Realizing you can tell a lot about someone based on what they need at the grocery store— the way they write their list, their handwriting and even the kind of paper they use—she concocted elaborate stories about the people who had written them, and then reinvented herself as those imaginary characters, dressing up and going to the store with their notes.

LEGO® OBAMA ■ Watched by more than 1,000 mini LEGO® people, a 4-in-high (10-cm) LEGO® model of Barack Obama was inaugurated in a replica presidential ceremony at LEGOLAND®, California, in January 2009. The detailed display also featured a LEGO® model White House, motorcade and even people lining up outside the portable toilets.

FAVRE TRIBUTE ■ In 2008, Carlene and Duane Schultz of Eleva, Wisconsin, created a corn maze bearing the image of former Green Bay Packers quarterback Brett Favre to mark the announcement of his retirement. The maze reads "Thanks" and shows Favre's upper body holding a football, with his No. 4 jersey.

HAIR SCREEN ■ For an exhibition at Hanover, New Hampshire, New York City-based Chinese artist Wenda Gu created an 80 x 13 ft (24 x 4 m) screen made from human hair. It contained 430 lb (195 kg) of hair, collected over a period of several months from no less than 42,350 haircuts.

RUNNING EXHIBIT ■ A British artist who won the prestigious Turner Prize with lights that switched on and off and whose previous installations include a piece of putty stuck to a wall, unveiled his latest work in 2008—runners sprinting through a gallery. Martin Creed's creation consisted of 50 athletes taking turns to dash 282 ft (86 m) along London's Tate Britain gallery every 30 seconds for four months. He came up with the concept to illustrate that it is not necessary to look at paintings in a gallery for a long time.

ARTISTIC LICENSE

www.ripleys.com

Ripley's Believe It or Not!

SLEEPING MASTERPIECES ■ Lee Hadwin of Henllan, Wales, draws strange and fantastical works of art—in his sleep. The sleepwalking artist—dubbed Kipasso—shows no interest in drawing by day, but at night he produces amazing pictures on any surface available—walls, tables, even clothes. Although he now leaves sketchbooks and charcoal pencils scattered around the house at night—particularly under the stairs, his favorite venue—he never has any recollection of doing the drawings when he wakes up. And if he tries to re-create them by day, the results are poor. "When I'm awake, I'm unable to do even a simple sketch," he says.

GOLDEN GANDHI ■ An Indian goldsmith has designed a statue of Mahatma Gandhi that is no bigger than a grain of rice. Kommoju Gunasekhar took 90 days and used 0.035 oz (1 g) of gold to design the ¼-in-high (7-mm) statuette, which depicts the bespectacled Gandhi holding a holy book in one hand and a stick in the other.

MACHINE FLUFF ■ Instead of discarding the fluff that collects inside her tumble dryer, Saira Lloyd turns it into works of art. The artist from Nottingham, England, wraps the collected fluff in saran wrap and, mixing it with fragments of skin, hair and dirt, creates unique sculptures.

LIBERACE LOOK-ALIKES ■ Las Vegas, Nevada, stages an annual Liberace competition, which is judged not only on piano-playing, but also on the contestants' ability to dress most like the great pianist—in sequins, caked makeup and glitter hairspray.

BUD-DING DESIGNER ■ A design student from Hertfordshire, England, drank 4,000 cans of Budweiser beer over a period of three years—and used the empties to build a car! After completing the life-size model 1965 Ford Mustang, Jack Kirby had a couple of cans to celebrate.

MAIL MOSAIC

Rather than throwing away her annoying junk mail, Arizona artist Sandy Schimmel decided to do something more interesting, and used it to create colorful mosaics in a process known as "upcycling." The vivid piece *All American Blonde* features pop icon Madonna and was actually created from political junk mail and tax forms.

Flammable Faces

Careful how you handle these innovative sculptures by Scottish artist David Mach. His portraits of iconic figures are constructed from thousands of colored matchstick tips packed closely together to create 3-D heads. David created this sculpture of Elvis, 2 ft (60 cm) in height, using 50,000 matchsticks imported from Japan. Each match was glued on to a glass fiber-mold in a process that took more than 500 hours to complete. His other matchstick creations include Marilyn Monroe and a matchstick version of Michangelo's *David*. As a fitting end to his art, David sometimes takes a match to his sculptures and lets them disappear in flames.

CAN CREATIONS ■ A firm from Staffordshire, England, sells models of planes, trucks and helicopters—all made from drinks cans. They will even personalize the gift using only cans from the recipient's favorite drink.

MATCHSTICK McLAREN ■ Michael Arndt from Hanover, Germany, spent six and a half years building a full-size model of a Formula One McLaren Mercedes racing car out of 956,000 matches. The car cost him $9,000 to build—that includes the 1,686 tubes of glue he used—and is ten layers thick in places so that it is strong enough to sit in.

GARAGE BOOTY ■ In January 2007, the American Folk Art Museum, in Manhattan, was about to stage an exhibition of rare drawings by Mexican artist Martín Ramírez when it received an e-mail on behalf of a woman from Auburn, California, saying she had some of his drawings—that had been lying in her garage for nearly two decades. In fact, she had 140 Ramírez artworks—and the total body of his previous known works only numbered 300. Some of his drawings have sold for more than $100,000.

MINI MONA ■ A British artist has painted a version of the *Mona Lisa* that is less than one-quarter the size of a postage stamp. Andrew Nicholls from Farnborough, Hampshire, painstakingly re-created Leonardo da Vinci's masterpiece in 1:70 scale to produce a replica just 7/16 in x 1/4 in (11 x 7 mm). Peering through a magnifying glass, he used a 0000 gauge brush, which consisted of just a few strands of brush tapered to a fine point, to layer his acrylic paint on a piece of card.

BACK TO THEIR ROOTS ■ In March 2008, a train station in the Beatles' home city of Liverpool, England, unveiled life-sized sculptures of the Fab Four—carved out of a hedge. It took expert gardeners 18 months to grow the topiary John, Paul, George and Ringo—plus their guitars and drum kit—and to shape the plants around handmade metal frames.

TOWERING CREATION ■ A matchstick model of London's famous Tower Bridge took Michael Williams of Shoebury, Essex, ten years to build—that's two years longer than the real bridge! He used more than 1.6 million wooden matchsticks—each painstakingly carved by hand—on his 6-ft-long (1.8-m) model, which has 156 working lights.

DIAMOND SKULL ▥ In 2007, British artist Damien Hirst covered an 18th-century human skull with 8,601 diamonds—almost three times the number on the coronation crown of Queen Elizabeth II. The centerpiece of the $100 million artwork, titled *For the Love of God*, was a 52-carat stone set into the forehead, and even the eye sockets were filled with hundreds of jewels. The teeth were taken from the original skull before being polished and reset in the cast.

MATCH CLOCK ■ In 2008, David Harding of London, England, built a half-size grandmother clock from 12,000 matches.

SECURITY FILM ■ Using footage she obtained of herself that had been filmed by closed-circuit TV security systems in Britain, Austrian film-maker Manu Luksch created a movie called *Faceless*. In the movie, all the other faces are blocked out so that she is the only person with a recognizable human face.

HANGING RHINO ■ Made by Italian artist Stefano Bombardieri, a full-size sculpture of a rhinoceros hangs several feet above the ground in a street in Potsdam, Germany.

LITERARY VISION ▥ Chinese author Chen Hong has written five novels—containing a total of 190,000 characters—despite having to dictate every word by blinking his eye. He was stricken with an incurable degenerative muscle disease in 1999, but manages to communicate with the help of a transparent board displaying phonetic symbols.

PAPER SHIP ■ Jared Shipman of Roseville, California, built a 320,000-piece model of the USS *Nimitz*, measuring 9 ft 1¾ in (2.78 m) in length, out of only paper.

LEAP DAY ▥ Performance artist Brian Feldman from Orlando, Florida, marked Leap Day (29 February) 2008 by leaping off a platform 12 ft (3.6 m) high every 3 minutes 56 seconds over a 24-hour period. He managed to complete 366 leaps in all, to match the number of days in the "leap" year.

GUM SCULPTOR ▥ Jamie Marraccini of Sterling, Virginia, makes ingenious works of art from chewing gum. Each sculpture contains hundreds—sometimes even thousands—of pieces of chewed gum molded into place. A collection of miniature human heads—titled *Fiesta de Huevos*—used 804 pieces of gum, while Marraccini used 4,212 pieces to make a 2 x 3 ft (60 x 90 cm) gum portrait of himself and his wife, which he took five years to complete. Although he can chew 50 pieces a day, Marraccini needs help with supplies and so hands out packs of gum to workmates and friends, along with laminated sheets of paper on which the willing helpers can return the chewed gum. He then groups the gum into color categories before using it in a sculpture.

DIAL-A-DRESS ■ In 2008, Jolis Paons, an innovative student at Indiana University's Herron School of Art and Design, made a lightweight dress constructed entirely out of pages from phonebooks.

PLASTIC FANTASTIC ▥ Artist Brian Jungen from Vancouver, British Columbia, Canada, created life-sized statues of whale skeletons made entirely from white plastic deck chairs. He specializes in turning everyday objects into works of art and has also created elaborate ceremonial native masks from running shoes.

FASHION BUG ■ When swarms of cicadas invaded the town of Sandwich, Massachusetts, in the summer of 2008, two enterprising teenagers saw a business opportunity and turned the dead insects into jewelry. Katheryn Moloney and Brady Cullinan charged $10 for a pair of earrings or a necklace made out of the lacquered carcasses of the bugs.

PAINTED SNAILS ▥ In 2008, an artist calling himself Slinkachu, from London, England, used nontoxic paints to decorate live snails' shells in pretty colors and patterns as part of a series of designs dubbed "Inner City Snail—a slow-moving street art project."

FISHY IDEA ■ Girls in Chengdu, China, latched on to a new fashion craze in 2008—wearing live fish around their necks as jewelry. They queued in their hundreds to buy sealed plastic pendants housing the fish, which can live there for three months, because the pendants contain water, fish food and two solid oxygen balls. At the end of the three months, the fish can be released.

MOWNA LISA ■ Tania Ledger from London, England, hired a 3-D art expert to re-create the "Mona Lisa" in grass in her front garden. Chris Naylor took two days to reproduce Leonardo da Vinci's masterpiece, using a small lawn mower and garden tools.

SUSHI MOSAIC ■ Twenty students in Mumbai, India, made a sushi mosaic measuring 163 sq ft (15.16 sq m) using 5,814 pieces of sushi in March 2008.

SALVEST SALVAGE ■ Jonesboro, Arkansas, artist John Salvest made a version of the U.S. flag, the "Stars and Stripes," from 90,000 cigarette butts. His works have also incorporated such everyday objects as business cards, spent coffee filters, wine corks and even nail clippings.

BALLOON BIKINI ■ Two U.S. fashion designers have created a range of clothing—from bikinis to party dresses—made entirely out of balloons. Each outfit designed by Katie Laibstain of Richmond, Virginia, and Steven Jones of Cincinnati, Ohio, contains around 300 twisted balloons and takes an average of ten hours to make. Even though the dresses can be worn only once, some of the designs have sold for $2,000.

COFFEE STAINS ■ Sunshine Plata of Manila, Philippines, paints with coffee grounds, creating lifelike pictures that look like brown watercolors—but, of course, their smell reveals their true nature.

PATERNAL POT ■ John Lowndes of Pembrokeshire, Wales, missed his daily pot of tea with his father so much that when dad Ian died, John had his ashes made into a teapot. Potter Neil Richardson mixed Ian's ashes straight into the clay so that the teapot was safe to use.

Rubber Robes

Artist Susie MacMurray from Manchester, England, stitched 1,400 rubber gloves together in a flamboyant long-sleeved dress design. Her other rubber glove designs include a strapless ball gown and a wedding dress made from rubber gloves and balloons woven into a mesh foundation.

BOTTLE LAMPS ■ In Kuala Lumpur in May 2008, Lisa Foo and Su Sim from Selangor, Malaysia, exhibited beautiful lamps in the shape of sea creatures and marine organisms—all made from recycled plastic water bottles.

KING KURTA ■ Craftsmen in Pakistan have made a *kurta*—a form of long shirt—large enough to be worn by somebody 175 ft (53.3 m) tall. The garment measures 101 ft (31 m) in length, which is 30 times larger than the average *kurta*, weighs an incredible 1,765 lb (800 kg) and took a team of 50 tailors 30 days to put together.

PIANO-PLAYING FLY ■ Belgian photographer Nicholas Hendrickx has been creating a buzz in the art world by taking quirky pictures of flies. Using his bedroom as his studio, Hendrickx employs miniature props to photograph flies apparently playing the piano, the guitar, skateboarding, cycling, flying a kite or relaxing on the beach. His art requires great patience, as he mainly uses living insects.

INFLATABLE ANIMALS ■ In 2008, street artist Joshua Allen Harris made sculptures of animals—including bears, seals and giraffes—from discarded plastic bags and then tied them to ventilation grates above New York City subway lines so that whenever a train rushed through underneath, the surge of air caused the animal to jump up and spring to life.

LIFELIKE ANIMALS ■ Thanks to Joe Wertheimer, people can enjoy the beauty of wild animals on their land without any of the upkeep. The Californian sculptor designs magnificent lifesize animals that, from a distance, are indistinguishable from the real thing. He has carved 18 African animals for a hotel in South Africa and four grazing sheep and a Texas longhorn bull for a client in Malibu.

HIGHWAY DEBRIS ■ To highlight the dangers of road debris, artist Ken Andexler built a sculpture 8 ft (2.4 m) high from 350 discarded items he found along a one-mile stretch of road in Naples, Florida. He included two baking pans, a diver's fin, tennis balls, a wrench, a paintbrush, rusted springs, and various items of scrap metal. The centerpiece was a sign spelling out "Lost and Found" in 176 cigarette butts.

Paper Faces

Dutch artist Bert Simons has cloned himself in paper. The Rotterdam sculptor makes realistic, lifesize, 3-D paper models of human heads with the aid of computer technology. He first creates a computer model of his subject and then flattens it into its component parts. Once a template is created, he prints it out on a sheet of paper ready to be cut out and reassembled (see below). By this method he has also created models of friends and even a turtle.

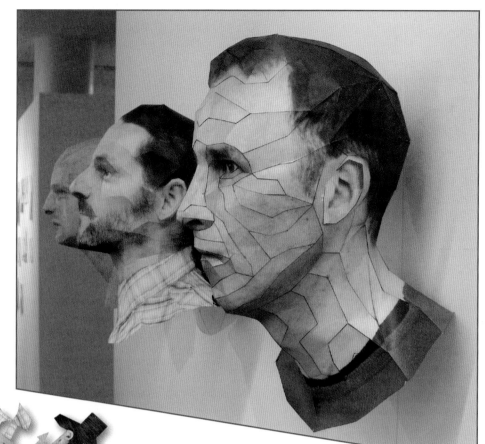

Cookie City

A model city 16 ft (5 m) long, 16 ft (5 m) wide and 8 ft (2.5 m) high was unveiled in Shenyang, China, at the end of 2007. The edible edifice was made with 25,000 cookies, weighed over 2,200 lb (1,000 kg) and featured many famous landmarks from the city, including the Imperial Palace and the TV tower.

GAS STATEMENT ■ Sick of paying high gas prices and irritated by the abandoned gas station that was causing an eyesore on her drive, artist Jennifer Marsh from DeWitt, New York, decided to cover it with a vast handmade blanket. Helped by artists from 15 countries and by more than 2,500 grade-school students in 29 states, Marsh covered the 5,000 sq ft (465 sq m) of the station. including the pumps, light stands and signs, with more than 3,000 colorful panels that were crocheted, knitted or stitched together to form a single blanket. The panels were made from such diverse materials as leather, silk and plastic shopping bags.

CLIP ART ■ American artist Joshua Mantyla creates sculptures from paper clips. He started off by making simple flowers, but has since progressed to such intricate artworks as a small motorcycle—complete with rotating wheels—and an oversized 3-ft (90-cm) mouse, the latter taking him some 3,000 hours to complete.

STYROFOAM PRESIDENT ■ In 2007, Fran Volz of Arlington Heights, Illinois, unveiled a Styrofoam sculpture of Abraham Lincoln. It took eight months to create the 250-lb (113-kg), 10-ft (3-m) sculpture, which was carved with the aid of an electric chainsaw.

Moving Masterpieces

Using the human body as a living canvas, artists who took part in the 2008 New Zealand Body Art Awards in Auckland put on a spectacular show. The artists came from a variety of professional backgrounds including fine art, special effects, makeup and theater, and were awarded points for the originality, design and application of their creations.

Carmel McCormick's lizard won the competition's Supreme Award, and her model, Levi, also won an award for Best Performance by a Model.

The Rain Forest Reptilian by Kim Stevenson won an award for Special Effects Fantasy.

The Airbrushed Body Art prize went to Yolanda Bartram for Cheeta (seen here) and Songe (top left).

LONG LINE ■ At Ireland's Rockland County Feis and Field Games in July 2008, 312 dancers stretched out to form a continuous dancing line that was more than 700 ft (213 m) long.

STOP-START ART Performance artist Matthew Keeney walked from the Capitol steps in Washington, D.C., to the Lincoln Memorial and back in February 2008, stopping each time he heard a car horn and then starting again when he heard another. The 3.8-mi (6-km) walk took him just under 3 hours.

SHARK PHOBIA ■ Hollywood actress Christina Ricci suffers from pool-selachophobia—she's scared that a shark might swim through a hatch in the side of a swimming pool.

ARTISTIC TYPE ■ Israeli artist and typographer Oded Ezer creates startling works of art from typefaces, especially Hebrew fonts. His short film, *The Finger*, presents an imaginary landscape composed of Hebrew letters.

PLAY-A-DAY ■ The New York City Off-Broadway Show, *365 Days/365 Plays*, is a compilation of the 365 plays that American playwright Suzan-Lori Parks wrote in 365 days.

PRIVATE CONCERT ■ A violinist who left a 285-year-old Stradivarius on the back seat of a New York City cab in April 2008 played a special concert to thank the driver who returned it to him. Philippe Quint accidentally left the $4-million violin in the airport taxi after a performance in Dallas, but following an appeal, driver Mohamed Khalil got in touch the next day to return it. The grateful violinist gave the driver a $100 tip and free tickets to his next New York concert and a 30-minute private performance in the taxi waiting area at Newark Liberty International Airport.

BRAD'S BAN ■ American actor Brad Pitt is banned from ever entering China because of his role in the movie *Seven Years in Tibet*.

ICE PIANO ■ As part of the 20th International Snow-Sculpture Art Expo in Harbin, China, during the winter of 2007–08, a company designed and built an ice piano that could be played by visitors. The life-size ice sculpture could also automatically play more than 30 classic piano pieces before, come the warmer spring, it melted away.

CHANGE OF CLOTHES ■ David Whitthoft of Ridgefield, Connecticut, wore a football jersey every day for 1,581 days straight—more than four years—before finally taking it off on his 12th birthday, April 23, 2008.

QUICK PICKER ■ Despite suffering from a rare muscular disorder, Todd Taylor of Palm Bay, Florida, can play the banjo at 210 beats per minute. A typical fast bluegrass song is 130 bpm. He demonstrated his skill by playing "Duelling Banjos"—a piece normally performed by two people—at such a pace that he had to superglue the picks to his fingers to stop them flying off. He is such a fast player that he has to change the strings of his banjo three times a day.

PERCUSSION POWER ■ Akron, Ohio, musician Link Logen played the drums for 86 hours 16 minutes straight in June/July 2008—that's more than three-and-a-half days. He survived the lack of sleep largely on coffee but at one point started crying because of the extreme mental and physical fatigue. "As I was playing," he said, "I literally went into a catatonic state."

BEAUTIFUL DAY ■ A painting that hung in U2's recording studio in Dublin was sold at auction for $10 million in 2008—19 years after it was spotted by the Irish rock band's bass player, Adam Clayton, in a New York gallery. The painting was "Pecho/Oreja" by American graffiti artist Jean-Michel Basquiat.

BEAR SUIT ■ A British artist produced a two-hour film that showed him spending ten nights in a Berlin museum while dressed in a bear suit. Mark Wallinger said that wearing the bear suit in the film, entitled *Sleeper*, enabled him to "look through the eyes of something that was of another culture."

PRIZED POEMS ■ A signed collection of poetry by William McGonagall (1825–1902), known as "The World's Worst Poet," sold at an auction in Edinburgh, Scotland, in May 2008, for £6,600—more than the selling price for a first-edition signed set of Harry Potter books.

BARGAIN BURIAL ■ To save costs, the body of William Shakespeare's friend and fellow dramatist Ben Jonson was buried standing up in Westminster Abbey in 1637.

WRAPPER DRESS ■ Vanessa Randall of Wayne, Maine, made her 2008 high-school prom dress from 3,000 gum wrappers. She started collecting the wrappers three years earlier, helped by friends and family.

BIRTHDAY PRESENT ■ Robert Louis Stevenson, author of *Treasure Island*, willed his birthday, November 13, to a friend because she was born on Christmas Day and never had a birthday celebration.

CANOE TOPIARY ■ Glenn Tabor of Leeds, England, has created something different in his front garden—a topiary sculpture of a huge Native American man paddling a 16-ft (5-m) canoe. "I was bored with having a normal hedge," he says, "and decided we should have something a bit eccentric." He used manual shears and an electric hedge-trimmer to make his creation.

LIBRARY LABOR ■ Polish historian Jan Alvertrandy (1731–1808), forbidden to copy historical documents from libraries in Upsala and Stockholm, Sweden, memorized the entire contents of 100 volumes. He read them day by day in the library and then wrote down every word he had learned at night.

HEAVY READING ■ The book *Greatest of All Time*, a tribute to boxer Muhammad Ali, is itself a heavyweight. It weighs in at an astonishing 75 lb (34 kg). Furthermore, it contains 3,000 pictures and nearly 600,000 words.

WHEAT MODELS ■ Scale models of British landmarks were unveiled in 2007—made from wheat. London's Big Ben clock tower, the Blackpool Tower and Edinburgh Castle were among the eight structures re-created in wheat for an exhibition aptly entitled "Land of Wheat and Glory."

MUSICAL METHANE ■ Practicing yoga with his sister, Paul Oldfield from Macclesfield, Cheshire, England, developed a talent of his own that would eventually lead to him blowing away audiences as the world's only full-time performing flatulist. Oldfield, who calls himself Mr. Methane, found that he could control his gas emissions to mimic the sounds of such diverse tunes as Johann Strauss's "The Blue Danube" waltz and Kylie Minogue's pop hit "I Should Be So Lucky."

FALL GUY ■ Four scaffolding waterfalls installed as an art project on New York City's East River in 2008 churned 2.1 million gal (8 million l) of water per hour. Designed by Dutch artist Olafur Eliasson, the tallest artificial waterfall was 120 ft (37 m) in height and the widest was 30 ft (9 m) wide. Eliasson is no stranger to mimicking nature. He had previously re-created the Sun in London's Tate Modern gallery with the help of 2,000 yellow lamps and numerous mirrors.

COMEDY ROUTINE ■ More than 80 comedians performed a nonstop comedy routine for 50 hours at New York City's Comic Strip in June 2008.

A colorful human head is revealed by one side of Brian's dissection of the Household Physician book.

Webs New Inter Diction is a painstakingly hollowed-out illustrated dictionary.

The other side of Household Physician displays equally intricate work.

MURDER MYSTERY ■ The publication of his debut novel *Amok* led to Polish author Krystian Bala being jailed for 25 years in 2007. A court decided that his murder-mystery novel was too close to the truth, after it was discovered that the supposedly fictional story bore striking similarities to a real-life incident in which Bala had allegedly tortured and killed a businessman seven years previously.

HIDDEN TALENT ■ Dutch artist Desiree Palmen creates amazing camouflage art by wearing suits that are hand-painted so that they exactly match her chosen background. First, Desiree photographs a scene and then she uses acrylic paints to meticulously transfer its detail on to a cotton suit. The artist then poses in the suit against the chosen backdrop—and immediately becomes virtually invisible.

TRAVEL FATIGUE ■ In 2008, technicians at a museum in Madrid identified 129 changes to Pablo Picasso's famous anti-war painting *Guernica*, caused by wear and tear from its many journeys around the world. Painted in 1937, the 11 x 25 ft (3.4 x 7.6 m) canvas was exhibited in dozens of cities on both sides of the Atlantic over the following 20 years.

SLOW READ ■ Ante Matec of Zagreb, Croatia, borrowed a book in 1967 and never got round to reading it. He returned it in 2007!

YOUNG WRITER ■ By the age of eight, English poet and writer Thomas Babington Macaulay (1800–1859) had penned a compendium of world history as well as "The Battle of Cheviot," a romantic narrative poem in the style of Sir Walter Scott.

BIDDING WAR ■ A painting sold for 1,700 times its maximum reserve price in 2007, because the winning bidder decided it was a self-portrait by the 17th-century Dutch artist Rembrandt. The painting—*The Young Rembrandt as Democrates the Laughing Philosopher*—was valued at just $3,400 by experts who considered that it was not by Rembrandt himself. So inconsequential was it that it had hung in a house in Gloucestershire, England, for several years. Yet at a London auction it fetched a staggering $5.8 million.

CAN CAN CHAIR ■ British interior designer Laurence Llewelyn-Bowen has created a stylish modern armchair entirely from recycled drinks cans. He designed the "Can Can Chair" using nothing but cans that he and his family collected from around the house.

HARDBACK

Like dissecting a dead animal, Brian Dettmer from Atlanta, Georgia, performs surgery on old books that nobody reads anymore, fashioning new and incredibly detailed pieces of art out of pages that have been hidden for years. The artist seals the edges of the books before cutting into them from the front, using a knife, tweezers and other surgical tools, to remove certain sections, while keeping interesting pictures and text intact. None of the material is altered, only removed; so that the elements of the finished piece remain in their original place in the book.

BOOK SENTENCE ▦ Keely Givhan of Beloit, Wisconsin, spent six days in jail in 2008—for having overdue library books.

SOLD SISTER ▦ In 2004, British singer James Blunt sold his sister on eBay! He asked for a knight in shining armor to bid for a damsel in distress when his sister couldn't find transport to attend a funeral in Ireland. The winning bidder offered her the use of his private helicopter, and three years later the couple actually married!

HEAD LICE ▦ Seven young artists from Berlin, Germany, with lice in their hair, lived in an Israeli museum for three weeks in 2008. The artists, who slept, ate and bathed in the gallery and who wore plastic shower caps to prevent the lice from spreading, said their exhibition fitted in with a theme of hosts and guests.

RARE VOLUME ▦ The only privately owned copy of the 711-year-old Magna Carta (an English legal charter) was sold to an investment company in 2007—for more than $21 million.

DRUM ROLL ▦ Eric Sader Jr. of Salina, Kansas, played a continuous drum roll for 1 hour 22 minutes 5 seconds at McPherson College in May 2008.

RUBBER ART ▦ Artist Chakaia Booker from New York City creates sculptures from old tires. She salvages them from streets, gas stations, auto body shops and recycling centers.

HEAVY DUTY ▦ No wonder fame sometimes hung heavy on his shoulders—some of Elvis Presley's bejewelled jumpsuits weighed more than 30 lb (12 kg)!

AUTO PARTS ▦ An auto parts shop in Moscow, Russia, decorated its forecourt with sculptures of people made solely from the spare parts of used cars.

DEATH CHANNEL ▦ A television channel devoted almost exclusively to death has been launched in Germany. Eos TV, run by producer Wolf Tilmann Schneider in conjunction with Germany's funeral association, is screened 24 hours a day, 7 days a week, on cable and the Internet, and its program lineup includes televised obituaries plus numerous documentaries about graveyards.

HIDDEN TREASURE ▦ Elizabeth Gibson of New York City found a painting in a garbage pile that was actually a stolen work by Mexican artist Rufino Tamayo and worth over $1 million.

mini art

Vladimir Aniskin takes miniature art to a whole new level of tiny. Rejecting canvas and normal paintbrushes, the Russian artist uses human hairs, poppy seeds and grape seeds and, unbelievably, casts shoes for the feet of real fleas that he picked off his cat. His pieces have to be seen—or not seen—to be believed!

Vladimir works as a scientific researcher by day, and does all of his micro-miniature artwork with the help of a microscope. It is a painstaking discipline and he rises early each morning before going to work to make his creations, working between heartbeats to keep an incredibly steady hand. He has placed a caravan of seven camels walking along the eye of a needle, each one only 0.0039 in (0.1 mm) high, and written out a classic Russian story, comprising 2,027 letters over 22 lines, quite clearly on a grain of rice.

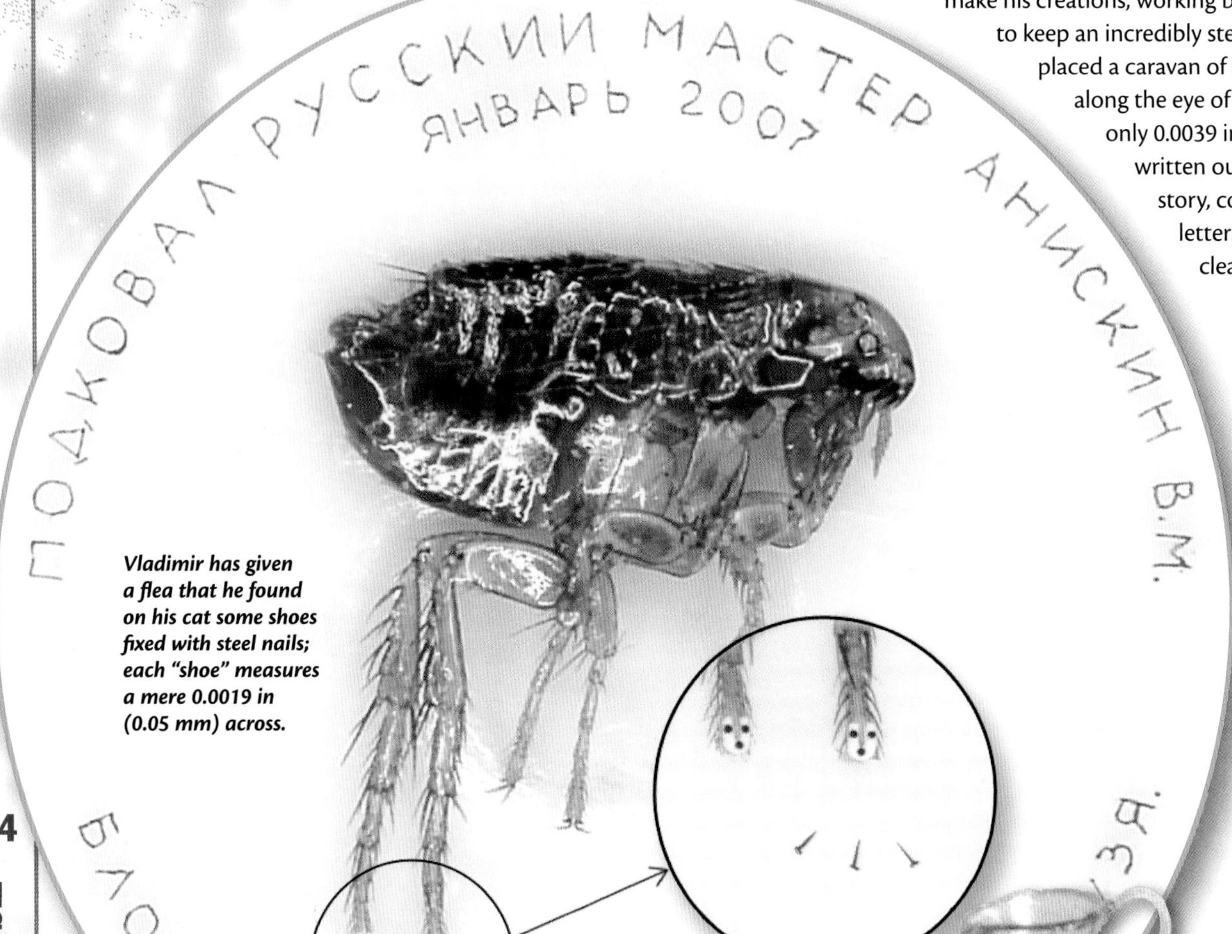

ПОДКОВАЛ РУССКИЙ МАСТЕР АНИСКИН В.М.

ЯНВАРЬ 2007

БЛОШКА МУСА... ПОНСОР... ...ЗЯ.

← ГВОЗДИКИ

Vladimir has given a flea that he found on his cat some shoes fixed with steel nails; each "shoe" measures a mere 0.0019 in (0.05 mm) across.

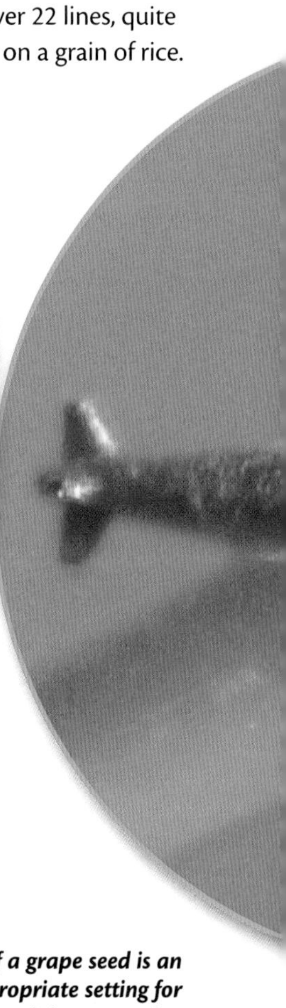

Half a grape seed is an appropriate setting for these mini grapes, wine glasses and decanter.

For this piece, the entire alphabet is written on the end of a hair only 0.0035 in (0.09 mm) across. The width of a human hair can range from 0.002 in (0.05 mm) to 0.005 in (0.13 mm).

HUMAN HAIR

GRAPE SEED

POPPY SEED

For this seasonal piece, Vladimir placed a snowman measuring 0.0019 in (0.055-mm) high on half a poppy seed, under a banner supported by specks of dust.

2006

HUMAN HAIR

A tiny submarine 0.015 in (0.39 mm) long on the end of a strand of horsehair and made of platinum.

A rosebud made of dust particles, only 0.002 in (0.065 mm) across and set inside a human hair like a glass vase.

HORSEHAIR

MATCH

The scale of Vladimir's work can be seen when comparing a matchstick head to a ⅛-in-long (3.5-mm) chess table, complete with gold and silver chess pieces as small as 0.006 in (0.15 mm).

Ripley's ask

Why did you start making miniature art?

In 1998, I accidentally came across a book about Soviet masters of microminiature art. I was impressed by the works that were described. Within myself, the desire arose to make something similar. The book did not describe the technology of making microminiatures; one thing was clear—I needed a microscope. Soon I managed to get a child's one-eyed microscope. It was extremely difficult to work with: it turned the representation from right to left and upside down. Finally, I managed to obtain a good binocular microscope, and I work with it to this day.

What problems do you have in your work?

The main difficulty in microminiature is one's heartbeat. If you use a needle with your fingertips, calm yourself and breathe smoothly, the tip of the needle begins to flutter to the beat of your heart. It is impossible to get rid of such fluctuation. You can only adapt to it—that is, to do particularly delicate work between the heartbeats. Another difficulty in microminiature-making is static electricity. It happens sometimes that the material sticks to the tool, and it is impossible to separate it without damaging it.

What materials and tools do you use?

Perhaps all materials are suitable for microminiature art. Each of them has its own properties, which can be successfully used in each particular case. Longevity is the main issue for the use of any material. If a material can undergo oxidation, it cannot be used. For instance, copper should not be used. Unfortunately. even specialists are unable to predict the behavior of material at micro levels; we all have to learn by experience. Some materials are particularly sensitive to moisture—for example, hair. The works Camels in a Hair and Rose in a Hair have been repaired several times.

How small do you think you can make art in the future?

If you consider the principle of microminiature, "small, even smaller, the smallest in the world," we can say the following: the objects to which you can apply this slogan should be easily recognizable by everybody. This can be, for example, chess, books or musical instruments. A micro violin must contain all the standard parts of a regular violin. When one reaches smaller and smaller dimensions, it is important to distinguish between art and modern methods of nanotechnology. Art is what is made solely by the human hand. In making microminiatures, I can identify several objectives worthy of hard work. This is the smallest alphabet, the smallest book, chess, musical instruments or other smallest objects made by the hand of man.

Do you have any ambitions for your miniature art?

I am planning to continue a series of micro-military orders that reflect the military honor of the Russian nation, as well as a series of Russian cartoon characters.

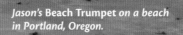

Jason's **Beach Trumpet** *on a beach in Portland, Oregon.*

Liminal Space *is a gallery-based installation piece.*

Beautiful Balloons

New York City artist Jason Hackenwerth creates surreal, mystical creatures—such as giant plants and alien monsters—solely from balloons. He spends up to $12,000 a year on balloons for his creations, which can be made from around 3,000 individual balloons and take 25 hours of work. Luckily, less than 10 percent of the balloons pop. Jason's sculptures are inspired by living creatures and human anatomy, and can last for months in the right conditions.

PEN PORTRAITS ■ Kenyan artist Troy Howe re-creates classic paintings with a ballpoint pen. Taking up to 16 hours on each work, he has drawn pen versions of Leonardo da Vinci's *Mona Lisa*, Johannes Vermeer's *Girl with a Pearl Earring* and a portrait of the U.K.'s Queen Elizabeth II.

EXPENSIVE PITCHER ■ A priceless 1,000-year-old Egyptian carved rock-crystal pitcher sold for around $6 million in England in October 2008—nine months after nearly being sold for just $200. A Somerset auction house had wrongly identified it as a 19th-century French claret jug, but luckily for the owner the first sale was declared void.

DESK CARVINGS ■ Chris Reeves from Hertfordshire, England, carved a complete nativity scene—including beautiful 3-ft-high (90-cm) wooden figurines of Mary, Joseph, and the Angel Gabriel—from a pile of old schoolroom desks.

EDIBLE NATIVITY ■ A farm shop in Crawley, Sussex, England, staged a nativity scene at Christmas 2008 with all the characters made from fruit and vegetables. The Three Wise Men were made of marrows, onions and apples, Mary and Joseph were made from butternut squash with lemon crowns, sheep were created from cauliflower florets, and baby Jesus was made from carrots.

DUMPSTER PARK ■ Oliver Bishop-Young from London, England, creates urban artworks in dumpsters. He has turned the yellow containers into a skateboard park, a swimming pool, a living room and even a miniature park complete with a park bench.

FOOD COVERS ■ A Japanese website has featured dozens of famous CD album covers made using traditional lunchbox food such as seaweed, egg, potatoes and ham—all on a standard rice base. Album-cover designs by the Obacchi Jacket Lunch Box site include *Voodoo Lounge* by the Rolling Stones and *In Utero* by Nirvana.

TOPIARY PUDDING ■ Roger and Valerie Holley from Somerset, England, spent five years creating a 20-ft-high (6-m) topiary Christmas pudding in their front garden. They merged and pruned two conifer trees into a round shape before adding plywood leaves, and berries made from toilet ballcocks.

www.ripleybooks.com

www.ripleys.com

206

ARTISTIC LICENSE

Ripley's—
Believe It or Not!®

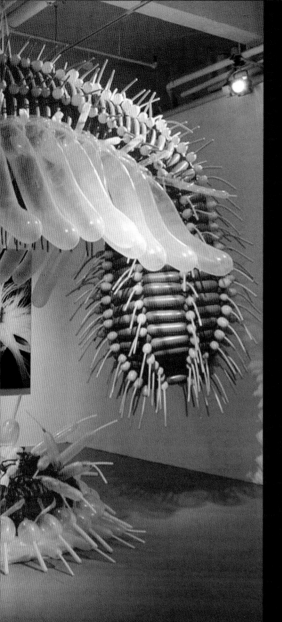

Jason's installation, Alien Rainforest, complete with human model.

LARD STATUES ■ A Gurkha chef in the British army won an award in 2008 for hand-carving a sculpture of a Buddha statue from lard. Lance Corporal Amrit Limbu—originally from Nepal—took 100 hours to make the intricate statue, preparing an inner structure from wire and muslin before adding 11 blocks of animal fat.

BARNEY ORDEAL ■ Colorado judge Paul Sacco has devised an unorthodox punishment for noise polluters—he forces them to sit in a room and listen to an hour of hits from such artists as Barry Manilow and Barney the dinosaur.

MOVIE CAMERAS ■ Retired Greek postman Dimitris Pistiolas has a collection of more than 930 vintage movie cameras. He started collecting them 64 years ago at age 15 and they cover every inch of wall in the basement of his Athens house. He nearly lost his prized collection to an earthquake but █████ a sense of impending doom, he had r████ome five hours before the quake to secure the cameras firmly in place.

CREATING A STINK ■ Belgian conceptual artist Jan Fabre's 2008 exhibit "Spring is on the way" consisted of rows of onions and potatoes hanging from an Antwerp museum ceiling. However, as the vegetables started to rot, visitors complained about the smell.

MONEY SEA ■ Seattle, Washington, artist Chris Jordan created a series of artworks based on American statistics. He made a sea of 426,000 cell phones—the number thrown away in the U.S.A. each day—and a forest of one million toothpicks, equal to the number of trees felled to manufacture the paper needed for the junk mail sent in the U.S.A. each year.

CONVERTED TOILETS ■ A public restroom in Munich, Germany, proved a popular tourist attraction after being converted into an art museum in October 2008. Built in 1894, the toilet house closed down in 1992 but reopened with paintings—including images of Barack Obama—hanging over the urinals.

BOTTLE MYSTERY ■ Puzzled residents of Stourbridge, England, awoke in 2008 to find beautiful drawings of cows and mice carved into their glass milk bottles. The mystery designs were the work of local artist Charlotte Hughes-Martin who planted the bottles at random addresses under cover of darkness.

WEIGHTY TOME ■ *Una Dotta Mano* (meaning "the learned hand"), an Italian velvet-and-marble-bound book depicting the life and work of Michelangelo, weighs an incredible 62 lb (28 kg) and is valued at more than $100,000.

CHOCOLATE MODEL ■ Italian artist Angelo Feduzzi made a 35-ft-high (10.6-m) scale model of London, England's Big Ben clock tower—from 17,600 lb (8,000 kg) of chocolate. The edible tower stood for a week in December 2008 before being sliced up and handed out to visitors at a Christmas food festival in the town of Macerata Feltria, Italy.

LIFE IN BLACK AND WHITE

Maverick artist Scott Blake creates well-known portraits made up from hundreds of humble bar-code bars.

He started to think about using bar codes in art around the time of the millennium computer-bug scare. While manipulating images on a computer, he discovered that some of the patterns resembled bar codes, and he decided to make portraits of famous faces using the everyday black-and-white lines that we usually ignore. Scott's first piece of bar-code art was of Jesus—he manipulated 940 barcodes over 48 sheets of paper and stuck them together to complete the face. A portrait of Elvis consists of hundreds of bar codes from real-life Elvis Presley products.

Scott has also created interactive pieces where scanning the bar codes on a portrait of an icon such as Bruce Lee or Elvis flashes up images of them on a screen. When scanned, every bar code on the picture of Bruce Lee will play a fight scene from one of his movies. Scott also works with tattoos, flipbooks and online art using bar codes. These include an automatic counter that will run through every possible bar-code number combination—over 100,000,000,000—for more than 300 years.

A bar-code portrait of martial-arts legend and movie star Bruce Lee has formed part of an interactive piece by Scott.

208

The further you hold the page away from your eyes, the clearer the King becomes.

❯ The first patent for a bar code was issued in 1952. The very first bar codes were orange and blue stripes, used to keep track of freight-train cars as they traveled around the U.S.A.

❯ International insect experts are interested in placing miniature bar codes on bees to help track more than 20,000 different species of bee.

❯ The first two numbers of a bar code always identify the country of origin. Each number of the bar code is represented by two black and two white bars of varying widths, which the scanner reads.

❯ The U.S. Army have used bar codes up to 2 ft (60 cm) in length to label large boats in docks.

Scott uses the bar codes at varying sizes to create the desired effect.

Scott's interpretation of Jesus, made from bar codes.

Scott standing in front of his portrait of Jesus.

ARTISTIC LICENSE

With stunts that definitely come under the heading "Don't do this at home," Chinese photographer and performance artist Li Wei appears to defy gravity.

One minute he is floating horizontally from a window on the 29th floor of a Beijing skyscraper, the next he is buried at an angle of almost 45 degrees with his head through the windshield of a car or he is submerged vertically, headfirst in a lake.

Li Wei's spectacular self-portraits, which sell for up to $8,000, do not use computer software. Instead, the 38-year-old farmer's son from Beijing often risks life and limb, using invisible steel wire supports to hang in midair vast distances above the ground.

Other photos are created with the help of a 3-ft-sq (0.3-sq-m) mirror with a hole in the center large enough to accommodate his head and neck. He then places his head through the hole and projects his image onto various historical and urban settings.

Li Wei has taken his hair-raising performances all over the world—to the U.S.A., Italy, Spain, Australia and Korea—including a series of startling photographs showing him crashing into walls and sidewalks.

It may seem that Li Wei has already achieved the ultimate in death-defying art, but his aim is to take it to a higher level by hovering from even taller buildings.

Among Li Wei's most celebrated works are his free-falling series of photographs, where he appears certain to have plunged to his death.

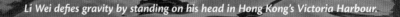

Li Wei defies gravity by standing on his head in Hong Kong's Victoria Harbour.

Ripley's ask

Why did you start performance art?

I studied oil painting first. In 1996, I started to do performance art. In the beginning, I used photos and video works only to record my performance art. Later, I turned to photography.

How do you describe your art?

My photos always immortalize me at the very limits of the absurd and are stupendous for their originality that, at times, borders on madness. My form of artistic experimentation is a metaphor for a restless existential state that puts stress on our physical condition by putting it to the test and going beyond the limits of human resistance.

How do you suspend yourself in the air?

I use iron wire on my back to hang myself up.

Is any of your work dangerous?

Yes, it's dangerous. That's why I'm fascinated with it.

What kind of reactions do the photos get? Are people scared by them?

People love my work. They react in different ways. Some think it humorous and others think it unique.

What are your future plans?

I'll try 3-D animation and also statues. I've made some statues full of broken mirrors. I'll do more and more in the future. Also, I won't stop performance art.

Wires strapped to Li Wei's back enable him to hover from skyscrapers.

In addition to wire supports, Li Wei uses his acrobatic skills to achieve striking poses.

Body of Art

Disregarding paper, canvas and clay, artist Emma Hack from Adelaide, Australia, uses human bodies as the medium for her work. Emma takes body painting to a new level, but because the human form is limiting—it never changes and there's only so much you can paint—she combines models with painted and computer-generated backgrounds. Her wallpaper designs are influenced by famous Australian designer Florence Broadhurst's papers of the 1960s and 1970s.

BLURRED FICTION ■ When Norman Mailer began to write his novel *Barbary Shore*, he had no intention of including a Russian spy, but gradually the character evolved to play a major part in the story. After the novel was finished, the U.S. Immigration Service arrested a man who lived just one floor above Mailer in the same apartment building. He was Colonel Rudolf Abel, said to be the top Russian spy working in the U.S. at that time.

REVERSE RECITAL ■ On hearing any French or Latin poem just once, French soldier and naturalist Baron de Ferussac (1786–1836) could recite it backward.

POETRY STUDY ■ Marc-Antoine Oudinet (1643–1712), who later became a famed French coin expert, memorized all 12 books of Virgil's "Aeneid"—10,000 lines of poetry—in a single week at the age of 12.

VALUABLE VASE ■ A couple who bought a "junk vase" for £1 at a garage sale in Scotland later sold it for more than £32,000 after it turned out to be an item of valuable glassware by French designer René Lalique.

SPELLING ERROR ■ V star Oprah Winfrey should have been called Orpah after the biblical figure. However, the midwife misspelled the name on the birth certificate.

BIG RIG JIG

Rearing four stories high into the air, a sculpture consisting of two 18-wheeler trucks fused together has wowed audiences at festivals across the U.S.A. Seen here at the Burning Man event in Nevada, the monster "Big Rig Jig" was designed and built by a team led by artist Mike Ross who has been creating large-scale sculptures for more than ten years. Viewers can actually crawl inside the structure, moving between the two trucks.

THE NAME'S BOND ◼ In 2006, David Fearn of Walsall, England, an avid 007 James Bond fan, had his name changed to James Dr. No From Russia With Love Goldfinger Thunderball You Only Live Twice On Her Majesty's Secret Service Diamonds Are Forever Live And Let Die The Man With The Golden Gun The Spy Who Loved Me Moonraker For Your Eyes Only Octopussy A View To A Kill The Living Daylights License To Kill Golden Eye Tomorrow Never Dies The World Is Not Enough Die Another Day Casino Royale Bond.

RECYCLED MATERIALS ◼ All of the attractions at the City Museum, St. Louis, Missouri, are made from recycled materials found within the city boundaries—including old bridges, roof tiles, construction cranes, chimneys and even two abandoned airplanes.

TOILET DRAMA ◼ Directed and written by Irish playwright Paul Walker, a March 2008 production of *Ladies and Gents* was staged in a public restroom in New York City.

SPIDER DRAWING ◼ Faced with paying an overdue utility bill, design director David Thorne from Adelaide, Australia, tried to settle the account by sending a drawing of a spider instead. He said he valued the drawing at $233.95—the amount owed—but his offer was rejected.

MODELS DROWNED ◼ Environmentally friendly artist Nick Crowe staged a series of models on a beach in Kent, England, in 2008 that were "drowned" whenever the tide came in. The models represented low-lying islands in the Pacific Ocean.

STICKY OUTFIT ◼ Charis Hill of Oriental, North Carolina, attended her high school prom wearing a gown made from five rolls of duct tape. She wore the leftover tape from the fifth roll as a bracelet. She even made shoes from duct tape, packing the tape to create a 1-in (2.5-cm) heel and then topping them with crisscross straps.

SECURE VAULT ◼ A group of museum curators kept relics from Afghanistan's National Museum safe from decades of conflict in a hidden vault that required seven keys to open.

KEYBOARD SNAKE ◼ Korea's Choi Jung Hyun has built a likeness of a viper from recycled computer keyboards.

WRONG GEAR ◼ As a young man, Hollywood star Sidney Poitier was sacked from his job parking cars—because he could not drive. He mixed up first gear with reverse and ploughed into another car.

Wire Art

Queensland, Australia, artist Ivan Lovett renders famous faces of rock in an entirely new way—he molds them from regular chicken wire. Busts of legends such as John Lennon and Mick Jagger have been formed from bent, twisted and layered wire, with each piece taking about three weeks to create.

"I started working on these mosaics in a class that taught computer graphics programs. I learned there are endless ways to use the programs; all you need is the idea. So with that approach, I began to experiment and quickly figured you could use Post-It® notes for pictures. So I ran some numbers and found a picture that I wanted to do. After I designed it, I began to plan it and look into the costs and getting hold of the supplies. I had a lot of fun working on it and it was an experimental project that turned out to fit my plan perfectly. As I am studying to become an art teacher, I want to be able to bring something new and original to the classroom. Basically, you don't have to be good at drawing to be an artist."

ACE ROCK STAR ART

A mosaic of rock legend Jimi Hendrix standing 25 ft (7.6 m) high is striking enough, but when you peer closer and see that it is created from 8,500 playing cards—more than 150 decks—the creation of David Alvarez, an art student from Leavenworth, Washington, really comes to life.

Among David's other work is a large mosaic of the singer Ray Charles made out of Post-it® notes, which is on display in the Ripley's Museum in Korea. To prove that you don't have to be able to draw to be great at art, David plans his pieces meticulously on a computer. For his card portraits, he then stacks the cards in the exact order they will be used on the wall. It took David 20 solid hours to complete the huge image of Hendrix.

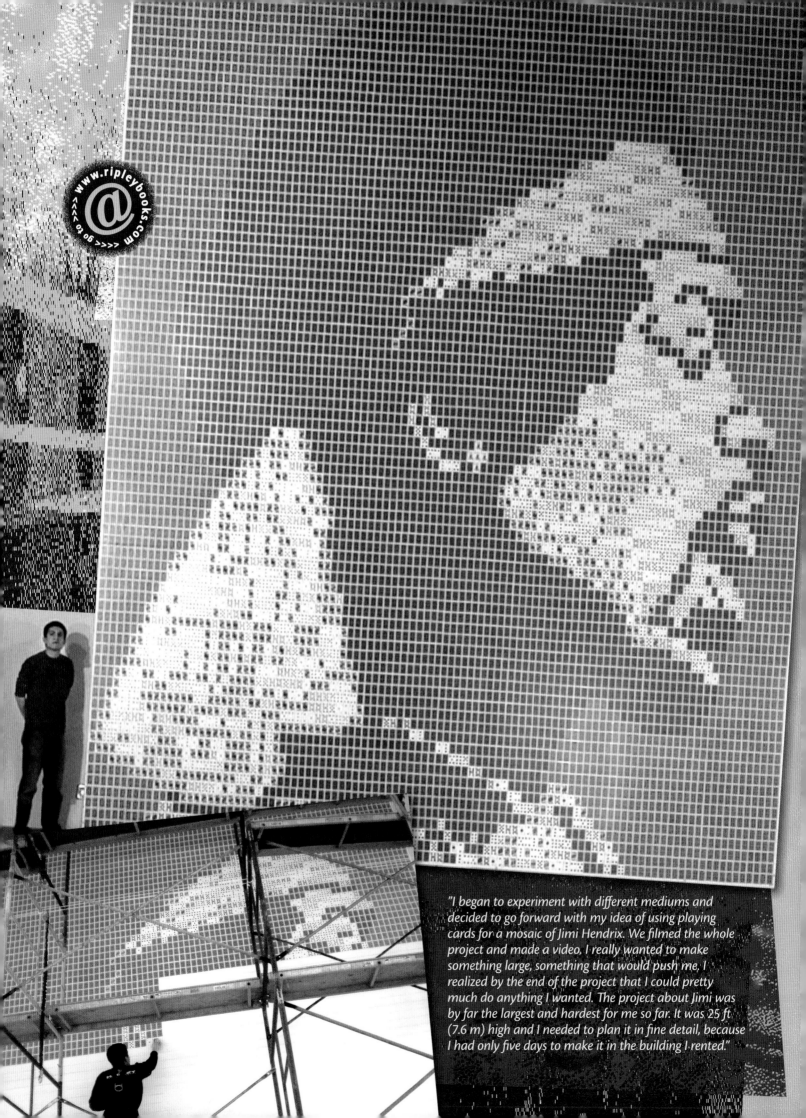

"I began to experiment with different mediums and decided to go forward with my idea of using playing cards for a mosaic of Jimi Hendrix. We filmed the whole project and made a video. I really wanted to make something large, something that would push me. I realized by the end of the project that I could pretty much do anything I wanted. The project about Jimi was by far the largest and hardest for me so far. It was 25 ft (7.6 m) high and I needed to plan it in fine detail, because I had only five days to make it in the building I rented."

CRAZY!

DO LOCUSTS ENJOY *STAR WARS*?	Claire Rind and Peter Simmons of the University of Newcastle, England, electrically monitored the brain activity of a locust while it was watching selected highlights from the movie *Star Wars*.
WHERE DOES NAVEL LINT COME FROM?	Karl Kruszelnicki of the University of Sydney, Australia, conducted an in-depth study into human belly fluff, determining how and when people get it and what color it is likely to be.
ARE DOG-BASED FLEAS MORE ATHLETIC?	French biologists Marie-Christine Cadiergues, Christel Joubert and Michel Franc discovered that fleas that live on dogs jump higher than fleas that live on cats.
WHAT DID I EAT 27 YEARS AGO TODAY?	Dr. Yoshiro Nakamatsu of Tokyo, Japan, has photographed and analyzed every meal he has eaten for nearly 40 years.
WHY DON'T WOODPECKERS GET HEADACHES?	Ivan R. Schwab and Philip R.A. May of the University of California explored why woodpeckers don't get headaches.
ARE ARMADILLOS A NUISANCE TO ARCHEOLOGISTS?	Brazilian archeologists Astolfo Araujo and José Carlos Marcelino conducted an experiment to show that armadillos can mix up the contents of an archeological site.
HOW OFTEN DO PEOPLE HAVE THEIR EYES CLOSED IN PHOTOS?	Australians Nic Svenson and Piers Barnes calculated that if a group of 15 people were to be photographed, the photographer should take five shots to (almost) ensure that nobody in the final picture will have their eyes closed.
HOW EASY IS IT TO SWIM THROUGH SYRUP?	Edward Cussler and Brian Gettelfinger of the University of Minnesota discovered that people can swim just as fast in syrup as they can in water.
HOW CAN YOU LEVITATE A FROG?	Andre Geim of the University of Nijmegen, the Netherlands, and Sir Michael Berry of Bristol University, England, conducted an experiment in which they used magnets to levitate a frog.
HOW DIFFICULT IS IT TO DRAG A SHEEP?	Seven Australian scientists filed a report titled "An Analysis of the Forces Required to Drag Sheep over Various Surfaces."

CREATED CREATURES

FLUORESCENT FISH	A Taiwanese company has created a species of genetically engineered fish that glow in the dark.
HUMAN SHEEP	Scientists in Edinburgh, Scotland, created Tracy, a sheep that was genetically modified so that her milk produced human protein, which could be used in the treatment of cystic fibrosis.
SEE-THROUGH FROG	Scientists in Japan have bred transparent frogs whose organs and blood vessels can be seen clearly through their skins.
CLONED DOG	In 2005, South Korean scientists successfully cloned a three-year-old Afghan hound, creating a puppy called Snuppy—short for Seoul National University puppy.
GENETICALLY MODIFIED MONKEY	In 2001, scientists in Oregon created a genetically modified rhesus monkey called ANDi (backward for "inserted DNA") in the hope that it would help them combat a range of crippling diseases.
MOUSE WITH HUMAN EAR	In 1997, Dr. Jay Vacanti of Boston, Massachusetts, grew a human ear on the back of a mouse.
GLOWING CATS	Scientists in South Korea have created cats that glow red under ultraviolet light.
FEARLESS MOUSE	By turning off specific receptors in a mouse's brain, scientists at Tokyo University, Japan, have created genetically modified mice that are not scared of cats.
GOATS WITH GAS ANTIDOTE	A U.S. biotech company breeds special goats that produce a nerve-gas antidote in their milk.
PROTEIN-RICH HEN	Scottish scientists are working to clone hens with eggs rich in certain proteins that could be used to make anti-cancer drugs.
CLONED CAT	In 2002, researchers in Texas cloned a domestic cat, producing a kitten that they named CopyCat.

Two teddy bears were propelled 18 mi (29 km) into space on a four-hour expedition in 2008. Wearing specially made space suits, the teddies endured temperatures of −31°F (−35°C) as they were strapped to seats attached to a weather balloon that had been launched from Cambridge, England. After completing their mission to monitor weather conditions in the stratosphere, the pair parachuted safely back to Earth.

≫ AMAZING SCIENCE

Out in Space...

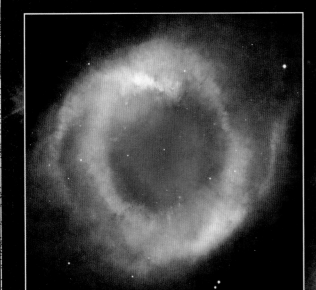

Snapping stunning photographs of galaxies millions of miles from Earth is the job of the Hubble Space Telescope, launched in 1990 at a cost of $1.5 billion, and named after the U.S. astronomer Edwin Hubble.

From its position in orbit some 353 mi (568 km) above the Earth, the camera is free from the Earth's atmosphere, giving it a far better view of space than telescopes on Earth despite moving at 17,500 mph (27,358 km/h). The telescope has sent many thousands of pictures back to Earth, and each week produces enough data to fill 3,600 ft (1,097 m) of books on a bookshelf.

Helix Nebula

NASA used nine different pictures taken by both the Hubble Space Telescope and a telescope in Tucson, Arizona, to produce this photograph of the Helix Nebula, because the nebula (an enormous cloud of dust and gas) is too big for one camera to capture. Formed from gases expelled by a dying star, like our Sun, it is 690 light years away— this means that light from the nebula takes 690 years to reach Earth, traveling a whopping 4,000 trillion Earth miles.

Sombrero Galaxy

The "Sombrero Galaxy" is so-called because it is shaped like the famous Mexican hat. What looks like a solid band of rock is actually a ring of space dust and, with its brilliantly bright core, it can be seen with small telescopes from Earth. It is 800 billion times the size of our Sun, 50,000 light years across—one light year is equivalent to about 5.8 trillion miles (9.3 trillion km)—and has a massive black hole in it. The galaxy is about 28 million light years away from Earth, and is estimated to be hurtling away from us at a speed of 700 miles per second (1,126 km per second) owing to the expansion of the universe.

SPACE FACTS

❯ The Earth orbits the Sun, a star, which is the center of our Solar System. Our Solar System is one of possibly billions that lie in our galaxy, the Milky Way. There are at least 200 billion stars in the Milky Way, which, in turn, is one of more than 100 billion possible galaxies in the known universe.

❯ Each year more than 14,000 tons of cosmic dust fall to Earth—that's equivalent to the weight of more than 3,000 African elephants.

❯ Our galaxy, the Milky Way, is 100,000 light years wide. In Earth miles, this is almost 600 quadrillion, or 600 thousand million million, miles. This means that if you traveled at 100 mph (161 km/h) it would take more than 600,000,000,000 years—600 billion—to get to the other side.

❯ We can see only 0.000002 percent, or around 2,500, of the stars in the Milky Way with the naked eye from any fixed point on the Earth.

Whirlpool

The Whirlpool Galaxy features "arms" of stars and gas laced with space dust. The galaxy is 31 million light years away from Earth.

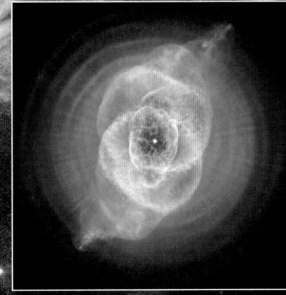

Cat's Eye Nebula

Like a great eye peering from a distant galaxy, the Cat's Eye Nebula was one of the first to be seen, more than 200 years ago, and can be found 3,300 light years from Earth. This particular nebula features dust rings in a circular pattern. Each ring of dust is thought to contain as much mass as all the planets in our Solar System combined.

Red Supergiant

A red supergiant star 20,000 light years away from Earth suddenly brightened for a few weeks— becoming 600,000 times brighter than our Sun. The Hubble Space Telescope caught the results some two years later as dust swirled around the star at the center, like the flash of a camera itself.

Child Genius

Babies at a hospital in Kosice, Slovakia, are introduced to culture almost as soon as they are born, as classical music is piped through headphones in the maternity ward. Reports suggest that listening to music at an early age can aid the development of young minds, with Mozart and Vivaldi being the most popular composers.

TINY BIBLE ▥ Scientists at the Technion Institute in Haifa, Israel, etched a copy of the Hebrew Bible on a silicon surface smaller than 0.01 inch square.

STILL TICKING ▥ A watch that was returned to its owner after being lost in 1941 was still working despite having spent 66 years on the ocean floor. The watch slipped off the wrist of Teddy Bacon, from Cheshire, England, while he was serving as a young officer with the Royal Navy in Gibraltar and was eventually discovered by workers who were dredging the harbor in 2007.

PLANT DIGNITY ▥ A law requires researchers in Switzerland to consider the personal dignity of plants that are used in scientific experiments.

ROBOT SOCCER ▥ Hundreds of teams from dozens of countries compete annually in a robotic soccer tournament called Robocup. The competition takes place in a different country each year and the organizers hope to develop a fully autonomous team of robots that can win against a human champion soccer team by 2050.

CLEANER CLOTHES ▥ A British company is developing self-cleaning clothes, using technology first invented by the U.S. Air Force. A solution of dirt-repellent chemicals is applied to fabrics with the help of nanoparticles, which hold the chemicals in place and also form a protective layer on the resulting clothing.

TRAINED FISH ▥ Researchers at the Marine Biological Laboratory at Wood's Hole, Massachusetts, have been training fish to catch themselves by using a recognizable tone to lure them into a net. The trained fish would be released into the ocean and once they have reached market size they would be enticed into an underwater cage on hearing a tone they associate with food.

JUMBO CALCULATOR ▥ Studies carried out on elephants at a Tokyo zoo suggest that they are cleverer than humans at mental math. In a test that involved dropping varying numbers of apples into two buckets and recording how often the participants correctly chose the bucket with the most fruit, the elephants scored 74 percent against the humans' 67 percent. In fact one Indian elephant, Ashya, scored an amazing 87 percent.

EMOTIONAL ROBOT ▥ Scientists at the University of the West of England in the U.K. have built a robot that reacts emotionally to the way it is treated. Heart Robot has a beating heart, a stomach that moves as it "breathes" and sensors that respond to movement, noise and touch. If it is cuddled, its breathing relaxes and its heartbeat slows, but if it is shouted at, it flinches, clenches its hands and its breathing and heart rate speed up.

SAFETY BEAR ▥ A talking teddy bear has been developed by Japanese scientists to help motorists find their way through traffic. The robot bear, which is 12 in (30 cm) tall and sits on the car's dashboard, has moving arms and neck so that it can point lost drivers in the right direction. It is also programmed to say, "Watch out!" in the event of sudden acceleration or braking and "You haven't been drinking, have you?" if it detects alcohol on a driver's breath.

Micro Magic

Baby bird or extra terrestrial? With this picture of a chicken embryo—an entry in a competition to find the best miniature science photographs—it is hard to tell. It demonstrates the art of "Photomicrography" whereby scientists use microscopes and computers to capture stunning close-ups of life that are too small for the naked eye to see. The subjects are often dyed so their structures can be seen more clearly, hence the bright color of this bug-eyed bird.

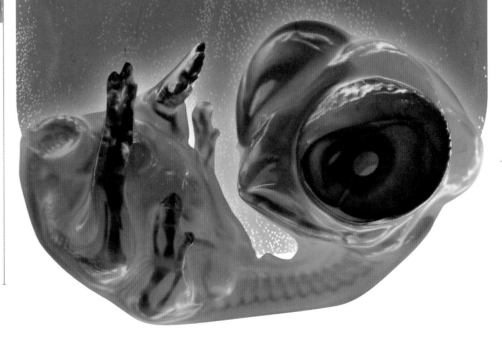

NORTH FACING ■ Scientists from the University of Duiburg-Essen, Germany, have deduced that cows automatically point north because they have their own in-built compasses—a relic from the days when their bovine ancestors needed a reliable sense of direction to migrate across the plains of Africa, Asia and Europe.

LIFELIKE DUMMY ■ To provide realistic training for medics, the University of Portsmouth, England, has devised a mannequin that not only moves and feels like a real patient, it can bleed, vomit, sweat, and even suffer heart attacks. The remote-controlled dummy, called iStan, is designed to replicate a human's anatomical structure, to the point of having bowels that make lifelike sounds.

DINOSAUR DUNG ■ A pile of dinosaur dung 130 million years old was sold at a New York auction for $960 in April 2008. The fossilized dung, from the Jurassic era, was bought by Steve Tsengas of Fairport Harbor, Ohio, to motivate employees in his company that treats dog and cat feces.

VITAL VENOM ■ Researchers in California believe that scorpion venom can be used in the body to transport chemicals that attack brain tumors. Initial trials show that a peptide found in the venom of the giant yellow Israeli scorpion can be used to target aggressive tumors by delivering radioactive iodine that destroys the tumor tissue.

SAME ANCESTORS ■ Studies of mitochondrial DNA reveal that if we go back far enough, we all have the same ancestors. Every person alive today is ultimately descended from a woman who lived in Africa approximately 140,000 years ago.

DANCING SUIT ■ The Pacer suit concept is the techno version of a one-man band. The sensors in the suit read electrical impulses from muscle movement so that you actually dance to create music—and should therefore always move in time. The suit can also be used as a form of therapy to aid the stimulation of specific muscles in the human body.

SHEEP SHADES ■ U.K.-based artist Julia Lohmann makes lampshades from sheep's stomachs. She buys the discarded stomachs from her local butcher for $10 and, following the insertion of a balloon to give it a bulbous shape, converts the organ into a lampshade, which she sells for $500.

INSECT INSPECTORS

Bees are being trained to sniff out bombs by U.S. scientists in New Mexico. The insects, which have a highly developed sense of smell, are rewarded with sugar water when they detect explosives. They are strapped into specially designed containers that leave their heads exposed so that they can be observed closely—when the bees smell the scent of explosives in the air they wave their proboscises around, expecting their reward.

BIG BIRD ■ A dinosaur recently discovered to have lived in Inner Mongolia, China, named *Gigantoraptor erlianensis*, stood up to 16 ft (4.8 m) tall, had a toothless beak, and may have been covered in feathers.

COMPUTER BEAVER ■ Artist Kasey McMahon from Los Angeles, California, has invented the Compubeaver—a computer housed in a dead beaver! She bought the beaver ready-stuffed and cut out the foam interior with an electric carving knife. After inserting the computer tower, she reinforced the animal with fiberglass.

HICCUP BLOG ■ A man from Lincoln, England, set up an on-line blog to find a cure for the hiccups that he'd had for five months. Christopher Sands recorded his woes in *The Hiccup Diary* on the networking site MySpace.

MOSS MAT ■ Nguyen La Chanh from Switzerland has invented a living bathmat made of moss. Her mat, which contains 70 pieces of ball, island and forest moss, feels soft underfoot, does not smell when it gets damp and is kept alive by the water that drips from the user's body.

NIBBLED PENCILS ■ A British company has launched a range of pre-chewed pencils in a bid to help children concentrate. It says that because the pencils look chewed already, students are less likely to put them in their mouths.

DRIP DRY ■ An Australian company has invented a suit that can be worn in the shower. Australian Wool Innovation says the suit, aimed at busy businessmen, has been specially designed so that it can be washed clean under the shower head, with no need for dry cleaning or soap.

Inviting 100,000 volts onto your head while standing in a swimming pool doesn't sound smart, but Peter knows what he is doing and achieves spectacular results. The foil stretches down into the saltwater pool, which conducts electricity and grounds it. Peter attaches wires to protect his face, but the experiment could go badly wrong if his body conducts the electricity to the water instead of the foil, and the electricity then returns to the Tesla coil to complete the circuit.

Peter generates huge showers of sparks.

Peter stands inside his **Dalek Cage** (also known as a **Faraday Cage**) electrical shield, which allows him to watch the show safely from inside.

Lightning Strike

Electronic adventurer Peter Terren from Western Australia enjoys playing with lightning in his backyard. What he calls the "Holy Art of Electrickery" involves creating wild-looking light sculptures using up to 500,000 volts. The centerpiece of his shows is an electrical device called a Tesla Coil. His experiments are potentially lethal given the vast electrical charges used, but even after sitting in a swimming pool in a foil hat as 100,000 volts of homemade lightning flashed about his head, the daring experimentalist reported "no sensation" at all.

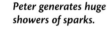

WHAT IS A TESLA COIL?

The Tesla Coil was invented by Serbian scientist Nicola Tesla in the late 19th century. It is an electrical transformer that generates extremely high voltages. The coil discharges electrical energy into the air, creating impressive arcs of sparks, or plasma, that resemble lightning. They are potentially very dangerous owing to the high voltages produced, often well in excess of 1,000,000 volts, and the electrical field created can light unconnected neon lights up to 50 ft (15 m) away.

An innovative and frightening car-theft-prevention device is one of Peter's many ideas. Any occupants of the car are safe from the electricity, because the car body acts as a protective cage.

LIGHT YEARS ■ A woman on the Isle of Wight, England, has a lightbulb that is still burning brightly after more than 70 years. Whereas most bulbs have a lifespan of between 750 and 1,000 hours, Mo Richardson's Swann-Edison filament bulb, bought in 1938, has been switched on for more than 600,000 hours.

PERFECT POSTURE ■ A small gadget attached to the skin is available that buzzes to remind the wearer to sit up straight, thereby reducing the risk of backache. Invented by Dr. Moacir Schnapp of Memphis, Tennessee, the iPosture vibrates discreetly if the wearer slouches by more than three degrees for one minute.

URINE POWER ■ In Singapore, scientists have managed to generate electricity from urine. When a drop of urine is added to a piece of paper soaked in copper chloride, the resultant chemical reaction produces electricity. The inventors hope that the paper battery can be used in disposable kits to help people monitor their health at home.

ROBOT CONDUCTOR ■ In May 2008, the Detroit Symphony Orchestra performed "The Impossible Dream" under the direction of a robot. The white metal conductor, which stood 4 ft 3 in (1.3 m) tall, was built by the Honda company and is known as ASIMO, which stands for Advanced Step in Innovative Mobility. Engineers had programed it to mimic a human conductor so that it nodded its head at sections of the orchestra, gestured with one or both hands and took a bow at the end.

PAPER AIRPLANE ■ The Japanese Space Program (JAXA) is developing a paper airplane that can survive a trip falling from the International Space Station all the way to Earth. The origami glider will be able to withstand wind speeds of 5,300 mph (8,530 km/h).

RAT ROBOT ■ A robot that is controlled by a blob of rat brain cells could provide insights into diseases such as Alzheimer's and Parkinson's. The 300,000 rat neurons are being taught to steer the robot around obstacles and, by studying what happens to the neurons as they learn, scientists at the University of Reading, Berkshire, England, hope to discover more about how memory works.

TIME MACHINE ■ Ever since his father died of a massive heart attack at age 33, Ronald L. Mallett, a professor of physics at the University of Connecticut, has devoted his energies to inventing a time machine so that he could travel back in time and save his father by telling him not to smoke.

HEAT LOSS ■ The protective tiles on NASA's space shuttle dissipate heat so quickly that they can be held by hand just seconds after leaving a 2,300°F (1,260°C) oven.

COOL CLOTHES ■ A Japanese company has invented a range of self-cooling clothes to help the wearer combat the heat of summer. Two small fans, powered by a rechargeable battery, are sewn into the back of the garment and circulate air across the person's skin, although some people have complained that the billowing air makes them look larger than they really are.

ASTRONOMICAL PREDICTIONS ■ The Antikythera Mechanism, a device retrieved in 1901 from the wreck of a 1st-century-BC Roman merchant vessel, could not only make calculations, it could also predict the future, including astronomical events such as the spring and fall equinoxes and the phases of the Moon. It could also locate the position of other planets in the Solar System.

YEAST GENERATED ■ Living yeast cultures generated electricity for the lights, sound and motion of Jon Karafin's 25-ft-tall (7.6-m), two-ton mechanical sculpture in Rochester, New York, in December 2007.

JET PACK ■ New Zealand inventor Glenn Martin has spent three decades perfecting a jet pack that could enable commuters to fly to work. He says the contraption, which carries five gallons of gas, should be able to fly an average-sized pilot 30 mi (48 km) in 30 minutes on a full tank. At its unveiling at a 2008 Wisconsin air show, it climbed to 3 ft (90 cm) off the ground and hovered for 45 seconds before returning to Earth.

SMART GLASSES ■ A pair of eyeglasses, incorporating advanced software, has been designed that can recognize objects. The Japanese Smart Goggle records everything the wearer sees, so that if you lose something you can tell the glasses what you're looking for and the technology will show you when and where you last saw it. The amazing robotic specs will also identify unknown plants and faces.

INTERNET INSECT ■ British scientist Dr. Richard Harrington discovered a previously unknown insect in 2008—on eBay. Thinking it would merely make an interesting curio, he had bought the fossilized insect encased in amber for $40 from a Lithuanian seller, but it turned out to be a long extinct and hitherto undescribed species of aphid, which was duly given the name *Mindarus harringtoni*.

SEA MONSTER ■ Norwegian scientists have discovered the existence of a huge prehistoric sea reptile that measured approximately 50 ft (15 m) long. The 150-million-year-old pliosaur, found on the Arctic island of Spitsbergen in 2006, is believed to have been so powerful that it would have been able to pick up a small car in its jaws and bite it in half.

ACCOUNT FROZEN! ■ John Shepherd-Barron came up with the idea of the ATM, which first went into service in London, England, in 1967, after being locked out of his bank. Today, there are some 1.5 million cash-dispenser machines around the world, including one at the South Pole to serve Antarctic researchers.

MONSTER PHONE ■ A Chinese man created a working cell phone that is 3 ft (90 cm) high and weighs 48 lb (22 kg). Mr. Tan, of Songyuan City, says the phone is an exact copy of his own model—but 620 times bigger. It has a built-in camera and Internet access, but has to be plugged into the main electricity supply as he hasn't been able to build a large enough battery.

PURIFYING TRICYCLE ■ To help people in the developing world who have to make long journeys to collect water, which is often unsafe to drink, California-based design firm IDEO has devised a tricycle that purifies water as the rider pedals. Called Aquaduct, it has a large water tank mounted over the rear axles. Pedaling draws water from this tank through a filter to a second, removable tank in front of the handlebars.

INVISIBLE OBJECTS ■ Scientists at the University of California have developed a material that can bend light around 3-D objects, rendering them invisible. The team believes the material, whose structure is transparent over a wide range of light wavelengths, could be used to make invisibility cloaks large enough to hide people.

MODIFIED MOUSE ■ A mouse with a blocked-up nose has been bred to help people afflicted with chronic sinusitis, a disease that takes away their sense of smell. The genetically modified mouse was developed by Johns Hopkins medical institutions in Baltimore, Maryland, to provide researchers with a tool for investigating sinus problems.

CORPORATE CLOUDS ■ U.S. entrepreneur Francisco Guerra has managed to create foam clouds shaped like corporate logos that can float 20,000 ft (6,000 m) into the air. The 4-ft (1.2-m) shapes—known as Flogos—are machine-made from tiny soapy bubbles filled with helium.

BANG

In the most ambitious experiment in human history, scientists have been attempting to unlock the secrets of how our universe began millions of years ago. The birth of the universe is commonly known as the Big Bang, and the scientists plan to re-create the conditions immediately after it occurred.

The ambitious experiment has been taking place 330 ft (100 m) below ground in a specially built 17-mi (27-km) circular tunnel running beneath the border between France and Switzerland. Two beams of tiny particles, called protons, are steered in opposite directions around the circuit at close to the speed of light, completing approximately 11,000 laps—a total of 187,000 mi (300,950 km)—every second. By smashing these particles together with tremendous force, scientists hope that new, even smaller particles will emerge, revealing insights into the nature of the cosmos.

Protons are found in the central part, or nucleus, of an atom. Atoms are the basic building blocks of life. They can join together to create molecules, which in turn form most of the objects around us—chairs, glass, even the air.

Hundreds of billions of protons are propelled around the tunnel so that they collide at a rate of 80 million per second. Although 200 billion protons are lined up to collide, they are so tiny—each is a trillionth the size of a mosquito—that only around 20 will actually clash. These collisions take place inside vast detectors in the tunnels and create temperatures 100,000 times hotter than the core of the Sun. Just one of the detectors weighs 13,800 tons.

The experiment, launched in September 2008, is the result of collaboration between more than 10,000 scientists and engineers from over 80 countries and 500 universities.

The 17-mi (27-km) tunnel is large enough to accommodate a passenger train.

JLG LIFTLUX 153-12

BANG!

The tunnel houses the $10-billion Large Hadron Collider, a machine called a particle accelerator. This machine uses radio waves to push beams of protons around the circuit and bunch the particles together in groups of around 100 billion. Each beam packs as much energy as a train traveling at more than 90 mph (145 km/h). At specific points around the tunnel, the beams' paths cross and they collide inside massive detectors that are ready to monitor the results of the impact and to see what is contained in the debris.

The experiment will create more than 15 million gigabytes of data every year—the equivalent of 21.4 million CDs—and took more than 13 years to build.

The central component of the Large Hadron Collider before it is placed in position.

The Large Hadron Collider stands 12 stories high and is designed to generate temperatures of more than a trillion degrees Celsius.

HIT AT SPEED OF SOUND

In 1978, at an institute in Protvino, Russia, scientific researcher Anatoli Bugorski leaned over an item of particle accelerator equipment that had malfunctioned. As he did so, his skull was penetrated by a proton beam moving at the speed of sound, causing him to be exposed to a flash of light brighter than a thousand suns and a degree of radiation 600 times greater than is usually fatal. He was expected to die within days but miraculously survived, although the entire left side of his face was paralyzed. His face was effectively divided in two. The right side continues to age normally, but the left side remains frozen in 1978. When he concentrates, he wrinkles only half his forehead.

TOOTH FOR AN EYE

In an astounding surgical feat, a man from Bellaghy, Northern Ireland, who was blinded in 2005, had his sight restored two years later after a complicated 16-hour operation that involved implanting part of his son's tooth in one of his eyes. Rob McNichol lost his sight after liquid aluminum exploded in his face at work, and damage to his eye was so severe that a conventional corneal implant wasn't appropriate and an operation involving stem cells was unsuccessful. He was sent to another specialist who suggested the unusual surgery known as Osteo Odonto Kerato Prosthesis (OOKP), which involves implanting a live tooth root containing a man-made lens into the eye. One of Rob's eight children donated his tooth and the operation was a resounding success. After two years in the darkness, Rob is understandably delighted to be able to see his family again and to resume such everyday activities as walking down the street and watching TV.

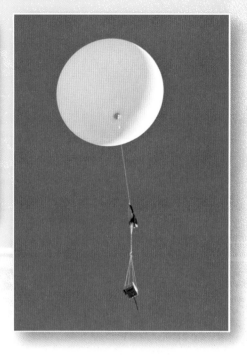

Space Balloon

You can rely on huge telescopes and satellites to see pictures of space, or you can do it yourself, like Tony Rafaat from Alberta, Canada, who made his own weather balloon with a camera attached. His balloon reached an incredible 117,595 ft (35,843 m) and traveled 62 mi (100 km) before it landed and Tony was able to retrieve it and reveal the stunning pictures it had taken on its journey.

LIGHT SHOW ■ According to new research by N.A.S.A. scientists, magnetic explosions taking place about one-third of the way to the moon are the reason why the Northern Lights (Aurora Borealis) and their southern equivalent (Aurora Australis) suddenly burst in spectacular shapes and colors and dart across the sky. These auroral flare-ups occur on average every two or three days.

FIRST DIRECTORY ■ The only known copy of the world's first telephone directory sold for $140,000 at an auction in New York in 2008. Twenty pages long, it contains the names and numbers of 391 subscribers in and around New Haven, Connecticut, and was issued in 1878—just two years after the invention of the telephone by Alexander Graham Bell.

CHEAP JIBE ■ A man from Brisbane, Queensland, Australia, attempted to sell New Zealand on eBay at a starting price of $0.01 Australian dollars. The price had risen to $3,000 before eBay closed the auction.

BLUE EYES ■ Genetic studies by scientists at Denmark's University of Copenhagen have found that all people with blue eyes have a single, common ancestor. By examining mitochondrial D.N.A. and comparing individuals in countries as diverse as Jordan, Denmark and Turkey, they found that all blue-eyed people inherited a genetic switch from brown at exactly the same spot in their D.N.A.

MECHANICAL MARRIAGE ■ David Levy's Ph.D. thesis at the University of Maastricht in the Netherlands explored the possibility of marriage between humans and robots.

SHARP NEEDLE ■ Scientists have created an object—a tungsten needle—so sharp that it tapers down to the thickness of a single atom.

COCKROACH BAIT ■ Belgian scientists have created smelly little robots that attract cockroaches from their hiding places into more open areas, where they can be easily crushed.

CUNNING FLIES ■ Researchers at the California Institute of Technology have discovered why flies are so hard to swat—because their brains are wired to avoid being hit. At the first sign of a threat, the insect repositions its legs and wings so that it can flee in the opposite direction and make a successful getaway.

BALANCING TRICK ■ Ballbot, a man-sized robot invented by Ralph Hollis of Carnegie Mellon University, Pittsburgh, Pennsylvania, moves by balancing on a spinning ball rather than using legs, wheels or treads.

KITCHEN WORK ■ In 2008, British scientists won a $2-million grant to research whether a robot can be safely employed to stir soup.

TINY TERROR ■ In China, in February 2008, scientists revealed the discovery of a new species of a 120-million-year-old pterodactyl with a wingspan of less than 10 in (25 cm).

SNOW SALE ■ Jim and Mary Walker of Loveland, Colorado, sold snow on eBay after their house was submerged by two blizzards in January 2007. They received hundreds of bids, eventually selling three snowballs for $200.

CAVEMAN RELATIVE ■ Manfred Huchthausen and Uwe Lange, two friends from neighboring towns in Germany, have discovered that they are both related to a Bronze Age caveman who died in their region 3,000 years ago. D.N.A. analysis of well-preserved skeletons that have been found in the Soese Valley showed that the two men actually share a great-grandfather 120 times removed.

Water Falls

Photographer Martin Waugh from Portland, Oregon, takes a scientific high-speed camera approach to shots of water drops and ripples, which results in stunning images of liquid sculptures that appear to show solid shapes. To capture the perfect "sculpture," Martin varies the color and texture of the water using dyes and soaps.

AROUND THE WORLD

90 MINUTES BY SPACECRAFT
Dozens of astronauts have orbited the Earth in a time of around 90 minutes.

67 HOURS BY AIRPLANE
Steve Fossett of the U.S. flew 23,125 mi (37,216 km) nonstop, solo, around the world in an airplane in 67 hours in 2005.

11 DAYS BY HELICOPTER
Starting and finishing in New York, U.S. pilots Scott Kasprowicz and Steve Sheik flew a helicopter on a 23,000-mi (37,015-km) round-the-world trip in 11 days 7 hours in 2008.

13 DAYS BY BALLOON
In 2002, Steve Fossett flew the balloon *Spirit of Freedom* around the world in 13 days 8 hours 33 minutes, covering 20,626 mi (33,194 km). Over the Indian Ocean, he reached a speed of 186 mph (300 km/h).

19 DAYS BY MOTORBIKE
Britons Kevin and Julia Sanders rode a motorbike on a 19,461-mi (31,319-km) round-the-world journey in 19 days 8 hours in 2002.

21 DAYS BY CAR
In 1997, Canada's Garry Sowerby and two British co-drivers drove a Vauxhall Frontera Estate car 18,344 mi (29,522 km) around the world in 21 days 2 hours 14 minutes.

50 DAYS BY YACHT
Accompanied by a crew of 13, France's Bruno Peyron sailed a distance of 27,000 mi (43,452 km) around the world in 50 days 16 hours 20 minutes in 2005.

60 DAYS BY POWERBOAT
The speed boat *Earthrace*, skippered by New Zealander Pete Bethune, circumnavigated the world in 2008, traveling 24,000 mi (38,624 km) in 60 days 23 hours 49 minutes.

80 DAYS BY MICROLIGHT
In 2007, India's Anil Kumar and Rahul Monga circumnavigated the world in a microlight airplane, covering 25,310 mi (40,732 km) in 80 days.

194 DAYS BY BICYCLE
Scotland's Mark Beaumont cycled 18,296 mi (29,445 km) around the world in 194 days 17 hours in 2007–8.

1,568 DAYS WALKING
Dave Kunst from Caledonia, Minnesota, walked 14,450 mi (23,255 km) around the world in 1,568 days from 1970–74. He estimated he took more than 20 million steps and wore out 21 pairs of shoes.

2,062 DAYS RUNNING
England's Robert Garside ran 30,000 mi (48,280 km) around the world in 2,062 days between 1997 and 2003.

BODY EXTREMES

49 DAYS WITHOUT FOOD
In 2004, Chen Jianmin went 49 days without food in Ya'an, China.

21 DAYS ON A HIGH WIRE
Jay Cochrane, from Toronto, Ontario, Canada, spent 21 days on a high wire in San Juan, Puerto Rico, in 1981.

5 HOURS 40 MINUTES HANGING BY BACK FROM HELICOPTER
New York's Criss Angel was suspended for 5 hours 40 minutes by hooks in his back that were attached to a helicopter that hovered above Times Square in 2002.

1 HOUR 30 MINUTES IN BATHTUB OF MAGGOTS
Christine Martin of Sussex, England, sat in a bathtub of maggots for 1 hour 30 minutes in 2002.

1 HOUR 12 MINUTES STANDING IN ICE
In January 2008, Dutchman Wim Hof stood immersed in 1,550 lb (703 kg) of ice for 1 hour 12 minutes on a street in Manhattan, New York.

45 MINUTES IN A BATHTUB OF SNAKES
Jackie Bibby sat in a bathtub with 87 rattlesnakes for 45 minutes in Dublin, Texas, in 2007.

17 MINUTES 4 SECONDS HOLDING BREATH UNDERWATER
In Chicago, Illinois, in 2008, David Blaine held his breath underwater for an astounding 17 minutes 4 seconds.

15 MINUTES HEADSTAND ON ROOF OF MOVING CAR
In 2006, Jewgenij Kuschnow balanced on his head on the roof of a moving car for 15 minutes in Munich, Germany.

45 SECONDS WALKING ON FIRE
Scott Bell of the U.K. walked across hot embers for 45 seconds, covering a distance of 320 ft (98 m) in Wuxi, China, in 2006.

33.6 SECONDS WITH HELICOPTER ON SHOULDERS
Austria's Franz Muellner bore the entire weight of a 4,000-lb (1,800-kg) helicopter on his shoulders for 33.6 seconds in Vienna in 2006.

33 SECONDS WITH CAR BALANCED ON HEAD
In 1999, John Evans of England balanced a Mini car on his head for 33 seconds.

12.22 SECONDS LIFTING 121-LB WEIGHT WITH ONE EAR
Zafar Gill of Pakistan suspended a 121-lb (55-kg) weight from one ear for 12.22 seconds in Germany in 2005.

Snake Manu
C. Manoharan from Chennai, India, becomes "Snake Manu" as he guides live snakes right through his head, entering his nostrils and slithering out of his mouth.

BEYOND BELIEF

WATERFALL Riders

Paddling a kayak down a tranquil river may be fun for some, but real thrill-seekers look for something a little more demanding. Those who can overcome their fear, after looking down at the white water below, brave the rocks and ride down crashing waterfalls.

Extreme kayaker Pat Keller of North Carolina plunged down the boiling waters of the 120-ft (36.5-m) La Paz waterfall in Costa Rica, looking like flotsam and jetsam in the deluge. He plummeted over the edge of the waterfall at the equivalent of around 300 ft (91 m) a minute. Once over the falls, Pat would have been dragged under the water before resurfacing.

Kayakers use different techniques, and at La Paz Pat rode the waterfall in the center of its 10-ft (3-m) width, so that he had the maximum amount of water each side. Pat used a curved round-bow boat that measured about 8 ft (2.5 m long), and was made of polyethylene plastic. It was buoyant and helped him resurface quickly.

Pat paddled away from his amazing endeavor, but broke his hand badly in the fierce impact at the bottom of the thundering falls. Later, he had to have surgery to correct the damage.

Pat appears exhilarated, despite his broken hand, after kayaking down La Paz waterfall.

Ripley's research

HOW IS IT DONE?

Kayaks used in extreme kayaking are often made from toughened yet flexible fiberglass to prevent shattering. They are being made shorter than they used to be and this increases the rider's control in the turbulent water, helps avoid them getting stuck in dangerous rock crevices and adds strength on impact after a steep drop.

Each stretch of water attempted is scouted out beforehand and the best line of attack planned to give the kayaker the best chance of making it out the other side. Special techniques are required using the paddle to steer out of danger: a "boof" is pulling a wheelie in a kayak, lifting the nose in a sharp shift of direction, either bouncing off a rock or in water. A high level of physical strength and fitness is also needed to maneuver the short boats to keep the nose up and prevent the craft submerging.

When extreme kayakers face a steep drop, they position their body over the kayak and hold their paddle close in, to prevent their spine taking the impact and avoid shoulder dislocations caused by the paddle pulling away from the body. Tucking close to the kayak with an arm over the face—known as the crash position—prevents the equipment from smacking into the kayaker's head as the water hits. A technique often used on the big drops is to "pencil" into the water in a vertical position to limit impact.

Another of the world's top extreme kayakers, fearless Jesse Combs of Oregon risked life and limb by paddling down the Mesa Falls in Idaho, facing violent currents and sharp rocks 70 ft (21 m) below.

KAYAKING CAPERS

> Shaun Baker has paddled over a waterfall with a 65-ft (19.8-m) vertical drop, traveled at 40 mph (63 km/h) on snow, and sped down huge sand dunes in the Sahara Desert, all in a kayak.

> Solo kayaker Satoru Yahata from Okinawa, Japan, arrived in Taiwan on June 18, 2007, after setting off from the Philippines, 435 mi (700 km) away, 16 days earlier. Yahata, in an 18-ft (5.5-m) kayak, was the first solo kayaker to successfully complete the trip.

> Extreme kayaker Tyler Bradt paddled down a 107-ft (33-m) descent over Alexandra Falls, Canada, and didn't flip once.

> Two British men were rescued from the North Sea when their attempt to cross the stretch of water from Scotland to the Faroe Islands in a kayak was cut short by bad weather and ill health. They hoped to row nonstop for 50 to 70 hours to complete the 220-mi (355-km) voyage.

> In 2001, British adventurer Pete Bray paddled a kayak across the Atlantic Ocean, braving frequent storms, gales and broken equipment, to complete the 2,892-mi (4,800-km) trip.

COCONUT CRAZY

Andres Gardin from Panama performs incredible feats of a dental nature. He has an appetite for coconuts, but not the milk inside—in Panama City in 2007, Gardin peeled the fibers off 500 coconuts in six hours using only his teeth.

CHIPPER GRAN ■ A great-grandmother celebrated her 100th birthday in 2007 by frying fish and chips in her shop. Connie Brown still works six days a week at the fish-and-chip shop in Pembroke, Wales, that she opened in 1928 with her late husband Sidney.

TIGER CUB ■ In 2007, an English golfer hit his third hole-in-one—and he was still only eight years old. David Huggins from Stowmarket, Suffolk, hit his first ace when he was four—two years younger than when Tiger Woods struck his first hole-in-one.

BRAVE SOLDIER ■ A British soldier serving in southern Afghanistan in 2008 threw himself onto an exploding grenade to save the lives of his patrol—and walked away with nothing worse than a bloody nose. Royal Marine lance corporal Matt Croucher from Birmingham survived the blast because his knapsack took most of the force of the explosion.

DANCING COP ■ On the streets of Provincetown, Massachusetts, police officer Donald Thomas has been directing traffic with exaggerated dance movements for more than 50 years—and he was still going strong in 2008 at the age of 81.

DOUBLE ACHIEVEMENT ■ Jeanne Stawiecki from Charlton, Massachusetts, has run marathons on all seven continents and climbed the "Seven Summits," the highest mountain on each continent—a feat all-the-more remarkable because she did not even start mountain climbing until she was 52.

COIN HOARDER ■ After begging on the streets of Calcutta for 44 years, Laxmi Das has finally saved up enough money—around $700—to open her own bank account and even qualify for a credit card. She had collected thousands of coins—weighing a total of 200 lb (90 kg)—in iron buckets at her shanty-town home.

PEAK FITNESS ■ In 2007, 76-year-old Michio Kumamoto from Tokorozawa, Japan, climbed Alaska's 20,320-ft-high (6,194-m) Mount McKinley, which is the tallest peak in North America.

SEVEN CONTINENTS ■ At just ten years old, Victoria White of Elizabeth, Colorado, completed a mission to ski on all seven continents. She and her father Ken spent a year traveling 75,000 mi (120,700 km) by air and 3,500 mi (5,630 km) by sea, finishing their journey at Winter Park, Colorado, in March 2008.

FAMILY FORTUNE ■ In 2007, the Leblanc family of Moncton, New Brunswick, Canada, had 13 living siblings ranging in age from 71 to 88.

LONG TOUR ■ In June 2003, 21 tourists spent more than 33 hours on a guided tour of the German city of Augsburg, listening to nearly 100 city guides who worked in shifts.

STREET WALKER ■ David Marsh walks 18 mi (29 km) a day in his job cleaning the streets of Wigan, England, which means that in his 40-year career Marsh, who has never had a sick day, has clocked up more than 169,000 mi (272,000 km)—the equivalent of walking around the world six times.

ROOKIE COP ■ Laurence Egerton became a rookie cop in 2007—at age 56. The former businessman joined the Wilmington Police Department in North Carolina.

FAMILY RIDE ■ Three generations of a Welsh family cycled across the U.S.A. from Cape Canaveral, Florida, to San Diego, California, in 60 days. Nine-year-old Ann Lintern accompanied her mother Julie Smith on a tandem while 62-year-old grandfather Victor cycled behind them during the 3,260-mi (5,245-km) journey.

KING RAT ■ Impoverished Bangladeshi farmer Binoy Kumar Karmakar won a color T.V. set after killing 39,650 rats during 2008. He was crowned the country's rat-killing champion after displaying the collection of his victims' tails to government officials.

PLASTIC WRAP ■ Seven-year-old Jake Lonsway from Bangor Township, Michigan, created a plastic-wrap ball that was so big he could barely see over the top of it! The ball, which had a circumference of 138 in (3.5 m) and weighed about 281 lb (127 kg), took Jake eight months to build in the garage of the family home.

TRIPLE TREAT ■ Playing in a baseball game for Portsmouth High School, Ohio, in May 2008, triplets Howard, John and Matt Harcha all hit home runs—in the order of their birth from oldest to youngest.

Stretchy Senior

In 1934, W.M. Keefe from New London, Connecticut, was able to touch his toes and then reach down a further 10 in (25 cm), despite being 73 years old.

SUPER SURFER ■ Rico de Souza rode a 30-ft-long (9-m), 224-lb (102-kg) surfboard for ten seconds off the coast of Rio de Janeiro, Brazil, in 2008.

GIRL PITCHER ■ A team in the Kansai Independent Baseball League in Japan drafted 16-year-old high school student Eri Yoshida, making her the country's first female professional pitcher to play alongside men.

Amazing Eyelids

Kung fu master Dong Changsheng from Changchun, China, attached hooks to his eyelids and pulled a 3,748-lb (1,700-kg) minibus carrying two adult men along the road. Dong has 35 years' experience in martial arts and achieves his extreme endeavors with the help of special breathing exercises.

BURNING RUBBER

The motorsport of Gymkhana requires drivers to drift sideways around seemingly impossible corners and spin through circles at breakneck speeds on a specially laid-out track. Expert stunt driver Ken Block is so adept at controlling his car that he can slide 360 degrees sideways round a moving target, such as a Segway scooter and its brave rider.

ROCKET MAN ■ Swiss adventurer Yves Rossy flew 22 mi (35 km) across the English Channel in 2008 with only a home-made rocket-powered wing strapped to his back. After Rossy was dropped from a plane 8,000 ft (2,440 m) above the French coast, the power from the four mini-jets attached to the 8-ft (2.4-m) carbon-fiber wing enabled him to make the crossing in less than 10 minutes at speeds of more than 125 mph (200 km/h). As his lightweight wing had no steering mechanism, he had to use his head and back to control the wing's movement.

BOXING VETERAN ■ Saoul Mamby of New York City is 60 years old and still boxes professionally against anyone in his weight class—no matter how old they are.

DIRT BUSTER ■ Twelve-year-old Kyle Krichbaum of Adrian, Michigan, has a collection of 165 vacuum cleaners and he vacuums his house five times a day. He got his first vacuum at age one, he dressed up as a Dirt Devil for Halloween at age two, and by age six, instead of going outside during school recesses, he often stayed indoors to vacuum the principal's office.

CHESS CHAMP ■ Twelve-year-old Peter Williams from Hampshire, England, has been playing chess since the age of five—and now he is so good that he can beat opponents even while blindfolded!

BREATHTAKING BLAINE ■ Brooklyn-born magician David Blaine managed to hold his breath underwater for more than 17 minutes on an April 2008 edition of *The Oprah Winfrey Show*. After inhaling pure oxygen to flush carbon dioxide from his blood, Blaine, wearing a silver wetsuit, was lowered into a sphere containing around 1,800 gallons of water. He had hoped to stay underwater for longer, but became aware that his heart was beating irregularly toward the end of the stunt.

WORD MEMORY ■ Listening just once to 140 random words, 18-year-old Rajiv Sharma, from Sarlahi, Nepal, was able to repeat 119 of them in ten minutes.

MARATHON WOMAN ■ In July 2008, Pauline Newsholme from Devon, England, ran her 69th marathon—at the age of 69.

HIGH TEE ■ Golf fanatic Andrew Winfield from Northampton, England, teed off from the summit of Africa's Mount Kilimanjaro in 2008—19,340 ft (5,895 m) above sea level. The 50-year-old climbed for a week with his specially adapted collapsible six-iron, before hitting his high tee shot.

GLOBAL TRAVELER ■ In May 2008, Kashi Samaddar, a Dubai-based Indian businessman, completed his quest to visit all of the world's 194 sovereign states—a journey that took him four-and-a-half years. The first country he visited was Uruguay and the last was the Serbian province of Kosovo.

DOMINO TOPPLING ■ In November 2008, 85 people from 13 countries gathered in the Netherlands to set up and knock over a chain of 4,354,027 domino blocks.

CARP CATCH ■ Forty-one teams of paired fishermen caught more than 18 tons of carp in 50 hours during the American Carp Society's 2008 Northeast Tournament in Baldwinsville, New York.

Skateboard Journey

New Zealander Rob Thomson embarked on the trip of a lifetime when he traveled 7,500 mi (12,000 km) on a skateboard. The trip lasted 462 days, and took him from Switzerland to Shanghai via Europe and the U.S.A. He even journeyed the entire length of China. Rob traveled solo and unsupported, carrying all his belongings on the specially modified skateboard trailer.

WHEELBARROW PUSH ■ David Baird, a 65-year-old British man, pushed a wheelbarrow 2,572 mi (4,139 km) across Australia in 112 days. He set off from Perth in September 2008 and reached Sydney in January 2009, having pushed between 10 and 12 hours a day.

VETERAN BODYBUILDER ■ Ray Moon of Thornbury, Victoria, Australia, has won four state and national bodybuilding competitions—at age 80. He began bodybuilding only in 2004 and does five fitness sessions a week, each consisting of 2.5 mi (4 km) on a treadmill and 45 minutes of weight training.

JET SKI ■ In January 2009, Roy Ogletree of Columbus, Ohio, traveled 1,080 mi (1,738 km) in 24 hours on a jet ski on Lake Lloyd in the infield of the Daytona Beach International Speedway.

Flying Feet

Jessica Cox from Tucson, Arizona, is one of a kind, being the first woman without arms to receive a pilot's license. Already able to drive a car, the motivational speaker was born without arms and prefers not to use prosthetic limbs, instead performing regular tasks with her feet.

IMPOSSIBLE X-RAYS

X-ray machines aren't just for broken bones and suitcases at the airport. Since x-raying a truck full of cola cans to find a prize-winning ring pull, photographer Nick Veasey from Kent, England, has forged a career by irradiating everyday objects to create pictures that show the inner beauty of the mundane.

Although he never found the ring pull, Nick has made stunning X-ray pictures of everything from a pair of training shoes to a 200-ft-wide (70-m) jumbo jet being serviced. He started out by hiring hospital machines and laboratories, using information gleaned from medical experts to find new ways of exploring the medium. Nick now uses a derelict radar station lined in lead to keep the potentially dangerous radiation from escaping. The X-ray machine inside is about 60 times as powerful as the type used in hospitals; the denser the object to be penetrated, the more radiation required.

Nick's final pieces are often a combination of traditional photography and X-rays, composed with a computer program after meticulous work blasting X-rays at objects captured on special film and converted into digital files with a 13-ft-wide (4-m) scanner.

One of Nick's most ambitious works to date is of a Boeing jumbo jet. He took 500 pictures of individual plane parts and then spent six months putting them together for the final image of a Boeing 777, the largest object ever to be x-rayed, with a wingspan and length of more than 200 ft (70 m). Some of the thinner parts of the plane were replaced with scale-model airplane parts because they wouldn't show up well enough on the X-rays, and Nick used skeletons rather than X-ray the real crew and ground staff working on the plane. The finished product was hung in an aircraft hangar at Boston Logan Airport, measuring 250 x 80 ft (76 x 24 m)—a 20,000-sq-ft (1,850-sq-m) X-ray. It was so convincing that some visitors to the airport thought the hangar was open.

A man riding a bike is captured in X-rays. Artist Nick Veasey creates seemingly impossible images by meticulously photographing individual parts and completing the images on a computer.

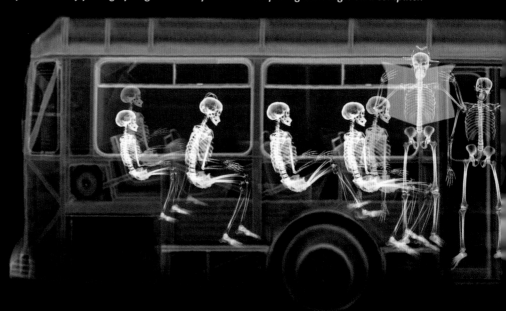

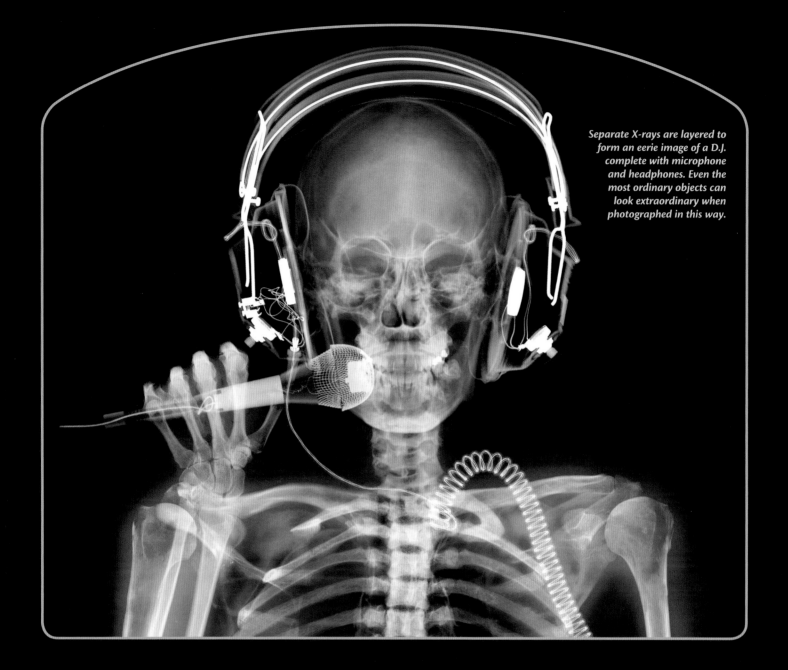

Separate X-rays are layered to form an eerie image of a D.J. complete with microphone and headphones. Even the most ordinary objects can look extraordinary when photographed in this way.

Nick went to the U.S. to capture a life-size bus full of people, using a $5-million X-ray machine that is normally used by U.S. Customs on the border with Mexico. The final life-sized photo was attached to the side of a real bus in New York and attracted so much attention it had to be taken down.

CHAIR FLIP

Aaron Fotheringham from Las Vegas, Nevada, can perform a back flip in a wheelchair. Aaron, who was born with spina bifida and has been almost permanently confined to a wheelchair since the age of eight, spends more than 30 hours a week at the skate park, using a specially adapted aluminum wheelchair with suspension and grind bars to help him perform his amazing stunts.

FIVE-YEAR RUN ■ In 2008, a British grandmother completed a five-year run around the world. Pulling her supplies in a cart, Rosie Swale-Pope from Tenby, Wales, survived freezing temperatures in Alaska, was hit by a bus in Siberia, came face to face with a polar bear in Greenland, suffered pneumonia and frostbite, was nearly swept to her death in a raging river and received 29 marriage proposals.

FAST DRIVE ■ Joshua Keeler, Joey Stocking and Adam Gatherum of North Salt Lake, Utah, traveled more than 7,000 mi (11,265 km) by road through each of the 48 states in the continental U.S.A. in 2008, completing the journey in just 106 hours and 43 minutes.

STREET CLEANER ■ Ding Youzhen of Dongtai City, China, cleans the streets around her home every day—even though she is 104. She has been tidying up the city's streets for free for more than 84 years.

FREE RIDE ■ Kris Mole from Southwick, Sussex, visited 26 capital cities on a six-month, 9,763-mi (15,712-km) trek around Europe without spending a penny. Instead, he begged rides, went days without food and slept outdoors when not offered a bed for the night.

OLD-TIMER ■ A 90-year-old D.J. announced her retirement in 2007 after 37 years at the turntable. Margaret Brelsford—or D.J. Master Maggie to her friends—played old-time dance music at Platt Social Club in Accrington, England.

JUNIOR LINGUIST ■ By the age of three, Seth Kinast of Hutchinson, Kansas, could recite the alphabet in Greek, count in German and Spanish, and had read almost 1,200 books.

GOLF BRAWL ■ A Florida golfer chose a four-iron to fight off an 11-ft-long (3.3-m) alligator as it attacked a diver who was looking for lost balls in a lake. Matt Johnson used the club and a rake to hit the reptile on the head as it grappled with unsuspecting diver Dwight Monreal at the Tampa Palms Golf and Country Club in April 2008.

GOLFING ACE ■ A 92-year-old blind golfer hit a hole-in-one in Florida in 2008. Leo Fiyalko, who needs help lining up his shots, struck the ace—his first-ever—while playing a 110-yd (100-m) hole in Clearwater.

MOWER RIDE ■ Accompanied by his dog Yoda, Paul Woods of Mystic, Connecticut, completed a 6,000-mi (9,660-km) trip from Alaska to Connecticut riding on a lawn mower. With the machine having a top speed of just 15 mph (24 km/h), the journey took him more than a year and a half.

MEMORY MAN ■ Despite being diagnosed with attention deficit hyperactivity disorder and dyslexia in high school, Dave Farrow from Toronto, Ontario, Canada, can memorize the exact order of 59 decks of playing cards all shuffled together—that's recalling 3,068 cards in order!

BIKE RIDE ■ Mark Beaumont from Fife, Scotland, cycled 18,000 mi (29,000 km) around the world in 195 days. He traveled through 20 countries, braving floods, robbers and being knocked off his bike in Louisiana when an elderly motorist ran a red light.

RIVER SWIM ■ In 2008, 21-year-old Katie Spotz of Mentor, Ohio, completed a 326-mi (525-km) swim of Pennsylvania's Allegheny River in a month. She swam for up to eight hours a day and on her best day covered 22 mi (35 km).

LOFTY AMBITION ■ Neil Sauter completed an eight-week, 835-mi (1,354-km) journey across Michigan in 2008—on aluminum stilts.

HOT SHOT ■ Randy Oitker of Plainville, Illinois, once hit five coin-sized targets with five arrows fired simultaneously from his bow.

EPIC WALK ■ Rick Wallenda, a descendant of the famous "Flying Wallendas" circus troupe, walked 2,000 ft (610 m) along a tightrope just 5/8 in (1.5 cm) wide, suspended 112 ft (34 m) above ground at Kings Island, Mason, Ohio, on July 4, 2008. Without safety nets or harnesses and using a 38-lb (17-kg) pole to maintain his balance, he completed the walk in 35 minutes.

PERFECT GAME ■ A 78-year-old blind man bowled 12 back-to-back strikes to record his first-ever perfect game at the Century Lanes bowling alley in Alta, Iowa. Dale Davis had given up his love for the sport after losing his sight to macular degeneration but, encouraged by his sister, he now plays six games a week even though he can't see the lane or the pins.

EVER PRESENT ■ Andria Baker of Constantine, Michigan, didn't miss a day of school from kindergarten all the way through 12th grade.

HAPPY EVER AFTER ■ Indian couple 103-year-old Pyara Singh and 101-year-old Hansa Devi celebrated their 83rd wedding anniversary in May 2007. They attribute their happy life together to disciplined living, controlled diet, and honesty.

AGED ABSEILER ■ Partially blind Eve Mobbs from West Sussex, England, abseiled down the outside of a multistory car park in 2008—at 92 years of age.

FLYING HIGH ■ Bob Brown from Nottinghamshire, England, was still pole-vaulting in his seventies. In 2007, he was selected to compete in the British Athletics League against vaulters less than a quarter his age.

BLIND CLIMBER ■ Even though he has been blind since the age of five, John Wimmer of Medford, Oregon, has conquered more than half a dozen mountains across the U.S.A. In the summer of 2008, accompanied by his guide dog Rasha and friend Diego Joven, Wimmer climbed 11,249 ft (3,429 m) to the summit of Mount Hood, Oregon.

MALL MARATHON ■ Boyd Otero of Zanesville, Ohio, has walked 20,000 laps—10,000 mi (16,000 km)—around his local mall in less than five years.

BACKWARD WALK ■ For five months in 2007, Bill Kathan Jr., 55, of Vernon, Vermont, walked across the U.S.A.—backward. He set off from Concord, New Hampshire, in April and completed his 3,330-mi (5,360-km) reverse march in Newport, Oregon, in September.

Human Spider

Known as "Spider-Man" for his death-defying exploits in scaling the outsides of buildings all over the world using only his bare hands and climbing shoes, Frenchman Alain Robert climbed Paris's 625-ft-high (190-m) Tour Total for the sixth time in 2008. Over the past 20 years, he has climbed more than 80 skyscrapers and monuments, including the 1,483-ft-high (452-m) Petronas Twin Towers in Kuala Lumpur, Malaysia, and New York's 1,250-ft (381-m) Empire State Building.

Confident that he could fly faster than a speeding plane, Swiss "aerialist" Ueli Gegenschatz took the challenge to race a plane over the Irish Sea. He descended from a height of 14,763 ft (4,500 m) and flew for an incredible 10.9 mi (17.6 km) from the island Inis Mor to Connemara Airport on the Irish mainland in a hi-tech suit that gives you "wings" to fly like a bird with no propulsion other than the wind.

The distances achievable in a wingsuit are variable, as Ueli explains. "It depends a lot on flying conditions, your fitness and of course the exit-altitude. The higher you exit the aircraft and the more tailwinds you'll get, the farther you can go."

He released his parachute just 650 ft (200 m) before landing, and touched down in Ireland in 5 minutes 45 seconds—more than a minute faster than the 120-mph (193-km/h) plane that makes the trip daily. Ueli himself averaged 155 mph (249 km/h) for his blistering flight high above the sea. The daredevil said that he was glad that he landed on dry land, as he had heard the Irish waters are very cold.

Ueli soars in a wingsuit over Mount Säntis—the highest mountain in Switzerland at 8,202 ft (2,500 m)—in 2004. He jumps from mountains, planes and other aircraft to fly in his special suits.

Ueli exits from a microlight aircraft to fly his wingsuit over Monument Valley, on the Utah–Arizona border, in 2004.

Ripley's ask

Did your dive work as well as you hoped?

Yes, I've been skydiving since 1989 and am experienced in controlling my body in any kind of free fall. Therefore, wingsuit flying was more like an additional way to get a much broader range in terms of free-fall duration and flying distance. It took a while to reach peak performance and each wingsuit is a challenge to take advantage of.

What goes through your mind as you fly?

I am totally focused on my flight so that my body and flight pattern go off well and as precise as initially planned. And for some ineffable moments, I enjoy the stunning immensity of being able to experience the original human dream to "fly like a bird."

Is it dangerous?

Flying a wingsuit itself is not dangerous if you have the knowledge, skills and ability to fly and control your body in free-fall. If you start flying a wingsuit from fixed objects like cliffs or buildings, you absolutely need to be aware of what you are doing. If you are not skilled enough or if you do not know about your personal limits, it can easily become very bad.

How much control do you have in the wingsuit?

Total control is required and attainable if you spend the time to learn how to fly your wingsuit. But it takes you five years to get five years of experience! You have to learn it step by step.

What has been your favorite flight?

I did find a few very special exits on some Swiss mountains, where I can jump off and stay very close to the cliffs for more than a minute. Performing flights with full speed and control near a wall is unbelievably intense, but every minute of the three-hour hike and climb up is worth the 90 seconds of flying down to the valley.

What is the next step for human flight?

Almost everything is possible. My aim is to improve my flying skills in duration and distance and to perform flights with more control and nearer to the ground. And, as birds don't need a parachute to land, it is a great dream and challenge for wingsuit pros to land from a flight without a parachute.

SERIAL JUMPER ■ Martin Downs from Yorkshire, England, skydived on six continents in eight days in August 2008. He started with a 10,000-ft (3,050-m) jump in Natal, South Africa, before moving on to Madrid in Spain, Caracas in Venezuela, Los Angeles in the U.S.A., Sydney in Australia, and Nhathang in Vietnam.

WONDER SHOT ■ A 74-year-old grandmother achieved a one-in-a-million archery shot by splitting one arrow with another – even though she is blind. Tilly Trotter from Devon, England, has been an archer for only two years and although she can see movement, she has no central vision, instead relying on her husband to tell her how near her shots are to the target.

TOY CATCH ■ After a 25-minute struggle, David Hayes from Wilkes County, North Carolina, caught a sizeable 21-lb (9.5-kg) catfish in 2008—with his three-year-old granddaughter Alyssa's Barbie fishing rod. At 32 in (81 cm) in length, the fish was 2 in (5 cm) longer than the pink plastic rod.

HUMAN CALCULATOR ■ Alexis Lemaire, a student at Reims University, France, worked out the 13th root of a random 200-digit number in his head in just 70 seconds in 2007. His answer of 2407899893032210 was the only correct solution from a possible 393 trillion combinations. He discovered his talent at age nine and began solving the roots of 200-digit numbers after finding that 100-digit numbers were too easy.

SEVEN MARATHONS ■ A blind British runner completed seven marathons on seven continents in seven days in April 2008. Dave Heeley, 50, from West Bromwich, ran a total of 183 mi (295 km) in the Falkland Islands, Rio de Janeiro (Brazil), Los Angeles (U.S.A.), Sydney (Australia), Dubai (United Arab Emirates), Tunis (Tunisia) and London (U.K.).

DAREDEVIL DIVER ■ At a Florida County Fair in 2008, Joe Egan of San Antonio, Texas, dove repeatedly from an 80-ft (24-m) platform into a pool 18 ft (5.4 m) deep—hitting the water at a speed of 60 mph (96.5 km/h). Filled with twists and flips, the dive took about two seconds and required him to enter the water feet first to avoid serious injury. Because of the impact, he could make the dive only 15 times a day.

SPRIGHTLY SPRINTER ■ In February 2008, Phillip Rabinowitz from Cape Town, South Africa, ran the 100 meters in 30.86 seconds—at the incredible age of 104.

ELDERLY GRADUATE ■ A 95-year-old great-grandmother graduated from college in 2007. Nola Ochs, who has 13 grandchildren and 15 great-grandchildren, received her bachelor's degree in General Studies and History at Fort Hays State University, Kansas.

BUNGEE JUMPS ■ New Zealander Mike Heard completed 103 bungee jumps from a bridge in just 24 hours in August 2008. He made his first 131-ft (40-m) plunge from Auckland Harbour Bridge head first, but soon changed to making the jump feet first to avoid getting unnecessarily wet.

YOUNG PROFESSOR ■ In 2008, New Yorker Alia Sabur was appointed a professor of physics at Konkuk University in South Korea—at the age of just 18. A child genius, she had earned her bachelor's degree at 14.

HIGH WIRE ■ Starting from opposite ends, Chinese high-wire walkers Adili and Ya Gebu passed each other on a single wire suspended more than 850 ft (259 m) above ground. Without safety wires or nets, they had to climb over each other in the middle of the wire that stretched almost three-quarters of a mile (1.1 km) over a valley in Gansu Province.

Eye-popping Ride

In 1954, Col. John Stapp of the U.S. Air Force found out what it feels like to travel from 0 to more than 600 mph (0–965 km/h) and back again in just a few seconds. Experimenting with the effects of G-force on the human body, he was strapped into a rocket-propelled sled on rails for the ride of his life. When the rockets were lit, the sled sent him from a standstill to 632 mph (1,017 km/h)—faster than a speeding bullet—in five seconds flat. It then hurtled into a water barrier and decelerated to a dead stop 1.4 seconds later. The force of this impact on Stapp's body felt like hitting a brick wall. His eyeballs shot forward in their sockets giving him two black eyes and temporary blindness. Pressure equivalent to 40 times the pull of gravity was exerted on his 168-lb (76-kg) body, making it weigh, for a moment, the equivalent of a staggering 6,720 lb (3,050 kg).

David Blaine had an amazing view of the sights over New York's Central Park—hanging upside down 40 ft (12 m) in the air for 60 hours, like a human bat. Doctors feared that he risked medical problems after such a prolonged spell the wrong way up, including losing his sight, but at the end of his stunt, Blaine dived from a 44-ft-high (13.4-m) platform, touched the ground for a moment and was then carried into the night sky by giant balloons.

HANGING TOUGH

INDEX

Ripley's Believe It or Not!®

Ripley's—
Believe It or Not!®

Atlantic City
NEW JERSEY

Bangalore
INDIA

Blackpool
ENGLAND

Branson
MISSOURI

Buena Park
CALIFORNIA

Cavendish
CANADA

Copenhagen
DENMARK

Gatlinburg
TENNESSEE

Genting Highlands
MALAYSIA

Grand Prairie
TEXAS

Guadalajara
MEXICO

Hollywood
CALIFORNIA

Jackson Hole
WYOMING

Key West
FLORIDA

Kuwait City
KUWAIT

London
ENGLAND

Mexico City
MEXICO

Myrtle Beach
SOUTH CAROLINA

New York
NEW YORK

Newport
OREGON

Niagara Falls
CANADA

Ocean City
MARYLAND

Orlando
FLORIDA

Panama City Beach
FLORIDA

Pattaya
THAILAND

San Antonio
TEXAS

San Francisco
CALIFORNIA

St. Augustine
FLORIDA

Surfers Paradise
AUSTRALIA

Williamsburg
VIRGINIA

Wisconsin Dells
WISCONSIN

ACKNOWLEDGMENTS

Page 4 (t/l) Tony McNicol/Rex Features, (t/r) LEGO and The LEGO logo are trademarks of The LEGO Group, here used with special permission. ©2009 The LEGO Group. ©2009 Lucasfilm Ltd & TM. All rights reserved, (b/l) Library of Congress, (b/c/l) www.tesladownunder.com, (b/r) Jason Hackenwerth Beach Trumpet 2007 Latex Balloons; 5 (t/l) Ashley Bradford, (t/c) RINSPEED, (b/l) Sandy Schimmel/Barcroft Media, (b/c) www.lichtfaktor.eu, (b/r) Chris Van Wyk; 9 AP Photo/Kyodo News; 10–11 Barcroft Media Ltd / SCRABBLE, the distinctive game board and letter tiles, and all associated logos are trademarks of Hasbro in the United States and Canada and are used with permission. © 2009 Hasbro. All Rights Reserved. Scrabble ® is a registered trademark of J. W. Spears & Sons Ltd., a subsidiary of Mattel, Inc. © Mattel, Inc. All Rights Reserved; 12 (t) www.SWNS.com, (b) Yawar Nazir/Scoopt/Getty Images; 13 John Little/Bizarre Archive; 14 (t) © EuroPics[CEN], (b) Discovery Channel "Wild Child"/Discovery Communications; 15 Canadian Press/Rex Features; 16 Reuters/Sukree Sukplang; 17 (t) © EuroPics[CEN], (b) www.toothpasteworld.com; 18–19 (c) © Bettmann/Corbis; 18 ChinaFotoPress/Photocome/PA Photos; 19 © Karen Kasmauski, 20 Barcroft Media; 21 Reuters/David Moir; 22 Dolores Calgi Foley; www.theyrecoming.com; 23 (t) Reuters/Ho New, (b) Tim Sloan/AFP/Getty Images; 24 (t) Bournemouth News/Rex Features, (b) © EuroPics[CEN]; 25 (b) www.SWNS.com; 27 © Joseph Sohm/Visions of America/Corbis; 28–29 Bill Counsell; 30–31 (b) Eric Gay/AP/PA Photos, 30 (t) Alan Blacklock NIWA; 31 (t) Lori Mehmen/AP/PA Photos, 32–33 (dp) Phil Yeomans/Rex Features; 32 (b) Pooktre; 33 (b) ChinaFotoPress/Photocome/PA Photos; 34 (t/l) Paul A. Zahl/National Geographic/Getty Images, (t/r) © NHPA/Photoshot, (b) Chris Van Wyk; 35 Steven Haddock/MBARI; 36 (t/l) © Ulises Rodriguez/epa/Corbis, (t/r) © Cameron French/Reuters/Corbis, (b/l) Reuters/Sergei Karpukhin, (b/r) Heinrich van den Berg/Getty Images; 37 Kenneth Libbrecht/Barcroft Media; 38 (t, b/r) Steve Nicol/Australian Antarctic Division, (b/l) Barcroft Media; 39 Steve Nicol/Australian Antarctic Division; 41 ChinaFotoPress/Photocome/PA Photos; 42 Henryk T. Kaiser/Rex Features; 43 Mieke Zuiderweg/Landov/PA Photos; 44 Joe Raedle/Getty Images; 45 LEGO and The LEGO logo are trademarks of The LEGO Group, here used with special permission. © 2009 The LEGO Group. © 2009 Lucasfilm Ltd & TM. All rights reserved; 46 Library of Congress; 47 (t) Time & Life Pictures/Mansell/Getty Images, (b) Library of Congress; 48–49 (scattered) © Connie Wade/Fotolia.com; 48 (b/l) Barcroft Media, (b/r, c) Susan Fessler; 49 (t) Kent Horner/NBAE via Getty Images; 50 Charles Sykes/Rex Features; 51 (t) Long Hongtao/AP/PA Photos, (b) Reuters/Claro Cortes; 52–53 Newspix/David Sheridan/Rex Features; 52 (t) Kirk Lee Aeder/Barcroft Media, (b) Peter Willows/Rex Features; 55 Keith MacBeth; 56–57 ©Jeffery R. Werner/IncredibleFeatures.com; 58–59 Library of Congress; 61 (sp) Francisc Stugren, (t) Photoshot/Imagebroker.net; 63 Caters News Agency Ltd/Rex Features; 64–65 Dan Burton www.underwaterimages.co.uk; 67 Camera Press/Images24.co.za; 68 (t) Reuters/Albert Gea; 69 Reuters/Yuriko Nakao; 70 (t/l) Manpreet Romana/AFP/Getty Images, (t/r) Narinder Nanu/AFP/Getty Images, (b) Sipa Press/Rex Features; 71 Reuters/Toby Melville; 72 Alfaqui/Barcroft Media; 73 (t) Pat Ferron/AP/PA Photos, (c/r, b) Kerrilee Beetham; 74 Martin Mejia/AP/PA Photos; 75 Reuters/China Daily Information Corp - CDIC; 77 Newspix/Rex Features; 78–79 Newspix/Rex Features; 80 Feature China/Barcroft Media; 81 (t) *MaxPPP*/Photoshot; (b) Richard Austin/Rex Features; 82–83 ZOOM/Barcroft Media; 84 (t) Newspix/Rex Features, (b) David Scholnick & Lou Burnett; 85 (t) Barcroft Pacific, (b) Mark Clifford/Barcroft Media; 86 Feature China/Barcroft Media; 87 (t) California Academy of Sciences, (b) Glenn Olsen/GB/Barcroft Media; 88 Otago Museum Dunedin New Zealand; 89 (t) www.swns.com, (b) Chris Van Wyk; 90–91 Kiyoshi Ota/Getty Images; 92 Newspix/Rex Features; 93 (t, c) Andy Rouse/Rex Features; (b) Andy Rouse/NHPA/Photoshot; 94–95 Stephen Douglass/Rex Features; 95 (r) Gary Roberts/Rex Features; 96–97 Reuters/Juan Medina; 98 (t) Mike Hutmacher/AP/PA Photos, (b) Barry Bland/Barcroft Media; 99 La Petite Maison/Solent News/Rex Features; 100 (t) Reuters/Yuriko Nakao, (b) Tian Xi/ChinaFotoPress/Photocome/PA Photos; 101 John Downer Productions; 102 Newspix/Rex Features; 103 UPPA/Photoshot; 104 www.firebox.com; 105 Barry Bland/Barcroft Media; 107 © Transtock/Corbis; 108 (l) Bill Call, Scripps Institution of Oceanography, (r) www.GoldenStateImages.com © Randy Morse; 109 Glenn Roberts, Motorcycle Mojo Magazine www.motorcyclemojo.com; 110–111 © Jeffery R. Werner/IncredibleFeatures.com; 112 © EuroPics[CEN]; 113 Solent News/Rex Features; 114 (r) Carl Court/PA Wire/PA Photos; 115 Andy Hazell; 116 (t) Rinspeed, (b) Volvo Cars of North America; 117 ZORB™ Ltd www.zorb.com; 118–119 (b) Reuters/Kai Pfaffenbach; 118 (t) © Harrod Blank Grass Bus © Gene Pool; 119 (t) Barry Batchelor/PA Archive/PA Photos; 121 Tony McNicol/Rex Features; 122 (t) Li Shuangqi/ChinaFotoPress/Photocome/PA Photos, (l) CNImaging/Photoshot; 123 Takashi Itoh; 124 (t) Greta Ilieva. Jellies by Bompas & Parr, (b) UPPA/Photoshot; 125 Photo by Matt Kuphaldt/Cake by Mike McCarey of Mike's Amazing Cakes/Commissioned by Misty Doty for John Doty; 126–127 Sven Dillen/AFP/Getty Images; 128 (t) Cameron Spencer/Getty Images, (b) Tony McNicol/Rex Features; 129 Reuters/Chor Sokunthea; 130 Reuters/Lucas Jackson; 131 (b) Paul Thompson/World Illustrated/Photoshot; 132 (t) Judi Bottoni/AP/PA Photos, © nata_rass/fotolia.com, (b) Reuters/Daniel Munoz; 133 Niklas Halle'n/Barcroft Media; 134 (l) Jean L. Zaun, (t) © steve-photo/fotolia.com; 135 (t) Jean L. Zaun, (c) © steve-photo/fotolia.com; 136 (t) Barry Snyder, (b) Logan Cramer III courtesy Denny's Beer Barrel Pub; 137 Sven Dillen/AFP/Getty Images; 138 Esther Dyson via Flickr; 139 (t) Reuters/Nicky Loh, (b) Reuters/Laszlo Balogh; 142–143 Jeff Chen/Trigger images; 143 (b) AP Photo/Rubin Museum of Art, Diane Bondareff; 144 © Sebastian Kaulitzki/fotolia.com; 145 (t, l) Blank Archives/Getty Images, (r) Hulton Archive/Getty Images; 146 (t) Hulton Archive/Getty Images, (b) Reinhold Thiele/Getty Images; 150 Blank Archives/Getty Images; 151 (t) Hulton Archive/Getty Images; 152 (b/r) Henry Guttmann/Getty Images; 153 Mark Ralston/AFP/Getty Images; 154 Solent News/Rex Features; 155 Steven Heward toothartist.com; 156 (b) Wong Maye-E/AP/PA Photos; 157 Animal Press/Barcroft Media; 158 East News/Rex Features; 159 Simon de Trey-White/Barcroft Media; 160 Neville Elder/Bizarre Archive; 162 Mark Clifford/Barcroft Media; 163 (t) Manchester Evening News, (b) Simon de Trey-White/Barcroft Media; 165 Fred Duval/FilmMagic; 167 James Kuhn/Rex Features; 168 Reuters/Fabrizio Bensch; 169 Reuters/Sheng Li; 170 Reuters/Andy Clark; 171 (b) Reuters/Stringer Shanghai; 172 EFE/UPPA/Photoshot; 173 UWE LEIN/AP/PA Photos; 174 (t) ChinaFotoPress/Photocome/PA Photos, (b) Dinodia Photos; 175 Newscom/Photoshot; 177 Matt Cardy/Getty Images; 178–179 (b) Reuters/Ho New; 178 (t) Bournemouth News & Pic Service/Rex Features; 179 (t) Dave Thompson/PA Wire/PA Photos; 180 mauisurfboardfence.com/photographer: John Hugg huggsmaui.com; 181 ZOOM/Barcroft Media; 182–183 Amytha Willard; 183 Marya Figueroa; 184 (t) Ray Asgar www.austinhelijet.com, (b) Ashley Bradford; 185 Frank Hormann/AP/PA Photos; 187 www.herbwilliamsart.com; 188–189 www.lichtfaktor.eu; 188 (t) www.lichtfaktor.eu, (b) Lichtfaktor with thanks to creativereview.co.uk, 189 (t/l, t/r, c/r2, b/r) www.lichtfaktor.eu, (t/c, b/l) Lichtfaktor with thanks to creativereview.co.uk, (c/r) Lichtfaktor with thanks to skymovies.com; 190 Skip Peterson/AP/PA Photos; 191 Rex Features; 192–193 www.underwatersculpture.com; 194 (t) Chris Jackson/Getty Images, (l, r) Elizabeth Thompson www.tulpastudios.com; 195 Sandy Schimmel/Barcroft Media; 196–197 (t) Solent News/Rex Features; 196 (c/r) © Nicholas Piccillo/fotolia.com; 198 Solent News/Rex Features; 199 (t) Rex Features, (b) Cai Bing/ChinaFotoPress/Photocome/PA Photos; 200 David Rowland/Rex Features; 202–203 Brian Dettmer and Kinztillou Fine Art; 204–205 www.aniskin.ru; 206–207 (c) Lyons Wier Ortt New York; 206 (l) Jason Hackenwerth Beach Trumpet 2007 Latex Balloons; 207 (r) Jason Hackenwerth Alien Rainforest 2007 Latex Balloons; 208–209 Scott Blake www.barcodeart.com; 210–211 Li Wei; 212 GB/Barcroft Media; 213 (t) Jim Hammer; 214–215 David Alvarez; 217 Geoffrey Robinson/Rex Features; 218–219 (dp) NASA and The Hubble Heritage Team (AURA/STScI); 218 (t) NASA, NOAO, ESA, the Hubble Helix Nebula Team, M. Meixner (STScI), and T.A. Rector (NRAO), (b) NASA and The Hubble Heritage Team (STScI/AURA); 219 (t) Credit for Hubble Image: NASA, ESA, K. Kuntz (JHU), F. Bresolin (University of Hawaii), J. Trauger (Jet Propulsion Lab), J. Mould (NOAO), Y.-H. Chu (University of Illinois, Urbana), and STScI. Credit for CFHT Image: Canada-France-Hawaii Telescope/ J.-C. Cuillandre/Coelum. Credit for NOAO Image: G. Jacoby, B. Bohannan, M. Hanna/ NOAO/AURA/NSF, (b) NASA, ESA, HEIC, and The Hubble Heritage Team (STScI/AURA). Acknowledgment: R. Corradi (Isaac Newton Group of Telescopes, Spain) and Z. Tsvetanov (NASA); 220 (l) Maria Zarnayova/isifa/Getty Images, (b) WENN/Newscom; 221 (t,r) Rick Scibelli/Getty Images, (scattered) © alle - Fotolia.com; 222 www.tesladownunder.com; 224–225 © CERN; 226 James Connolly/PicSell8; 227 (t) Tony Rafaat/Barcroft Media, (b) Martin Waugh/Barcroft Media; 229 Barcroft India/Barcroft Media; 230–231 Lucas J. Gilman/Barcroft Media; 230 (r) Darin Quoid; 232 Elmer Martinez/AFP/Getty Images; 233 (b) Feature China/Barcroft Media; 234 William T Knose Jr; 235 (t) Rob Thomson, (b) Linda Abrams, Ercoupe "Sky Sprite"; 236–237 Untitled X-Ray/Nick Veasey/Getty Images; 238 Barry Bland/Barcroft Media; 239 Emmanuel Aguirre/Getty Images; 240–241 (dp) © andrew downes/red bull photofiles; 241 (t) © andrew downes/red bull photofiles, (c) © loïc jean-albert /red bull photofiles, (b) © christian pondella/red bull photofiles; 242 (c) Keystone/Getty Images; 243 (sp) KPA/Zuma/Rex Features, (b) Bryan Bedder/Getty Images

Key: t = top, b = bottom, c = centre, l = left, r = right, sp = single page, dp = double page

All other photos are from Ripley's Entertainment Inc.
Every attempt has been made to acknowledge correctly and contact copyright holders and we apologize in advance for any unintentional errors or omissions, which will be corrected in future editions.

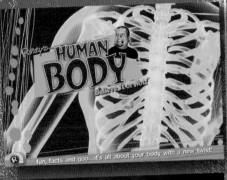

ANNUALS

Prepare to be Shocked!

Ripley's Believe It or Not!

TAKE A LOOK AT THE WORLD'S WEIRDEST FACTS

5

collect them all!

Ripley's Believe It or Not!®

ALL NEW

SEEING IS BELIEVING

4

Ripley's Believe It or Not!®

The Remarkable... Revealed

TAKE A LOOK AT THE WORLD'S WEIRDEST FACTS

3

Believe It or Not!®

ALL NEW

Expect... The Unexpected

TAKE A LOOK AT THE WORLD'S WEIRDEST FACTS

With **all-new** stories and pictures in **every** edition of this bestselling series, our books entertain, shock and amaze! Collect all of the eye-opening, mind-boggling and sometimes stomach-churning Ripley's Believe It or Not! titles.

Feast your eyes on an amazing array of extraordinary images.

Gasp at literally thousands of brilliant reports on the brave, the talented and the downright bizarre.

Interviews and in-depth research features give an insight into some of the incredible tales featured.

Want to know more? Check out www.ripleybooks.com for video clips and more about many of the books' features.

Ripley's Believe It or Not!® Planet Eccentric!

2

TAKE A LOOK AT THE WORLD'S WEIRDEST FACTS

Ripley's Believe It or Not!®

1

TAKE A LOOK AT THE WORLD'S WEIRDEST FACTS